Siblings in Therapy

Life Span and Clinical Issues

Siblings in Therapy

Life Span and Clinical Issues

Edited by

MICHAEL D. KAHN, Ph.D.
KAREN GAIL LEWIS, Ed.D.

W. W. NORTON & COMPANY · *NEW YORK* · *LONDON*

Published simultaneously in Canada by Penguin Books Canada Ltd.,
2801 John Street, Markham, Ontario L3R 1B4.

Printed in the United States of America.

Firts Edition

Library of Congress Cataloging-in-Publication Data
Siblings in therapy.
    Includes index.
    1. Brothers and sisters.   2.   Psychotherapy.
I.   Kahn, Michael D., 1936–   .   II.   Lewis, Karen Gail.
RC489.F33S56   1988   616.89′14   88-9981

ISBN 0-393-70058-5

W. W. Norton & Company, Inc., 500 Fifth Avenue, New York, N.Y. 10110
W. W. Norton & Company Ltd., 37 Great Russell Street, London WC1B 3NU

1 2 3 4 5 6 7 8 9 0

From Mike

To Ruthie:

Who said, long ago "Whither thou goest, I will go," and then gave me the joy and solace which helped make ours a journey of adventure.

From Karen

To the 5 sets of siblings in 3 generations of my family, ages 8 to 84. Still loving and bickering and loving to bicker.

Acknowledgments

I am delighted to have the opportunity to thank all of those people who helped to bring this book about siblings to fruition. An edited book, particularly one like this with all original contributions, is, after all, a truly collective enterprise, representing many years of effort by many people, all of whom have their own debts of gratitude to those who nourished their work. As an editor, I wish to thank them all even though I have never, in that sense, met all of them.

My own acknowledgment of appreciation has to begin with my parents, Helen and Lester Kahn, each of whom was an only child and in this way served as the original inspiration for my curiosity about sibling relationships, i.e., "What would it be like to have a sibling connection?" This wondering was compounded by my being an only child too, by always having best friends who were onlies as I was growing up, and by eventually marrying an only, my wife of now 30 years, Ruth. In this land of onlies, Ruth and I agreed that sibling relationships could be valuable, honorable, and fun, and we have throughly enjoyed raising our three children, Kim Lee, Tamara, and Ben. They became the first laboratory in which she and I could observe real sibling interaction.

Later on, through Ruth's work teaching and working with poor families, and in my 25 years of being a family therapist, university professor, and researcher, I learned an enormous amount about brothers and sisters of all ages, interviewing thousands of sets of siblings and working with students and other therapists about their cases. I am indebted to all of them for the lessons I have learned—about life, about struggle, about success, and about relationships. My longtime colleague, Stephen Bank, with whom I actively collaborated for 10 years (1973–1982), also deserves my gratitude; our work on the sibling relationship was certainly a forerunner to the thinking contained in this book, and together, interviewing families and in countless hours of discussions, we learned how much the therapist is a privileged observer and chronicler of intimate life.

My co-editor, Karen Lewis, is to be admired for her enormous energy and boundless capacity for hard work. Karen's spirits never sagged in the three years of bringing this book to fruition and during all the brainstorming sessions we did on the telephone weekday and weekend nights, cross-country at 1 a.m.

Laura Roth never failed me with the tight typing deadlines I imposed on her, and Florence Hoberman was that indefatigable buffer, organizer, and vital emissary who helped me pull together the myriad details always involved in a project of this scope.

Our editor, Susan Barrows, deserves our enormous gratitude. Susan was always available for consultations, would work on the tiniest details or help with larger conceptual ideas, and is that rare gem in today's hurly-burly publishing industry, an editor who is knowledgable, considerate, and committed.

Finally, each contributor is to be congratulated not only for writing a fine piece of work, but also knowing how to put up with the deadlines and demands of these two editors. Karen and I share a great deal of satisfaction that we were able to bring together all of these "siblings" to cooperatively create an original and, we hope, valuable piece of work. Now, like a typical only, I welcome the chance to pull back into comforting solitude and to savor the fruits of that labor.

M.D.K.

The idea for a book on siblings was sown in the spring of 1984, when my oldest niece celebrated her bas mitzvah. This was the first extended family gathering held by my generation. As we sat around that evening, I felt overwhelmed by the power and the intensity of the multiple relationships of the three generations: my parents and their siblings, my two brothers, Doug and Steve, and their children. So much was happening in the room, so much had been happening for years, and so much was being repeated. I knew more needed to be understood about the sibling relationships in each generation. Therefore, as this book finally comes to fruition, I want to express my deep gratitude to my parents, aunts, and uncles for teaching me about sibling relationships. I hope my brothers and I can replicate some of the patterns that will be enhancing to our later years. And I hope we can learn from their legacy which ones to avoid.

I would also like to thank my work family, which has been a major source of gratification during these past three years. To Susan Wooley, Ph.D., Wayne Wooley, Ph.D., Lee DeRhodes, MSW, and Marsha Basquette, B.A. — I greatly appreciate your energy, creativity, and support, but mostly your friendship. I want to add a particular thanks to Susan for providing me with a model of a productive and caring professional woman, and to Lee for the special experience we shared as cotherapists. In addition, I want to thank Nora Stevenson and Shelly Harp, secretarial staff, who — although having never met Michael Kahn — know his address by heart. They were forever helping me, "get this off to Mike today, please." And a special thanks to Jon Kamholtz, Ph.D., for teaching me how to edit a book.

This book would not exist without the thousands of siblings I have worked with over the past two decades. Thanks to them for sharing with me their love and anger, their struggles with each other, and their rewards from the struggle.

This book would not exist without the wonderful contributors who joined Mike and me in our excitement about this topic. Their eager participation (and their promptness) eliminated much of the reputed difficulties of an edited book.

My acknowledgments would be incomplete without a very warm thanks to you, Mike, my co-editor. Your enthusiasm, together with your editing acuity, has made the creation of this book a marvelous experience. I especially appreciate your willingness to look at our own professional sibling issues when we bumped in different directions. Parenthetically, I understand the telephone company wants to thank both of us for the many, many hours we spent each week talking late into the night.

There is something special about siblings — family siblings as well as professional ones. This book could not exist without both.

K.G.L.

Contents

Acknowledgments   vii
General Introduction   xv
  Michael D. Kahn and Karen Gail Lewis
Contributors   xxi

I. SIBLING DYNAMICS: GENERAL ISSUES

Introduction   1

1. Intense Sibling Relationships: A Self-Psychological View   3
  Michael D. Kahn

2. Enchantment of Siblings: Effects of Birth Order and
  Trance on Family Myth   25
  Morton S. Perlmutter

3. Basics of Family Structure and Sibling Position   46
  Walter Toman

4. Ethnic Patterns and Sibling Relationships   66
  Eve Primpas Harriman Welts

II. WHEN SIBLINGS ARE CLOSE: THE EARLY YEARS

Introduction   89

5. Young Siblings in Brief Therapy   93
  Karen Gail Lewis

6. Clinical Interventions with Large Family Systems:
   Balancing Interests Through Siblings   115
   Dennis E. McGuire and Patrick Tolan

7. Untangling Incestuous Bonds: The Treatment of
   Sibling Incest   135
   Marsha L. Heiman

8. Psychotherapy With Siblings of Disabled Children   167
   Milton Seligman

9. When Parents Separate or Divorce: The Sibling System   190
   Lee Combrinck-Graham

10. Stepsiblings in Therapy   209
   Elinor Rosenberg

11. Children of Alcoholics: Their Sibling World   228
   Rosalie C. Jesse

III. BALANCING CLOSENESS AND SEPARATENESS:
     LATE ADOLESCENCE AND EARLY ADULT YEARS

   Introduction   253

12. Symptoms as Sibling Messages   255
   Karen Gail Lewis

13. The Tilted Family   273
   Clark W. Falconer and Colin A. Ross

14. The Vortex: Siblings in the Eating Disordered Family   297
   Laura Giat Roberto

15. My Brother's Keeper: Siblings of Chronic Patients
   as Allies in Family Treatment   314
   Ethan G. Harris

IV. SETTLING OLD SCORES: THE MIDDLE YEARS

Introduction 339

16. The Stolen Birthright: The Adult Sibling in
    Individual Therapy 341
    Stephen P. Bank

17. Blueprints from the Past: A Character Work Perspective
    on Siblings and Personality Formation 356
    Sandra Watanabe-Hammond

18. Siblings and the Family Business 379
    Robert Carroll

19. Sibling Issues in Cotherapy and Coauthoring 399
    William J. Doherty

V. FACING THE PROBLEMS OF AGING: THE LATE YEARS

Introduction 415

20. Relationships Among Adult Siblings Who Care for
    Their Aged Parents 417
    Mario Tonti

21. Interpersonal Relationships Among Elderly Siblings 435
    Victor G. Cicirelli

Index 457

General Introduction

As editors of a book on a broad-ranging subject that is close to our hearts, we know that the reader who begins by examining these few introductory pages may not always share our enthusiasm — a not uncommon experience for those who may have paused here because they were merely curious, or were searching for the contribution by a colleague, or were hopeful of finding a particular special subtopic of their own interest. Yet we also think that the very nature of what we have focused on — *the sibling relationship* — inevitably raises questions, contradictions, ambivalence, excitement, and a certain hesitation in both clinicians and the general public. It is the purpose of this book to demystify and demythologize relationships among brothers and sisters and, through the writings of 22 seasoned clinicians and theoreticians of differing orientations, to expose the reader to the complexity of the subject.

While it has required three years for this book to be brought to fruition, it has really taken many more years for our field to understand what siblings mean to one another. More than 65 years (roughly 1890–1955) passed before the modern field of psychotherapy acknowledged the full impact of the family on the development of the individual, although references to family influence were always present in the psychoanalytic literature. Once family therapy began to make headway, it was almost another 30 years (1955–1982) before the importance of sibling relationships was more fully developed by one of the editors (Michael D. Kahn) and his colleague Stephen Bank in *The Sibling Bond* (1982). It would be presumptuous, however, to overlook the fact that the pioneers of family therapy, such as Nathan Ackerman, Carl Whitaker, Sal Minuchin, Ivan Boszormenyi-Nagy,

Murray Bowen, Virginia Satir, and Don Jackson, among others, all skillfully worked with siblings as part of their approach to working with the family. By bringing family members of several generations together, they not only created a new conceptual framework and paradigmatic shift for the understanding of human problems in context, but also began to systematically use the sibling(s) of the identified patient as a therapeutic resource. In doing so, they made it easier for our generation of therapists to take the next step, articulating just how and precisely when siblings can and do influence each other's lives.

Yet it must strike the reader as curious that in a culture which places so much emphasis on family enrichment, family roots, and overcoming the vicissitudes of family life, it has taken so long for clinicians and theorists, professionals and the public, child development specialists and experts on the aging to more completely understand the sibling relationship. This most enduring of life's intimate ties outlasts those with our parents by 20–30 years, and remains as a constant despite aging, despite divorce, and despite children growing up. We hope the breadth of this volume will help identify and describe the important influence of these ties across the life span.

We have, as editors, carefully chosen different contributors to lay bare the anatomy of sibling ties with four very different purposes in mind:

1. To present, across the life span from early childhood, to adolescence, to adulthood and the later years of life, issues in which brothers and sisters cross paths in important ways. We have deliberately chosen a number of contexts (clinics, psychiatric hospitals, private practice settings, businesses, etc.) where such intense interactions take place.

2. To describe clinical issues of importance that embroil siblings. Thus, there are, among others, chapters on alcoholism, sexual abuse, eating disorders, physical and emotional handicaps, divorce, remarriage, family business, conflict, chronicity, favoritism, and caring for elderly parents.

3. To include representatives from a wide spectrum of therapeutic approaches. While some of the contributors use individual approaches as well, all are committed to a family systems perspective. All work with the sibling group as an important

subunit of the family, keeping one eye on the influence of the parents, the other on the concerns of the individual. The chapters describe a range of family therapy approaches, such as the structural, strategic, Milan, psychodynamic, self psychological, family of origin, symbolic-experiential, and integrative schools.

4. To include theoretical issues that can inform a number of approaches for many kinds of problems. We therefore consider that many of the theoretical chapters make groundbreaking contributions to the literature of family systems as a whole, with new findings reported on birth order, tilted families, intense sibling relationships, the meaning of symptoms, ethnicity, colleagueship and friendship, large families, young children, and the ties among elderly siblings.

The long-standing enigma of the sibling relationship is partially understood by our recognizing that it often defies accurate and easy-to-document description. When children are asked, they are usually not able to accurately discuss their relationship with their brothers and sisters. For many adults, this relationship is often consciously relegated to fourth place behind the loyalty to one's spouse, parents, and children. Furthermore, the ties between siblings in earlier America were often broken early, when children in large families left home as soon as physically possible. Yet in our modern world, it is often the parents who, in one way or another, physically and psychologically leave; in such circumstances, siblings depend on one another, even when that dependence is fraught with pain, anxiety, and disappointment. Curiously, and in seeming paradox, dependence among siblings also occurs at the opposite extreme, when fortunate parents, whose lives unfold productively and whose plans for their families evolve with a certain harmony of spirit, find development of their children to be expectable, optimal and desirable. In such cases siblings often enjoy their relationship, forming a different kind of bond in which they become each other's friends, models, good-natured competitors, companions and trailblazers. Our contributors describe the influence of siblings both in the highly charged atmosphere of families where there has been turmoil and conflict, and conversely, in families where things have gone well.

We do not consider that, ipso facto, siblings are always an important influence; when children are born many years apart, are stepsiblings in experientially very different families, or are raised with an attitude of detachment or disdain, they may by adulthood elect infrequent contact or shrug off the relationship as of little or no consequence. Spouses who are less invested in sibling relationships may also claim a higher priority. Yet the existence of such distant relationships does not detract from those families where the influence is obviously important and even profound. And we hasten to point out that over the years we have learned as clinicians, therapists and theoreticians that there are many instances where the sibling influence is subtle and hidden. As therapists, with careful and sensitive probing, with an eye towards the problems within the family, we are often in the best position to uncover that influence. Under these circumstances, the sibling relationship may begin to loom larger than the parents or children ever suspected, increasing everyone's awareness and enormously increasing our therapeutic efficiency. The sibling relationship is therefore a resource for us, as well as an influence and integral part of each brother's and sister's life.

We cannot also introduce this book without briefly mentioning two aspects of being a sibling which have dogged the literature and too easily conjured up rigid and fixed associations about our field of inquiry. We are speaking of sibling rivalry and birth order. While we deplore the books which fuel popular myths with unsubstantiated (and linear) speculations about these issues, they seem to linger in the public mind, and of course, operate in many families, helping determine expectations about each child's development. We have therefore included chapters on both topics, but the authors have been mindful to frame their assumptions in a larger dynamic and systemic perspective.

Thus, while birth order hypotheses fuel popular assumptions (for example, "olders are more responsible, but neurotic, while youngers succeed less often but have more fun"), our contributors who have written about birth order look at it in a more discriminating way and take into account the powerful myths that operate in families. They carefully avoid the fixed predictions that birth order position will ultimately determine an individual's fortune, fate and destiny. Similarly, we are aware (as the early psychoanalysts were) that an older child's secure niche in the family, may be seriously shaken by the birth of a new sibling—one early writer called this the "dispossession theory" (that is, being kicked out of mother's nest)—thus laying the foundation for resentment and sibling rivalry. But we have observed many families where such events are skillfully and sensitively handled by the parents, and where the children grow up with a caring and loving attitude toward one another. Therefore we claim — with the weight of thousands of clinical cases behind us — that sibling rivalry is not inevitable, although fights and quarreling among siblings are common. Sibling relationships can be, and often are, positive. When rivalry dominates, we always find that other systematic and dynamic issues are fueling the fires of resentment and hate.

Finally, we are delighted to state that our culture appears to be freeing itself from the sexist shackles which led parents to value their sons over their daughters. In our more egalitarian climate, sisters have fewer reasons to resent their brothers, while brothers have to accept that, if privilege and power are to be theirs, it has to earned, not handed to them by the accident of birth. All of our authors, and we as editors, share the goal of helping families overcome the evils of sexism and the damage that accrues to families where it occurs unchecked. Along with this observation, we would also like to note that, although we have permitted our contributors on occasion to use the pronoun "he" to encompass both genders, this is a literary convenience, not a slipshod escape into a gender preference.

And lastly, and without apology, we would be remiss to try and present all of our authors as long-established "sibling experts." We invited some clinicians to work with us because, even though they had never written about siblings per se, we knew them as skillful people and sensitive thinkers, who, in working with families and individuals had dealt·extensively with siblings. In dialogue with us, their insights were refreshing. Their experiences in putting their thoughts about sibling relationships into writing will, we believe, be similar to yours, the reader, who will come to recognize important patterns and phenomena that will enlighten your own work. We have all been made wiser by this collaborative venture and, in the best spirit of an evolutionary science, hope we may one day receive the benefits of your input to this field of inquiry.

— *Michael D. Kahn*
Karen Gail Lewis

Contributors

Stephen P. Bank, Ph.D.
Adjunct Associate Professor of
  Psychology,
Wesleyan University;
Co-Director, Bank and Hiebel,
Family and Child Associates
Middletown, CT

Robert Carroll, M.D.
Assistant Clinical Professor of
  Psychiatry
University of California-Los
  Angeles
Los Angeles, CA

Victor G. Cicirelli, Ph.D.
Professor of Developmental and
  Aging Psychology
Purdue University
West Lafayette, IN

Lee Combrinck-Graham, M.D.
Director, Institute for Juvenile
  Research;
Clinical Associate Professor and
  Director of the Division of Child
  and Adolescent Psychiatry,
Chicago Medical School,
University of Illinois,
Chicago, IL

William J. Doherty, Ph.D.
Associate Professor and Director,
Marriage and Family Therapy
  Program,
University of Minnesota,
St. Paul, MN

Clark W. Falconer, M.D.
Assistant Professor,
Department of Psychiatry,
University of Manitoba-Winnipeg
Winnipeg, Canada;
Director of Training in Systems
  Therapy,
Health Sciences Center,
Winnipeg, Canada

Ethan G. Harris, LICSW
Director of Family Therapy,
Framingham Day Hospital,
Framingham, MA

Marsha L. Heiman, Ph.D.
Private Practice,
Metuchen, NJ

Rosalie C. Jesse, Ph.D.
Director,
Alvarado Center for Counseling and
  Psychology,
La Mesa, CA

Michael D. Kahn, Ph.D.
Professor of Psychology,
University of Hartford,
West Hartford, CT;
Clinical Associate Professor of
  Psychiatry,
University of Connecticut School of
  Medicine,
Farmington, CT

Karen Gail Lewis, Ed.D.
Coordinator,
Family Therapy Eating Disorders
  Clinic,
University of Cincinnati Medical
  Center,
Cincinnati, OH

Dennis E. McGuire, ACSW
Assistant Professor,
Carthage College;
Faculty, Family Systems Program
Institute for Juvenile Research,
Chicago, IL

Morton S. Perlmutter, Ph.D.
Associate Professor,
School of Social Work,
University of Wisconsin-Madison,
Madison, WI

Laura Giat Roberto, Psy.D.
Director, Center for
  Eating Disorders,
Adjunct Associate Professor
College of Health Sciences,
Old Dominion University
Norfolk, VA

Elinor Rosenberg, ACSW,
Clinical Assistant Professor,
Department of Psychiatry,
University of Michigan Hospitals,
Ann Arbor, MI

Colin A. Ross, M.D.
Assistant Professor,
Department of Psychiatry,
University of Manitoba,
Manitoba, Canada

Milton Seligman, Ph.D.
Professor and Chair,
Counseling Psychology Program,
University of Pittsburgh,
Pittsburgh, PA

Patrick Tolan, Ph.D.
Assistant Professor,
Department of Psychology,
De Paul University, Chicago

Walter Toman, Ph.D.
Professor of Psychology,
Institut für Psychologie,
der Universitat Erlangen-Nurnberg,
Erlangen, West Germany

Mario Tonti, DSW
Director of Community Services,
Bellefaire/Jewish Children's Bureau,
Shaker Heights, OH

Sandra Wantanabe-Hammond, BS,
  OTR
Family Institute of Chicago,
Chicago, IL

Eve Primpas Harriman Welts,
  MSW, LICSW
Lecturer,
Department of Psychiatry,
Harvard Medical School,
Cambridge, MA;
Attending Social Worker,
McLean Hospital,
Belmont, MA

Siblings in Therapy

Life Span and Clinical Issues

I

Sibling Dynamics

GENERAL ISSUES

While we have divided this book into various sections depending on the major themes which dominate at different points in the life cycle, certain issues pervade throughout the life span. In this first section, we present four chapters which deal with important themes that occur in a variety of siblings situations. The clinical examples underscore that powerful social, biological, cultural, and familial forces influence and shape the pattern of sibling relationships.

Kahn, using concepts from self psychology, opens the section with an examination of origins of intense sibling ties, whether loving or hateful. He points out the deep and important developmental needs that siblings can provide for one another, such as merging, mirroring, idealizing, and twinning, and how these affect the object and self representations the individual carries through life. The implications for including siblings in therapy and noting the importance of the earlier sibling relationships on the psychic structure of the individual are explored.

Perlmutter then considers the important prevailing myths about first-born, second-born, and later-born children and how they operate in our culture and in many families. Since some of these myths jeopardize or impair the development of relationship-seeking acts in some children, the clinician must know how to counter their effects. Perlmutter, using an Ericksonian approach, engages families through

1

hypnosis and discusses how the perceptions about each child's birth order position can be altered.

In a very different contribution about birth order dynamics, Toman reviews his almost 30 years of research on this topic. The structural features of families — birth order, gender of the children, identification with the parents, the impact of loss, and the siblings relationship due to "complementarity" — are outlined, and implications for therapy are discussed.

In the concluding chapter, Welts illustrates how immigrant parents may differ from their children, whose sibling relationships are based on different and newly derived norms. Working with children of parents from differing ethnic groups is discussed, as well as the contrasts which exist in major ethnic groups on such issues as gender preference, birth order, emotional expressiveness, separation and autonomy.

1

Intense Sibling Relationships: A Self-Psychological View

Michael D. Kahn

I am distressed for thee, my brother Jonathan

—Second Samuel, Spoken by David upon the death of Jonathan

The words from the Old Testament jump into sharp focus, giving me pause. My awareness of sibling dynamics drifts back instantly to the more commonly cited Biblical reference, "Am I my brother's keeper?"—a more familiar and yet indeterminate phrase, tentative, uncertain, implying nonresponsibility, inviting indifference, even abandonment, of any possible concern and compassion by one person for the other. When one thinks of the sibling references in the Bible, the most frequent are of fratricide and rivalry, disappointment and revenge— Tamar and her two brothers, Absalom and Amnon, Cain and Abel, Joseph and his brothers, Jacob and Esau, and the two good sons of Noah, Shem and Japheth, who contrast with their brother Ham, the bearer of the father's curse, forever exiled and humiliated. Always set against a backdrop of parental misguidance and misjudgment, these personifications of sibling strife are metaphors which have set a pattern in the Western mind of brother against brother, sister against sister. The negative connotation surrounding sibling relationships generates an expectation that for many, unfortunately, becomes a living reality in families where parents are uninvolved, insensitive, or abusive (see Bank and Kahn, 1982; Bank and Kahn, 1981). And yet

3

the statement about Jonathan by David* is of compassion and love, an inner resonance of one person with another, the taking in of the pain of one person's death by one who survives—in short, what we in the 20th century have come to term "empathy."

This chapter sets forth some of the particular contributions of the self psychological view to the understanding and treatment of intense sibling relationships. By "intense" I do not just mean "high access," a term I have used previously (Bank and Kahn, 1982; Kahn, 1986a) for brothers or sisters who are close in age, have similar experiences, attend the same schools, and are encouraged or forced to share activities, possessions, friends and roles. Intense bonds among siblings occur when there is a compelling need by two or more children for object relatedness which is not being gratified by an adequate adult caretaker. Intense relationships can also occur when the parent or parents want their children to have a close relationship. Projecting their own needs onto the children, parents can form an idealized version of closeness which the children live out; alternately, a more negatively charged relationship can develop because the parents transfer their own unhappy and unsatisfied interpersonal demands onto their children. An intense sibling relationship can occur when circumstances, sometimes out of the parents' control, force the children to turn to one another out of a basic and inherent human striving for relatedness. As a species, we require gratifying and reliable human contact—nothing less will suffice (not television, not teddy bears, not narcotics of any kind)—for nurturance, for a sense of wholeness, and for the optimal structuralization of mind (Pine, 1985; Stern, 1985; Stolorow, 1985). Intense relationships can also occur for brief periods, when the children's developmental needs for close human contact, a mirroring response of delight and enjoyment, or the wish for an idealized counterpart of themselves are best satisfied by a close-at-hand companion, a sibling who looks like, feels like and is like no other person, the next best thing to oneself.

---

*Although Jonathan and David were not biological brothers, they loved each other, played with one another and were each other's constant companions. David was the son of Jesse, Jonathan the son of Saul. Each were loved by Jonathan's father, the King Saul, but David was alternately loved and exiled. These words uttered by David upon hearing of Jonathan's death, precede David's becoming King of Judah.

PRINCIPLES OF SELF PSYCHOLOGY

Self psychology, the basis from which this chapter is written, is a major evolutionary departure from the biologically-based concepts and linear epistemologies which underlie traditional psychoanalytic theory. It was developed by the late Heinz Kohut (1971, 1977, 1984) as an outgrowth of his psychoanalytic treatment of adult patients. Increasingly, Kohut noted the sensitivity of these individuals to narcissistic slights, their alternating between craving for affection and approval and conversely withdrawing into defensive postures where self-absorption and self-indulgence dominated. Not incidentally, he noted a proliferation of such defensive patterning in the society at large, a phenomenon explainable only by examining the cultural and environmental ambience of these patients as children, not from exploring the vicissitudes of their instincts or biological drives. As Eagle (1984) has pointed out, certain classes of pathology are due more to developmental defects and arrests than to internal conflicts.

Gathering a growing group of sympathetic colleagues around him (e.g., Arnold Goldberg, John Gedo, Michael Basch, Paul and Marion Tolpin, Anna and Paul Ornstein, etc.), Kohut noted the important role of the analyst's countertransferential responses to these patients. Therapy often required maintaining an affectively charged mirroring stance of empathy and concern in spite of the patient's incessant and often contradictory demands for closeness and distance, constancy and change. The use (or abuse) of the therapist in this way had a rather impersonal quality about it; the therapist typically felt ("neutrality" notwithstanding) that *who* he was to the patient was less important than *what* he was being used for, namely an *object* to gratify the *self* of the patient. The "selfobject" came to be known as the dependable other person whom the young child needed in order to develop an adequate sense of self. The term "selfobject," a key concept in self psychology, is a clue to what has come to be accepted as phylogenetically necessary for the development of a cohesive self, for the creation of a stable set of mental configurations in the structuralization of mind, and for the restoration of the optimal potential of the individual through his connection to gratifying contextual elements. In the self psychological view, the therapist can become a major selfobject for the patient, able to be empathic and to create

reciprocal empathic resonance in the patient's self structures. What I
hope to document and explore here is how siblings can be major
selfobjects to one another.

Since the reader by now is probably itching to learn about intense
sibling relations, I do not want to dwell too long on the variations
and permutations within the self psychology field, but a nicely suc-
cinct summary of some of the major points has been provided by
Ernest S. Wolf. The following are paraphrased from his 1984 article:

1. Introspection is the method of access to one's own subjective
   experience; empathy and vicarious introspection give access
   to the subjective experiences of others.
2. The center of attention in self psychology is the self in an
   environmental matrix that functions to shape and maintain
   the structure of the self. Selfobjects are objects that function
   to maintain the self.
3. The healthy development of the self depends on the maturation of a given set of potentials that are activated and sustained
   by an appropriately functioning selfobject environment.
4. Faulty relations between the self and his/her selfobjects, particularly during a phase of vulnerability of developing nascent structures, lead to developmental arrests, to chronically
   weak or damaged self structures, and consequently to defensively distorted self-selfobject relations in the present. (pp.
   143–144)

Note that this is an avowedly contextually focused perspective, and
one in which the quality and quantity of important caregiving from
the selfobject determine the structural nature of the individual's experience of himself and the world at large. When therapists attempt to
correct these developmental deficiencies utilizing this view, they permit selfobject transferences to develop and enter the phenomenological world of the patient from an "experience near" rather than an
"experience distant" position (see Kahn, 1987). The therapist therefore becomes the reparative optimal selfobject. This is no small task.
Moreover, examples in the self psychology literature are more often
derived from psychoanalysis than from once-a-week psychotherapy.
Family therapy examples from this perspective have seldom been reported (for exceptions see Brighton-Cleghorn, 1987; Kahn, 1986b).

OBSERVATIONS ABOUT SIBLINGS

Having laid some groundwork, now let me plunge into the heart of our topic by stating certain principles and observations about siblings gathered over more than 20 years of careful clinical study. Concepts from self psychology will become apparent to the reader:

1. In the century-long development of theories of psychological structures, there had long been an assumption that children developed within a stable world of concerned adults, permanently anchored ecologies, satisfying ideologies, and coherent social matrices.

2. The world has changed dramatically; assumptions of object, environmental, and ideological constancy are archaic, naive and dangerous given the volatile and violent changes occurring with ever-increasing rapidity.* Psychotherapy, whether individually or family focused, requires reparation of context, symbolized and actual, whenever possible. Focusing on only the self and not the selfobjects in the person's intimate life or the selfobject representations a person carries within him leads at worst to therapeutic failure or at best to therapeutic interminability.

3. Conceptions about reality are never "fully formed." The relative plasticity or rigidity of people's beliefs about their personal past is influenced by rapid and sometimes incoherent social change. In the search for some object constancy, there is a regression to the self and familiar selfobjects. For some, self-absorption becomes an island in a sea of inchoateness. Beliefs about personal history, as Carlos Sluzki (1983) has pointed out, are always cognitive constructions of subjective reality, not reflections of a "true" external reality.

4. Memories of sibling transactions are particularly indeterminate and arbitrary. The nature of sibling life is always some-

---

*This chapter is being written on October 20, 1987, the day after the New York Stock Exchange crashed by more than 500 points. The President of the Stock Exchange, using apocalyptic language, called it a "meltdown." More shares were traded in one day than in the entire year 1957. On the same day, U.S. Naval forces bombarded two Iranian oil derricks in the Persian Gulf in an undeclared war that President Reagan, in refusing to comply with the War Powers Act, rationalized as having similarly occurred 140 times in U.S. history. Millions of Americans continued to try and comfort themselves by watching news reports of a little girl who had been saved after falling into a backyard well.

what secretive, usually outside the view of the parents (indeed, it often derives its power and charm precisely because parents are not able to intrude on it or choose not to). The relationship, begun early in life without a coherent linguistic map to mark it, usually cannot be adequately described by any of the siblings. Therapists and other interested observers have to be content with a reasonable reconstruction of what has actually happened between any two children, regardless of when in the life span one is asking for that information. Unless there is total fusion, no two siblings ever see the same thing the same way.

Bizarre exception: From the *Chicago Sun Times*, Tuesday, December 9, 1980:

> London (AP) — Greta and Freda C., 37 and identical twins, are so alike in the way they look, think, speak, move, dress and live that scientists say they seem to share one mind. They do everything together, and they scream or sulk if parted. Most uncannily, they talk in unison when under stress — speaking the same words in identical voice patterns that create a weird echo effect. . . . a senior psychiatrist who asked not to be identified, said: "Their total parallel identity, particularly their constant oneness in speaking, takes them far beyond any other sets of identical twins known to psychological medicine. This must be the nearest thing the world has ever seen to a daily unrehearsed dazzling display of telepathy." . . . Arrested for breach of the peace after jealously hounding the common object of their romantic adoration (a former neighbor), the twins appeared in court . . . each wearing one pink mitten and one brown woolen glove. . . . Officials had given some details of their life described by (their) social worker as "one mind in two bodies." (p. 3)*

5. Parents in the United States are less involved in the caretaking of their children than in years past. James Coleman (1987) has defined this as the withdrawal of "social capital." By social capital he means the norms, the social networks, and the relationships between adults and children that contribute to children's growing up. It is the interest, even the intrusiveness, of adults in the activities of children. With an

---

*One must assume that such intense reciprocal fusion rarely occurs between siblings, although identical twins often delight in demonstrating to outside observers through "twin games" how they are of "one mind in two bodies" (see Bank and Kahn, 1982; Engel, 1974).

increase in financial capital in many households who choose to have no children ("DINKS," i. e., double income, no kids) and a decrease in financial capital in households with many children (the povertization of American childhood, i.e., approximately 25% of children in the United States now grow up in poverty), many adults are either underwhelmed or overwhelmed with regards to the emotional and social capital they commit to children. In a culture that increasingly does not value children, siblings may have little choice but to depend on each other. Close at hand, relying on one another for contact and companionship, siblings become each other's agents for intense emotional experience. In their mutual self-selfobject relationships, needs for love, hate, yearning, hope, envy, anger, twinning, merging, mirroring, idealization, and identification are partially, but incompletely gratified. The parents may be oblivious to any or all of the emotional transactions between the children, content as long as the kids "play" and do not make noise and moved to action only if "fighting" reaches intense proportions.

6. While sibling relationships for many young children are growing in importance, the nature of those experiences between very young, psychologically immature beings is often discontinuous, disruptive, and disharmonious. Any break in the emotional match between a child and his or her caregiver will create an internal sense of fragmentation and defensive posturing, sometimes of an assertive social nature and sometimes characterized by withdrawal into private, autoplastic space (Wolf, 1984). If a brother or sister needs to merge with a sibling in order to experience "oneness" with the selfobject, the other child may experience this as being engulfed. If, conversely, a brother or sister needs to defensively withdraw, the child who has been the needed selfobject may experience inner emptiness or abandonment. Quiet parallel play or noisy, chaotic bickering and fighting are often the behavioral analogs of these intense internal states.

7. In an attempt to create object constancy within a larger world of fragmentation and an intimate world of dishar-

mony, siblings will often carry "frozen images" of each other throughout life. These simplifications and object representations of one another as "good," "bad," "unreliable," "loyal," "fair," etc., are often psychological mooring points against which each child forms his or her own self-representations. While parents form their own myths about the qualities of each child (Bank and Kahn, 1980–81; Bank and Kahn, 1982; Perlmutter, Chapter 2), siblings juxtapose self and sibling object representations against one another, creating a map of the family which may or may not be realistic. The freezing of these characterizations and representations may become so rigid that the siblings hate or love each other throughout life, avoiding one another in the former case (what Bank and I (1982) and Schacter (1985) have called "sibling deidentification") or in the latter case living out a mutually dependent, mutually satisfying relationship which sometimes takes precedence over any other. To relinquish a frozen image of an intensely connected sibling forces each person to reorganize his own self representations.

8. In order to gain a sense of strenth and inner calmness, one sibling may idealize another (usually a younger will idealize an older but the reverse also occurs). The idealized sibling will often maintain a close relationship with the adoring sibling as long as it is possible to reap narcissistic gratification from the mirroring received. Such complimentary stances of adored idealized sibling and adoring mirroring sibling can be broken by the birth of another child in the family, developmental change in one of the siblings, or any other drastic occurrence in the family life cycle.

9. To buffer themselves against the pangs and disappointments which inevitably occur in any intense sibling relationship (developmental change inevitably happens and with it a breakdown in the harmony created by two constancy seeking individuals), young children will need to create transitional space filled with satisfying part representations of the valued brother or sister. While transitional objects (Winnicott, 1951, 1965) have typically been described as filling the void created by the infant loosening his tie with the mother during early phases of the separation-individuation process,

I have noted many "twinning" phenomena in which part representations of a close sibling are imagined, fantasized, and created, assuaging the loss of the sibling who was once a close and constant companion. While Kohut (1971, 1977) noted the occurrence of twinning transferences with adult patients, we here see this development in early childhood as the attempted resolution of the rupture of a previously intense, constant sibling relationship. This filling of the "intersubjective matrix" (Atwood and Stolorow, 1984) with "twin" representations often underlies the search for satisfying friends and colleagues in adult life, i.e., longing for a "best friend" or even imagining that one's partner or spouse is just like oneself, a twin or almost-sibling.*

10. Intense bonding between siblings in unhappy families will sometimes spill into sexual tension and incestuous relations. While family therapists often treat such cases as sexual abuse, and the offender sibling (usually an older brother) is viewed as a victimizer of a weaker sibling (usually a younger sister), there are a number of cases in which actual sexual relations between a brother and sister have continued for as long as eight or ten years, well into late adolescence (see Bank and Kahn, 1982, for an extensive review of the literature and analysis of such situations). Such secret and prolonged relationships, quite different from abusive ones, usually remain hidden until one of the adult siblings reveals the secret in individual therapy. I have called this type of sibling incest "nurturance-oriented," in contrast to the more commonly known power-oriented incest, which is exploitative and coercive. Nurturance-oriented incest may not be that uncommon; some estimate sibling incest to occur five times as often as the more frequently discussed father-daughter incest. When it is described by one or both participants, the processes of merging and idealization are quite striking. The sister usually idealizes her brother, who is a parent substitute, providing attention, caring, nurturance and excite-

---

*"Projective identification" has often been used to describe such phenomena but it seems too barren and mechanistic. The notion of "twinning" lends a more phenomenological-based bilateral quality to the relationship, in which each person imagines and anticipates the thinking of the other.

ment; the brother merges with his sister and feels loved, excited, and powerful. This is in contrast to the neglect, misunderstanding, or physical abuse they receive from their parents. Together, forming a bonded unit in secret coalition against their parents, the sibs often feel they are the most important people in each other's lives. They usually separate regretfully, stopping their sexual relationship in middle adolescence. In my experience such siblings seem to have been so affected by this intense relationship that their personality traits, sexual adjustment, and eventual marital partner choices are irrevocably and adversely influenced by what previously occurred. Nevertheless, they often feel indebted to one another, tacitly acknowledging that for an important developmental stretch of time there was no one else who gave them love and attention. They have, in other words, become each other's selfobjects.

11. Real abuse, sexual and physical, does of course take place between siblings. The most common form, repeated hitting of a weaker brother or sister, is so frequent as to have been excused or minimized by our culture as expected and tolerated. But sibling "rivalry" is insufficient to describe the sometimes compulsive hitting or fighting that goes on. Repeatedly offering oneself as the recipient of another sibling's violence, repeatedly and seemingly stupidly being unable to avoid doing the hitting is not just circumstantial. Instead there is a ritualistic quality to this compulsive clashing between two particular siblings in which over and over the violence occurs, with one child seemingly putting himself at the mercy of the other. We are struck by how such violent dramas seem the only way such children feel intensely, how pain, hurt, disappointment, revenge and humiliation are the sharpest ways they feel at all, how such experiences are in stark contrast to the emotional deadness of the families they grew up in, and how the hitting is one way of saying, for both the aggressor sibling and the victim sibling, "I am alive. Someone needs me, pays attention to me, thinks about me. I am not alone." Not incidentally, we are interested in how frequently sibling violence is the precursor for

subsequent spousal abuse in adult life. Intense bonding, through violence, is not unusual in our culture.

12. Finally, we cannot resist noting that many outstanding recent Hollywood movies have been about sibling relationships: *Crimes of the Heart, Fanny and Alexander, Ran*, The Color Purple,* and *Hannah and her Sisters* have the sibling bond as their central themes. While the great movies of the 1950s dealt with the fall from grace or denouement of parent figures (e.g., *Death of a Salesman, Come Back Little Sheba*) or love relationships (e.g., *Street Car Named Desire*) films of the 1980s have emphasized sibling relatedness as enduring, even outlasting all other intimate ties. This shift to egalitarian relationships, away from hierarchical domination, becomes in art, as well as in life, a psychological challenge. Such a way of relating becomes a treasured ideal. It forces individuals to shift away from such fixed perceptions of difference as greater/lesser, powerful/weak and superior/inferior and to struggle with more ambiguous concepts of equality and fairness. Ahsen (1984) has referred to this as the Rhea complex. In such a perspective, the Oedipus complex is only one constellation of forces an individual goes through developmentally. Equal sibling or sibling-like relatedness in adulthood forces one to transcend the Oedipal notions of dominance and submission and to attempt the achievement of cooperative effort, mutual concern and empathy.

CLINICAL EXAMPLES AND THERAPEUTIC STRATEGIES

The following clinical examples and ensuing therapeutic strategies demonstrate many of these principles. Since some of the phenomena I have been describing occur at different points in the life cycle, the illustrations will be presented in a more or less straight developmental sequence. It is of course impossible in one chapter to do justice to the many ways these issues are dealt with in individual and family therapy, but the reader is urged to refer to the author's other writings on the subject.

*This modification of the great *King Lear* parable demonstrated siblings destroying one another once parental power no longer held sway.

Seeing Things Differently But Still
Feeling the Same

   Linda and Sarah, identical twins with an older brother and sister, found themselves in the middle of an acrimonious divorce process between their parents when they were only three years old. The girls' mother received custody of the children. Mother's subsequent tumultuous relationships and father's withdrawal left Linda and Sarah to emotionally fend for themselves. Their older siblings seemed to have adjusted better to the breakup of the family.

   The twins were not only each other's constant companions but, like many close-in-age siblings in times of stress, were also tacitly assigned the care of each other by their parents, who were too busy, too distraught, and too overwhelmed to give Linda and Sarah separate attention. They were always together; Linda took the lead, speaking for Sarah, initiating the games they played, being the dominant, active twin throughout childhood and adolescence. Finally, they ruefully chose different colleges knowing they had to achieve separate ways of dealing with the world. By their mid-twenties they had nonetheless moved to the same city — Sarah in business, married, Linda single, in graduate school. Once again they resumed that constant companionship that had marked their earlier years. When Linda sought therapy for herself, her overriding concern was her guilt and ambivalence about Sarah, whom she fought, loved, needed, measured herself against, and seemed unable or unwilling to separate from. Such intense ambivalence is not unusual in twins or close-in-age siblings who have needed and depended on each other in childhood and who feel both sad and confused about gaining independence from one another later in life. Linda, in fact, wanted to enter therapy with Sarah, a metaphorical statement about wanting simultaneously to separate and to stay close together, and still needed Sarah to mirror her.

Linda: We are a reflection of each other. I am the complement of who she is. We are always opposites. Wherever I am in my life, it's not where she is. So if I try and be a more distant person, it is because she is so close. At the core we try to be different. It seems to be a coincidence, but it's *so* unconscious. Unfortunately, who she is, is who I am.

But Sarah, the less dominant twin, while having some of the same needs, approaches it differently, revealing her old need to merge:

Sarah: I wouldn't be the same person if it weren't for Linda. I have this need to be close to my family and Linda gives me that sense. It's weird trying to have a close family since it's really like two separate families, the one with my mother and the one with my father. But with Linda it's different. I had the sense of being dependent on people and Linda let me be dependent. I much prefer to let people handle my responsibilities and I have to fight the urge so I can learn independence. Linda made it easy for me to be not independent. She acted as a mother figure.

Successful therapy with Linda and Sarah meant respecting the intense bond, formed early in life, between these two intelligent, sensitive women. They needed to differentiate into "opposites" (see Linda's statement) and yet maintain a sense of ongoing continuity (see Sarah's statement). Interpreting their wish to be so close within a calm, trusting atmosphere where they were seen together with no threat of separation, allowed, in self psychological terms, "transmuting internalization" and assimilation of new cognitions. Subsequently inviting mother and father to meet with their daughters in separate sessions helped consolidate and integrate the parents into a tangible, palpable sense of "family."

Transitional Phenomena

Two other sisters, 13 months apart in age (the Irish fondly call such "Irish twins"), came from an intact family and, unlike Sarah and Linda, did not experience disruption and trauma in their early years. Separation and individuation went fairly smoothly, with Cathy, the younger sister, apparently delighting in being able to always play with her older sister, Betsy. The older sister let Cathy tag along and play with her toys, and talked to, taught, and teased her younger, admiring sibling. Their parents, both only children, had very much wanted their daughters to have a close and positive relationship. But at three and a half years of age, Betsy needed more distance, needed to assert herself without hurting Cathy, whom she dearly loved. Enter "Beacie and Crusty," two imaginary siblings, who, as the now 26-year-old

Betsy told the therapist, "had no gender, no physical appearance, just an outline of two human shapes." Betsy continued:

> They were my friends, not Cathy's. I would have them come to dinner, Mom would hold the door open and I would set plates for them, they would sit in their chairs and I would put food on their plates. When my parents wouldn't notice, I'd eat some of it or mush it around to make it look like they'd eaten. . . . I remember feeling good that Mom indulged me in this. Cathy and I were always together, and we were usually playing outside with Cathy crawling and then being in the sandbox with me, but then Cathy began to understand that Beacie and Crusty were my friends. I would talk to them and give them orders out loud and tell them what to do, and let them come in the house. I never fought with them—they just did what I told them and Cathy understood this.

Beacie and Crusty, the imaginary siblings apparently "stayed" around for a half a year. Cathy, now 25, remembers them also:

> I felt I didn't know Beacie and Crusty. They were Betsy's friends. But I was jealous that I [Cathy must have been three by then] didn't have any such companions, and so one night I tried to invent some and have them for dinner too, but it didn't work. They didn't seem so real. It had bothered me that Beacie and Crusty didn't exist, that they were invisible and still got a place at the table, and besides, Betsy was my friend; we did everything together. I remember that Betsy once had a friend over to play in the sandbox. I felt mad and jealous and pretended, off on the side, to have fun with a drum. I sang real loud, hoping Betsy and the friend would come over. It worked because they then played with me. I guess I was jealous of Beacie and Crusty too but it didn't work with them. I couldn't imagine them the way Betsy did.

As a little girl Cathy was of course unaware of how Beacie and Crusty were an externalized image of Betsy and Cathy, of how Betsy with her emerging need to be separate from her sibling could put something exclusively hers, the imaginary siblings, between her and her sister. This holding-on to the sibling bond through an imagining process was a transitional phenomenon which allowed Betsy to have some breathing space and to create harmony between her internal and external worlds without loss or serious disruption. As adults, Betsy and Cathy continue to enjoy a vital, warm, and now less intense relationship. They are each other's best friends and role models, although Cathy still feels some "guilt" about living her life differently from her sister. While valuing the relationship, she uses transitional phenomena in her own way. The facts that she works in her sister's previous place of employment and that she has a good friend from college who looks very much like her sibling are no accidents; transitional sibling objects can be satisfying throughout the life cycle (see Horton, 1981), for an explanation of solacing objects in adulthood).

The Search for Object Constancy

In many families siblings define for each other the ongoing sense of family, particularly when events change things irreparably. At those times the children may react violently and angrily or tenderly to one another, or they may swing wildly between the two extremes. It is important for therapists to recognize the need to continue to shore up the sibling connection in spite of the vicissitudes the children go through and the different developmental needs of each child. Therapists may be thrown off-track because the intensification of the sibling relationship may appear as rivalry, hostility, or disavowal, but underneath the kids probably need one another as never before (Kahn, 1988). These principles are illustrated by a family of three children who went through five dramatic changes within 14 months.

The children, Billy, 16, Suzanne, 12, and Debby, 7, were far enough apart in age to not necessarily have high access or a high dependency on one another. But two months after their parents divorced (following a three-year battle for sole custody which ended bitterly in a shared custody arrangement because neither parent could "win"), mother was found dead of an aneurysm. Ten days later father's girlfriend moved into the house with him and the children and three months later she and the father married, as they had planned. Shortly thereafter, the new step-mother became pregnant and eventually gave birth to a boy. The new parents talked of selling the house and moving. The children appeared devastated under the successive and sudden impact of (1) a custody fight, (2) divorce, (3) death, (4) father's remarriage, and (5) the new sibling.

The therapist talked to the siblings together and held entire family sessions with the father and stepmother present. In the sibling sessions the children, led by the vocal older brother, proclaimed their hatred for their new stepmother. Debby, the youngest, who sat in the family sessions subdued, whiny, and sucking her thumb, came alive in the sibling meetings, throwing off the pseudo-compliance which marked her relationship with her stepmother. The children were united in wanting their Dad to hear their concerns, in wanting certain possessions of their mother's (which mother's parents had carted away), in wanting some restoration of the old rules of the household, and in not wanting to move or endure any more changes. And yet, in the full family meetings as at home, it was not unusual for severe teasing or scapegoating to occur, or for Billy and Suzanne to gang up on little Debby, or for Suzanne to suddenly punch Debby in the nose or arm. The children's need to nurture each other, to have what I have been calling object constancy, and to maintain the sense of the old family was evident in the sibling sessions and the way they played and shared when they were alone together at home or visiting relatives. However, faced with the serious devastation of their former lives and the frustration of dealing with their father and new stepmother, they could only retaliate and display unhappiness with each other. They could and seemed almost willing to sit still for sibling abuse.

Therapy therefore dealt pragmatically with the restoration of the old sense of family, where possible, and development of the parents' sensitivity to each child's needs. With the parents' softening, the need for abusive object constancy between the children diminished, replaced more and more by attitudes and acts of compassion and caring, particularly by the older two children towards their younger sister.

The Unresolved Aspects of Sibling Abuse

Of course, many children do not get to a therapist at a time of crisis. They may be forced to carry the ill effects of a hostile, painful, and intense sibling relationship with them all their lives. In some instances they may recognize the contextual elements that played a role in the abuse, and the responsibility of the parents in permitting it; alternatively, such affects may be split off, with the abusive sibling remembered only as evil, mentally "diseased," or a villain.

One brother states:

> I think the problem of sibling abuse isn't dealt with or even recognized. I was cruelly and brutally abused by my brother, ten years older, beginning when I was a little toddler. Both my mother and my father

sat back and let him abuse me as much as he wanted to. They refused to restrain him or to protect me or shield me in any way. It's a good thing he left home before I started seventh grade, for I'm sure I would have stabbed him if I had had to take much more of his abuse.

I have deep emotional problems as the result of having been beaten up by my older brother and very deep resentment towards my parents because they refused to restrain Jimmy and refused to protect me.

In other families, with a pattern seen all too commonly, the oldest child may be saddled with the burden of taking care of younger brothers and sisters. Parentified and yet feeling guilty about protesting, such caretaker siblings may become abusive towards their younger charges, hating them for the burden they feel stuck with and occasionally exploding, as one eldest sister of seven siblings put it:

I was only 13 and Shirley was 11; we were too close and she was always the favorite. She got everything, she went everywhere, she never had to do any housework or take care of any kids, or anything of that sort. She always went on vacation, she was always off someplace new every summer. She was always favored as far as clothes and money and stuff.

One time, I wanted to go out and Shirley didn't want to watch the kids. . . . so it ended up that I went out, and she cut up all my clothes with a scissor. . . . Oh I was mad when I came home and I beat her up. I really beat her up. She didn't get out of bed for a week. That is the one and only time I really got mad or lost my temper with her. (Bank, 1985)

Other caretaker siblings internalize this rage completely. They, needing their siblings as selfobjects, compulsively act out the role of burdened pseudo-parent, taking on too much responsibility, never complaining, never asserting their own needs, later exhausting themselves in their adult work roles by acting like a "big brother" or "big sister" to too many colleagues. Their intense relationships with their younger siblings — accepting their resentments, nurturing them, needing them to shore up their own identities — become characterologically ingrained. Long-term individual psychotherapy, emphasizing both the sibling dynamic and parental neglect, is the preferred way of working through these issues.

Sibling Love and Incest

Too intense sibling love can, as I have previously pointed out (Bank and Kahn, 1982; Kahn, 1986a) define a person's self-concept, dictate partner choice, orchestrate sexual behavior, or spill over into actual and prolonged sibling incest. Abend (1984) described two patients whose eroticized play with and idealized attachments to older siblings set the pattern for later choice of love partners. In families where children's needs for mirroring responses, selfobject ties, and connection to idealized and affirming sources of warmth and affection are particularly thwarted, sex play between siblings may reach intense incestuous proportions. The younger sibling, usually a sister, will in such instances be unable to establish sufficient self-demarcation and will be vulnerable to guilt, shame, and anxiety that keep her locked into the relationship. The older sibling, usually a brother, will do what he can to maintain his self-selfobject tie to his sister, recognizing that through sexual intimidation and arousal he can maintain a vital responsive connection, which contrasts with what his parents are able or willing to give him. Children, as Stolorow (1985) has pointed out, will adapt themselves to whomever they can and however they can in order to preserve self-integrity and inner coherence.

A sexualized sibling relationship of the type I have been describing usually ends when the social network of the adolescent makes its continuance unconscionable or when someone alerts appropriate professionals. However, before this happens, guilt, self-denigration and confusion about other possible sources of self-affirmation keep it going for a long time. A grown-up survivor of such a process describes it (Houseman, 1982):

> I participated . . . that was the horror of it. Somehow I always saw myself as an equal participant and an unconscious instigator. Something evil in me made those events take place. I was the problem. He was only acting out natural urges in response to my stimulus. I was seven when it began and maybe sixteen when it ended. I was never threatened. He never said that he would do this or that to me if I told. Yet I certainly was putty in his hands. I never understood my control, but I clearly and totally experienced my guilt.

The contextual reasons for the incest were there.

> As my parents' marriage progressively weakened. . . .my older brother John carried more and more responsibility for my mother's emotional needs, and eventually, assumed a parental role, caring for me, his little sister. He was a responsible, intense young man always. What carefree childhood he was allowed had ended long before I was born.

And her own needs and confusion began to express themselves:

> The only time that I was noticed by family members was when I was perceived as the problem. As a result, my childhood struggle was to maintain a low profile, all the while hungering for love, companionship, affection, warmth. Another member of my family offered me that [my brother]. But it came only through participating in sex, an act in itself which was awkward and uncomfortable. It never made sense to me for I felt no passion. A seven year old . . . no seven year old . . . knows or understands sex. . . . By the time I was eleven I was scared, continually fearing the shame of discovery and pregnancy.
>
> But, I could not turn him down. I was a child who knew fear, and loneliness. Within each relationship, I was an object.

Her dependency on her brother was profound:

> Even my brother must have had mixed feelings towards me. I had received a welcome at birth not accorded him. Yet, I was also the vehicle for his successes. You see, he raised me. He really did. He taught me to read. He taught me to be a good little girl. He instilled in me good moral values and worthwhile ambitions.
>
> Yet, John also seduced me. He used me sexually. And I let him because I was grateful for the kindness which he showed me by wanting to be with me. I was in debt to him, whatever his motives.

At this point in her life she is finally able to assert her indignation at what her brother did to her.

> But, now I call him aggressor and hold him responsible as he never saw fit to do. He had the age, the experience, and the capacity for responsible action . . . even if he did not choose to make use of them. . . . He had understanding beyond mine. He had choices that were never allowed me. He abused the trust of a child. And, he stole my innocence, leaving me to replace it with self-contempt.

Eventually, after many years of other disappointing and self-damaging relationships with men, this very brave woman was able to overcome the effects of the sibling incest.

Her eloquent words give testimony to how important it is for clinicians to carefully understand the contextual, familial, and individual reasons why such phenomena occur. The decision to use family therapy, sibling therapy, or individual therapy for sibling incest should be made on a case-by-case basis, depending on the emotional responsiveness of the participants. Any and all of these approaches can be helpful (see Heiman, Chapter 9), but none of them should be rushed into, given the exquisite pain and hurt felt by the survivors. In the case of "Sarah Houseman" we witness the long-term aftereffects of prolonged, nurture-oriented incest used for self-stabilization. This woman decided, after one frustrating and humiliating attempt, to no longer contact her brother or associate with him. Having named him the aggressor, she was able to clarify her own role in the incest. But she left the door open for future therapeutic work with her brother in a letter to me. As with many siblings it is difficult for her to envision a complete cutoff of the relationship.

CONCLUSION AND IMPLICATIONS FOR THERAPY

As seen in the descriptions of a number of important sibling events and dynamics, brothers and sisters have intense needs for and interactions with each other. Using self psychological principles allows us to understand the inner psychological, not just behavioral, nature of the events and the motives that propel siblings, even when the effects are painful or destructive, to seek each other out, to depend on each other, and to value the relationship. Although no two siblings see the same things the same way, they construct their own views of reality and of themselves in a way sometimes more powerful and enduring than that provided by the parents. Close-in-age, close-at-hand, high-access siblings, propelled by the wish to merge with and idealize another human being, will try to find affirmation of emerging self organization in each other. These processes, occurring at nascent periods and lacking a highly articulated consensual verbal map, will by definition be incomplete, leading the siblings to feel confused about the events they shared and yet affectively highly connected — or in a word, bonded. The processes which fuel highly charged events need to be understood, preferably at the time they take place or later, rather than not at all, lest misunderstandings become "frozen," affecting both personality traits and later patterns of interaction.

Therapists need to explore sibling dynamics even when the presenting problem(s) do not appear sibling based. In a culture which is increasingly peer-oriented, communitarian, and less hierarchical, the sibling relationship becomes for many the most powerful and enduring intimate connection available. In individual therapy, adult brothers and sisters should be asked about the effects of their sibling bond, sibling transference (and sibling countertransference) phenomena should be noted, and carefully selective, strategic sessions with those siblings should be considered. In family therapy, careful attention to the sibling system, with and without parents present, will often yield important information, uncover misinformation, and consolidate the sense of family and object constancy important for each person. My own experience as an individual and family therapist is that when I pay attention to sibling issues, my efficiency and effectiveness in reaching important goals increase enormously.

Since we are engaged in a highly complex, hermeneutic science, it behooves us to learn as much as possible about the perceived reality of each of our patients. Failing to recognize the effects of intense sibling relationships and events is to ignore an important piece of that reality and to compromise our therapeutic effectiveness. It matters less that we have different approaches to different problems and call ourselves self psychologists, strategic family therapists, feminists, or structuralists; any and all of these philosophical and pragmatic stances can be enhanced by our becoming aware of the struggles and satisfactions within the sibling system.

REFERENCES

Abend, S. M. (1984). Sibling love and object choice. *Psychoanalytic Quarterly, 8*, 425–430.

Ahsen, A. (1984). *Rhea complex: A detour around Oedipus complex*. New York: Brandon House.

Atwood, G. E. & Stolorow, R. D. (1984). *Structure of subjectivity: Explorations in psychoanalytic phenomenology*. Hillsdale, NJ: Analytic Press.

Bank, S. P. (1985). Personal communication.

Bank, S. P. & Kahn, M. D. (1981). Freudian siblings. *Psychoanalytic Review, 67*, (winter), 493–504.

Bank, S. P. & Kahn, M. D. (1982). *The sibling bond*. New York: Basic Books.

Brighton-Cleghorn, J. (1987). Formulations of self and family systems. *Family Process, 26*(2), 185–202.

Eagle, M. N. (1984). *Recent developments in psychoanalysis: A critical evaluation.* New York: McGraw-Hill.

Engel, G. L. (1974). The death of a twin: Mourning and anniversary reactions: Fragments of 10 years of self-analysis. *International Journal of Psychoanalysis 45*(1), 23-40.

Horton, P. C. (1981). *Solace: The missing dimension in psychiatry.* Chicago: University of Chicago Press.

Houseman, S. (1982). Personal communication.

Kahn, M. D. (1986a). The sibling system: Bonds of intensity, loyalty, and endurance. In M. Karpel (Ed.), *Family resources: The hidden partner in family therapy.* (pp. 235-58). New York: Guilford.

Kahn, M. D. (1986b). The self and the system: Integrating Kohut and Milan. In S. Sugarman (Ed.), *The interface of individual and family therapy.* Rockville, MD: Aspen.

Kahn, M. D. (1987). Book review. *Journal of Marital and Family Therapy, 13*(2), 215-217.

Kahn, M. D. (1988, March). Hansel and Gretel or Cain and Abel: Attachment, bonding, and differentiation among siblings in divorcing and remarrying families. Paper presented at the 65th Annual Meeting of the American Orthopsychiatric Association, San Francisco.

Kohut, H. (1971). *The analysis of the self.* New York: International Universities Press.

Kohut, H. (1977). *The restoration of the self.* New York: International Universities Press.

Kohut, H. (1984). *How does analysis cure?* Chicago: University of Chicago Press.

Pine, F. (1985). *Developmental theory and clinical process.* New Haven: Yale University Press.

Schacter, F. F. (1985). Sibling deidentification in the clinic: Devil vs. angel. *Family Process, 24*(3), 415-427.

Sluzki, C. E. (1983). Process, structure and world views: Towards an integrated view of systemic models in family therapy. *Family Process, 22*(4), 469-476.

Stern, D. N. (1985). *The interpersonal world of the infant: A view from psychoanalysis and developmental psychology.* New York: Basic Books.

Stolorow, R. S. (1985). Toward a pure psychology of inner conflict. In A. Goldberg (Ed.), *Progress in self psychology. Vol. I.* (pp. 193-201). New York: Guilford.

Winnicott, D. W. (1951). Transitional objects and transitional phenomena. In D. W. Winnicott (Ed.), *Through paediatrics to psychoanalysis: The collected papers of D. W. Winnicott.* New York: Basic Books.

Winnicott, D. W. (1965). *The maturational processes and the facilitating environment.* New York: International Universities Press.

Wolf, E. S. (1984). Disruptions in the psychoanalytic treatment of disorders of the self. In P. E. Stepansky & A. Goldberg (Eds.), *Kohut's legacy: Contributions to self psychology.* (pp. 143-156). Hillsdale, NJ: Analytic Press.

2

Enchantment of Siblings: Effects of Birth Order and Trance on Family Myth

Morton S. Perlmutter

Most of us believe that our personal and family myths are fictions, but during more than 25 years of practicing individual and family therapy, I have found the opposite to be true. Our myths are founded in real personal experience and in turn become the maps by which we understand and appreciate those experiences. Many of those experiences are beyond our cognition and do not lend themselves to open discussion. Rather, we depend on our memories of events, out of which we negotiate myths, recalling feelings and fleeting recollections of actions and reactions between ourselves and other participants in the event. Thus, the myth becomes real while the experience recedes.

Our myths are stories of past events and our mythologizing is their enactment. I have come to view mythologizing as an unconscious process involving natural hypnotic trance states. Natural trance is familiar to all of us; the common experience of driving a car for a brief period and then seeming to awake, as if from a light sleep, is an example. At those times we may wonder how we were able to avoid an accident, but being in natural trance merely means that we are employing both our conscious and unconscious minds simultaneous-

I am indebted to Liz Briskin, M.S., for her help, critical ideas, phrasing, and guidance through the treacherous shoals of my sexist socialization. I am also thankful that she is married with me.

ly. In mythologizing we also employ both our conscious and unconscious.

In the course of my clinical work, I routinely employ strategies that capitalize on the trance states experienced by family members in their mythologizing. I may, for instance, join their trance by speaking and behaving so as to remain in the story being enacted, to maintain their hypnotic state. I may reframe or alter their interpretations of ongoing mythologizing. I may even tell a story in which I introduce metaphors that counter the dysfunctional ones they are employing. At other times I might induce the trance and the myth purposefully, encouraging their mythologizing in order to understand and appreciate their myth, the map they use in interactions about specific familial experiences. But whether or not I or family members induce this trance, it is always present as the basis of their mythologizing.

BIRTH ORDER AND FAMILY SYSTEMS

Some years ago, I became interested in the myths created by sibling groups, particularly those myths associated with birth order characteristics. Since then I have discovered that sibling pairs or groups develop myths that are partially if not totally independent of the family myth. Frequently the mythologizing of siblings appears to be a factor in conflicts between parents and sibling groups. At times sibling mythologizing confuses and angers parents, leaving them feeling impotent.

To date, most clinical practice, research and theory concerning the relationship between ordinal position and the development of a family's system reflect little concern with the role of birth order in the family system's formation, organization and ongoing systemic functions (Ernst and Angst, 1983). Most research and theory is aimed at quantifying, or in some other way describing characteristics associated with ordinal position. Only a few investigators have paid any attention to interactions between parents and children with regard to birth order effects. To my knowledge, none has addressed the formation of family system as a function of ordinality.

Family therapists and theorists hold many unspoken but operant assumptions that betray their perception of birth order as linear, but the family system as circular or ecogenic (Ernst and Angst, 1983). In fact, most research and clinical paradigms concerning the relationships between birth order and the development of the family system are linear and causal, rather than systemic. Few attempts have been made to understand the processes by which the linear order of birth is transformed into an ecological system; in addition, there have been few attempts to reconcile this apparent contradiction.

A brief review of family system theories leads to the conclusion that the field has focused most of its energies on processes of differentiation in families and little on the morphogenesis of the family systems from which individuation and differentiation are directed (Van den Berghe, 1979). Individuation from the family system, rather than the structural evolution of the family system, has been the primary focus. One explanation for this lack of attention to the emergence of the family system lies in our cultural ideas concerning the relationships between individuals and family. Research and theory-building exist within the context of a culture that values autonomy and independence and is highly individualistic (Bellah et al., 1985). Such a context is almost certain to produce clinical practice, research, and theory that pay only lip service to the systems processes of joining, confluence and sharing, while emphasizing individuation, differentiation, and separation (Belenky et al., 1986; Gilligan, 1982).

Autonomy and individuation may be thought of as masculine world views, while sharing and joining may be thought of as feminine. Systems emerging from either value set will certainly replicate themselves, but systems based on confluence and joining will have a much different history and future from those based on individuation and separation. The apparent linearity of birth order clearly reflects masculine epistemology. We have come to accept a kind of clinical-theoretical mystique in which it is assumed that family systems emerge from the addition of individual ordinal positions of the children to the parental unit. But little is known or understood about just how that process functions or from what process the system emerges.

Several years ago I stumbled on the clinical research concerning birth order and family systems conducted by Jerome Bach and his colleagues (1980) at the Bach Institute in Minneapolis, an outpatient family therapy center. While their theory of birth order and family system formation was primitive, it nonetheless conveyed the central idea that each child is born into a family that is different for her/him than for preceding and succeeding siblings.

Following Bach et al.'s early clinical investigations, Hoopes and Harper (1987) extended the theory. They more rigorously investigated the development of affective, ideational, and behavioral characteristics associated with each child's ordinal position. Equally important, they paid attention to the family's systemic development. Their findings point to the reciprocal nature of family systems. As each child is born into the family, the family map changes and its metarules, the rules by which rules are made, and rules themselves evolve in a systemically ecological order. With the birth of each child, communicational complexity increases, as do task demands and role functions. Based on clinical research, Hoopes and Harper hold that systemic changes occurring with the birth of each child produce contextual conditions which require each offspring to respond differently; in short, each child exists in a different context. The responses of the children from their particular ordinal positions produce systematic differentiation in the family.

Hoopes and Harper further generalize that there is a high degree of homogeneity across families among characteristics of children in the same ordinal position. Hence, according to their model, all first children will possess response characteristics peculiar to that position, as will all second and third children, etc. Second children are born into a family in which their parents have developed parenting styles with their first child, resulting in much different types of interactions with their second, and so on throughout the family sibling pattern. Consequently, firstborns are often distant, remote and apparently unrelating. Secondborns model older siblings and parents. Their interactions are often characterized by polarized behavior and affect, arguing logically at one moment and emotionally the next. Third children generally have to fit into the established system and are required by their parents to get along with their oldest and next oldest siblings, thereby developing greater conciliatory skills. I refer the reader to Hoopes' and Harper's work for more extensive details about birth order characteristics. Their research points up that these characteristics emerge from the system of interactions between parents and children. Consequently, a first child response characteristics are shaped specifically because he or she is the parents' first child. In effect, the first child is a "laboratory" experiment in which the parents must invent new behavior, experience new feelings, and rely on minimal prior learning vis-à-vis their new offspring.

The birth of the first child also signals the onset of familial, rather than marital, mapping process. It is explicative and has no historic anchors, save for parental histories. As the family map unfolds with the birth of each child, characteristic responses associated with each child's ordinal position represent themselves as different mapping strategies within the context of the same family system (Hoopes and Harper, 1987). Systemic demands for homeostasis and identity create a situation of paradox. On one hand, each child's strategies for mapping the family must necessarily be different. On the other hand, maintenance of the system requires a high degree of homogeneity of affect, ideation, and behavior. A central task in the family is to negotiate a process in which these disparate conditions are synchronous and systemic.

ORDINALITY AND FAMILY MYTH

In 1974 I began an investigation of family myths. I had earlier hypothesized that families create stories from the threads of historic familial events in order to cope with the socio-emotional results of those events (reported in Perlmutter, 1979). For example, in my family, "the myth of my loneliness" emerged from my status as an only child. Further, I agreed with Ferriera's (1963) finding that myths serve to maintain family homeostasis, but postulated that they also promoted and gave the family tangible evidence of its own identity (Perlmutter and Wikler, 1976).

During the course of these investigations, my colleagues and I became aware that certain types of myths were consistently clustered around specific ordinal positions. Many of the families we studied and observed in our clinical practice held myths about the idiosyncrasies of only and firstborn children, the guilt of second children, and the emotional "sweetness" of third children. We were struck by the consistency of these myths not only across families but also across several generations of the same family (Perlmutter, 1986; Perlmutter and Sauer, 1986).

Further investigations disclosed that myths about children appeared to be associated with developmental stages and emerged after the children demonstrated characteristics associated with their ordinal position (Perlmutter and Wikler, 1976). For instance, the myth of the only child as "loner" resulted from the relative isolation of the only child and her/his autogenous orientation to the world (Perlmutter, 1974). "Autogenous" refers to world views that emerge more from idiosyncratic perception, than from interaction with others—in this case, siblings. Because no sibling context for learning and practice exists, only children tend to learn self-reliance and independence to a greater extent than children in other ordinal positions.

As the family begins to develop its own identity, family members use rules and metarules that are peculiar to their system. Parents and children engage in what I have come to call the cooperative transactions of relationship-seeking acts (RSA's). Relationships are composed of complex acts in which each actor seeks to know the feelings of all other actors toward him. It is the consistency among such RSA's which creates the pattern we call a relationship. In order for the actors to know what others feel about them, all must first agree on the rules and strategies to be used to transmit affective information. It is a highly cooperative game (Perlmutter, 1974).

When children attempt to transcend or mitigate the effects of their family myths, their RSA's are usually directed toward altering their parents' views of them. Children usually desire recognition for their current developmental skills and for who they are in the existential present; they resist being seen as actors in an ongoing family myth. Nevertheless, the acts children choose to extricate themselves from their myths often reinforce the family's perception of them. Children's repertoire of ways to effect change is usually so limited that they do, in fact, behave in ways congruent with their family myths. This creates a condition in which children are left feeling impotent— the harder they try to change the myth, the more true it becomes in their parents' eyes. It is a paradox known to all of us—the more we change, the more we stay the same. No matter how hard they try, children effect only first-order change, and they become stuck in a cooperative venture (Perlmutter, 1983, 1984, 1985). Whether children seek complementarity or symmetry in their RSA's, the parents usually find themselves in reciprocal positions. The maintenance of the family myth becomes a game with its own rules and metarules; as long as these are consciously or unconsciously obeyed, all family members remain players. For instance, the fact that little Janie is smarter than Johnny has little merit in a family in which a myth of male superiority must be maintained, no matter what the cost to Janie.

Our studies have extended our theories about mythologizing, the emergence of the family system, and birth order (Perlmutter and Sauer, 1986). We have found that, while the myth is a story with a factual historical past, such as "Johnny is good in sports," its vitality lies in its currency as a complex family regulatory process, that is, "sports" may prevent family members from dealing with the pain of their historical roots. The process of family mythologizing is one in which the myth is enacted, just as a story is enacted in the context of a stage play. The enactment of the myth, like the play, requires the willing suspension of disbelief.

All stage plays have "stage business" that helps the audience make the shift from its reality to the reality of the stage. That business is a hypnotic induction that exploits the human ability to enter natural trance states, and every stage performance depends on induction and trance. The playbill and the dimming of the houselights help to move us from one reality to another. So too with each family myth. It begins with an hypnotic induction, followed by a prolonged trance state involving all members of the myth who have been initiated into the comedy and/or drama (or both) of the myth. Induction into the trance of our myths is usually natural and flows from routine family interactions. It may be a topic, a gesture, or even an odor which triggers the group trance. The induction, like the dimming of house-lights in the theater, consciously and unconciously signals the players as well as the audience to begin. As in the staged play, the actors in the family myth are their story and literally act their parts in trance — to the extent that no other internal reality is able to make a difference (Zimmerman, Collins, and Bach, 1986).

SIBLING GROUPS, ORDINALITY AND MYTH

Sibling groups function quasi-independently in the context of larger family systems. Sibling pairs or groups function more on the basis of *differences* among ordinal positions than does the entire family system, which requires greater *homogeneity*. The internal logic of the sibling group is essentially that of accommodation to the linearity of birth order and to individual characteristics, while the internal logic of the family system is the mitigation of difference for the sake of synchronous functioning. Differentiation, according to birth order characteristics, is the generally accepted operating principle for sibling groups. The formation of alliances excluding and often opposing the parents affords siblings different relationship patterns than those found in the total family context.

Members of sibling groups generally have a clearer understanding and greater appreciation of birth order differences than do their parents. Parents struggle to homogenize differences in order to make their system functional. That is not necessarily the case among siblings. While detentes and rapprochements among siblings are common they often cannot be celebrated if parents demand the absence of conflicts or its comfortable resolution in order to sense functional closure in a system for which they feel responsible. Paradoxically, while birth order is linear and imposes a logic of difference, the family system is analogic and imposes a logic of sameness. It is a testimony to human ingenuity that families are able to grow, endure, and successfully function.

During the course of many family therapy cases, I have become aware of the myths many families hold about sibling subunits. Stories about "John and Ned always fighting," or "Sally and Joe always taking Mom's side" are common. Conversely, listening to the siblings, I have heard entire stories about the "way Mom and Dad are" and their unchangeability. Clearly, not only do entire family systemic myths exist, but myths exist among parents and sibling subsets as well. John and Ned might well have myths about Mom's and Dad's need to mythologize their children's constant "fighting," while Sally and Joe have myths about Mom's need for allies in her marital struggles. I now routinely separate siblings from parents during therapy, giving each subunit the opportunity to engage in mythologizing.

The mythologizing of the siblings serves different functions for them than for their parents. Sibling mythologizing helps to synthesize and integrate individual siblings' characteristic response patterns, patterns associated with their ordinal positions, into the larger and more functional context of the family system. Sibling mythologizing also enables brothers and sisters to define the parameters of their relationship in the context of the family system. By preserving their sense of difference while pretending to be the same, they are able to help support family stability.

Sibling group mythologizing is often unconsciously and unintentionally induced by the parents. In one family, both parents were convinced that the children were incapable of cooperation and comfortable relationships among themselves. Mom and Dad's constant reference to these beliefs facilitated their children's myth that they were incapable of getting along. This was carefully told to me by the siblings who agreed with the family myth, but behaviorally contradicted it by telling me about it in the most cooperative manner. Mom's and Dad's fights, they explained as one example, upset the third child much more than the first or second, the third child being the one who tends to feel most responsible for their parents' marriage. Her upset may cue the second child, who can depict the parents' fight as a repetitive affective/cognitive pattern, while the first sibling generally offers unidimensionally rational and logical explanations for the parental fights. The third child soon learns to couple her perceptions with both rationality and affective patterns in order to make sense of the context. The first child's rational logic is reinforced, as is the pattern recognition of the second sibling. In that way a mutually reinforcing sibling group functions to create myths about parental fights and sibling responses.

In another example, the oldest child may side with Dad, the middle one with Mom and the youngest one with the inequity of the total parental fight, thereby creating a pattern of mythologizing about the nature of ongoing conflict among the parents. The first example illustrates function of mythologizing in maintaining symmetrical relationship among the siblings and between the sibling system and the parental dyad. In the second example sibling mythologizing maintains complementary relationships among the siblings and between them and their parents. In the first example, birth order differences indigenously enhance homogeneity in family identity, while in the second the characteristics of each ordinal position fit together cooperatively to maintain differentiation as the form of family identity.

Sibling subunits also demonstrate systemic independence from the total family system in ways that cannot be observed unless they are physically separated from their family. Zimmerman, Collins, and Bach (1986) have developed a conceptual schema regarding ordinal position and family processes. In their scheme, the birth of each child alters the family mapping process as well as its family map. The birth of the first child signals the need for different rule-making strategies than those employed by the marital pair alone. Their process and their map change. For the first time rules need to be more explicit, although they become more implicit with practice.

The second child learns to respond to the implicit nature of those rules, while the third child responds to observable rules enacted in the course of interaction between older siblings and parents. Fourth children tend to see first the whole and then its parts and usually accept rules only if they can be integrated into the whole. Consequently, myths emerge that enable the accommodation of differences in rules for each sibling. Family myths about first children's autonomy and independence make sense when viewed in the context of the second child's family map. Sibling group mythologizing most frequently organizes on the basis of these differences, while familial mythologizing organizes despite them. Consequently, therapeutic approaches to working with sibling groups must be of an entirely different order than those employed with the entire family.

SIBLING GROUPS AND THERAPY

It has become clinically fashionable and reasonable to view family problems from an ecosystemic perspective (Bernal and Ysern, 1986; Keeney, 1979). The tendency to view problems in the context of the total system has obscured our awareness of peculiar functions and dysfunctions of sibling subsystems. Intimacy, for instance, is a much different order of business among siblings than between children and parents (Perlmutter and Hatfield, 1980). In one interview, three sisters in their late teens and early twenties were able to joke about their sexual encounters playfully and happily. But when they attempted the same type of humor with their parents, they encountered painful recriminations and increasing emotional distance. The inclusion of parents in the systemic therapy of dysfunctional sibling intimacy can sometimes be a serious clinical error.

As another example, sexuality among opposite-sex siblings is usually worked through in a way much different than that employed between parents and children. Similarly, anger and conflict usually have different meanings among siblings than between parent and child. Consequently, siblings often need to deal with these issues among themselves, thereby allowing their mutual differences from the entire total family system to be aired. If not, issues may become confused and boundaries blurred as parents naturally assume guilt, shame, and responsibility, stepping in to help with problems which do not or need not directly involve them. Obviously, each system needs help, but the different needs and functions of parental and sibling systems call for different approaches.

"JOHNNY, JIMMY, AND ERNIE"

These three adolescent boys were brought to my office by their parents, who were themselves seeking relief from constant struggle around sexual problems. Dad accused Mother of "frigidity" while Mother suspected Dad of "playing around." The boys, Johnny, 15, Jimmy, 13, and Ernie, 11, let it be known that their parents' struggles came to light when Mother caught Ernie masturbating and Dad was asked to intervene. Dad refused and told Ernie to "talk to his brothers," which he did. Mother was furious that Dad's "permissiveness" had further allowed Ernie's behavior to "run rampant." During the course of the third of the initial five assessment sessions, Dad laughingly said that Ernie's brothers "could talk with him just as easily about sex" as he could. Mother became angry and tearful, saying that Dad, "just didn't care about the family anymore," to which he replied that she was "scared shitless of sex — all she wants me to do is cut their peckers off." The boys laughed and appeared as if they shared a unified "sibling front."

I separated the spousal dyad from the siblings and saw each group separately for approximately six months. During that time, they met with me as a family on four occasions, as a way of checking on their progress and noting what issues in their family relationships needed work. During the family therapy sessions, Johnny attempted rationality, Jimmy was polarized between logical and emotional arguments, and Ernie simply tried to please everyone. But the mythologizing process was firmly in place and the harder they tried, the deeper into that process they moved.

The parents worked on Mother's fears that Ernie's pubescence had signaled an increase in Dad's sexual appetites and Dad's denial that he was inappropriately colluding with his sons against Mom. Mom didn't want to believe that as boys reach adolescence they may become sexually active and sometimes promiscuous. It was easier for Dad to accept this since he had lived through it himself. In session, Dad had said to Mom, "I know you feel that way because you had a screwy relationship with your older brother." Although they viewed that relationship as "screwy," it was really stereotypic in that

Mom's brother was allowed broad sexual expression while she was restricted.

In the family Mom and Dad created, the more sexually aware the boys became, the more anxious and sexually inhibited she grew. As the boys noted their mother's anxiety, they increased their sexually taunting behavior by leaving open copies of *Playboy* in their rooms and making frequent sexual allusions to Mom. Dad seemed to enjoy these regular exchanges between mother and sons. This in turn fueled her anger and reinforced her sons' sexual mischief. The boys developed stories about their mother and father's sexual life, and their parents developed diagnoses about their sons. The household was frequently upset by blaming and accusation. The parents and the brothers became more firmly entrenched in their attitudes, feelings and behaviors on the occasion of each conflict. They all knew their roles and every eruption was practice for the next. Their mythologizing had become a well-established, long-running family drama.

One myth held that Mom was asexual and completely disinterested in things sensual. Another myth was that Dad was appropriately sexual and expressive. A third myth contained an expectation that the sons were to emulate Dad's sexuality.

The parent's sexual problems were directly related to their emotionally and sexually inhibited socialization. Mother and Father had been carefully schooled by their parents to abhor sex and sensuality alike. Mom's arousal of sexual feelings during her pubescence was brought into sharp focus as she observed her older brother's flagrantly sensual behavior, which was forbidden to her. Dad was inhibited sexually because he was so focused on performance he could not feel his own sensations. Nor could he appreciate or validate his partner's.

They were involved in the familial enactment of social myths that hold women to be sexually constricted and men to be sexually competent. Dad's collusion with his sons against his wife was a reenactment of his relationship with his own father when he was a child.

Unconsciously, Mom and Dad married each other for the same reason. They were both terrified of sexual expression. Their marriage became a fertile ground for conflict. The more he demanded sex, while being emotionally and sexually inadequate, the less she was interested. The more terrified and asexual she felt, the more angry and demanding he became.

Once they became aware of these conscious and unconscious sexual prescriptions and proscriptions, they began to practice new behaviors. They even went so far as to expand their heretofore restricted and puritanical social group, to include couples and families who were generally more sexually liberated. Mom and Dad both became aware of the myth that Dad was "fooling around." They understood it as behavior that reflected the only recourse to express her anger toward her husband. Mom's behavior was full of self-blame for her supposed sexual inadequacy which was converted to her belief that Dad was sexually unfaithful. Dad's aggressive defensiveness only reinforced this misperception. In marital therapy Mom and Dad were able to resolve many of their sexual conflicts, even though they both maintained a high degree of modesty.

Johnny, Jimmy, and Ernie used their therapy time to strengthen their fraternal bonds. Johnny coached Jimmy's sexual mentoring of Ernie by providing corrective feedback to Jimmy. Sibling therapy proceeded by enabling the three of them to freely express feelings about their parents' restrictiveness. But, these feelings of anger and resentment were short-lived. The separation of the two systems, the parents and the siblings, coupled with parental changes, enabled Johnny, Jimmy, and Ernie to concentrate on their own sibling processes. They were better able to relate to one another's sexual development. For example, Jimmy would tenderly joke with Ernie about nocturnal emissions causing Ernie much discomfort. Johnny, on hearing Ernie's demands that Jimmy stop teasing him, pointedly told Johnny, "Knock it off. Christ," he went on, "you know how it feels to have someone make fun of you. God! especially about when you come at night." After this, there were many more frank and open discussions among them, both during and outside of therapy sessions. Jimmy was better able to feel Ernie's discomfort and empathize, while providing him with sexually explicit information he checked out with Johnny.

The separation of parents and siblings had the salutory effect of helping each more fully develop and strengthen their own systems, independent of the other. Mom and dad drew closer and focused more on themselves than on their sons.

The siblings separated in very important ways from Mother and Dad, leaving—or allowing—them to finally resolve their own sexual dilemmas.

Bank and Kahn (1982) define the sibling bond as "a connection between themselves, at both the intimate and public levels." I consciously used this definition as the operational metaphor in the treatment of Johnny, Jimmy, and Ernie by strengthening their bond, using characteristics associated with their ordinal positions. I used Johnny's firstborn style of teaching and assuming authority to aid Jimmy. As the secondborn, Jimmy was frequently polarized between his thoughts and his feelings, and Johnny's directness — while troubling — was eventually appreciated. Johnny's approach to life was more linear. I helped him accept and use Jimmy's ability to see patterns of relationships as a way of furthering his ability to get along with others.

I asked Jimmy to tell his brother the words he used to describe his parents' relationships. I then asked Johnny to repeat those words and free-associate to them. After that I asked Jimmy to try to give more exact definitions to his brother's associations. By having them use one another's strategies, they became more comfortable with both their process and content.

While firstborns often feel lost because they have difficulty apprehending relationship patterns, second children generally have a much easier time of it. Ernie, born third, not only saw relational patterns more clearly than his brothers but also had a greater appreciation of their complexity.

The boys together developed a new myth about their parents. It had to do with Mom and Dad's sexuality, although it was thinly disguised. During one of the total family sessions, there was some discussion about the parents' sexual values. Somehow the term "generation gap" was transmogrified into "generation crap" by Dad. Johnny and his brothers thought it was the perfect metaphor for their parents' sexual attitudes. I began to use it as an induction into the trance of the myth of parental (sexual) naivete. When, during our monthly family sessions, Mom or Dad berated their sons for their sexual innuendos, and the boys reacted, I asked, with feigned innocence, if that was "generational crap." The siblings carried that into their therapy sessions and used it at home as well, as a punctuation to end the parent-sibling group bickering. The significant change came about as the metamessage of "generational crap" shifted from contempt to gentle warmth and chiding. Within each group, stories emerged about the irreconcilable generational differences. As each group came to believe in that irreconcilability, the "sexual conflicts," with the exception of a few minor skirmishes, ended.

Both Mom and Dad suffered from conflicts emerging from their childhood sibling patterns. So on several occasions I asked Mom's and Dad's older siblings to join the therapy sessions. They did so voluntarily and themselves, individually and as a sibling group, benefited from the strengthening of the bonds with their respective siblings.

Over time Dad ended his collusion with his sons and Mom came to appreciate her sons' sibship as a separate entity. She evolved a myth of her sons' fraternal unity which replaced the earlier myth of "lascivious sexuality." It was eagerly accepted by the boys.

LILA IS LAZY; LINDA IS LOVABLE

Linda, 31, and Lila, 39, brought their mother into therapy because of their three-member family's chronic squabbling. Since Dad had died seven years earlier, their relationship consisted of an unending series of arguments. Years earlier, Dad had apparently been the peacemaker between the "three girls," his term for them.

Both Linda and Lila shared the extremely large family home with their mother. Each of them had what amounted to her own living quarters. Their family had always been wealthy and father's death left them even more financially secure.

Linda and Lila both had professional degress and practiced their professions both locally and internationally. Each had attained high status and high salaries. Continuing to live at home, complete with servants, afforded them the supports they wanted to actively pursue their careers. I was never asked to deal with any issues surrounding their living arrangement. Although I had my own questions about it, the family refused to answer them.

During the first two sessions, it became apparent that the conflicts between Linda and Lila were like a magnet that drew mother to them. She became the replacement for the peacemaker, the role her husband had played. The siblings—grown women—fought with each other about who had more privileges, who was more loved by Dad and Mom, and who had more power in the family. Mother was totally confused by these screaming matches. No matter how she tried to end them, there was no resolution. She explained the context for these

fights by describing each daughter's characteristic behavior patterns—Lila's "laziness" and Linda's "lovability." The sibling conflicts
escalated with each telling. I saw the three of them several times
before I decided to ask Lila and Linda to come in together, without
mother.

Each sister told her version of the family myths of "Lila's laziness"
and "Linda's lovability." Lila, being an only child for her first eight
years, had developed many characteristics associated with first and
only children. Lila took a lot of responsibility for Linda during her
infant and toddler years, while mother worked. Lila was hurt and
angry about Linda's lack of gratitude for her efforts. Linda had learned
early on to be the family "baby" and charmed everyone who had
contact with her. She exuded "cuteness" as a child, which matured
into lovability as an adult. Lila, being more aloof and distant, resented those characteristics in her sister.

A family myth arose, out of Lila's constant struggles to be as
lovable as her sister, that she was lazy because of her constant attention to love and approval-seeking at the expense of her assigned
household chores. Lila, on the other hand, always seemed, to Linda
and mother, to be able to accomplish both. The more Linda struggled
for the kind of attention Lila got, the more resentful she became. She
learned to focus her caretaking on her sister but Linda accepted it as
her due. Each told her stories in natural hypnotic trance and in the
typically automatic manner characteristic of mythologizing (Perlmutter and Sauer, 1986).

Using hypnotic techniques such as suggestion, I assisted them in
editing their myths in such a way that they learned to view each other
quite differently (Lankton and Lankton, 1983; Ritterman, 1983).
This was a form of reframing-in-trance. In this process, I invent or
borrow a story much like the one being told and enacted by the
sibling group but with modifications. The modifications are aimed at
changing perceptions and the ways listeners map or understand the
meaning of one another's behavior. If the old map, the old myth, is
no longer operative, a new one must be invented. Linda became able
to laugh at the myth of her lovability. She shared openly that she "was
a real bitch but would never let anyone see that side of me. Every time
I got bitchy, you know, wanting my own way," she went on, "Dad
would really come down on me—hard. He was a real son-of-a-bitch,
Jesus!" Lila and she shared a deeply felt sisterly laugh as Lila told

Linda of her endless hard work to "look as good to Dad as you did. No matter how hard I worked, no matter how many household chores I did, Jesus, Dad would always find fault and tell me that I didn't pull my load like you did." Linda laughed and said, "I'm the lazy one, but I always found the easy way. I'd kiss up to Dad whenever I did anything and I always told him that I did it for him. God, he was a sucker for charm!"

Linda and Lila negotiated new myths about Dad's meaning to each of them. Their mythologizing about Dad and Mom's ignorance about his relationship to his daughters took on the characteristics of sorority sisters sharing secrets that were for their ears only. They became quite close and placed rather tight boundaries around their relationship. Mom, in the few subsequent sessions, expressed her relief and gratitude that her "girls had gotten so close." Mom's ecstasies about her daughters' newfound relationship brought giggles from Linda and Lila. They alone were the repository for family secrets and the developers of a new myth that was rightfully theirs and theirs alone.

Mother was also ambivalent. While she felt unburdened of her role as peacemaker, she also felt lost without it. The ambivalence also reflected the sameness/difference dialectic noted earlier. It is an ambivalence that is still not fully resolved, and I suspect is never fully resolved for any parent.

IMPLICATIONS FOR SIBLING THERAPY

Bank and Kahn (1982) have suggested five reasons why therapists avoid sibling therapy:

1. Therapists are taught little or nothing about the subject because a unified body of knowledge has not existed until now.
2. The authoritative parental role of the therapist may be undermined or subverted when working with siblings.
3. Aspects of therapeutic caring differ between sibling and other therapies.
4. There are discrepancies and omissions in the ways family therapists view power in family relationships.
5. Therapists' resistances to including siblings in therapy emerge from therapists' own sibling experiences.

I suggest still another reason for the exclusion of siblings from therapy, namely, our assumptions are unconsciously sex-role biased. Our therapies are built on a masculine epistemology. That view holds dominance, control, and power to be essential forces in family life. Consequently, the drive for cooperation and sharing requisite in sibling relationships is no better understood by therapists than by families seeking their help.

The theories out of which family therapy grew and in which most of us were trained employ concepts of hierarchy and power inherent in sex-role stereotypic assumptions. No matter how systemic we become, often erroneous assumptions about hierarchy and power in families seem inescapable.

More recently, however, feminists, writing about women's world views and feminist perspectives on family therapy, have offered new insights into and alternatives to our theoretical and clinical biases (Avis, 1985; Belenky et al., 1986; Gilligan, 1982; Layton, 1984; Noddings, 1984; Simon, 1984; Taggart, 1985). Inherent in their thinking is a different epistemology in which joining and sharing, intrinsically ecogenic functions, take their places alongside control as a characteristic of family systems. The idea of shared space, thinking, and control readily admits sibling subunits to the realm of therapeutic possibility. Identity is no longer viewed as being solely a function of parental affiliation but can now be understood as emerging from several contexts (Bank and Kahn, 1982; Gilligan, 1982). Siblings, therefore, must be considered by family therapists as important to our clinical enterprise. Anything else continues to promote sex-role biases that rob families of their opportunities for healthy change and therapists of opportunities to help more effectively.

CONCLUSION

I have attempted to specify some conditions concerning sibling therapy by highlighting the development of family problems as a function of myths generated from characteristics associated with birth order. Each child's birth changes the familial context and children's characteristic ways of behaving change to meet their context. First children, for instance, must process family information differently from third or fourth children. Consequently, every child perceives the family differently. In turn, each child will be perceived according to the characteristic way of perceiving. It is out of this complexity that each child's familial reputation is built, and from which mythologizing about each child emerges. Mythologizing is the enactment of a myth or story. It occurs in a trance state in which the story-telling and attendant rituals are performed automatically. Induction into mythologizing follows the same modes as does induction into any trance state. These inductions can be sensate, psychologic, or social, such as the anniversary of an event or celebration of a holiday. Sibling units develop their own mythologizing not only separate and apart from their parents but also as the result of parent-child interactions.

Some sibling conflicts do reflect parental dysfunctions, no doubt. But too little is known about the ecology of sibling groups to believe that siblings exist only as reflections of parental systems. Too many of our family therapies operate on these assumptions.

If we turn our clinical attention to sibling groups and subunits, we will find that they too have their own ecosystems, with their own internal logic. Their mythologizing is, more frequently than we know, peculiar to their own system. Sibling mythologizing enhances individuation from parents while maintaining familial ties. Sibling bonds are more closely linked, I believe, to successful friendship bonding than to parent-child bonds.

Our avoidance of sibling issues in therapy has created clinical ideology in which only the individual or the total family unit is defined as a unit of treatment.

Sibling issues must be more clearly understood and addressed. In addition, the sibling relationship patterns of therapists and their implications for therapy must also be investigated. Finally, we know very little about the relationships among birth order, family mythologizing, and therapeutic effectiveness. Some forms of mythologizing are dysfunctional while others promote family satisfaction and health. Numerous questions still need to be addressed. Among them are: From what types of families do our therapists emerge? And, what are the operant mythologizing patterns among help-seeking families?

REFERENCES

Avis, J. M. (1985). The politics of functional family therapy: A feminist critique. *Journal of Marriage and Family Therapy, 11*(2).

Bach, J., Anderson, A., & Rhetts, J. C. (1980). *The growth of the family*. Unpublished manuscript. Minneapolis: The Bach Institute.

Bank, S. P., & Kahn, M. D. (1982). *The sibling bond.* New York: Basic Books.

Belenky, M. F., Clinchy, B. M., Goldberger, N. R., & Tarule, J. M. (1986). *Women's ways of knowing: The development of self, voice, and mind.* New York: Basic Books.

Bellah, R. N., Madsen, R., Sullivan, W. M., Swidlen, A., & Tipton, S. M. (1985). *Habits of the heart.* Berkeley: University of California Press.

Bernal, G., & Ysern, E. (1986, April). Family therapy and ideology. *Journal Marital and Family Therapy, 12*(2).

Ernst, C., & Angst, J. (1983). *Birth order: Its influence on personality.* Berlin: Springer-Verlag.

Ferriera, A. (1963). Family myth and homeostasis. *Archives of General Psychiatry, 9.*

Gilligan, C. (1982). *In a different voice.* Cambridge, MA: Harvard University Press.

Hoopes, M. M., & Harper, J. M. (1987) *Birth order roles and sibling patterns in individual and family therapy.* Rockville, MD: Aspen Publishing.

Keeney, B. (1979, June). Ecosystemic epistemology: An alternative paradigm for diagnosis. *Family Process, 18*(2), 117–129.

Lankton, S. R., & Lankton, C. H. (1983). *The answer within: A clinical framework of Ericksonian hypnotherapy.* New York: Brunner/Mazel.

Layton, M. (1984, May–June). Tipping the therapeutic balance: Masculine, feminine, neuter? *The Family Networker, 8*(3).

Noddings, N. (1984). *Caring: A feminine approach to ethics and moral education.* Berkeley, CA: University of California Press.

Perlmutter, M. S. (1974). *The ontology of relationships.* Unpublished paper, School of Social Work, University of Wisconsin-Madison, Madison, Wisconsin.

Perlmutter, M. S. (1979, April). *Developmental stages of family myth formation.* Paper presented at The American Family Therapy Association Meeting, Chicago.

Perlmutter, M. S. (1983, October). *Family myths.* Paper presented at the Annual Meeting of the American Association of Marriage and Family Therapists, Washington, DC.

Perlmutter, M. S. (1984, October) *Family myths and birth order.* Paper presented at the Annual Meeting Workshop of the American Association of Marriage and Family Therapists, San Francisco.

Perlmutter, M. S. (1985, October). *Family mythologizing and birth order.* Paper presented at the Annual Meeting Institute of the American Association of Marriage and Family Therapists.

Perlmutter, M. S. (1986). *Mythologizing as a regulatory process in family systems.* Unpublished paper. School of Social Work, University of Wisconsin-Madison, Madison, WI.

Perlmutter, M. S., & Hatfield, E. H. (1980, Spring). Intimacy, metacommunication and second order change. *The American Journal of Family Therapy, 8*(1).

Perlmutter, M. S., & Sauer, J. S. (1986). Induction, trance and ritual in family mythologizing. *Contemporary Family Therapy, 8*(1).

Perlmutter, M. S., & Wikler, L. M. (1976). *Family myths and family types.* Unpublished paper. School of Social Work, University of Wisconsin-Madison, Madison, Wisconsin.

Ritterman, M. (1983). *Using hypnosis in family therapy.* San Francisco: Jossey-Bass.

Simon, R. (1984, May-June). An interview by Richard Simon from ideology to practice: The women's project in family therapy. *The Family Networker, 8*(3).

Taggart, M. (1985). The feminist critique in epistemological perspective: Questions of context in family therapy. *Journal of Marriage and Family Therapy,* 11(2).

Van den Berghe, P. L. (1979). *Human family systems: An evolutionary view.* New York: Elsevier.

Zimmerman, N., Collins, L. E., & Bach, J. M. (1986, Fall). Ordinal position, cognitive style and competence: A systemic approach to supervision. *The Clinical Supervisor,* 4(3).

3

Basics of Family Structure and Sibling Position

Walter Toman

HISTORICAL BACKGROUND

Depth psychological concepts about early influences of persons and events upon a growing child's motivation, personality and mental health have been advanced and defended throughout our century. Anecdotal evidence correlating such early influences with outcomes later in life has been compiled on a broad front, ranging from psychotherapy and education to mental illness, psychosomatic disorders, crime, juvenile delinquency, indigence, and professional careers. While psychotherapists and clinicians have defended their observations, often these have amounted to no more than individual case histories.

Social scientists were more demanding and empirical. They wanted several cases of a kind and some statistical significance. They wanted groups of cases—at least two groups drawn from the same population, but different from each other in the characteristic under study. They wanted to look for differential effects of the independent variable. In such pursuits they often gathered no more than sporadic statistical evidence. Psychologically, sociologically, ethnically or even geographically, their fishing grounds were too far apart.

On the basis of my own clinical work as a psychoanalyst and psychotherapist, it dawned on me in the early 1950s that these two kinds of efforts needed to be integrated. Inconspicuously and innocuously to the therapeutic process, I began collecting data from my own clinical work and the work I supervised, not only about the subjective aspects of a patient's life and relationships, but also about objective givens, including significant persons, particularly family members. This extended beyond the parents to a patient's siblings, to the siblings of the parents and their children, and in turn to the grandparents. Knowing at least whether the grandparents had been around or not during the childhood and youth of the parents seemed relevant for obvious reasons: If they had not been around, it constituted an early parental loss and potential psychological trauma for the parent (Toman, 1959a,b,c, 1961, 1965). If a patient had a partner or a spouse and/or children, they were included in these explorations as well.

Needless to say, losses of persons *anywhere* in the family background constituted potential psychological trauma. Inquiring about loss enabled us to uncover psychological responses and consequences the loss generated in family members or in the patient.

In addition to losses of family members, the structure of the family itself is of crucial importance. Freud's (1915–17) father-mother-child constellation is the basic pattern considered by psychoanalysts, but in effect is merely a beginning. It's father-mother-boy and father-mother-girl for the two genders. Then, heeding Adler's (1973) criticism that Freud primarily emphasized the family situation of the only child, suppose we consider a family of two children, a boy and a girl. If they are not twins, the family structure is affected by who has come first. It is still different if the family has two girls or two boys.

SIBLING CONFIGURATIONS AND SIBLING POSITIONS

We have already spotted the four basic combinations of two children considering merely age rank and sex. Looking at each of the two children separately, we get eight basic sibling positions (Toman, 1959a,b,c, 1960, 1961, 1965):

Older brother of sister	b(s)
Younger brother of sister	(s)b
Older brother of brother	b(b)
Younger brother of brother	(b)b
Older sister of brother	s(b)

Younger sister of brother	(b)s
Older sister of sister	s(s)
Younger sister of sister	(s)s

Any sibling configuration of three or more children is composed of some of these basic sibling positions. Take older brother of brother and sister, b(bs), or a middle sister of two brothers, (b)s(b), for example. Obviously, the boy is the older brother of a brother and of a sister, b(b) and b(s). The girl is both a younger and an older sister of a brother, (b)s and s(b). A younger brother of two sisters, (ss)b, on the other hand, has two sibling relations of the same type: s(b) and (s)b. In contrast, only children, whether boys or girls, have no sibling position.

Let us stick with the two-child family a bit longer. Due to having been around for some three years, on average, before the younger sibling is born, an older sibling is likely to take on a role of responsibility, guidance, and care vis-à-vis the younger one. If the older one hesitates, perhaps dreaming of the times when he or she was still the only one, the parents will usually pressure him into that new role.

A younger sibling, on the other hand, has ordinarily never been without the older one. The younger is likely to become dependent upon the guidance and care of the older sibling. As he or she grows up, however, the younger sib begins to resist or evade the older one at times, as well as to emulate and even outdo the older child.

Whatever conflicts arise between the two siblings from such a predicament, we have found them ordinarily to be more pronounced and severe when we are dealing with two brothers or two sisters than when the siblings are of the opposite sex.

Empirical Studies of Sibling Position

Adler (1973, 1978) is known for his early explicit attempts at describing general characteristics of some sibling positions. He omitted others, among them some of the basic ones, and was not very systematic in other ways. Our studies of personality characteristics and social attitudes, including relationships with persons of the same and the opposite sex, were more thorough than Adler's and revealed comparatively clear patterns. It turned out that children in a particular sibling position, older sister of brothers, for example, showed more similarity with children of that same position in other families than they did with siblings in their own.

Focused studies by myself and fellow researchers in Boston and later in Erlangen, as well as by other social scientists (for surveys see Ernst and Angst, 1983; Sutton-Smith and Rosenberg, 1970; Toman, 1974, 1976; see also Croake and Olson, 1977; Strodtbeck and Creelan, 1968), showed that sibling position characteristics tend to account for some 10 to 20% of the variance in a person's long-term social behavior, his social interests and preferences. If a person occupies an identical or similar sibling position as his same-sex parent, the characteristics of that sibling position can sometimes account for up to 50% of a person's variance in long-term social behavior.

In order to test whether the personality and social role portraits of basic sibling positions I had assembled in the first edition of *Family Constellation* (1961) would withstand a hard data test, Löhr (1966) gave excerpts of those portraits to high school students and asked them to select those that best fit their siblings. A comparison of the portraits thus chosen with the actual sibling positions of the siblings showed a significant coincidence ($p < .01$). Subjects trying to recognize themselves in one of those portraits succeeded too, but at a lower level of statistical significance ($p < .05$). This, by the way, is a general phenomenon that we have encountered many times when people appraise portraits of their own sibling position and those of others, such as siblings, cousins or friends: They recognize others in those portraits with more subjective conviction than they do themselves. Others, however, seem to recognize them better in those portraits.

Theoretical Considerations

Why should sibling positions or sibling roles matter anyway? The term "sibling role" seems fitting because sibling positions develop in a social context—the family. Hence the question may be rephrased: Why should a social context like the family exert an influence on its children, and why should it be strong enough to notice? In fact, why should or might it be the strongest of all social contexts—stronger than other social context in which people assemble, associating partly by destiny or fate, partly of their own free will, and to which they keep returning at different and variable intervals and for different and variable lengths of time, such as neighborhood, playground, school, clubs, place of work, vacation resort, or cafeteria?

The family is usually the strongest context because it is the first or oldest in a person's ontogeny, the most exclusive, comparatively speaking (subjectively there is no other at first), the most enduring, and the most pervasive of all social contexts. Living with and relating to other persons start here; even when a child is in school, on the playground or with neighbors at times, he or she always returns home, at least under ordinary circumstances.

How could it be otherwise? What else would a child have to go by when entering and staying in new social contexts than the patterns of interaction and relationship experienced at home? The child is prepared for interactions and relationships with parent- and sibling-like persons, with people like mother and father or brother and sister.

And how will the child fare in new social contexts? We explicated our assumptions and findings in the duplication theorem (Toman, 1961, 1971), which says: Social relationships in new social contexts tend to be viewed in the light of social relationships in familiar social contexts. Hence those social relationships in new social contexts that are similar to social relationships in familiar contexts are easier to enter and to maintain than are those that are less similar.

A Field Experiment in Nursery School

In that vein we were able to show that children in nursery school tend to behave according to the duplication theorem (Toman, 1975/6). Oldest siblings were inclined to lead child-centered activities in nursery school. Other children, especially youngest siblings, wanted to follow them. Oldest siblings heeded the teacher's wishes more than younger siblings did. Also children who had siblings only of the other sex were likely to play with children of the other sex rather than of the same sex. Children who had only siblings of the same sex sought contacts with children of the same sex rather than the other sex.

After the children had been in nursery school for at least half a year, this picture began to change with the addition of new types of contacts. Some youngest siblings attempted to initiate activities themselves and to lead others. Some children also sought playmates of the sex opposite from their siblings. Our explanation: Youngest siblings wised up to the fact that, in contrast to home, the other children in class were not older (more mature) than they were themselves. If younger siblings in nursery school acted like their older siblings, they seemed to meet with more acceptance than they did at home. Through identification with their older siblings, moreover, they may even have had more to offer at times than the older siblings in their class.

We also assume there is a tendency or even a need in all new social contexts eventually to try those interactions and relationships for which one has been less well prepared. All new contexts become more familiar after a while and can serve in turn as examples for other new contexts. Just as the family is the context upon which to draw in nursery school, family and nursery school are the contexts upon which to draw in school or on the playground, and so on. We suspect, though, that the older and more enduring contexts remain more influential. They sit deeper in the person. They are harder to escape.

Compatibility of Sibling Roles in Marriage: More Field Experiments

Developmentally the nursery school study should perhaps have been our first, but historically another and bolder "experiment" had preceded it. If sibling roles truly had an influence on actual long-term social behavior, this should even be evident in partnerships and marriages. Partners who had siblings of the opposite sex in their families of origin would be more at ease with each other than partners who did not. They might be happier, more likely to have children, and less likely to separate. Similarly, couples consisting of an oldest and a youngest sibling might be better off with each other than partners who were both oldest siblings or both youngest.

Combining both aspects — sex of partners' siblings and age ranks of partners among their siblings — would lead us to expect that an oldest brother of sisters and a youngest sister of brothers would be a good match, and so would a youngest brother of sisters and an oldest sister of brothers. In both cases the partners enter a peer relationship with each other that is familiar. Their sibling roles are complementary to each other. They have married someone like their respective siblings.

In contrast, an oldest brother of brothers and an oldest sister of sisters would be among the poorer matches, comparatively speaking, and so would the youngest brother of brothers with the youngest sister of sisters. In both cases the partners have had limited experience of life with a peer of the opposite sex and have occupied identical age ranks. Their learned sibling roles may lead to both a gender conflict and an age-rank conflict.

There are seven intermediary degrees of conflict between complete complementarity of sibling roles of partners and complete age-rank and gender conflict of their sibling roles. However, for the sake of simplicity, let us ignore those seven here.

What do we assume when one or both partners have had no siblings? Singletons, we assume, would be less well prepared for a partnership of peers than persons who have had siblings. They would rather be looking for a parent. However, only children do differ from one another. Here another factor has to be taken into account—the sibling role of the same-sex parent in his or her family of origin. But let us set the case of only children aside for the time being and stick with the supposedly best and poorest matches, as appraised by degree of complementarity or conflict of sibling roles. If our assumptions are correct, couples with complementary sibling roles should be rare among those partnerships or marriages that end in divorce, whereas couples with both an age-rank and a gender conflict of their sibling roles should be relatively frequent.

I had found this to be the case in a sample of 16 divorced couples that I had come across in Boston while teaching at Brandeis University. I matched them with 16 intact marriages of the same age, educational background and social strata and found nine complementary or partly complementary matches among the 16 intact marriages, but only one among the 16 divorced couples. ("Partly complementary" is something like an older brother of a brother and a sister married to the middle sister of two brothers: b(bs)/(b)s(b), the slash indicating partnership; each partner has at least one sibling relation among several that is complementary to at least one of the other partner's.)

Thus, our assumption was proven correct in this instance. However, matching one group to another is a complex affair amenable to the unconscious biases of the researcher. We were itching to do a more substantial test. The opportunity arose when I moved to the University of Erlangen-Nürnberg. The German Research Association (Deutsche Forschungsgemeinschaft) sponsored a large-scale study of more than 2300 families in Nürnberg and Zürich. We had access to the families through the schools, all families studied had children, and we had an incidence of 108 divorces in our sample. This was within the sampling error of divorces in the population (which amounted to 5% for that generation of families with children).

We searched through all cases of complete complementarity looking for divorced couples and found none at all. In contrast, checking all those couples who had both an age-rank conflict and a gender conflict of their sibling roles, we found that 16% of them had ended up divorced. Only 84% of them were still married, whereas 100% of the completely complementary matches and 97% of those with partly complementary matches were still married. Couples where both spouses had been only children had a 9% incidence of divorce.

In other words, the pivotal groups of matches demonstrated that sibling roles and their compatibility or conflict still had an effect even decades later. Sibling characteristics are overlaid by many other factors, to be sure, but they do show in marriage. And the duplication theorem provides an explanation. To my knowledge, no other hypothesis or theorem explains this effect.

Distrusting our data in the tradition of Vienna's old school of philosophy of science (e.g., von Schlick, 1938), we checked and rechecked repeatedly the different degrees of complementarity. We tested whether including all intermediary degrees of sibling role conflict and only children married to spouses with siblings uncovered a greater incidence of divorce among lower degrees of complementarity. It did. We checked whether that was also true of parents who had a child together but never got married to each other. It was. We tested whether those among the divorced couples who had stayed married for at least 10 years were better matched by sibling roles than those who had divorced sooner. They were (Toman, 1971, 1974, 1976).

Perhaps it was not complementarity of sibling roles but merely size of spouses' families of origin—in other words, number of spouses' siblings—that was conducive to staying married rather than divorcing. This was true. Divorced couples came from smaller families of origin. In order to rule out size we kept number of siblings "constant," selecting only those of the divorced couples who, among the two of them, had four or five siblings. We found that even then low

degrees of sibling role complementarity were significantly more frequent among the divorced than expected by chance.

Turning again from the subsample of divorced parents to the entire
sample of 2300 families, we began checking whether number of
children springing from marriages of different degrees of complementarity was in any way telling. We found that complementary and
partly complementary parents had about half a child more than the
average, whereas parents one or both of whom had been only children had about half a child less than the average.

At one point we wondered whether the population at large, as
represented by our sample, heeded the duplication theorem and chose
complementary partners by sibling roles more frequently than
chance. They did not. However, trying what statisticians have come
to call "configuration frequency analysis" (see Toman, 1955, for an
early example) and splitting them up for age, we found a clear effect.
Those couples who had married above the median age (of 27 years
for the husband and 24 years for the wife) had significantly more
complementary matches than the average, whereas those marrying at
an early age had significantly fewer complementary matches.

Confirming Evidence By Other Researchers

Our empirical studies (Toman, 1959a,b,c, 1961, 1965, 1971,
1974, 1976) have apparently intrigued psychologists, psychotherapists, sociologists and social workers. Some of them have done studies of their own which confirmed our findings.

Baxter (1965) questioned college freshmen about apparent conflict
prevailing among their parents and their parents' sibling positions.
Those parents who had an age-rank conflict of sibling position had
more apparent conflict than those with age-rank complementarity.
However, sex conflict of parents' sibling roles did not differentiate
parents with high and low apparent conflict.

In a study by Kemper (1966) of 256 executives, brothers of younger sisters who had married sisters with older brothers, had more
satisfactory relationships with their spouses than the average, also
than brothers with older sisters married to sisters with younger
brothers.

In Handy's (1968) study of college students, partner satisfaction
was greater with complementary matches than with noncomplemen-

tary matches of sibling roles. Yet the absolute frequency of complementary matches was no greater than in random matching of students by computer. The latter finding coincides with one of ours: The population as a whole seems to go in all directions of matching. They do not particularly, even unconsciously, seek sibling role complementarity when they are young.

In one experiment, 64 pairs of college students were studied. They had been computer-selected from 500 persons, controlled for race, social status, family size, age spacing between siblings, physical attractiveness, and religious preference, and then ordered into four groups by complementarity of sibling roles: complementary by sex and rank, by sex only, by rank only, by neither. There was a significant relationship between complementarity and satisfaction of dating as reported in questionnaires and indicated by the number of actual dates (Mendelsohn, 1973; Mendelsohn et al., 1974).

Among female as well as male college dormitory roommates, interpersonal problems tended to be more frequent between those with conflicting age ranks of sibling roles than with complementary sibling roles (Scheidt and Smith, 1974, 1976).

Nonconfirming Evidence and Possible Explanations

Some studies of sibling role compatibility have failed to show the expected effects. Sibling role compatibility was not telling with couples consulting a family agency (Levinger, 1965; Levinger and Sonnheim, 1965), with newlywed student couples (Pinsky, 1974), with dating couples (Critelli and Baldwin, 1979), and with college roommates (Schuh and Williams, 1977). Compared with the studies they were meant to check, however, the nonconfirming ones appeared to contain more possible flaws, particularly in choice of criteria for satisfaction or success of subjects' relationship and in control group selection. However, one study went a long way to test the influence of sibling role compatibility on partnerships and failed, at least in part. Discussing it in greater detail may illustrate the types of problems one can encounter in this area of research. Birtchnell and Mayhew (1977) hired a market research organization to study a "British national representative sample" of 982 subjects reporting "successful marriages" and 1012 subjects reporting "unsuccessful marriages." They found no significant difference in complementarity of sibling roles of partners between the two groups. In that study, however, 27% indicated a particular fondness for an opposite-sex sibling. Of those, men who were especially fond of an older sister tended to marry a woman with a younger brother or no sibling more often than chance. No corresponding choices were found for women or for men who were fond of a younger sister.

This particular effect observed with men fond of an older sister belongs to those configuration frequency analyses of subgroups that I have mentioned and recommended. I can think of a number of other subgroups to study, such as those among the unsuccessful marriages that actually ended in separation or divorce versus those that did not. Self-rating of success or failure of marriage alone may not be a sufficient criterion to divide the sample in two groups. Children or no children, ages of children, age of parents at time of marriage, time until the first child arrived, duration of marriage and a few more easy-to-obtain characteristics of family structure would be meaningful moderators to define subgroups or refine the criteria of success.

Beyond that, I am not sure what selection principles prevailed when the market research organization approached its subjects for data-gathering. It could also be that the British respond differently from Americans or Germans to such questions. From small samples of families that I studied myself in London in connection with two research projects on "individual friendship systems" (Toman, Gasch, and Schmidt, 1972; Toman, Hörwick, and Möckel, 1986), I was surprised by the British subjects' eloquence and independence in love and partner relations, as well as by their pervasive social strata thinking. Belonging to the working class, being a teacher, moneyed, titled, Irish, Episcopalian, from Chestershire, living in a platformed or detached home or on an estate — all seemed to them to be impermeable boxes. It could be that those variables loom larger in British minds than do the paraphernalia of daily life, closeness to a partner or compatibility at home. They may also loom larger than they do in the United States or in Germany.

Birtchnell and Mayhew (1977) also checked whether with British undergraduates there was more complementarity of sibling role between them and their closest friends than expected by chance. There was not, perhaps for reasons similar to those outlined above.

In contrast to these British findings, in an early study (Kassel, 1962) we found that complementarity of sibling rank was a factor in friendships and that those who reported no friend at the time had lost a friend of conflicting sibling rank and/or sex more often than chance. This was confirmed with friendships in school (von Hintzenstern, 1968). Our research projects on "individual friendship systems," including *all* friends that the subject remembered, whether the friendship was still on or not, confirmed it too. Pooling all friendships listed by all subjects showed that those with compatible sibling roles lasted significantly longer than did those with incompatible ones. The study also revealed how complicated friendships are. Above all, they come in configurations. Different friends offer a person different things. What one cannot provide, another might. That way friends seem to serve a person best and also tend to get from the person what they like the most (Toman et al., 1972, 1986).

General Commentary

Failure of some of the reported studies to display the expected effects is no reason to discard the sibling role compatibility-incompatibility theorem. The studies that confirmed it appear better founded than those that did not. Birtchnell and Mayhew's study, while attempting to get a representative sample of the population, may have been scattered too widely, so that local and regional effects have perhaps blurred the long-term social behavior trends contained in the data.

Some of our best results had regional biases, like a number of randomly chosen schools and classes in Nürnberg and Zürich (Toman, 1971, 1974, 1976) or a number of psychotherapeutic clinics in the Ruhr district (Langenmayr, 1975, 1978). It is always possible to check how far off the samples are from the current census. In major respects ours were well within the statistical limits. The advantage of regional samples of comparatively complex data sets is, however, that the condition "other things being equal" is more likely to be met. Chances are better that the social frame of reference is about the same for all subjects studied. The relationships found within the data sets tend to be freer of sampling errors.

Let me illustrate this by another example. Freyn (1974) investigated whether teachers tend to grade primary school students differently depending on the teachers' sibling positions. Among the male teachers of a school system he selected oldest and youngest brothers of brothers only as well as of sisters only. The students were of both sexes. He found no difference. They all seemed to judge their students comparably, with one exception: Those teachers who had been youngest brothers of sisters showed a slight trend toward grading girls better than boys. However, when sibling positions of the students were taken into account too, Freyn found a significant interaction. In their grades teachers favored those students who had a sibling position either identical with or complementary to that of the grading teacher. Metaphorically speaking, teachers showed (unconscious) preference for those pupils with whom they could identify themselves, as well as those in whom they could identify one of their own siblings.

PARENTS AND CHILDREN: FAMILY CONSTELLATIONS

Having established that complementarity of sibling roles is neither phantom nor sheer nonsense, let us return to the family.

In some crude ways fathers are like many other fathers (typically a bit older than their wives, taller and physically stronger, with deeper voices, usually the breadwinners, etc.). Mothers are like many other mothers (typically younger, smaller and prettier than their husbands, more tolerant of fussy or sick children, more of a homemaker, and so on). On closer look, each father is, of course, a personality in his own right, each mother too, and some of their personality characteristics derive from their respective families of origin and from their sibling positions or roles. This is one of the ways variety enters the system. Compatibility or incompatibility of spouses, as well as conflict with parental roles, may result. In fact, parental behavior that may work well for one configuration of children may not be so good for another. Let us offer an example.

If parents are the older brother of a sister and the younger sister of a brother, b(s)/(b)s, and if they have two children, a boy first and a girl next, the family structure can be symbolized this way, putting the children between two slashes and father on the left, mother on the right:

$$b(s)/bs/(b)s$$

By their sibling positions the parents are optimally compatible. What's more, the children have come in the same order as the parents are used to from home. Hence the son can easily identify with father and the father with his son, the daughter with the mother and vice versa. And the son can relate to mother in a similar way as mother has been used to with her brother and her husband, and the daughter can relate to father as he has been treated by his younger sister and his wife. Son and daughter can treat each other as they see their parents do it. All is bliss, it seems, other things being equal. Their relationships both of identification (with the same-sex parent) and interaction (with the opposite-sex parent) are smooth and easy.

This could be quite different when the children come in the reverse order, a girl first and a boy next:

b(s)/sb/(b)s

Now the boy may find it difficult to identify with father if father thinks a boy should take care and charge of a girl, but the boy thinks the girl (his older sister) should take care of him and let him do as he pleases. The girl, on the other hand, may want to take on responsibility and leadership, but gets no such example from her mother. She may have troubles identifying with her mother, who appreciates guidance and care from a man, whereas she, the daughter, by her experience with her younger brother, wants to lead and take care of men. The daughter's relationship with her father may be complicated by a similar conflict. Perhaps father wants the girl or woman to rely on him and lean on him and let herself be guided, whereas she wants to mother father.

In other words, with just a little change in the succession of children, misunderstandings and conflicts may arise. To an extent they are built into that family constellation.

Let us see for a moment what might happen when that family has a third child, another girl:

b(s)/sbs/(b)s

In the growing relationship with his younger sister, the boy can now also practice what the parents are accustomed to and tend to encourage. He can take care and charge of a little female. As for relations to the other sex, he is at last becoming as father wants him and beginning to treat mother too in that way. And the little girl looking up to her brother is developing those "feminine virtues" that father cherishes and mother displays. Where does that leave the older sister? If she tries to cut into the game and take charge of the little one, which in fact she probably could do better than the boy, she may meet with additional displeasure from the parents. She should "leave that little couple alone," the parents seem to be intimating. She "should mind her own business!" "Which business, if not taking care of little siblings?" she may ask in return, and if the parents listen, they might find ways to change their own behavior and include her. If they don't, and if they should discover years later that they need family counseling or therapy, it is likely that the older sister will be the designated patient (see Toman, 1974, 1976, 1979).

The situation is different again when that family has two boys or two girls instead of boy and girl or girl and boy. In the first case both boys will probably identify with father, although one of them perhaps better than the other, and in their relation with mother there might be a scramble—three males competing for the favors of one woman. Likewise, two girls can identify with mother, one often better than the other, and both of them, together with mother, may play for father's favors.

The situation is still different if the parents are differently matched, such as younger brother of sister with older sister of brother (complementary relationship), younger brother of brother with older sister of sister (sex-role conflict), older brother of sister with older sister of brother (rank conflict), or younger brother of brother with younger sister of sister (sex-role and rank conflict).*

There are altogether 16 such basic matching patterns, plus three in which only children are involved (husband the only child while the wife has siblings, wife the only child while the husband has siblings, and both of them being only children). Those patterns can combine with any of four different configurations of two children and, of course, with eight configurations of three children or 2^n different configurations when n is the number of children in the family. With such a multitude of possibilities, basic sibling roles and basic family patterns help us make sense of complicated family structures.

As for basic identification and interaction bonds between parents and their children, we have concluded, from a variety of clinical and statistical evidence, that, among other things, a parent tends to iden-

*These possible outcomes will undoubtedly be made more complicated due to the rapid social and gender role changes now occurring in both Western Germany and the United States.—*The editors.*

tify better with a child in the identical or similar sibling position as the parent himself had among his siblings. And a parent is likely to interact more easily with a child in the identical or similar sibling position as the parent's sibling.

Other simple structural features that would be important to consider are the age distance between siblings, between parents, and between the parents and the oldest child. Two siblings separated by more than six years tend to become quasi-singletons. A husband who is more than about 11 years older than his wife often becomes a bit of a father to her, a wife who is more than about five years older than her husband a bit of a mother to him. A father who is older than 38 when he has his first child often turns somewhat grandparental in his attitudes toward his children, and so does a mother who is beyond 34. In contrast, a mother of 18 and a father of 20 at the time of birth of their first child frequently become their child's siblings rather than his or her parents, psychologically speaking. An actual grandparent is often taking care of the child.

Losses of Family Members

Loss of a parent is likely to be psychologically very traumatic when it occurs during the first six years of life, traumatic when it occurs between 7 and 15 years of age, and more or less manageable after that. Sibling loss is usually less traumatic than parental loss, loss of a younger sibling than oneself less traumatic than loss of an older sibling (Toman, 1959a,b,c, 1961, 1965; see also Bowlby, 1951).

The structural change that the loss of a family member inflicts upon the family is always worth trying to figure out psychologically. Some important questions are: Who in the family takes on the part of the person lost? How well is he or she equipped to do it, among other things by age and sibling role? And how can the remaining family members accept it? These questions apply also to a newcomer to the family who might be considered as a replacement of the lost person; How well does he or she fit into the family structure, among other things by his own family background, his age, his own sibling role?

Besides permanent losses of family members there are temporal losses (e.g., a father returning after two years of absence), partial temporal losses (e.g., a father seeing his children only weekends), and partial qualitative losses (e.g., learning that mother had been married once before, or that father is an alcoholic). Temporal losses tend to be less traumatic than permanent losses, qualitative losses to become apparent only in individual or psychotherapeutic appraisals.

Clinical Considerations and Principles for Therapy

Whether the conflicts between, and losses of, family members do indeed have traumatic effects on a person's further social and psychological development remains to be seen in each individual case. We can say, though, on the basis of our research as well as our clinical and psychotherapeutic work of some 30 years, that the objective and life situational givens of conflict and loss clearly matter in a person's subjective responses. In an average of four out of five cases, our assumptions about psychological difficulties and developmental disruptions tend to be borne out.

Telling patients in psychotherapy about the objective facts of family constellations is another story. In fact, the patient cannot do much with it if he hears it. Whatever he can see, understand, feel and possibly change in the future must come from his own memories and experiences of the past and present as they emerge in his mind during therapeutic sessions and in between, hopefully under the unobtrusive, friendly, and selfless guidance of the psychotherapist.

Some psychotherapists ask: Why should I bother to think about the objective givens and their possible implications and stuff my memory with those details from a person's life when all that counts are his feelings and wishes and longings and fears and furies? I answer: You are doing it anyway. Using your memory, that is. You can't help it. Besides, there are not really that many objective givens and details. If need be, the therapist can take notes and think about them later.

In any case, since psychotherapy amounts to getting a better mix of a patient's early and partly irrational and unconscious wishes with his rational interests in reality, both past and present, the therapist has to know reality. Having some knowledge of a patient's reality will enable the therapist to appraise the patient's responses and his reality concept.

Any pathology of responses and concepts about reality, it seems, can be meaningfully estimated only in relation to the degree and circumstances of objective environmental disruption that the patient has suffered. As a matter of fact, only in relation to environmental traumas can something like a possible constitutional weakness be inferred. Only when we have probed all conceivable aspects of a patient's life for external and potentially traumatic conditions, particularly in his early childhood and youth, and found none, can we hypothesize an organic or inherited deficit as a cause of his psychopathology.

If there is such a deficit or constitutional weakness, the goals of psychotherapy tend to be fundamentally different. Such a person may take inordinately long to grow up to an independent life of his own. Psychotherapy may have to be supportive therapy as long as it goes. The help offered may be above all for the patient to accept that he will not be able to live without some assistance and care of another person, preferably a person who is or has been spontaneously taking an interest in him despite his continued, if decreasing, comparative immaturity.

Directly or indirectly, the patient's family background — or lack of it, in some instances — will always be involved in the therapeutic discourse. It pays for the therapist to know and think about it, but, as mentioned before, there is no need to talk shop about it or give the patient any messages from a book or from the therapist's experience with other patients. The patient would not really appreciate that, at least not in the long run.

This has been my message to psychotherapists, some of whom had been jubilant about the content of my book, *Family Constellation*, when it first appeared in 1961, and who were spilling it to patients like a gospel. No, the patient will have to work it all out at his own pace, with his own insights, and his own conclusions. This is true even in family therapy where, unfortunately, teaching and practicing family life under the explicit and conspicuous instruction of the family therapist have replaced therapy proper in some camps. Not that the family therapist cannot become a teacher of family life with some of the families. But not right away. Not without giving the family a chance first in the ordinary or classical way of psychotherapy, at least for a while.

REFERENCES

Adler, A. (1973). *The practice and theory of individual psychology* (2nd ed., P. Radin, Trans.). Tatowa, NJ: Littlefield. (Original work published 1920)

Adler, A. (1978). *Understanding human nature*. New York: Fawcett. (Original work published 1926)

Baxter, J. (1965). Parental complementarity and parental conflict. *Journal of Individual Psychology 21*, 149–153.

Birtchnell, J., & Mayhew, J. (1977). Toman's theory tested for mate selection and friendship formation. *Journal of Individual Psychology, 33*, 9–17.

Bowlby, J. H. (1951). Maternal care and mental health. London: World Health Organization.

Critelli, J. W., & Baldwin, A. C. (1979). Birth order: Complementarity vs. homogamy as determinants of attraction in dating relationships. *Perceptual Motor Skills, 49*, 467–471.

Croake, J. W., & Olson, T. D. (1977). Family constellation and personality. *Journal of Individual Psychology, 33*, 9–17.

Ernst, C., & Angst, J. (1983). *Birth order: Its influence on personality.* New York: Springer.

Freud, S. (1915–17). Introductory lectures on psychoanalysis. In J. Strachey (Ed. and Trans.) *The standard edition of the complete psychological works of Sigmund Freud.* (Vols. 15 and 16). New York: Norton.

Freyn, W. (1974). *Lehrer-Schülerverhaltnis und Schulerfolg.* Inaugural dissertation, Universität Erlangen-Nürnberg.

Handy, L. C. (1968). An examination of two of Toman's family constellation hypotheses concerning the relative success of mate selection. *Dissertation Abstracts, 28*, 4873–4874.

Kassel, H. (1962). Geschwisterkonstellation und gegengeschlechtliche Freundschaften. Seminar paper, Universität Erlangen-Nürnberg.

Kemper, T. D. (1966). Mate selection and marital satisfaction according to sibling type of husband and wife. *Journal of Marriage and Family Living, 28*, 346–349.

Langenmayr, A. (1975). Familiäre Umweltfaktoren und neurotische Struktur. Göttingen: Vandenhoeck and Ruprecht.

Langenmayr, A. (1978). Familienkonstellation, Persönlichkeitsentwicklung, Neuroseentstehung. Göttingen, Toronto, Zürich, Hogrefe.

Levinger, G. (1965). Complementarity in marital adjustment: Rejoinder. *Journal of Individual Psychology, 21*, 147–148.

Levinger, G., & Sonnheim, M. (1965). Complementarity in marital adjustment: Reconsidering Toman's family constellation hypothesis. *Journal of Individual Psychology, 21*, 137–145.

Löhr, G. (1966). Wiedererkennen von Geschwistern an Hand von spontan selbstverfassten Charakterbildern bei Jugendlichen. Diplomarbeit, Universität Erlangen-Nürnberg.

Mendelsohn, M. B. (1973). Successful heterosexual pairing, sibling configuration and social expectancy. *Dissertation Abstracts International, 33*, 4521.

Mendelsohn, M. B., Linden, J., Gruen, G., & Curran, J. (1974). Heterosexual pairing and sibling configuration. *Journal of Individual Psychology, 30*, 202–210.

Pinsky, H. J. (1974). The effect of sibling constellation on mate selection. *Dissertation Abstracts International, 35-B*, 3031–3032.

Scheidt, F. J., & Smith, M. E. (1974). Same-sex dyads and Toman's theory of birth order compatibility. *Psychological Reports, 34*, 1174.

Scheidt, F. J., & Smith, M. E. (1976). Birth order compatibility and same-sex dyads: A replication. *Journal of Social Psychology, 99*, 291–292.

Schuh, J. H., & Williams, O. J. (1977). Room-mate compatibility. *College Students Journal, 11*, 285–286.

Strodtbeck, F. L., & Creelan, P. (1968). Interaction, linkage between family size, intelligence, and sex role identity. *Journal of Marriage and Family Living, 30,* 301–307.

Sutton-Smith, B., and Rosenberg, E. G. (1970). *The sibling.* New York: Holt, Rinehart and Winston.

Toman, W. (1955). The multiple attitude test: A diagnostic device. *Journal of Abnormal Social Psychology, 51,* 163–170.

Toman, W. (1959a). Family constellation as a basic personality determinant. *Journal of Individual Psychology, 15,* 199–211.

Toman, W. (1959b). Die Familienkonstellation und ihre psychologische Bedeutung. *Psychologische Rundschau, 10,* 1–15.

Toman, W. (1959c). Family constellation as a character and marriage determinant. *International Journal of Psychoanalysis, 40,* 316–319.

Toman, W. (1960). *Introduction to psychoanalytic theory of motivation.* New York: Pergamon.

Toman, W. (1961). *Family constellation.* New York: Springer.

Toman, W. (1965). *Familienkonstellationen.* München: Beck.

Toman, W. (1971). The "duplication theorem" of social relationships as tested in the general population. *Psychological Review, 78,* 380–390.

Toman, W. (1974). *Familienkonstellationen.* (2nd ed.). München: Beck.

Toman, W. (1975/76). On the extent of sibling influence. In K. F. Riegel & J. A. Meacham (Eds.). *The developing individual in a changing world* (pp. 701–709). 2 Vols. The Hague: Mouton.

Toman, W. (1976). *Family constellation* (3rd ed.). New York: Springer.

Toman, W. (1979). *Familientherapie.* Darmstadt: Wissensch. Buchgesellschaft.

Toman, W. (1987). *Familienkonstellationen.* (4th ed.). München: Beck.

Toman, W., Gasch, U., & Schmidt, R. (1972). *Individuelle Freundschaftssysteme.* Bad Godesberg, research report of Deutsche Forschungsgemeinschaft.

Toman, W., Hörwick, E., & Möckel, K. (1986). *Individuelle Bezugspersonensysteme, insbesondere Freundschaften.* Bad Godesberg, research report of Deutsche Forschungsgemeinschaft.

von Hintzenstern, G. (1968). Schulfreundschaften und Familienkonstellation. Diplomarbeit, Universität Erlangen-Nürnberg.

von Schlick, M. (1938). *Gesammelte Aufsätze.* Wien: Gerold.

4

Ethnic Patterns
and Sibling Relationships

Eve Primpas Harriman Welts

Sibling interactions, as this chapter will point out, are always influenced by ethnicity. Many clinicians, unaware of ethnic factors, label behaviors normal within a particular ethnic group as pathological. They do not understand that pathology, like beauty, is often in the eyes of the beholder. Some therapists not only ignore the ethnic dictates of families, but compound the error by assuming that all siblings behave similarly or have equality within the family. Failed attempts at therapy due to disregarding these basic elements may prevent families from ever attempting other therapy.

For example, it would be helpful for a therapist treating the Lupo family (see below) to know that Italian men, at least to the world outside the family, are dominant, while Irish women typically run their households. Therapists trained to value independence and individuality must realize that Italians may interpret these values as undesirable and selfish. They believe that family members are bound to work out their relationships and problems without outside interference (Rotunno and McGoldrick, 1982). In working with families where males dominate, it is foolish for a therapist to urge women to take control. An Irish woman might not find a feminist perspective dystonic; however, if she is married to an Italian man she needs to be supported both in her right to equality and in her sensitivity to her husband's belief that he must take primary responsibility for the family decisions. When parents represent two different cultures, their children are often given very different models, leaving them very confused about choices as to what works best for them.

The following case, like many others encountered by the author, did not initially present itself as having a sibling focus, but it became apparent to the therapist that sibling involvement was vital to the overall outcome in this family. However, before this could happen, the therapist needed to understand the ethnic polarities which existed, values which could either drive these siblings apart or weld them into a cohesive working group. Therapy addressed both ethnic and sibling issues.

The Lupo Family

Mario Lupo, Italian, and Margaret, his Irish wife of 28 years, came to therapy for marital counseling. Now that the children had grown, Margaret struggled with loneliness and role displacement. Mario vehemently prohibited her taking an outside job or going out with friends in the evening without him. Typically, Mario handled all major bills and controlled the finances.

They had two sons, Mario Jr. and Nicholas, and a daughter, Regina. Mario had rarely helped with the children when they were young but had become very involved and authoritative when they were teenagers. He was proud that he had gotten both sons to become owners of a franchise business similar to his own and had loaned them the money to get started. Nicholas remained financially dependent on Mario; not only did he borrow money to set up business, but he and his family were living at low rental in a home owned by Mario and Margaret. Both Nicholas and Regina had married Italians and their spouses had become involved with their in-laws' marital disputes as well. (It is not unusual in Italian families for in-laws to fight out the battles; the therapist should not take this as too great an infraction of family boundaries.) Mario Jr. had married a British-American woman who, true to her ethnic style, supported her husband but did not directly involve herself in discussions with her in-laws. This couple moved to another state.

In marital therapy, Margaret described her struggle for some autonomy and for Mario's friendship. His response was, "How can you be my friend? You're my wife." Margaret, seeing changes in her friends brought about by the feminist movement, realized her needs were being stifled. While options were open to her, she knew that her marriage would also end if she pushed her husband too hard for changes. She sought support from Mario's two sisters when he was especially outrageous, but they remained completely loyal to their brother and did nothing to change him. The therapist did not attempt to engage Mario's sisters in the therapy, as it would have added more women for whom Mario had little respect. To lessen opportunity for criticism, Margaret seldom spoke to Mario and she continued to subordinate her wishes to gain his approval. However, her tolerance of his emotionality and outbursts decreased as she began to assert herself.

Mario had been seeing a male psychiatrist for medication since experiencing a manic episode two years before; however, he had stopped taking his medication and severed contact with his doctor. With the children all out of the home, Margaret could no longer stand Mario's constraints, complaints, and demands. She moved out. We could speculate that Margaret could no longer tolerate Mario's shouting and constant emotional volatility as a consequence both of her culture and of her shyness. Mario pleaded for her return. He claimed that he had not previously understood her pain and that he would change his behavior, give her "freedom," whatever she wanted. Mario and Margaret perceived their situation so differently that the therapist had difficulty comprehending that they were talking about the same events.

With parental permission, in an attempt to gain some objectivity, the therapist then asked the adult children to come in together. Initially they spoke positively of both parents but criticized Margaret for not being more tolerant of Mario's behaviors, which they saw as normal. None of them accepted Margaret's explanation of intolerable emotional pain while living with their father, though they each described their own difficulties with him and said they could not have continued being part of that household. Feeling forced to take sides, they were caught in cultural pull, total loyalty to family (Italian) or cutoff (Irish) (see McGoldrick, 1982). They were even unable to peaceably interact among themselves. Nicholas's wife, Anna, allied with her father-in-law, whom she correctly perceived to be in charge of the family money, perjuring herself in court against her Irish mother-in-law. Margaret, true to her Irish self, refused to engage with Anna in the family shouting matches. Regina tried to remain loyal to her father but gave up when he flaunted his affairs with younger women. She was "disgusted" when he moved a young girlfriend into the Lupo family home. She tried to cut herself off from the family. Unable to maintain that stance, she sought therapy to help reconcile with Nicholas and his children shortly after her own first child was born.

It was then that therapy of the sibling group began by engaging Regina, the only one available and willing to attempt to reach out to her brothers to help change the family situation. She was coached by the therapist to accept the break with her brother Mario, who had moved away, and not pursue him, as this only further distanced him and his wife from the family. Eventually, Nicholas, realizing that both Mario and Regina might remain out of his life, changed his passive stance. While the therapist was careful to listen to the expressed needs of the three spouses, work focused on connecting the sibling group, restoring much of their childhood closeness. In time, they reunited, made face-saving through their desire for the children to have the cousin relationship so valued on the Italian side. Even though their parents divorced, the siblings were committed to preserve the family of origin as a cohesive group through their ongoing relationship.

In this case, if the therapist had allowed the focus to be the inappropriateness and intrusiveness of the in-law behavior, a family split would have been supported. Instead, these siblings, who have little tolerance for separate lives, are continuing the family tradition of making relatives their closest and most trusted friends.

SIBLINGS AND ETHNICITY

It is primarily within family groups that behavior receives situational definitions and role attributions (Spiegel, 1982). Most children first learn to interact with other children in their sibling group. They then try to behave as they did with their siblings when they contact peers outside the family. Their expectations and behavioral patterns are brought to adulthood and reflected in marriage and parenting. In cyclical fashion, sibling relationships are patterned by the family. Child-rearing practices, emotional expressiveness, cultural value systems, goal orientations, and expectations and responsibilities for siblings during all life phases are all factors which influence childhood development.

Immigrants are especially vulnerable to the development of conflicts between generations. In immigrant families, knowledge of language and American customs plays a key role between the younger, more Americanized generation and their elder family members. Proficiency in English unites the siblings, excluding the parents and older generation. Children are exposed to peers and acculturate easily. Later, in an attempt to integrate the disparate directives of two cultures, they attempt to dissociate themselves from the old culture. They may ridicule their parents, reject ethnic food, and set themselves apart from their elders. In this situation younger siblings are more apt to model their older siblings than their parents. Parents may blame the new culture or criticize its values, or fathers may blame mothers, charged with the responsibility of controlling the behaviors of their children. These conflicts between the parents make them less available to their children and usually strengthen the bond among the siblings (Jalali, 1982).

SOME ETHNIC PATTERNS WHICH INFLUENCE SIBLING RELATIONSHIPS

Rules are most often organized around age and sex, as they are the most important determinants of authority. Differences in birth order, gender, physique, appearances, coloring, intelligence, energy levels, and other factors all influence sibling relationships. Among these, competence, industriousness, and determination fuel competitiveness for parental approval and support. Cultural patterns are more fixed on the roles and responsibilities ascribed to the oldest and, most often, the eldest male. Four major ethnic determinants which affect sibling relationships seem to be birth order, gender, separation/individuation, and emotional expressiveness.

Birth Order

Primogeniture, the right of the eldest son to inherit the property, title, and material possessions of the parent to the exclusion of all other children, persists in a variety of cultures. It was introduced into

England at the Norman conquest and still prevails in England in modified form. Even when primogeniture is not practiced, conflicts may arise among siblings over inheritances. Other methods of distributing the older generation's wealth foster rivalries and add potential for manipulativeness and competitiveness among siblings. The Irish, for example, do not practice primogeniture, with fathers often deciding only late in life which of the sons will inherit the land (Arensberg and Kimball, 1968). This keeps the sons engaged as long as possible. As always with uncertainty, anxieties and competitions run high.

Although some siblings attempt to establish a more egalitarian relationship during adulthood, age hierarchies continue to be compelling. In the Asian family, for example, the oldest son is the most important child. He is expected to be a role model for his siblings and to have authority over them. Younger siblings are expected to follow the guidance of the oldest son, not only as children but throughout their adult lives (Shon and Ja, 1982). The youngest daughter, on the other hand, is expected to care for her elderly parents. The positions of oldest son and youngest daughter have been associated with the highest rates of psychopathology in Chinese culture, suggesting that the social roles that go with these positions may at times be highly stressful (Kleinman and Lin, 1981). Latin American, Southern European and Near Eastern parents also accord authority to the older siblings and, in most large families, usually delegate some supervisory and caretaking functions to them. This focus often triangulates the child.

In many immigrant families where a father and mother both work, an older sibling may act as a substitute parent or "parental child" for younger siblings. Younger boys and girls are left at the mercy of older, more powerful sibs who have an opportunity to pass onto their younger siblings the hardships they endured in being initiated to a more adult status. Minuchin (1974) writes that, if the parents abdicate their responsibilities, a child may be forced to become the main source of guidance, control, and decision-making when he or she is developmentally unprepared to handle such a role. Adolescents may reflect their stress through delinquency, sexual impulsiveness, or inappropriate handling of younger siblings when the demands of the household conflict with their age-appropriate need to be with peers.

However, children in this position do not always see the parents as the "enemy." Greek children are included in most social activities and are rarely left with nonfamily babysitters. The parents do not perceive themselves as abdicating responsibility. Elder siblings are conditioned to expect to care for and be responsible for their younger sibs, generally resulting in close bonding among the siblings, as it does in many other groups in which the children do not interact as much with the parents as they do with each other. In Puerto Rican families, for example, parents consider it an expression of gratitude for children to assume responsibility for younger siblings and older parents (Garcia-Preto, 1982).

Power and Preference Through Gender

Notions of sibling power structure are hardly new and are rife in the *Bible* and literature. In the 1700s Samuel Johnson wrote "A child is afraid of being whipped, and gets his task, and there's an end on't; whereas, by exciting emulation and comparisons of superiority, you lay the foundation of lasting mischief; you make brothers and sisters hate each other." In many ethnic groups boys are valued more than girls, a practice begun for economic and survival reasons which fosters a hierarchy of superiority/inferiority, dominance/submission among siblings. The unevenness is distancing. Nevertheless, children rarely attribute their dislike of a sibling as a predictable consequence of the system; rather, they see it as some deficiency in themselves.

Role definition varies greatly among ethnic groups; further, some stress gender differentiation more than others. Often a woman's cultivation of and identification with her son are both a pathway to power and compensation for her helplessness in a male-dominated society. In Latin, Mediterranean, and similar male-dominated cultures, girls are taught obedience and are discouraged from being assertive. Clearly, whether on their own or in identification with their mothers, sisters in these families look to their brothers for guidance, protection, and support (Welts, 1982). Likewise, in West Indian families there is a strong bond between mothers and sons, and a son is doted on regardless of his sibling position. If her husband is absent there is a tendency for the mother to depend on her sons rather than her daughters (Brice, 1982).

Iranian mothers are very affectionate toward their children, especially so with their sons. They attempt to persuade their sons rather than give them orders, but they try to dominate their daughters.

Their sons' naughtiness and aggressiveness are affectionately praised at the same time that they are scolded. Both parents are more permissive with their sons than their daughters (Jalali, 1982). Girls are expected to be submissive, to give in to their brothers, and as a consequence Iranian brothers tend to bully their sisters and sometimes tyrannize them.

Boys are especially valued when family name and lineage are passed through sons. Since having a son is a Greek wife's main source of prestige and validation, preference for male children carries that additional importance. Others, like French-Canadians, welcome children of either sex but prefer males and indulge them more. Greek boys are taught by their parents that they are superior to their sisters who, in turn, are taught to accept their inferiority. While a sister is likely to be greeted with great joy in a British-American family, the brother of an infant girl in a Greek family is apt to hear, "Well, girls are nice, too."

A child's sense of worth can be negatively affected by messages of lesser value given in metacommunication. A therapist seeing a girl from a Mediterranean family might wonder why she is so passive, why, though she may be doing well academically, she shows little motivation for expanding her life to fit her potential. If the girl is pushed to succeed, competing with her brothers, the loss of support from her parents may be too much for her to withstand.

The following example is from the individual therapy of Georgia, a woman in a Greek family, who was trying to examine the difference in her behavior toward her husband and her brother. It illustrates the subtle gender dynamics that permeate adult life and relationships.

Georgia

At this time the family consisted of aged parents and four middle-aged children, Bill, Tina, John, and Georgia, in that order. Tina lived out of state. As is typical in Mediterranean families, mother's role was to encourage family connectedness by providing Sunday family dinners. Mother's failing health and advanced years now prevented her from maintaining the custom at her house. Georgia, a responsible daughter, took over.

Father always told stories of his youth and life achievements at the end of a meal. Georgia commented to John that she had never heard these stories before and wanted to capture them on videotape. John had heard them often. She wondered how she could have missed them, having been present at the same meals. John responded, "You never heard them because you were so self-centered you never bothered to listen to anyone but yourself." Georgia found this a devastating concept, incongruent with her picture of herself. She had been raised to defer to her older brother.

The therapist encouraged Georgia to contact her sister. It was reasoned that if her sister, her constant companion as a child, had heard the stories, she must accept John's impression and further explore her distorted memory; if Tina had not, there would have to be another explanation. Quizzed, Tina knew none of the stories.

As the two sisters thought back to their childhood, the explanation became evident. As soon as people were through eating, father would begin to "hold court" and tell his stories. Mother would direct both girls to the kitchen, far removed from the dining room, to do the dishes. Confronted with this recall, John was a bit sheepish. He saw how little he had understood the different childhood his sisters had experienced in the same family. He gained intellectual understanding of his "entitlement" around women and saw that he was expecting his sister to replace his mother. He began to work on more equal interaction with his sisters and stopped assuming that Georgia should replace mother. Meanwhile Georgia gave up the sense that she alone should shoulder her mother's family responsibility. Had the therapist not referred to the sibling of the same sex for validation, Georgia might have been seen as a woman who needed assertiveness training, when in fact her behaviors were acceptably assertive in all other areas of her life.

Autonomy and Individuation

An extremely important cultural differential is the degree to which separation/individuation is supported. When "centrality" is encouraged, one is more likely to find three-generational households or families living in very close proximity. In three-generational households, the older generation often demands continued role functioning as the authoritative parents. They ask to be respected, obeyed, and awarded deference by both younger generations. The second and third generations may relate more as siblings to one another, depending on the degree to which the oldest generation maintains control, lack of separateness, and power.

Autonomy and individual achievement are not particularly emphasized in Latin American, Native American, Mediterranean, Near Eastern and Asian families. The family controls the individual. Affiliation and cooperation are stressed, while confrontation and competition are discouraged. When this is carried to an extreme degree, it can conflict with some basic American institutions. For instance, when an urban American Indian family establishes itself with employment or when a student from such a family receives a stipend or fellowship for himself, problems develop: Unemployed parents move in, and siblings consume food, wear out clothing, and take up time needed for study and advancement. This tradition hinders more promising careers than perhaps any other obstacle to full participation in the life of the contemporary urban American society (Attneave, 1982). In Black families it is not unusual for an older child to drop out of school and work to help a younger sibling finish. Later, the educated child may contribute to the education of the younger children in the family.

"Reciprocal obligation" is the label McAdoo (1978) has given the process of helping those who have helped others in times of need. Today, in the U.S., upwardly mobile students and professionals, many from India and Pakistan, send their children home to be raised by grandmothers until they are old enough to manage for themselves. This extracts a debt to be repaid later in life when the grandparents expect to be cared for by their children and grandchildren. They are not able to understand or accept the adult child's right to have spouses, jobs, or interests which would interfere. Therapists trying to help their clients accept more American priorities are surprised at the depth to which that obligation is felt.

In working-class Greek-American families, some parents leave their young children in Greece with grandparents until they can be sent to school here. Naturally, these arrangements affect sibling bonds. Away from the parents, children hold on even more tightly to each other. Few therapists seem to explore these separations as having created mourning and anxious attachments.

The separation process is so difficult in Jewish families that it is not uncommon for the children to remain emotionally dependent and physically close to the parental home. Pressure to achieve and thus eliminate "family" embarrassment is frequently as great from the sibs as the parents, forcing all the children to go to college (Herz and Rosen, 1982). My clinical experience suggests that these young adult siblings are anxious to "equalize" resources by helping one another, thereby eliminating the guilt of being the "haves" while their sibs may be the "have-nots." The success of one's siblings is like insurance or money in the bank, to be claimed if you find yourself in need.

Emotional Expressiveness

Emotional distance of the parents promotes a closer sibling bond. Mediterranean, Irish, German, Scandinavian, Polish, and Asian children do not often hear parental feelings articulated, although Mediterranean and Latin-American families may be very expressive in other ways. Jealousy and competitiveness between Greek extended family members is intense, as it is with Mexicans and Italians (Papajohn and Spiegel, 1975). In the British-American family, children often complain that their parents relate to them in a detached manner (McGill and Pearce, 1982). (*Mary Poppins* illustrates the closeness fostered between the children by that parental style.)

When emotional expression is strictly controlled, overt and direct aggression is rare within the family. Aggression is channeled mainly through indirect means: teasing, ignoring, silence, averting the glance, or staring balefully. Within the Greek family, children learn that teasing is part of being loved. They do a great deal of it within the sibling group (Welts, 1982). Teasing is intended to toughen them and make them cautious. Teasing and ridicule are especially common in Irish family relationships. Unfortunately, this easy ability to joke can leave family members frozen in emotional isolation when it comes time to get close to someone outside the family (McGoldrick, 1982). Such a covert way of expressing closeness is often overlooked by British-American and Jewish therapists, since teasing is often viewed as purely hostile by their ethnic background.

Winawer-Steiner and Wetzel (1982) write that the overall German family climate is more favorable to tasks and doing than to nurturance and showing feelings. While there is less emphasis in German-American families on expression of emotions, they seem to be sensitive to issues pertaining to justice between family members and between generations. The Germanic style of handling emotions is very different from that of the Mediterranean nations. In German tradition people are not encouraged to show emotions openly or to display affection, grief, or anger in public. Children are rewarded less for airing their feelings than for politeness in verbal expression, appropriate table manners, or fulfillment of their household chores. The lack of emotional sharing among siblings is a pattern that follows them through life; it is often mistaken for lack of feeling or caring.

Irish families often designate a good child and a bad one, and they may ignore aspects of a child's behavior that do not fit his or her designated role (McGoldrick, 1982). Since the reasons for these "rules of the family game" are not visible to the other children, anxieties run high. An escalating pattern of competition for parental approval occurs among the children. In addition, as a consequence of sexual repression, they also avoid tenderness, affection, and intimacy. Siblings in Irish families are therefore often emotionally isolated from each other; when things go badly, the family atmosphere may become sullen, dour, and puritanically rigid (McGoldrick, 1982).

Within the Italian family all emotions are viewed as acceptable. Italians do not have problems with disallowed feelings as some cultural groups do. Although there are clear values of right and wrong behavior, they are often based on how the behavior will affect the welfare of the family. Characteristically colorful in their talk, they also express more of their emotional tension and hostility when under stress than many other groups—notably the Irish, to whom they are often compared (Rotunno and McGoldrick, 1982). For Italians, words are not meant literally. They give expression to the moment; their purpose is not logical and measured and can be easily disqualified by less dramatic speakers.

These differences of emotional expression are extremely important in intermarriage. Mediterranean spouses, used to emotionally expressive sibling interaction, will not understand that their words may be emotionally overwhelming or devastating to their non-Mediterranean spouses, especially when expressed in anger. When treating couples caught in this bind, it is often useful to explore contacts of the spouses with their siblings-in-law. My experience has shown that both extended families shy away from large gatherings of both families when the cultures have different styles of emotional expression.

ADULT SIBLINGS

As people get older they often reconnect with siblings, as they are called on to manage and make decisions for their aging parents, make funeral arrangements, and settle estates. This intensity revives childhood patterns of behavior. The earlier years of their adult lives and the cultural influences of their spouses play a large part in determining how these crises will be managed.

As discussed by McGill and Pearce (1982), British-American adult siblings are not apt to see each other much, their style of withholding feelings creating more distance from one another. Private property and money, the source of British-American family fights, are the means by which British-American older parents control the behavior of their adult children. Many British-American adult siblings therefore frequently have little contact, often not even meeting, calling, or writing, except for yearly Christmas cards. They simply feel they have little in common and therefore no reason to get in touch. Leaving home at an early age probably contributes to the British-American sense that adult siblings have little in common, since their maturation takes place away from their siblings.

Many cultures expect children to take care of their parents in their old age. For example, in Chinese-American families the oldest son must provide the major emotional support to his mother and grandmother and may be used as a pawn in a power struggle between an overinvolved mother and a detached father or as an intermediary to link uncommunicative family members. He is obligated to take care of the educational and character development of his younger siblings and bring honor to the family by being a good student and financial supporter. Raising the youngest daughter usually represents the last task of the parents; she is their final hope of a child who will not abandon them by leaving. She may resent being left with the responsibility for her parents as her older siblings leave home, and additionally, feel the sting of the unfair treatment she gets as a daughter in relation to her brothers (Lee, 1982). Like the Chinese, Mediterranean daughters, rather than sons, are generally expected to care for sick or aging parents. In the current society, since so many women work, sisters frequently resent the lack of responsibility of their brothers who were so favored growing up, especially since a son's closeness with his mother continues even after he marries.

Some, like the Portugese adult children who do not marry, are expected to remain home forever. A single young adult, particularly a daughter, who leaves the parental home prematurely, seriously risks ostracism by the family and community (Moitoza, 1982). Once married, Portugese, like other Mediterranean, as well as Near-Eastern, adult children, usually live near their parents. Often they live in the same house, or at least in the same neighborhood, and maintain frequent, even daily, contact. This is true of both sons and daughters. Sons are often responsible for the financial support of aging parents, while daughters (often the oldest daughter) are responsible for their physical care. This sharing of responsibility results in less conflict, and the siblings remain more attached throughout adulthood.

In Mexican and other hispanic families, because of sibling closeness and lifelong association, life cycle events in the family of one sibling may have repercussions in the family of another sibling. Children who are orphaned or whose parents are divorced may be included in the household of relatives, along with adults who have remained single, become widowed, or divorced. Kinship ties up to the third and fourth cousins are often close. Even the children's godparents or compadres may be considered part of the extended family. Quarrels and resentments among adult siblings are common, and emotional expression is overt. Quarrels may be caused by the favoritism of the parents for one sibling over another, by disagreement over inheritance, by unpaid debts, or by the persistence of a controlling attitude on the part of an older sibling that is no longer acceptable to a younger one. Rifts among siblings, however, are seldom permanent. Life cycle rituals or crises, such as illness or loss of job, usually reunite these siblings (Falicov, 1982).

A strikingly common pattern for the Irish is in marked contrast to these more enmeshed systems. While Irish siblings may meet for holidays out of a sense of loyalty, there is often a sense of emotional isolation and they may not actually enjoy each other. In Irish families tensions and anger may build up over long periods of time without resolution and finally lead to an emotional cutoff of the relationship (McGoldrick, 1982).

SIBLINGS IN FAMILY THERAPY

In therapy a genogram should be obtained and should include information on the extended family, especially since there is a tendency in some cultures for individuals to live in families-of-origin at every developmental stage. Often taking history may involve exploring several cultural backgrounds which interface in the nuclear unit. Since few of us have clinically experienced a great many ethnic groups, we can only look for the variables that determine how a family will reflect ethnic heritage. Since sibling relationships are significant both through the developmental years and later through a generalized transference outside the family, sibling relationships should be explored carefully. The clients themselves are the best teachers about their family system.

Through the process of making the genogram, clients often come to better understanding their sibling relationships, as well as those with their parents. Clients should be helped to see how ethnic expectations have influenced their development as to sense of responsibility, self-worth, obligation to self or family, life goals, individuation/differentiation and ability to adapt these in their current life. Family rules around age and gender and extra- and intra-familial stressors inhibiting adaptation to American norms should be examined.

The degree of sociocultural isolation or integration is an extremely important parameter to assess. When families are composed of many ethnic backgrounds, it is crucial to get a detailed history of which aspects were favored and with whom primary identifications were made. Strictly ethnic names do not necessarily mean that the children have been raised with a particular religious or ethnic affiliation. To stereotype too quickly is a real danger to any therapy. Even within a family, different children may identify with differing ethnic aspects of their background and this may interfere with a cohesive sibling relationship.

It has been my clinical experience that if differentiation between family members of both generations is a goal, this can be achieved more quickly when siblings are brought into the therapy. Seeing siblings together offers greater support to the individual and offsets parental pressures. Clearly, those ethnic groups which inhibit individuation experience stress when faced with conflict between important traditional ethnic values and integration into the broader societal system. The resistance against integration often becomes strident and is misunderstood by therapists as pathological when traditional parents encourage their children to maintain their symbiotic ties. If the therapist persists in trying to free the siblings from their enmeshment, failure of treatment will surely follow. These concepts are especially important to black families experiencing "victim system stress," since members, attempting to compensate for the stress, are apt to form overly closed systems, maternal overcentrality, fused identities, and emotional cutoffs in their attempts to establish equilibrium (Hines and Boyd-Franklin, 1982; Pinderhughes, 1982).

Since immigrant children of any ethnic group generally have an easier time learning English than adults, they are often asked to interpret for their parents in family therapy sessions. Speaking for one's parents is contrary to many ethnic groups' expectations that children should be quiet in front of strangers (Garcia-Preto, 1982). This gives the sibling group an unusual advantage and power, a role reversal between the usual parent and child dynamics. Separating the children from their parents to ascertain information often puts them in greater fear of their being misrepresented to the parents. Furthermore, one child may fear speaking openly, threatened that a competitive sibling will distort the message once it is retold to the parents.

Irish siblings for example, often fear being pinned down and may use words and manner to avoid clearer meaning or refuse to talk at all about matters too emotionally laden. Helping Irish patients uncover "family secrets" to resolve childhood conflicts is hampered by their characteristic inability to approach their parents on previously "taboo" subjects. Carefully engaging the siblings may enable patients to overcome this obstacle.

The following case highlights the difficulties of emotional expressiveness when important events have not been discussed with the children and resolved. Once again, this case example did not initially come to the therapists' attention as a sibling issue.

Dierdre

Dierdre, from an Irish background, never knew her father, who had died when she was an infant. Alone, mother raised Dierdre, her older brother and her sister. Father was never talked about. Dierdre began to explore her own early development and family history during her hospitalization for depression following the birth of her first daughter. She had attempted suicide prior to her hospitalization.

The fear that her father had actually suicided rather than died from natural causes had threatened Dierdre's sense of worth since she was a small child. She had never been able to bring herself to question her mother about the events of her father's death. Only after years of therapy did she confide her fears to her sister. They then began to see a family therapist together. They checked newspapers and verified that their father had not suicided. In therapy, they gained an adult perspective on their mother's reticent behavior as stemming from the ethnic directive not to dwell on the past, but instead to attempt to shield children from painful truths and to avoid intense, emotional discussions.

Dierdre's fantasy that her father had committed suicide had left her in great fear of abandonment by men. The fear had intruded itself in her marriage as a lack of trust of her husband, inhibiting their intimacy. It was only after the family therapy with her older sister, who had urged her to pursue her search, that her relationship with both her husband and brother improved.

The Short Family

In a British-American family, the ethnically-fueled style of privacy and secrecy worked against two sisters in this case.

Henry and Mary Short, both British-American, were the parents of two daughters, four years apart. The girls were so close as young children that they had developed their own exclusive language. For ten years their father, untreated for manic-depressive illness and alcoholism, had mentally and physically abused both of them. When a senior in high school, Elizabeth, 18, the younger child, went to a school adjustment counselor to get protection from her father's incestuous attacks. The girls had never openly articulated the real problems to their mother nor discussed his attacks. The mother, Mary, had known about the problems but had never sought professional help as she believed doing so would be a violation of family privacy and she could not tolerate the shame and embarrassment she thought she would feel. Instead, the girls had been drilled in evacuation techniques, to escape the house if their father was out of control or drunk. There were no discussions between mother and daughters about these visibly intolerable behaviors.

When Elizabeth finally sought outside help, the family system could no longer remain closed. Everything was breaking down. The older sister, Abigail, 20, was then a senior in an out-of-state college.

Recently diagnosed a manic-depressive, she was in therapy and medicated. The father, Henry, involuntarily hospitalized for the first time in the many years of illness, was also diagnosed as manic depressive and was medicated with significantly positive results. He consistently denied any memory of the events alleged by his daughters.

Henry and Mary were referred for marital therapy in anticipation of Henry's hospital discharge. One year after the therapy began, the therapist was permitted to meet with the girls because Elizabeth was hospitalized, depressed and suicidal.

In full family sessions, history was vague and only brief answers had been given to direct questions. No information was volunteered and no relevant connections were offered. But in the sibling sessions, each sister opened up. In those sessions, they talked about their childhood isolation and validated their mutual victimization. While the dynamics of this case are similar to other cases of incest, the ethnic factor was an important contributor to the time and energy required to build a therapeutic relationship and to help them share themselves with outsiders in any way. Seeing the siblings together allowed the therapist to more effectively challenge the family rule of "not talking."

Where other cultures might regard questions about credentials and authority of a therapist as rude or intrusive, the Jewish family views them as perfectly reasonable, legitimate, and necessary reassurance that one is getting the best available help. Jewish families utilize verbal anger, criticism, and argument as ways of dealing with problems. Expressing thoughts and feelings in Jewish families is not only a method of catharsis but an important aspect of family interaction. Writing on the Jewish family, Herz and Rosen (1982) describe that, along with the very high value placed on the family, there is an emphasis upon maintaining geographical as well as emotional closeness between the generations. If there is a rift or serious division, Jews may carry deep resentments from one generation to the next.

The Gold-Bertram Family

Simon and Deborah Gold came to family therapy upon the psychiatric hospitalization of their adolescent, heroin-using daughter, Mona. The parents were confused and ashamed by their daughter's behavior, preoccupying themselves with this child's treatment to the near exclusion of their three other children, Sarah, Daniel, and Wendy. The mother's younger brother, Robert (an attorney who also handled legal affairs for their business), his wife, Amy, and the maternal grandparents, Mr. and Mrs. Bertram, were overly involved and enmeshed in the Gold family and business affairs.

It should be noted that in this therapy there were two significant sets of siblings—Deborah and Robert in one generation, the patient and her three siblings in the next generation. While sibling issues were never meant to be the focus of the therapy, it became apparent that an understanding of sibling dynamics was critical to this ongoing, long-term therapy.

Simon, the father, had cut off from his family of origin. He had never had a close relationship with his siblings. Even prior to Simon's marriage to Deborah, the Bertrams had considered him inferior to their daughter. These feelings intensified following his imprisonment, "taking the rap" for a family member in an illegal business matter in which he had been only peripherally involved. His time in federal prison was a secret known only to the family and a few others in the business world. The Bertrams had not been at all supportive to Deborah and her children as Deborah made weekly visits to the prison three hours away. Deborah remained bitter about her ordeal.

At the time of Mona's hospital admission, Deborah was president of the Golds' rapidly growing business. She created jobs for her parents, who denied their years and diminished functioning. Deborah never questioned that it was her obligation as the daughter to care for her parents and to protect her younger brother, as she had always done as a child. The Bertrams expected to be treated as though they retained earlier parental authority, disregarding business protocol and embarrassing Deborah frequently with intrusions during meetings or phone calls. They reflected their disappointment in Simon by ignoring him in decision-making, as though the family business belonged to the Bertrams rather than to Simon and Deborah, a collusion in which Deborah participated.

The therapist pointed out Deborah's acceptance of the family pattern preference for her male sibling. Simon, a passive man, had reinforced his exclusion by avoiding confrontations and limiting himself to solitary aspects of the business, alien to the skills of any of the Bertrams. Deborah had never told Simon how angry she was at him. As Deborah began to talk the anger away, the Golds began to see that

Deborah's brother Robert was being allowed, inappropriately, to dominate them. Deborah was coached alone in therapy to put Robert in a better perspective regarding the business. Deborah and Robert were then seen together to help Robert recognize how he had side-stepped the responsibility for his aging parents and had isolated his sister by perpetuating the myth of family "disappointment" in the man she had married. Gradually, in sibling and marital therapy, Deborah began to see her husband's strengths, as well as her own. Soon she was able to let Robert be a younger brother and no longer put him in the special, overly entitled place granted him by his parents. She was able to coalesce with her nuclear family, empowering Simon to take a firmer stance in the business and within the family. Family therapy with the Bertrams and the Golds helped to set boundaries, separating family of origin, nuclear family and family business. Though Mr. and Mrs. Bertram still tried to bypass their daughter and her husband, Deborah remained assertive and stopped it.

Meanwhile, seen as a subsystem in family therapy, the three Gold children began to get more involved with the family business. As their career choices moved them gradually into the family business, they collectively confronted their father's passivity. They ignored their grandparents' attempt to control, remained loving and respectful, but firm in their resolve to preserve *their* family business. Distant to one another as small children (father's sibling legacy) they began to relate more to one another, dampened their competitiveness, and developed a closer bond as their common goal of future security and prosperity crystalized.

Simon and Deborah were helped to take control of their own nuclear family, to be less fused with the business, and to support their children's more positive relationships, closer than their own sibling relationships had been. As Deborah resolved her resentment toward her husband and brother, her daughters improved their relationship with their brother. The children, no longer angered by Robert's forceful opinions and intrusions, were ultimately able to enjoy him as an uncle and revived their earlier closeness with their cousins without hostile competitiveness.

Until Bank and Kahn wrote *The Sibling Bond*, most family therapists were ignoring sibling interactions as independent of the parental influence. Adding an ethnic approach, family resistance to change may be lessened and therapy will not direct families toward behaviors which contradict their personal and cultural value systems.

REFERENCES

Arensberg, C., & Kimball, S. (1968). *Family and community in Ireland* (2nd ed.) Cambridge: Harvard University Press.

Attneave, C. (1982). American Indians and Alaska native families: Emigrants in their own homeland. In M. McGoldrick, J. Pearce, & J. Giordano (Eds.). *Ethnicity and family therapy* (pp. 55–81). New York: Guilford.

Bank, S. P., & Kahn, M. D. (1982). *The sibling bond*. New York: Basic Books.

Brice, J. (1982). West Indian families. In M. McGoldrick, J. Pearce, & J. Giordano (Eds.). *Ethnicity and family therapy* (pp. 123–132). New York: Guilford.

Falicov, C. (1982). Mexican families. In M. McGoldrick, J. Pearce, & J. Giordano (Eds.). *Ethnicity and family therapy* (pp. 134–161). New York: Guilford.

Garcia-Preto, N. (1982). Puerto-Rican families. In M. McGoldrick, J. Pearce, & J. Giordano (Eds.). *Ethnicity and family therapy* (pp. 164–184). New York: Guilford.

Herz, F., & Rosen, E. (1982). Jewish families. In M. McGoldrick, J. Pearce, & J. Giordano (Eds.). *Ethnicity and family therapy* (pp. 364–390). New York: Guilford.

Hines, P., & Boyd-Franklin, N. (1982). Black families. In M. McGoldrick, J. Pearce, & J. Giordano (Eds.). *Ethnicity and family therapy* (pp. 84–106). New York: Guilford.

Jalali, B. (1982). Iranian families. In M. McGoldrick, J. Pearce, & J. Giordano (Eds.). *Ethnicity and family therapy* (pp. 289–309). New York: Guilford.

Kleinman, A., & Lin, T. Y. (Eds.) (1981). *Normal and deviant behavior in Chinese culture*. Hingham, MA: Reidel, 1981.

Lee, E. (1982). A social systems approach to assessment and treatment for Chinese American families. In M. McGoldrick, J. Pearce, & J. Giordano (Eds.). *Ethnicity and family therapy* (pp. 527–550). New York: Guilford.

McAdoo, H. (1978). The impact of upward mobility of kin-help patterns and the reciprocal obligations in black families. In *Journal of Marriage and the Family,* 4(4), 761–776.

McGill, D., & Pearce, J. (1982). British families. In M. McGoldrick, J. Pearce, & J. Giordano (Eds.). *Ethnicity and family therapy* (pp. 457–478). New York: Guilford.

McGoldrick, M. (1982). Irish families. In M. McGoldrick, J. Pearce, & J. Giordano (Eds.). *Ethnicity and family therapy* (pp. 310–336). New York: Guilford.

Minuchin, S. (1974). *Families and family therapy*. Cambridge: Harvard University Press.

Moitoza, E. (1982). Portugese families. In M. McGoldrick, J. Pearce, & J. Giordano (Eds.). *Ethnicity and family therapy* (pp. 412–435). New York: Guilford.

Mostwin, D. (1979). Emotional needs of elderly Americans of Central and Eastern European background. In D. E. Gelfand & A. J. Kutzik (Eds.). *Ethnicity and aging*. New York: Springer.

Papajohn, J., & Spiegel, J. (1975). *Transactions in families*. San Francisco: Jossey-Bass.

Pinderhughes, E. (1982). Afro-American families and the victim system. In M. McGoldrick, J. Pearce, & J. Giordano (Eds.). *Ethnicity and family therapy* (pp. 108–122). New York: Guilford.

Rotunno, M., & McGoldrick, M. (1982). Italian families. In M. McGoldrick, J. Pearce, & J. Giordano (Eds.). *Ethnicity and family therapy* (pp. 340–362). New York: Guilford.

Shon, S., & Ja, D. (1982). Asian families. In M. McGoldrick, J. Pearce, & J. Giordano (Eds.). *Ethnicity and family therapy* (pp. 208–228). New York: Guilford.

Spiegel, J. (1982). An ecological model of ethnic families. In M. McGoldrick, J. Pearce, & J. Giordano (Eds.). *Ethnicity and family therapy* (pp. 31–50). New York: Guilford.

Welts, E. (1982). Greek families. In M. McGoldrick, J. Pearce, & J. Giordano (Eds.). *Ethnicity and family therapy.* (pp. 269–287). New York: Guilford.

Winawer-Steiner, H., & Wetzel, N. (1982). German families. In M. McGoldrick, J. Pearce, & J. Giordano (Eds.). *Ethnicity and family therapy* (pp. 247–267). New York: Guilford.

II

When Siblings Are Close

THE EARLY YEARS

Childhood is usually a time when siblings are the closest—physically and emotionally. From birth on, brothers and sisters are often intensely involved with one another, whether that means cooperative playing and sharing or constant fighting. During these years, siblings share much of their living space—at home, to and from school, after school hours, in the evenings, and on weekends. They often sleep in the same bedroom, wear each other's clothes, share the same friends and toys. In fact, they probably spend more hours together than with their parents. Life events or crises that affect one child in a family inevitably affect the others. And more so than at any other time in the life span, what affects the parents resonates through all the children.

Childhood and early adolescence become a practice ground for all future relationships. During these years, children learn how to love, share, negotiate, start and end fights, hurt others, and save face. It is a vitally important time, for these early learnings have life-long ramifications. The basis of healthy relationships in adult life starts with establishing clear lines of communication, appropriate boundaries, and rules of clean fighting in childhood.

The six chapters in this section move from the basics of why and how to include young siblings in therapy, to understanding the uniqueness of a particular type of family organization, to the complexities of the sibling relationship when a life crisis affects one child or the whole sibling subsystem.

Lewis describes how the relationships among young siblings are different when they are alone from when their parents are present. She outlines three types of situations when it may be helpful to see siblings together: when there is a problem between the siblings, when there is a family crisis, and when there is insufficient family structure. She also addresses parental and therapist anxiety about the siblings' being seen together without parents and offers concrete suggestions for preparing the office and structuring the assessment or treatment process.

McGuire and Tolan offer suggestions for understanding the organizational features of large families, which constitute a significant percentage of the clinical population. Large families, of course, include older as well as younger children. Four problems that manifest themselves in large families are imbalance between the family and extrafamilial system, too narrow individual labels, overresponsibility of the older siblings, and sacrificed youngest siblings. Working from a structural/strategic approach, McGuire and Tolan offer therapeutic suggestions for the assessment and treatment of these families.

With all the attention today on parent-child incest, Heiman's chapter on more common sibling incest is welcomed. After making the distinction between power-oriented vs. nurture-oriented incest, she describes the preconditions for the former: motivation, overcoming the internal and the external inhibitions, and overcoming the victim's resistance. Heiman identifies three treatment phases: (1) assessment, including interviewing the victimized sibling, the parents, and the offending sibling; (2) the reorganization of the family structure, using structural family therapy strategies; and (3) healing the wound and restoring the family to a higher level of functioning.

In the next chapter, Seligman approaches a child's disability from the perspective of the siblings—what do they need to help them deal with and accept the disabled sibling and to keep the disability from negatively interfering with their own lives. He presents seven important issues that need attention: information, caretaking responsibility, contagion fear, anger and guilt, communication, parental attitudes, and the effects of the disability on the siblings.

The final chapters in this section focus on major life events that cause a crisis in the sibling subsystem. Combrinck-Graham takes a pragmatic perspective on divorce's effect on children (and vice versa): "Divorce is neither good nor bad for children. It is an event, one of many, that changes children's lives." She accuses the mental health system of pathologizing the divorce process and its effect on children. Using many examples from her clinical practice, she describes three basic tasks for children during the separation or divorce process: taking care of their parents, taking care of themselves, and getting on with their own development.

Moving from divorce to remarriage, Rosenberg describes the ambiguities of this new union of two separate families. To help this new family that does not have a chance to evolve but more abruptly appears, specific issues need to be addressed. She identifies nine characteristics of stepsibling relationships: instantaneous relationships, lack of shared family history, common experiences of loss, conflicting loyalties, fluid boundaries, shifts in sibling positions and functions, abrupt change in family size, sexual issues, and incongruity between individual and the family life cycle tasks.

The final chapter in this section focuses on family alcoholism. While there has been an emphasis in the literature on children of alcoholics, the focus is usually on one individual child in the family not on the effect of the drinking on the sibling subsystem. Jesse describes her professional journey through the last 15 years in working with these children, focusing primarily on the latency aged child whose behavior is expressing the difficulty of growing up with alcoholism. Then she describes the way siblings in different birth orders show their reactions. Alcoholism may temporarily bring the siblings together during a crisis, but eventually the result is increased sibling rivalry and lack of intimacy.

While the life crises addressed in this section affect siblings at other points in the life cycle, they are included here since we felt that the vulnerability of children makes these topics particularly relevant during these early years.

5

Young Siblings in Brief Therapy

Karen Gail Lewis

A school therapist was asked to see John, a ten-year-old boy who was increasingly aggressive in class and whose work had been deteriorating. In a family meeting, Mother reported that at home John was aggressive with his six-year-old brother. They used to be "pals." She had no idea what might have caused him to become so "mean."

A family therapist in private practice was referred a couple who sought help with their marriage. After three visits, the wife admitted she had been having an affair with a man she really loved and wanted a divorce. The couple's two children, a ten-year-old son and an eight-year-old daughter, have been fighting more than usual. The parents say the children do not like each other.

A family therapist in a community mental health center was referred Candy, an eight-year-old girl, for bedwetting and thumbsucking. The referral person also wanted a therapist to see the girl's next youngest sibling, a brother whose stealing had progressed from the home, to school, and now to the community. On further exploration, the therapist learned that the third child was apathetic in school, while the youngest had been a failure-to-thrive infant. The parents were living together; mother was an alcoholic holding a job between drinking bouts and father was perpetually unemployed.

As we will see, these examples suggest at least three different types of situations when seeing just the siblings together might be the treatment of choice or a useful adjunct to family therapy. Focusing on families with children under 13 years of age, in the pages that follow I will provide some guidelines for thinking about when to meet with only the sibling subgroup, describe diagnostic and ongoing treatment goals, highlight parents' and therapists' concerns about such a meeting, and offer some clinical examples.

SIBLING RELATIONSHIPS

While family therapists think of an individual's problems as a part of a family drama, and usually try to see the whole family in therapy, too often they do not see the uniqueness of the sibling relationship. Siblings are a subgroup of the family. At the same time, they are a separate system unto themselves. They spend much time together in their own autonomous world without parental influence: to and from school, in the bedroom, on weekends, while dinner is being fixed. Outside of the parental purview, they have their own set of relationships and alliances. They have their own rules, history, hierarchy. They have their own code of ethics and their own loyalty bonds (Bank and Kahn, 1982; Minuchin, Montalvo, Guernez, and Schumer, 1967).

The level of access among siblings can affect their degree of loyalty and intimacy. Children with high access are close in age and share friends, clothes, bedroom, etc. Those with low access are usually more than eight years apart, with few overlapping daily life events (Bank and Kahn, 1982).

There are many ways in which the bonding between siblings, even those with high access, can be blocked. Sibling bonds can be damaged by transgenerational complementary roles requiring, for example, one child to be a clown and the other an egghead, one to be an overachiever and the other an underachiever. Parents' using one child to meet their own needs or to serve as a buffer between them also causes a barrier for the siblings, with the "chosen" child often rejected from the sibling group. Brothers and sisters who might otherwise be close are sometimes called upon to join with one or the other parent in the marital battle. Another common family occurrence that interferes with the siblings' developing relationship is (most often) the maternal role of "telephone operator." This is the mother who becomes central to all family communication, particularly among the children. Sibling intimacy is bound to be limited if mother is always between the children, leaving them little emotional privacy. Developing intimacy is also hindered if mother (or father) is between them as they attempt to sort out their own conflicts.

OVERVIEW OF THE LITERATURE

More has been written about involving young children in family therapy than about sibling therapy. And most of what has been written about young children in therapy has been in the context of the whole family, not just about the siblings. Salvador Minuchin and Carl Whitaker are probably the best known among those family therapists who specifically attend to young children, although neither of them sees only the children. Minuchin, for the most part, focuses on siblings for the purpose of shifting triangles and restructuring the family (Minuchin, 1974; Minuchin and Fishman, 1981). The sibling relationship itself does not seem primary. He may, however, have parents move to another side of the room or sit behind the one-way mirror when he wants to work with the sibling subsystem.

Whitaker joins the family through the children. He is noted for sitting on the floor and playing with infants or play fighting with young children. He may even ignore the parents while interacting with the children. He sees children as speakers of the real issues in the family and as a barometer for the family's strength and affect (Whitaker, 1967; Whitaker and Keith, 1981). He makes contact directly with each child, rather than encouraging sibling interactions.

The Sibling Bond (1982) was the first book to address therapy among siblings. Bank and Kahn suggest that therapists should help brothers and sisters live separate and independent lives, yet have the ability to enjoy closeness, intimacy, and dependency. Sibling issues that need assessing are level of access, career, identification patterns, loyalty and trust, sexuality and aggression, and the parents' sibling experiences.

A major proponent of attending to young children in family therapy, Lee Combrinck-Graham has edited a book introducing readers to a variety of settings and illustrating problems where children are central in family treatment. She is also editing the first handbook of family therapy with young children (Combrinck-Graham, 1986; in press).

Family therapists are just beginning to look at the use of the sibling subgroup as a target for intervention in times of family disruption, when the family as a whole is not available, or when the sibship is troubled. The stepsibling relationship in divorced and/or remarried families is one area that has attracted considerable attention (Eno, 1985; Nichols, 1986; Rosenberg, 1980). Sibling therapy has been suggested for children separated from their families through foster home placement (Lewis, 1986b) and for children from multiproblem families where there is inadequate or no parental control and guidance (Lewis, 1986a; Rosenberg, 1980). In these families, the therapist can foster bonding among the brothers and sisters to transcend the actual living situation. Kahn (1986) has given guidelines for therapists who work with younger siblings who are either enmeshed or disengaged.

SEEING SIBLINGS TOGETHER

For simplicity's sake, I have categorized three types of situations where seeing siblings for one or several sessions may be helpful: (1) when there is a problem between the siblings; (2) when the family is experiencing a particular crisis; (3) when there is no stable family structure. In the first two categories sibling therapy occurs within the context of family therapy—the siblings are seen separately for a specific goal and then family therapy resumes. In the third category the children are usually seen without parental involvement, since the parents often are not emotionally or physically available. (Length of treatment is discussed in a later section.)

Problems Between the Siblings

There are several ways in which sibling conflict comes to the therapist's attention. On occasion, a mother will call asking for therapy because of sibling rivalry. More often, a therapist is seeing the whole family and the embittered relationship between the siblings is mentioned or becomes apparent in the therapy session. When a therapist is seeing only one child, the problems with other siblings may be mentioned, as with John in the opening example.

Children are not born hating their brothers and sisters. Something happens to turn normal sibling squabbling into a destructive process. Parental preferences and parental intrusion in their children's relationship are two common contributing factors to sibling friction.

Another common factor is rigid transgenerational roles placed on siblings, leaving them in open conflict or in guerrilla warfare. This often occurs when mother and father have their own unresolved sibling issues, which then get replayed with their children. When a triangulated or parentified child is overinvolved with one or both parents, brothers and sisters may resent the sibling who has crossed into the adult hierarchy. They may scapegoat or abandon that child. Another cause for sibling conflict may be related to an unequal distribution of natural abilities, e.g., one child excels in many areas (Pfouts, 1976).

Sibling antagonism is a cause for concern, but so is sibling fusion—that is, siblings' relying on each other for emotional support and companionship. While parents rarely ask for help with this, the therapist may see the fusion in the family sessions. Fusion may reflect a pseudo-togetherness in response to parents' injunctions for them to be close or a mutual dependence resulting from certain life events (Bank and Kahn, 1982). Seeing the siblings separately gives the therapist a chance to evaluate their behavior when the parents are not present.

The last example in this category may not overtly relate to a sibling problem. When one child cannot get along with peers—whether the child is aggressively or passively isolated—seeing the siblings together may identify a sibling indifference or a covert subterfuge. If there is no sibling problem, therapy can provide a setting in which the better adjusted brothers and sisters teach the troubled child how to make friends or avoid conflicts with peers.

A Particular Family Crisis

When a family is in crisis, a family therapist is likely to see all family members together. When the crisis results from parental actions, such as separation or divorce, the children may benefit from talking together, without their parents present. In front of the parents, the children may have difficulty expressing the depth of their anger, fear, hurt, and shame. Marital conflicts often lead to parent-child alliances which cause rifts between the children. With each child siding with one parent, the marital battle can be continued through the children. Separate meetings are especially useful when children are not living with the same parent. Brothers and sisters need a chance to reestablish a relationship with one another, untarnished by their parents' hatred.

When the crisis is a remarriage, the situation becomes complex. Formation of the new family can reactivate unresolved issues for one or more of the children. In addition, the reality of adjusting to new brothers and sisters, new sibling positions, new living conditions, and new rules can be overwhelming. Therapy with all of the siblings can provide a forum for airing the feelings and solving some specific issues (Eno, 1985; Nichols, 1986; Rosenberg, 1980).

Sometimes in family therapy a crisis occurs for one child, such as sexual abuse or a physical disability. The whole family must deal with the effect of the crisis on the child and the family, but it may also be useful to give the siblings an opportunity to talk separately. A sibling meeting can help them talk within their own sibship about their anger and/or fears, express their lack of information, and share their worries about parental reactions to the problem.

Unstable Family Structure

As used here, an unstable family structure exists when children have no consistent, adequate parental system: One or both parents are minimally functional, e.g., alcoholic or depressed; parents are not fulfilling their executive roles; parents are absent and the children live together without adult caretaking. Another example is when the children have been placed in foster homes or group homes or have been institutionalized. Sometimes siblings are placed together as a unit, but more often they are separated.

When the children are left to take care of themselves or when the children are placed in separate foster homes, seeing them together helps create a sense of family; it is a way to develop a "we-ness" (Lewis, 1983, 1984, 1986b). For children not living together, the therapy session may be the only time they see each other. The therapy can help build a connection that transcends the separation and that allies them against what may seem a hostile world, since they may not be able to count on their parents or on a consistent foster family.

Siblings living together without a strong or consistent parental executive role need to establish their own working hierarchy so they can function smoothly. Abusive or neglectful parenting may lead to abusive or neglectful sibling relationships. Therefore, these young children need to learn how to care about each other, how to trust, how to enjoy playing together, how to solve problems, how to protect each other from abusive parents or foster parents, and mostly, how to like each other.

ASSESSMENT OR TREATMENT

The therapist can see the siblings together for a one-time assessment or evaluation, for periodic meetings in the midst of ongoing family therapy, or for time-limited or ongoing sibling therapy. A sibling assessment can occur at any point during the family's therapy. The therapist may recommend the meeting in order to evaluate the style or quality of the sibling relationship without parents present or to give children more privacy in addressing a specific topic. This evaluation meeting may be with all the children or with just a certain age subgroup.

Periodic sessions with the siblings can be beneficial when the siblings repeatedly get stuck around a particular problem, when there is generalized dyadic or triadic tensions, or when parental upheavals are creating disturbances among the siblings. In these meetings without parents, the children can learn to separate their feelings towards one another from their parental loyalty. Sometimes a single evaluation is sufficient; other times a series of periodic sessions is needed to provide the children with the privacy to sort out and express their feelings.

At times the treatment of choice is ongoing or time-limited sibling therapy. This is most often recommended for children without a stable family structure, as well as for children living in foster homes or for families where the parental system is inadequate and the siblings need to pull together to take care of themselves. This sibling therapy can focus directly on the effect of the family problems on each child as an individual and on the sibship. Unfortunately, necessity often prevents potentially beneficial long-term sibling therapy, since these families are highly mobil and the children experience frequent foster home changes.

There are very few situations when meeting with the siblings separately—in any of these formats—is contraindicated. The best reason for not seeing brothers and sisters together is the lack of a specific need to do so. Another good reason is intense parental anxiety about what the children might say without the parents present.

Parental Anxiety

Parents may express anxiety when a therapist wants to meet with just their children. The hesitation may be expressed openly, "I know this is silly, but I feel real uncomfortable not being there when you talk to the kids." It may be unconsciously expressed through missed, canceled, or late appointments for the children. Or parents may be quite agreeable to the meetings, but the children become more inhibited in sibling sessions than during the family meetings. Sometimes it is easy to recognize the anxiety and hence to talk openly about the parents' fears and worries before the sibling therapy session. This can help avert later reactions.

Some of the common fears underlying parental anxiety are that the children say unkind things about parents or the home life, that secrets (or lies) will be revealed, that the children will not behave well reflecting badly on their parenting, or that the parents will feel excluded. However, the most common response is a general discomfort with no specific concerns. Mothers, in particular, are used to being integrally involved in their children's lives and therefore may have difficulty being excluded from the sibling session. Without looking for and addressing the feelings aroused by parental exclusion, the sibling session may be counterproductive.

> The Lawson family sought help for their seven-year-old daughter Mina, who had developed a handwashing ritual. In the first two family sessions, both Mina and her eight-year-old brother Tony sat quietly, politely answering all questions. Their lack of spontaneity concerned the therapist, who scheduled a meeting with just the children in order to better understand what they may be feeling.
>
> The therapist asked Tony and Mina how they felt coming to the sibling session. Sitting very properly with hands folded, Mina said her mother told her to answer all the questions honestly, and "if you can't say anything good, don't say anything at all."
>
> It seems the mother did not have a clear understanding of the purpose of the meeting, and whatever exposure she dreaded had not been identified. The children were in a double bind: If they used the evaluation session well—talking about real feelings—they would be disobedi-

ent to the parental dictum—perhaps saying unkind things. It would have been more productive if the children had heard their parents airing their worries about what might happen in such a meeting, with a resolution that did not put them in the double bind.

FAMILY THERAPISTS AND YOUNG CHILDREN

Parents are not the only ones who may feel hesitant about just the siblings being seen in therapy. Consider this: The therapist is the only adult present with the children; the therapist is in the room as a stranger to an already formed group with its own alliances and secrets; children make a lot of noise; there may be confusion, with the children moving in different directions. A well-behaved, unfrightened and loving group of siblings can be a delight. However, when children enter the therapy room, their anxiety is usually high; they are there for some problem, and unless they are quite withdrawn or compliant, they are likely to hide their fear behind a high activity level. Not unreasonably, the therapist may feel left out and anxious. I recently conducted an informal survey of family therapy colleagues, asking whom they saw in their practice, and discovered that many of them do not include the young children. There are probably lots of reasons. Children are unpredictable, eliciting a range of emotions from otherwise reasonable adults. Children "are sweet, innocent, and demanding. They teach us how to love and expose us to our rage. They steal time, order, logic, and self-esteem. They expand self-esteem, enhance the family, and press for its destruction. They bring their parents closer together, and they drive their parents apart" (Keith, 1986, p. 3).

Children expect us to be wise yet they show us our foibles. They are humbling to the therapist who relies on language for communicating. Another "obvious and important, yet often overlooked reason for excluding children, particularly younger children, in family therapy, is that they are children. They will not behave or speak like adults—they play and act as children do" (Zilbach, 1986, p. 11).

Working with children may revive our fears of regression or remind us of our unresolved childhood issues or our own sibling experiences. For therapists with no children of their own, or for those with minimum exposure to children, or for those with little tolerance of others' children, the movement, noise and activity of the young can be annoying. We expect our therapy patients to resemble the 17th century portraits of young children—child bodies with adult faces (Aries, 1965)—to participate in a therapy session like adults, to sit quietly and to talk our verbal language.

There is little doubt that children will talk, but their language may not be the digital communication of adults (see Haley, 1976, for discussion of digital and analogic communication styles). I recall one of the first children I saw after graduate school. During individual play therapy Tory often made weird noises and body movements. For example, he would stiffen himself with an extended arm and fist and then slowly turn in a circle. I was ready to proclaim him very disturbed, just short of catatonic or psychotic. Although this was a child guidance center, and many of the therapists were parents, only one person at the case conference recognized the movements of the then popular Bionic Man. With that knowledge, I was finally able to understand Tory's communication; he assumed this posture when we discussed events in which he felt powerless and helpless. If one lacks knowledge of child development and of the meaning of play, as well as a child therapist supervisor, it makes sense to avoid working directly with young children in families.

There is another aspect of therapists' hesitation that needs to be considered. Seeing children without their parents is fertile ground for triangulation. Someone—parents, children, therapist—is going to be squeezed out, and too often it is the parents. Children can be endearing; therapists can become quite attached and join the kids against the parents, feeling they should be giving more or doing things differently. This puts the children in a bind. Either they loyally resist the therapist, avoiding the conflict of which "parent" is doing a better job, or they use the therapist's investment as a wedge against parents. ("My therapist says I need to express my anger more," as Lucy pulls Billy's hair.) Not surprisingly, parents may resent the therapist. This inevitably leads to reality being mistaken for transference when the therapist interprets the parents' negative reactions to the therapist.

The literature may not be a valid barometer of what clinical work with siblings actually goes on, for many therapists may be seeing brothers and sisters together but not writing about it. However, it probably is a valid reflection of the trends in training, since the American Association for Marriage and Family Therapy, the official accrediting agent for family therapy training programs, has no specific requirements for child development courses (AAMFT, 1975). Without basic knowledge of children and without close supervision, there is no impetus and no support for family therapists to pay particular attention to young children.

SETTING THE STAGE

Preparing the Office

Once a therapist decides to see the siblings, the office needs to be prepared for helping the children "talk." Children talk through toys. The toys do not need to be elaborate and most therapists have the basic equipment already in their office—paper and pencil or magic markers. Additional inexpensive toys include puppets, clay, soft material for hitting or throwing (e.g., sofa pillows), lightweight punching bag, scissors, paste. Some games require little or no props, such as the squiggle game (Winnicott, 1971) or mutual storytelling (Gardner, 1971). Discussing the presenting problem can be turned into a game by having the children, for example, "Name three things that worry you the most about your sister's illness," of "If you could turn each other into an animal, what animal would you choose?" The purpose of toys is to encourage expression and interaction. While some therapists rely on board games, such as checkers, such games, unless used skillfully, often allow children to hide their feelings behind the rules. Therapists' personal biases will always win out in furnishing a room for children. I personally hate paints and thereby ban them from the threshold of my door; in contrast, I love sitting on the floor with stuffed animals and puppets.

Goals

If during the family therapy sessions the therapist decides to meet with the siblings, the goals should be clearly spelled out for the parents and the children. The therapist should have specific assessment issues in mind, for instance: "When parents are not present, can Billy alter his role as the passive brother and can Charlie show more empathy for his less athletically skilled brother?" "How do the children feel about the upcoming marriage between mother and her friend Tim, since father has been dead only one year?"

The Sibling Therapy Session(s)

There are some basic differences between a one-time evaluation session and time-limited or ongoing therapy with siblings. A diagnostic or evaluation session must be complete in itself. No more anxiety than can be managed within the one session should be stirred up. While these meetings are evaluative, the therapist needs to consider the children's behavior in light of how their parents feel about the meeting, their typical reactions to new situations, the tensions that may have occurred in the car or are left over from a playground fight. They could be showing their very best or their very worst behavior.

These sessions should be structured so that the evaluation questions will be answered. By *structured*, I mean including specific activities addressing these issues — for example, spreading paper out on the table and asking the siblings to draw pictures of the worst thing they remember about the day Daddy moved out or of how angry they get at a brother or a sister.

In time-limited or ongoing sibling therapy, specified goals are just as important, but there may be less need to smooth out the affect at the end of the hour, since the children will be returning. Leaving an art project incomplete, for example, provides a transition to continuation of the themes during the next session. Nonstructured activities or free play are also suitable for ongoing therapy, enabling the children to use their own unconscious to direct the content (topic) and the process (materials/interactions) of the play. (The structure of a one-time periodic session is similar to that of an evaluation, while periodic consecutive sessions should be treated as time-limited therapy.)

Siblings' Anxiety and Play

Siblings often experience anxiety during the therapy session. While a certain amount of anxiety may be useful, when children become wild it can be counterproductive. For some children, free play can be overstimulating, increasing their anxiety and leading to out-of-control behavior. These children can benefit from more structured play.

On the other hand, some children become immobilized by their anxiety or try to avoid anxiety-provoking topics. These children use free play to flee from emotionally charged issues, such as the presenting problem. When that occurs, parallel play (Lewis, 1986c) can be useful. In parallel play, the therapist plays separately from the children but addresses the anxiety-provoking themes. For example, when parents are physically violent with each other, the therapist might have two puppets reenact a parental fight, with one parent walking out. The children can pretend to ignore the therapist's play, they can quietly watch, or they can join in, taking over the puppets.

ROLE OF THE THERAPIST

The therapist's role with young siblings is a cross between being a group therapist and a family therapist. In family therapy, the therapist is the unrelated one, the outsider. The therapist must find a way to join without being intrusive. In group therapy, the therapist is the central figure, since the members all know the therapist but not each other. The task is to get the group members to relate to each other. When the group members are young children, the level of responsibility increases. Initially, sibling therapists juggle dual tasks—joining while establishing themselves as the authority. Their task is to help the children express their conflicts and feelings. Their helping style varies with the goals of the meeting.

The therapist's role with fighting siblings is to allow the conflict to occur within the session. Then, directly or through play, the therapist helps them express their range of feelings and find less destructive ways to deal with the tension. If the children learn to understand what underlies the conflict, they may be able to generalize from one conflict to another.

With siblings seen because of a family crisis, the children may need only temporary support to share their feelings and to avoid isolation during the crisis period. For families where the parents are preoccupied with the turmoil, as with a divorce or remarriage, the children can benefit from relying on each other to provide mutual nurturing during the immediate stress. If parents were competent and giving before the crisis, the older siblings have had a model for caretaking. The therapist's role with these families is to nurture or channel what is already present and to help the siblings use their caring for each other to cope with this temporary family disorganizational period. Obviously, many siblings act out their anxiety, anger, sadness, and other feelings about the family crisis through fighting with each other. When this occurs, the role of the therapist in the sibling session is the same as with any siblings in conflict.

The therapist's role is different for children who come from families lacking a solid family structure. Many of these children have not had consistent nurturing. Their transferences may be intense, activating more caretaking from the therapist. These children need to develop reliance on each other, rather than depending solely on the therapist. Therefore, the therapist needs to help them connect with each other. The therapist can move in to teach them how to support and emotionally take care of each other, and then become less involved, leaving the children to rely on each other.

While stages of treatment are never concrete, there are essentially five evolving and then diminishing roles for therapists with these children (Lewis, 1986b). In stage one, the therapist is the invisible member of the group. The children first arrive at the therapy as a family unit; the therapist is the outsider. This stage may last only a few minutes, until they begin talking to the therapist, or it may be longer, as the children ignore the therapist and get very involved in the toys.

Stage two begins as the children accept the therapist, who then becomes a central member of the group, organizing the activity and intervening in conflicts. In this stage, the children generally turn to the adult as the key provider in the room. This is important for establishing trust, so that in a later stage interventions will be respected. In the third stage, the therapist acts as a matchmaker, bringing the children together. This is done directly by such questions as, "Elaine is playing alone, why don't you go play with her?" or "Rudy needs help in building this tower; Jamie, can you show him how to put the pieces together?"

In the fourth stage, the therapist coaches the siblings on how to play together, pay attention to each other's needs, and assist each other. In this stage, the therapist supports the natural sibling hierarchy, teaching the older children how to be more appropriately responsive to the younger ones. Ideally, therapists may wish to relieve the older child of such unfair responsibility. The reality, though, is that in many homes it is a well-functioning sibling hierarchy that helps a family run smoothly. The final stage is when the therapist becomes the former therapist, that is, when the children are no longer disabled by their individual and family issues and can turn to each other for support and direction. This may be an idealized post-therapy stage that is never actualized, but it suggests what is possible as the siblings grow older.

CLINICAL EXAMPLES

I have chosen one clinical example from each of the three categories of situations that can benefit from sibling therapy: when there is a problem between the siblings; when there is a family crisis; and when there is an unstable family structure. Each example describes the presenting problem and the treatment goals, gives a brief statement of what happened in the treatment, and is followed by a possible explanation for what occurred. In the first family the siblings were seen together only once; in the second family the recommendation was for periodic sessions; and in the third the children were seen in time-limited treatment.

Example One: A Problem Between Siblings

When siblings are fighting with each other, they may be reacting to one child's triangulation in the marriage, they may be paralleling their parents' marital problems, or they may be reflecting unresolved family-of-origin issues. While family therapy is most appropriate, a diagnostic sibling session offers an opportunity to see if the siblings' issues can be separately addressed.

> The referral comes for Lori, age 10, who is becoming more withdrawn in school and not doing her homework. After several family sessions, the family mythology is identified. Lori is like her father—quiet, super sensitive and emotionally fragile. Gail, two years younger, is said to be like mother—verbal, sometimes caustic, tough, and able to take care of herself. Gail appears the older child, either taking care of Lori or fighting with her. Gail sometimes becomes vicious. Lori's response is always to appear helpless and to call for an adult. However, when the girls are separated during the summer, they write to and call each other frequently.
>
> A recommendation is made for an evaluative sibling therapy session. The diagnostic questions are whether Lori can stand up for herself when parents are not present and what the girls dislike about each other, separate from parental projections.

During the sibling session, Lori and Gail are asked to draw a picture of themselves when happiest together and another picture when maddest at each other. They sit so they cannot see each other's papers. While the events they choose to represent the maddest and happiest times are different, the pictures are strikingly similar. In the maddest pictures, one or both parents are present; in the happiest pictures, no parent is drawn. For each picture, the therapist asks questions about what is happening, what has just happened, and what will happen next. For Gail's happy picture (the girls are playing marbles in the family room), the therapist asks what would happen if mother or father came into the room. Gail hesitates for a second and then says, "I guess we'd begin fighting." She has no explanation for that.

In family therapy the following week, the recommendation is made for the family to continue meeting together, with occasional meetings with just the girls. The goal of the sibling sessions would be to give them a forum, apart from transgenerational shadows, to bury the complementary patterns of strong Gail and weak Lori, to find and acknowledge what they do like about each other, and to find more appropriate ways to channel their dislikes. Practicing this apart from the parents makes it easier to maintain the changes in front of them. The parents will then need help to support the changes and to reverse the sibling hierarchy so Lori will be treated as the older child.

Example Two: A Family in Crisis

When a family is in crisis, one or all of the children may be reacting to the stress through their relationships, through underachievement in school, or with peers; alternatively, they may be dealing with the stress internally. If an evaluation or treatment is recommended for the siblings, the goal is to help the children identify the stress without letting the feelings spill onto other people. When they deal with the stress together, one sibling may not have to carry the affect for the others.

Michelle, age nine, stopped eating two weeks before the referral. She is the middle of three children: Her older sister is 12 and her younger brother is seven. A month before the referral, mother had been hospitalized and diagnosed as having multiple sclerosis. Three years before mother started having epileptic seizures, and last year the family business went bankrupt. The parents said they had been talking with children about each of the troubles but not dwelling on them.

They said the children got along very well, and that no other child seemed to be reacting to this series of problems.

Two family sessions were held before a recommendation was made for a diagnostic meeting with just Dana, Michelle, and Brian. The goal was to assess each of the children's reactions to the recent onslaught of crises and to test the hypothesis that Michelle was expressing anxiety for the other two.

In the sibling session, the children were given a brief reminder about the purpose of the meeting—"to talk about Michelle's not eating and any feelings you may have about what's happening in the family." Without much delay, Michelle told of her terror at seeing mother's seizures and her fear of mother's dying. Dana, crying, recanted on her prior statement, "I don't worry about it at all," and said she worried about mother's becoming incapacitated and about the extra responsibility she knew would fall on her. Brian then quietly asked a question he said he had been afraid to ask before—would they be able to live together if mother died or would they be parceled out to different relatives. Spontaneously, all three said they would stick together.

At the following family session, the parents reported that the children had refused to tell them what happened during their session, but Michelle was eating again and seemed happier, and there was a warmth between the children that parents had not seen for several years.

What allowed for the change was probably not a skillful therapeutic intervention. Most likely, it was just giving the children time to talk about their fears. While mother's illness had been discussed within the family and during the family therapy sessions, the opportunity for the children to talk together without the parents seemed to free them to discuss their deeper level of concerns. I suspect that the prior discussions were from parent to each child, whereas in the sibling meeting the children talked together. Dana's showing her vulnerability around the issue may also have freed Michelle to eat.

Example Three: Unstable Family Structure

A family without a stable structure often has multiple problems; frequently each child struggles alone, emotionally pulling away from the others. The referral for treatment often is for a specific problem with one child. However, sibling therapy can help the siblings learn to care about and rely upon each other; it can help them develop a "we-ness," since the unity of the family as a whole is missing. The treatment goal then is to address the specific presenting problem(s) while building a bond among the brothers and sisters. While ongoing therapy may be beneficial, as mentioned before, it may not be feasible. Since the dropout rate is high with these children, a short-term (time-limited) renewable contract may be more realistic (Lewis, 1986a, 1986b).

A child welfare worker referred Tammy, age 11, who was running away from home, stealing, and sometimes appearing disoriented. Tammy was the second of seven children, ranging from 12 to three years of age. She had been acting as the oldest for the past six years, since her older brother Tommy moved in with his maternal grandmother. The parents had been known to the welfare system for many years because of periodic neglect and occasional physical abuse to one of the younger children. The parents consistently refused to get marital therapy or alcohol counseling. All of the children were having problems in school and with peers, and they fought among themselves. Since there was the possibility of the children's being removed from the home, a four-week time-limited treatment was recommended. Even if the children were placed out of the area, it was believed that for the limited number of sessions the child welfare worker might agree to bring the children to therapy.

Tammy needed help with her out-of-control and disoriented behavior. All the children, though, needed to deal with Tommy's return and the most recent threat of foster placement. Our first goal was to help each child with daily adjustment problems. Other goals included preparing them to cope with the inevitable future family disruptions, building a sense of family unity, reshuffling the hierarchy to include Tommy while protecting Tammy from feeling ousted, and teaching them how to play and to fight with each other. These were obviously lofty goals for four sessions, but the hope was to at least begin making inroads in each area.

There were efforts to talk (verbally and through play) about the problems each child was having in school, about Tammy's stealing and her disoriented behavior (which ceased after the first session). When sibling fights occurred in the sessions, Tommy and Tammy would attempt to resolve them by hitting or screaming at the squabblers. The therapist coached Tommy and Tammy to deal in less abusive ways with the younger ones, and then supported their efforts. "Bess, Tommy is telling you not to hit Benny with your shoe; he is telling you how to get him to leave you alone. He has a good idea, why not try it?" It is quite likely that what made Bess tell Benny to stop bothering her was the therapist's input, but Tommy felt good about the results, and it gave him confidence when he tried it later with one of the other children.

As anticipated, the children were placed in foster homes between the second and third therapy sessions, the boys and girls in separate homes. As hoped, the welfare worker did agree to let the children finish the last two weeks. By coming to therapy, they were able to see each other once a week and to talk about their fears of the separation and the newness of the foster homes. They learned about each other's homes and discussed their worry about what would happen to their parents. Through directed play, the therapist helped them share the difficulties in the new homes, and helped them offer strategies to deal with them. Out of this, Tammy suggested biweekly telephone calls between the two homes. The therapist helped her coordinate the idea with Tommy and then each oldest discussed with the others in their home how to present the idea to the foster parents.

No long-term follow-up was possible, but two months later the child welfare worker said the children were making adequate adjustments in the homes and in the new schools. The biweekly telephone calls had not continued, but there were occasional calls between the two homes. One of the older children, she did not know which, had suggested an outing with the two families. It was in the planning stage.

It is presumptuous to assume to know what led to the smooth adjustment in the new foster homes. While there are probably multiple factors, I would like to think that the therapy had an impact. It is likely that the specific behavioral problems disappeared because of the caring and support the children were getting from each other and the therapist. It is also likely that emphasizing the sibling hierarchy allowed the older children to show caring for the younger ones, who valued the attention. All of this, of course, is basically guesswork. What was definitely clear was that the children left each of the four sessions making verbal and physical contact—something they had not been doing prior to therapy.

CONCLUSION

Of all the life stages, childhood may be the time when siblings need each other the most. From infancy on, brothers and sisters with high access are companions. They use each other to learn about playing and fighting, about intimacy, interdependency, competition, and personal boundaries.

While many family therapists do meet with the young children of a family, this is usually done in the context of the family meetings. This chapter has attempted to expand therapists' thinking about seeing only the siblings in therapy—through a one-time evaluation, periodic sibling meetings, or ongoing or time-limited therapy. Three categories of situations have been proposed when separate meetings can be beneficial.

There are many ways for siblings to cope when their families are torn by continual parental or transgenerational tensions. Some pull together for mutual support; others isolate themselves. When children become entangled in family projections, legacies, and triangles, they often play out the adult conflicts in their own relationships. Some siblings are able to insulate their relationship from the greater family aura; others are affected by the multiple triangles and transgenerational legacies all the time. Still others are affected only when parents are present; when alone they have their separate relationships with each other.

For siblings whose family is experiencing an immediate crisis, an evaluation session without parents may prove useful. When brothers and sisters are struggling individually in the family confusion, sibling therapy sessions provide a chance for them to share their feelings as well as their different views of what is happening. The mutual support, as well as alternative explanations or perceptions, can be relieving.

In families without a stable structure, the children may experience a series of struggles—lack of permanent shelter, of consistent nurturing, of assurance of food or physical safety. Involving these siblings in therapy may have a different meaning. Through sibling therapy they have a chance not only to resolve behavioral or relationship problems but also to develop a connectedness with blood relatives that could transcend the uncertainties that lie ahead of them in life.

While a case can be made for seeing young children together sometimes, many therapists do not do so. Several possible explanations have been presented. However, the most likely one is that therapists have just not thought about it. Our hope is that this chapter and the others in this book will provide the food for such thoughts.

REFERENCES

American Association of Marriage and Family Therapy. (1975). *Manual on accreditation*. Washington, DC: American Association of Marriage and Family Therapy.

Aries, P. (1965). *Centuries of childhood: A social history of family life*. New York: Vintage.

Bank, S., & Kahn, M. (1982). *The sibling bond*. New York: Basic Books.

Combrinck-Graham, L. (1986). (Ed.), *Treating young children in family therapy*. Rockville, MD: Aspen.

Combrinck-Graham, L. *Children and family therapy: Contexts of child mental health*. New York: Guilford. (in press)

Eno, M. (1985). Sibling relationships in families of divorce. *Journal of Psychotherapy and the Family, 1, 2*.

Gardner, R. (1971). *Therapeutic communication with children: The mutual storytelling technique*. New York: Jason Aronson.

Haley, J. (1976). *Problem-solving therapy*. New York: Harper Colophon.

Kahn, M. D. (1986). The sibling system: Bonds of intimacy, loyalty, and endurance. In M. Karpel (Ed.), *Family resources: The hidden partner in family therapy*. (pp. 235–258). New York: Guilford.

Keith, D. (1986). Are children necessary in family therapy? In L. Combrinck-Graham (Ed.), *Treating young children in family therapy* (pp. 1–10). Rockville, MD: Aspen.

Lewis, K. G. (1983). Sibling therapy. *Family Therapy News, 14*, 12. Washington, DC: American Association for Marriage and Family Therapy.

Lewis, K. G. (1984). Sibling therapy, Part II. *Family Therapy News, 15*, 7. Washington, DC: American Association for Marriage and Family Therapy.

Lewis, K. G. (1986a). Sibling therapy with multiproblem families. *Journal of Marital and Family Therapy, 12*(3), 291–300.

Lewis, K. G. (1986b). Sibling therapy with children in foster homes. In L. Combrinck-Graham (Ed.), *Treating young children in family therapy* (pp. 52–61). Rockville, MD: Aspen.

Lewis, K. G. (1986c). Systemic play therapy: A tool for social work consultation to inner-city community mental health centers. *Journal of Independent Social Work, 1*(2).

Minuchin, S. (1974). *Families and family therapy*. Cambridge: Harvard University Press.

Minuchin, S., & Fishman, C. (1981). *Techniques in family therapy*. Cambridge: Harvard University Press.

Minuchin, S., Montalvo, B., Guernez, B., & Schumer, F. (1967). *Families of the slums*. New York: Basic Books.

Nichols, W. (1986). Sibling subsystem therapy in family system reorganization. *Journal of Divorce, 9*(3), 133–31.

Pfouts, J. (1976, May). The sibling relationship: A forgotten dimension. *Social Work*, 200–204.

Rosenberg, E. (1980). Therapy with siblings in reorganizing families. *International Journal of Family Therapy, 2*(3), 139–150.

Whitaker, C. (1967). The growing edge — An interview with Carl Whitaker. In J. Haley and L. Hoffman (Eds.), *Techniques of family therapy*. New York: Basic Books.

Whitaker, C., & Keith, D. (1981). Symbolic-experiential family therapy. In A. Gurman and D. Kniskern (Eds.), *Handbook of family therapy* (pp. 187–226). New York: Brunner/Mazel.

Winnicott, D. (1971). *Therapeutic consultation in child psychiatry*. New York: Basic Books.

Zilbach, J. (1986). *Young children in family therapy*. New York: Brunner/Mazel.

6

Clinical Interventions
with Large Family Systems:
Balancing Interests Through Siblings

Dennis E. McGuire and Patrick Tolan

Although there is fairly extensive literature in the social sciences on large families, little has been written on the treatment of large families and nothing on the treatment of the sibling relationships within large families. This omission may be due to the belief that large families (four or more siblings) are vestiges of a bygone era or that family size is clinically irrelevant. In fact, although family size decreased from an average of 4.8 in 1900 to 2.8 in 1980, large families (more than six) still represent 12% of the population (Current Population Reports, 1985; McCubbin and Dahl, 1985). Moreover, the actual number of large families may be underestimated by these reports because they count only large families that are formed by marriage of the biological parents. In addition, many large families consist of three-generation households such as grandmother, her children, and their children or are formed by second and third marriages.

Thus, large family systems still constitute a substantial portion of the population. Further, there is some evidence that large families are overrepresented among clinical populations (Howe and Madgett, 1975), suggesting they have significantly more problems in managing their development. The view taken here is that large families make up a sizable proportion of our caseloads and by virtue of their size share some distinct systemic characteristics that should be considered. Understanding these characteristics can enhance a therapist's effectiveness with these families.

We believe, like the other authors in this volume, that attending to sibling relationships is critical in family treatment. This is particularly true with large families where the sibling group is often the central and most influential subsystem for the child. Because of size and complexity of these families, much of the socializing and caretaking occurs in the sibling subsystem. Older brothers and sisters become surrogate parents. Also, in contrast to smaller families, in large families it is functional and efficient for the executive concerns of the parents to be shared with and delegated to siblings. We have found that in most cases failure to attend to the centrality of siblings and the multiple sibling configurations when working with large families can fatally impede the clinical process, leading to poor treatment results and/or dropouts. Recognizing and accessing the unique aspects of the sibling subsystem can open avenues for therapeutic change which are simple, brief, and effective.

Beginning with a brief review of the available research literature, we will discuss a systemic view of large families and how it fits with a structural-strategic treatment approach that emphasizes siblings. Following this, defining characteristics of large families, typical presenting problems, and guidelines for assessment and intervention with siblings are presented.

RESEARCH ON LARGE FAMILIES

To date, almost all research on large families has focused on family size as a direct, linear, and detrimental effect on the family members (Tolan and McGuire, 1987; Wagner, Schubert and Schubert, 1979, 1985). An exception is Bossard and Boll's (1956) study highlighting the advantages of large family membership. A body of research, primarily based on large statistical studies, has suggested that children from large families have lower intellectual, emotional, and behavioral functioning skills than children from small families (Nye, Carlson, and Garrett, 1970; Rutter and Graham, 1976; Wagner et al., 1979). The obtained results are explained as reflecting the limited parental time and attention per child in large families, which is seen as impeding normal disciplining and guidance. Also, some of these studies suggest that the larger proportion of children to parents lowers the overall intellectual level of the family, decreasing the "environmental opportunity" to learn (Zajonc, 1976).

These results have been criticized methodologically and later studies have not found direct detrimental family size effects (Mednick, Baker, and Hocevar, 1985). Reevaluation of the research literature suggests that these early studies and their conclusions are too simplistic. The effects of family size in all areas of psychosocial functioning are complex and depend on interaction with such other influences as socioeconomic status and ethnicity. From a systemic perspective it is useful to compare family size with other influences on behavior and search out the clinical implications.

PROFILE OF CHILDREN FROM LARGE FAMILIES

Large family systems are distinguished in several ways. They tend to be more complex than smaller ones. Along with marital, parental, and sibling subsystems that constitute all families, several sibling subsystems coexist. Common subsystem distinctions are by birth order and gender (Tolan and McGuire, 1987). Because each sibling is a member of several sibling subsystems, there are shifts in sibling "alliances" depending on which subsystem organization is prominent at the moment.

In general, large families are more rule-governed than smaller families (Wagner et al., 1985); i.e., privileges, responsibilities, and discipline may be determined more by the rule than by the individuals involved. Thus, the individual relationship between parent and child will be less central in decisions than in smaller families (Hurley and Horn, 1971). In part this is due to the number of children, which limits the parents' direct attention to each child and promotes effective use of parental energy (Nye et al., 1970); in part it maintains family values of fairness and equal treatment (Bossard and Boll, 1956). As a reflection of the rule-oriented family organization, discipline is communicated less through verbal reasoning around each incident and more through an expectation of compliance to previously set rules (Elder and Bowerman, 1963). As a by-product, children of large families report they feel less parental approval than children from smaller families (Nye et al., 1970).

Because large families are so oriented to the group, they instill less of an individualistic orientation than most families. Members are likely to feel more bound to their family than those from smaller families (Bossard and Boll, 1956). Sharing is strongly emphasized. Therefore, one's identity is more intimately tied to interdependence with others than to individual accomplishment. Ownership is often transient, with material goods expected to be handed down to younger siblings. Economic resources must be spread farther than in other families of the same socioeconomic status; therefore, personal possession is considered a luxury (Espenshade, Kamenske, and Turchi, 1983). Similarly, privacy is less emphasized in large families, since both central living spaces and bedrooms are shared (Bossard and Boll, 1956; Espenshade et al., 1983).

As a result, children from large families score lower on measures of self-concept and/or report feeling more alienated and may be less emotionally expressive than children from smaller families (Kidwell, 1981). On the other hand, members of these families tend to be more cooperative, altruistic and responsive to others. They exhibit more self-control and feel more comfortable with interdependence than the general population (Bossard and Boll, 1956; Eysenck and Carlson, 1970; Wagner et al., 1979).

Although large families are overrepresented among clinical populations (Tuckman and Regan, 1967), cohort studies suggest that their members are not more likely to evidence psychological symptoms (Mednick et al., 1985; Touliatos and Lindholm, 1980). Symptomatic children from large families are more likely to exhibit learning problems and inhibitions, and less likely to exhibit problematic aggressive behaviors than children from smaller families (Searcy-Miller, Cowen, and Terrell, 1977; Boone and Montare, 1979). However, of those children having aggressive problems, children from large families tend to be more extreme than the general population (Murrell, 1974; Wadsworth, 1979).

SIBLINGS IN LARGE FAMILIES

The research on siblings in large families is rather limited. However, there are three studies which are of particular importance. Bossard and Boll (1956) surveyed the adult siblings from 100 large families. Their report stands to date as one of the most informative statements on large families, despite its age and reliance on retrospective accounts. They report that because of the size and complexity of large families, the siblings' roles as socializers and caretakers are central to their sibling relations. Older siblings are usually required to take on parental responsibilities. In a sense, the parents raise the older children and older children raise their younger siblings. As parental figures, older siblings are more tolerant than parents of the younger ones' misbehavior and are fairer in assigning tasks and consequences. Interestingly, 69% of the older siblings in their sample reported being satisfied with their parental responsibilities; only 11% of younger children reported resentment concerning the sibling parenting, while 44% reported resentment of their adult parents.

Bossard and Boll also noted several other characteristics of the children in their subject families. For example, sibling rivalry and conflict were surprisingly low, with strong feelings of closeness and connectedness occurring and continuing into adulthood. On the other hand, children from large families had a narrow assignment and ascription of formal roles and informal attributes (characteristics). Also, a child's esteem was defined less by individual accomplishments and more by doing his part as one of many. Similarly, attitudes toward socializing, use of leisure time, and vocational activity were family-centered and highly influenced by siblings. The individuality of each child was suppressed by the needs and demands of the "large" group.

Minuchin, Montalvo, Guerney, Rosman, and Schumer's (1967) seminal study of large poor families offered several basic structural concepts. They noted that large families had strong boundaries between the family and the outside. As the family size increased, sibling power increased, particularly when there was a dysfunctional parental subsystem. While the centrality of the siblings maintained the family to some extent, it also blocked development of adequate generational boundaries to allow discipline and executive functions to occur. Minuchin et al. determined that treatment required enhancing parental authority and competence while supporting appropriate sibling functions.

Bank and Kahn (1975) provided an analysis of the sibling subsystem's functions and were the first to emphasize its utility and power in family therapy. They said sibling relations can be as influential on family members as the parental-child relations or extrafamilial influences. Most pertinent to this chapter's topic, they outlined five autonomous functions of siblings in the family: identification and differentiation, direct service, mutual regulation, translating functions, and dealing with parents. However, there are major differences for siblings from large families on four of these. These distinctions provide a synthesis for understanding the function of siblings in large families and are basic to utilizing a structural-strategic therapeutic approach with these families.

Identification and Differentiation

As in parent-child relations, the identification of self with other siblings and the differentiation of the "me" from the "not me" are important parts of a child's development. In large families, the increased number of individuals and the diversity of personality styles provide a greater array of identification and differentiation figures. However, the process of identification then becomes more complex and less direct, particularly for later-born siblings. Perhaps as a partial solution to this complexity, large families, like other large systems, ascribe a narrower range of functions and characteristics to its member (Barker, 1968), which then stabilize and generalize beyond the family roles and childhood years (Bossard and Boll, 1956). Thus, if the attribute is positive ("gutsy," "go-getter," "humorous"), it can serve as a resilient organizer of self-esteem which extends across situations and time. If the attribute is negative ("dumb," "lazy," "crazy"), the effect can be equally powerful but in a devastating manner. Despite effectiveness in other situations and a wide range of positive abilities, the member's esteem and identity will be "ruled" by this narrow negative ascription. In large families, the siblings are central to ascribing these roles and maintaining their ascription.

Direct Service

As described by Bank and Kahn (1975), siblings also provide valuable services for each other, such as teaching skills, lending money, and helping out with work. Among large family siblings, the need to share and to cooperate in the use of limited resources often changes the form and quality of these direct services. Whereas among small family siblings the exchange of services is mostly centered around specific goods, such as money and clothes, in large families the exchange often centers around such intangible services as group support, advice, and mediation in other sibling relationships or extramarital systems. An example of the latter comes from the first author's first school dance at age 15; not only was a prized dress shirt furnished by an older brother, but the older siblings offered advice on grooming as well. Several brothers and sisters were present and offered emotional support during the evening, suggested dance partners, and recommended when to walk the girl home.

Mutual Regulation

Bank and Kahn (1975) state that as "mutual regulators" siblings listen to each other and provide feedback that either promotes or inhibits further development of ideas and feelings. They also can allow experimentation with new roles and behaviors without the "emotional obligation or guilt" of parent-child relations. As Bossard and Boll (1956) note, siblings in large families are especially fair and honest in encouraging and criticizing each other's behaviors. Thus, they can become very effective mutual regulators. However, they can also overemphasize conformity to the group's definitions of appropriate behavior at the expense of individual initiative and creativity, with effects such as the narrow role ascription defined above.

Translating Functions

Bank and Kahn (1975) used Zuk's (1966) concept of a "go between" to define the transacting function between siblings. As they explained, siblings mediate the transactions among themselves, between siblings and parents, and between the family and the outside world. With their increased numbers and greater influence, large families' siblings are often better able to moderate or buffer harmful parental or extrafamilial influences (Tolan and McGuire, 1987). However, this moderating function may break down when older siblings leave home and younger siblings are left to directly negotiate with parents. Also, the systemic organization may be overreliant on the sibling mediation, leaving parents with limited negotiating ability. Thus, in some families the sibling group may have too much control and too many parental responsibilities, as was reported by Minuchin et al. (1967). Additionally, the family effectiveness can be limited because important extrafamilial agencies and institutions will not deal with older siblings in what is considered a parental role, even though the siblings have adequate skills and the family's legitimate authority to act in this role.

Another transaction function of siblings in large families is to help maintain strong boundaries between "inside" and "outside" the family. The sibling group tends to shield its members from peer and other extrafamilial affiliations and influences and to act as an intermediary between parents and extrafamilial systems. Thus, these children may have limited peer interests.

As these research projects suggest, the large family system is more complex and the sibling system more central than in smaller-sized families. The autonomous functions of the siblings can regulate and promote behavior in several predictable and distinct ways. The centrality of siblings, the complexity and shifting nature of subsystem organization, and their strong boundaries with the extrafamilial can make understanding how to work with large families difficult. However, structural-strategic methods with a focus on siblings and on the need to balance the interests of competing subsystems (Koestler, 1979) provide an effective way of intervening.

TREATING THE LARGE FAMILY

In the structural-strategic approach the focus is on the contextual patterns (organization) of interactions that maintain a problem. The goal is to create a functional system that maintains appropriate organizational hierarchies and boundaries between its parts or subsystems (Haley, 1981; Minuchin and Fishman, 1981).

However, rather than emphasizing elevating the parental subsystem and viewing siblings only in their relation to parents, we contend that the sibling subsystem merits direct attention. Like the parental or marital subsystems, it cannot be viewed as totally separate from the family, just as a family cannot be understood apart from its larger context. Nevertheless, focusing attention on the siblings can give us useful information and a powerful avenue for therapeutic change. With this focus the problem is conceptualized not only in terms of hierarchy and boundaries but also in terms of the need to balance the interest and demands of the competing subsystems comprising the sibling group and, at higher levels, the family and the extrafamilial.

Problems develop when a child is unable to balance different interests and roles with the needs of the whole sibling subsystem. For example, if the family requires that the child assume many parenting functions, that child may have underdeveloped interests or abilities to receive parenting. Also, such an imbalance may result in the child's having little time or energy left for peer or academic interests.

General Guidelines

Large families may be difficult to engage for therapists who are unfamiliar with their organizational features or who underestimate their complexity. The following guidelines may be helpful.

(1) With the increased importance of the sibling group, key members of this group must be consulted or included in the decision to attend therapy. In some families it may be necessary to suggest that parents consult with older siblings to get their support for the therapy. However, in resistant families, it may be necessary for the therapist to talk directly to siblings in order to engage them in therapy.

Permission must be obtained from the parents to speak directly with older children. In granting permission, the parents will often identify the senior sibling or siblings who are most responsible for decision-making. It is usually, but not always, the oldest child. Once parental and key siblings agree to therapy, problems engaging other family members are rare.

(2) It may be useful to see the siblings without the parents, especially if most are adolescents or older. Siblings are likely to talk more freely when seen without parents and it is often easier for the therapist to determine the critical autonomous functions and transactional sibling patterns. The siblings may also be seen in smaller groups to assess the different subsystems and to determine alignments and splits with potentially serious repercussions for family functioning. Also, certain sibling subsystems may need specific attention to increase therapeutic leverage. Older siblings with executive authority may be seen to elicit their support around a therapy plan prior to introducing it to the others. Also, if younger siblings are seen separately from the older ones, it is advisable to ask permission of such older caretaking siblings, as one would ask a parent in smaller families. Seeing younger sibling groups alone can be particularly useful in challenging negative ascriptions maintained by the siblings as a total

group or in creating opportunities for younger siblings to exhibit executive functions.

(3) In planning therapy it is usually advantageous to see all siblings, including those who no longer live at home. Long after leaving home older siblings often retain caretaking functions and command considerable respect from and influence on their younger sisters and brothers. Moreover, these siblings can provide understanding and support for family members while also being very direct with suggestions and criticisms, especially if a younger sibling and the parents are in direct conflict. It is advisable, however, to include these siblings on a time-limited basis (usually one to three sessions). It is important to remember that these siblings have left home successfully; they should be engaged without jeopardizing their own autonomy. The developmental thrust of children leaving and remaining out of the home needs to be supported.

(4) It is important to assess all pertinent levels of the family system and related contexts, including the parent-sibling relations and familial-extrafamilial relations. Although focusing on siblings has advantages, flexibility to intervene at other appropriate levels or to utilize multilevel interventions must be retained.

CLINICAL PROBLEMS OF LARGE FAMILIES

Beyond these guidelines for engaging large families, there are four major types of problems that lead to dysfunctional behavior. Each problem, its systemic basis, and what is needed to reestablish balance are described below and followed by clinical examples.

An Imbalance Between Family
and Extrafamilial System

The strong sense of loyalty and affiliation among large family siblings can serve as a source of self-esteem and may smooth adjustment to the world, as in the author's first dance. In other cases, however, where siblings or the family group view themselves as different or antagonistic to extrafamilial systems, this loyalty may hinder a child in balancing the interests of each. This distinction of "difference" by the family may relate to a number of factors: socioeconomic, ethnic, or class differences with the major culture and institutions;

financial hardships; or the absence of an important family member. Efforts of family members may be focused almost exclusively on the family's struggle to survive and to maintain the family's interests. Thus children have little time for school or peer functions. The net effect is that the members see themselves as apart from the larger, extrafamilial system. Involvement with peers or other outsiders may be viewed as disloyalty. Individual outside interests are not supported. This organization often manifests as poor motivation in school or severe conflict in peer relations.

Because siblings are likely to be "closer" than parents to the child's experience of the differentiation process, they can more readily promote the interest of the child in extrafamilial pursuits. Also, they can provide direct service by dividing up a sibling's too-demanding family responsibilities among themselves to provide time and energy for outside interests.

In cases where a child's problem results from the inability of a large family to balance family and extrafamilial interests, the interventions must bridge the gap between the family and important extrafamilial systems. In intervening with large families, it is important to remember that, along with other executive functions inside the family, older siblings may have responsibility and parental permission to negotiate for the family with extrafamilial systems. These siblings are often well versed in family matters and quite capable of making executive decisions for the family. In some cases, in fact, the problem may relate to the failure of the outside agency or individual to accept an older sibling as a valid representative of the family, rather than to the family's unwillingness to negotiate.

For example, several young children from a large family were referred to a school psychologist for a number of school problems, including truancy and underachievement. Even though the school had threatened these children with expulsion, the psychologist and other school personnel had been unsuccessful in their attempts to meet with the parents to resolve these difficulties. Apparently, each time a school representative would call the home, one of the children would protectively report that the mother was too busy to talk and/or the father was asleep or at work. A consultation with one of the authors about the case resulted in the psychologist's agreeing to negotiate a meeting with a senior member of the sibling group. Jan was readily identified by the younger symptomatic family members and a meeting was arranged with her at her high school. To the surprise of the psychologist, she was well aware of the problem and agreed to meet with school staff the following day. At this meeting she was joined by two other older siblings, who immediately agreed to monitor the behavior and school work of their younger sisters and brothers. Subsequent to the meeting the performance of all of the younger siblings improved substantially. Six months later, at a regularly scheduled PTA meeting, the mother thanked the psychologist for the help. She explained that, although these problems were very important, the family was having a lot of difficulty at that time and she knew that Jan and her other older children were quite capable of handling these problems for her.

Too Narrow Individual Labels

Problems may manifest in large families through too-narrow labeling or attribution of roles and characteristics to individual members. The power of group influence may also prevent individuals from accessing and exhibiting other aspects or "parts" of their personalities (Lerner and Schwartz, 1986). As indicated above, this label often becomes a self-fulfilling prophecy organizing the child's interaction with the world in general. Thus, labels such as "troublemaker" or "selfish" not only inhibit the person's cooperation within the sibling group, but may also generalize to outside the family. Because siblings are the primary developers and maintainers of these ascriptions, the group needs to develop more adaptive alternative ascriptions or more complex ascriptions which also include some competencies. One intervention is to meet with the siblings in subsystems to increase the opportunities for members to exhibit more varied role behaviors. Other approaches include introducing evidence of abilities other than the ascribed ones through reports of such behavior in other settings and relabeling the negative characteristics to show their positive systemic functions.

For example, Bob, the fifth of seven children, was referred to a therapist for school problems. Although Bob demonstrated above-average intelligence on achievement tests, his grades were poor. When the therapist met with the sibling group it seemed that Bob was a relatively quiet and unassuming young boy who was positioned on either side by siblings who were bright and ambitious. As a result he was characterized as the "good-natured but somewhat slow or help-less one." Thus, little was expected or demanded to him at home or in school.

To challenge this label the therapist introduced evidence of Bob's achievement potential to the other siblings. In addition, his school failure was reframed as "*playing* dumb again." Although initially surprised, the siblings found that in using this phrase to describe him they began to see him as obtaining special help and favors when he actually was quite competent. Subsequently they demanded that he do his share of chores and at the therapist's urging pushed the parents to organize a time and place for Bob to do his homework. Also, his passivity was positively connoted by the therapist's labeling him "good natured." He was called a "diplomat," emphasizing his consid-erable skill in gently moving others toward a goal. Following this, Bob was called upon to be responsible for such important family matters as fielding calls from boys interested in his sisters and nego-tiating a disagreement between the parents and some siblings about curfew hours. These labeling changes were continually reinforced by the sibling interactions. They proved sufficient to alter Bob's behavior at home and school and to end his role as a school failure.

The Overresponsible Older Siblings

In looking at the different ordinal positions of large family sib-lings, we have found that children in several sibling positions, partic-ularly at the youngest and oldest extremes, are most at risk. Older siblings, because they are often delegated an inordinately large share of the parenting and caretaking responsibility for younger siblings, may have difficulty finding time for age-appropriate peer and school interests. Encouraging parents to take more responsibility for the younger children and balancing individual and familial responsibili-ties through more equitable distribution of these responsibilities among all siblings are two commonly needed interventions. In either case, focus on sibling relations is an efficient method of changing the families.

As an example, a family of six children and a single parent was referred because the oldest daughter, Nora, age 16, was failing her junior year in high school. She was quite capable of academic success but was often tardy or truant. In the meeting with the family, the therapist learned that the mother left home for work at five in the morning. The job of sending the five children (ages 5 through 14) to school was left to Nora. Several of her problems resulted directly from this responsibility. First, her school started earlier than that of her younger siblings. She took her caretaking responsibility as oldest child very seriously and would not ask for help or delegate to others. Instead she was tardy for school and jeopardized her school performance. Since she was expected to take on these duties, she did not tell her mother of the conflict; she did not want to bother this already burdened woman.

The therapist recognized the importance of Nora's role in the family and her good intentions, but introduced one important shift. The mother was asked to educate the daughter that a good leader delegates and uses the resources of those under her command. It was recommended she utilize the younger siblings' feedback to the oldest daughter to convince her that they wanted opportunities to share responsibilities. In the coming weeks, with the mother's encouragement, the daughter began to delegate more responsibilities to the other siblings; this allowed her more time for school and other self-interests. Siblings who left for school later made sure the youngest got to school on time. In addition, mother reported that advising her daughter and seeing how her children could support each other gave her the confidence to resolve the longstanding problem of her alcoholic husband's periodically returning to the home and disrupting the family's organization.

In some cases the problems with an older sibling develop because the child is given too little responsibility for the sibling position, rather than too much. For example, in a family of two parents and six children (ages 1 to 16), the oldest, Peter, was arrested for a number of serious acts of vandalism. The initial interview revealed that he had spent a good portion of his childhood at his grandparents, and had returned home recently because of their illness. At home Peter was treated more or less as an outsider by other siblings, with no position or status in the family. Another sibling, Judy, was functioning in the eldest position and had been ascribed its rights and responsibilities.

The goal of therapy was to integrate Peter into an appropriate older sibling position in the family. The therapist mediated a series of negotiations between Peter and Judy, age 14. Not only was she the most affected by his entrance and the incumbent change, but she had the most direct power to support the change. Although she initially balked at the possibility of sharing her authority with her brother, citing his lack of skills and his irresponsibility, after hearing of advantages to her of the change she supported it. The therapist noted that her brother could help her in caring for younger siblings and act as an ally when negotiating for the siblings with parents. Also, she would then have more time for her own interests. She was told that he would need some advising as he took on this role, which eased the process of her relinquishing the position. After an initial lag, Peter became more comfortable with his new role responsibilities. His problematic behavior in the home and other settings diminished. In time both he and his sister were able to balance their home responsibilities with appropriate interests outside the family.

The Sacrificed Youngest Sibling

Our experience has been that the majority of large family children presenting at clinics are the lastborn members. The parents are often exhausted by the time the younger children are born. Also, the parents' marital relationship may be developmentally pushing toward the "postparental" stage once the oldest siblings reach young adulthood or begin to leave home. The length of the parenting stage is so extended in large families that parents may feel unable to rekindle and therefore renegotiate marital intimacy. Moreover, some parents may have difficulty facing the impending loss and solitude of the "empty nest" that can accompany the postparental stage of marriage (McCubbin and Dahl, 1985; Tolan and McGuire, 1987). The youngest child may function as the mediator and distraction from this developmental problem (Haley, 1981). In addition, the caretaking roles learned by older children as prerequisites to developing their own independence and to leaving home are not passed on to the youngest siblings. For all of these reasons, youngest children may "sacrifice" their own development toward independence in order to stay home.

In dealing with this type of problem, a therapist may focus primarily on siblings remaining at home but should try to include grown siblings as well. The sibling system needs to be organized to help buffer marital issues that can interfere with independent development and to "model" leaving home skills. Older siblings should be asked to determine how vacant leadership positions should be filled in order to bolster needed confidence. These interventions can structure the siblings' interaction to enable the youngest siblings to be competent at home and therefore leave appropriately.

As an example, a large family in which the three oldest siblings were out of the home and functioning well was referred because several of the remaining siblings were symptomatic. The younger siblings complained that things were not the same since their older brothers and sister left, that the family seemed to have ended. After initial consultation with the whole sibling group, the goal of establishing an "eldest" sibling among those remaining at home was developed. The oldest sibling of those remaining at home had not been involved with the family since the exit of her next oldest sibling; instead she was very involved with her friends and her boyfriend. Once encouraged by her oldest siblings, however, she was quite willing to assume this new role in the family. To aid this transition several of the grown siblings advised her on how to manage sibling affairs. In addition to this sister's learning new skills and gaining self-esteem, the temporary reinvolvement of the older siblings helped end the demoralized atmosphere of the remaining siblings. The relabeling of the older siblings' exit from "the end of the family" to "a shift in roles of those at home" allowed the family to return to a normal course of development.

In some large families the youngest is "sacrificed" to "save the marriage." In such families, many of the older sibling members probably exited precipitously and are wary of any reinvolvement, even to aid a sibling. The family atmosphere is analogous to a sinking ship — and the sibs feel like escaping rats. In this case, it is critical to emphasize that the sibling system is an autonomous and major determinant of the family's existence and meaning and that changes in sibling functions can change the family. By separating marital problems from the family's existence, the sibling group can be engaged in cooperative problem-solving.

As a case example, Robert, age 21, was the youngest and last child at home in a family of 13 children. He was seen in therapy by court order for exposing himself at work. He had been labeled "marginally retarded" and assigned to a community program where his adjustment was poor. Family therapy was recommended.

In meeting with Robert and his parents the therapist learned of longstanding marital discord including threats and physical fights. Robert's problems served as the only distraction and were used to explain why the discord existed. Robert's siblings, having had their fill of the parents' problems, left home as soon as they were able. Their antagonism toward the parents continued and they rarely came to visit, even though most lived within five miles of the home. Robert was essentially isolated from his siblings. Moreover, Roberts' characterization as "mental" or "slow" by family members seemed to explain his difficulties and mitigate against any expectation or encouragement that he act more his age and/or leave home. For his part, Robert acted in accordance with these labels, although he admitted secretly to the therapist that he stayed at home primarily to "keep my parents from hurting each other."

Treatment with Robert and his parents was not successful. A new strategy was then developed by the therapist and the consultant. This involved inclusion of the other siblings in therapy, with the goal of using the siblings' power to aid Robert's transition to adulthood. Although extensive planning and outreach were required to overcome initial resistance, all siblings within the general geographic area agreed to attend a session. The group was seen without the parents.

At the beginning of this meeting the therapist offered evidence which effectively challenged the idea that Robert was of low intelligence. Also Robert's conscious forestalling of his own development to monitor the parents' relationship was shared and emphasized. In response, the older siblings discussed their own difficulties and reluctance to leave the home. This repeated theme was used to encourage the siblings to organize to help Robert be more independent. They impressed upon Robert that his parents would have to resolve their own difficulties and agreed to "spread" responsibilities to maintain contact with the parents and to "keep the family going." Robert's sensitivity and loyalty were noted; this gave him a measure of respect he had not previously had. He was then able to respond maturely and with intelligence, becoming an active participant in siblings' discussions. Over several sessions Robert was seen individually or with one or more siblings to ensure implementation of the plan and maintenance of the change. It was obvious that his developing confidence and dignity were tied to his identity as a sibling. In particular, a sincere interest in becoming independent and a more realistic view of his responsibilities for and control over his parents' marital problems emerged. Meanwhile, his parents were seen in couple therapy and in sessions with Robert. They were skeptical of his abilities and unsupportive of his moves towards independence. Marital disputes focused more on Robert's "problems." However, the siblings' position that these were two separate issues ultimately prevailed and the parents eventually focused more directly on their discord. At one-year follow-up, Robert had made an agreement to share housing with one brother. He had graduated from the community program and was employed. No other incidents of exposing himself had occurred. As he described it, he had graduated to "adult life."

CONCLUSION

As the literature review and clinical examples presented show, there are several distinct qualities of large families that are pertinent to clinical interpretation. Most prominent of these is the centrality and complexity of the sibling subsystem. This centrality not only increases the influence of the sibling role on members' behavior and perceptions, but also requires a focus on sibling relations in therapy. Straightforward application of assumptions about hierarchy, boundaries, and organization to large families can result in failed or harmful interventions. However, modifying these assumptions, recognizing the influence of autonomous sibling functions, and focusing on sibling relations in instrumenting change can lead to effective interventions and desired outcomes.

REFERENCES

Bank, S., & Kahn, M. D. (1975). Sisterhood-brotherhood is powerful: Sibling subsystems and family therapy. *Family Process, 14*, 311–337.

Barker, R. G. (1968). *Ecological psychology: Concepts and methods for studying the environment of human behavior*. Stanford, CA: Stanford University Press.

Boone, S. L., & Montare, A. (1979). Aggression and family size. *The Journal of Psychology, 103*, 67–70.

Bossard, J. H. S., & Boll, E. S. (1956). *The large family system*. Philadelphia: University of Pennsylvania Press.

Current Population Reports (1985). *Household and Family Characteristics*. (Series P-20, No. 371, March).

Elder, G. H., & Bowerman, C. E. (1963). Family structure and child rearing patterns: The effect of family size and sex composition. *American Sociological Review, 28*, 891–905.

Espenshade, T. J., Kamenske, G., & Turchi, B. A. (1983). Family size and economic welfare. *Family Planning Perspective, 15*, 289–294.

Eysenck, H. J., & Carlson, D. (1970). Personality in primary school children III. Family background. *British Journal of Educational Psychology, 40*, 117–131.

Haley, J. (1981). *Leaving home: The therapy of disturbed young people.* New York: McGraw-Hill.

Howe, M. C., & Madgett, M. E. (1975). Mental health problems associated with the only child. *Canadian Psychiatric Association Journal, 20*, 189–194.

Hurley, J. R., & Horn, R. L. (1971). Shifts in child-rearing attitudes linked with parenthood and occupation. *Developmental Psychology, 4*, 324–328.

Kidwell, J. S. (1981). Number of siblings, sibling spacing, sex, and birth order: Their effects on perceived parent-adolescent relationships. *Journal of Marriage and the Family, 43*, 315–332.

Koestler, A. (1979). *Janus: A summing up.* New York: Vintage Books.

Lerner, S., & Schwartz, R. (1986, October). *Working systemically with individuals.* Paper presented at the Annual Meeting of the American Association for Marriage and Family Therapy, Orlando, FL.

McCubbin, H., & Dahl, B. B. (1985). *Marriage and family: Individuals and life cycles.* New York: John Wiley.

Mednick, B. R., Baker, R. L., & Hocevar, D. (1985). Family size and birth order correlates of intellectual, psychosocial, and physical growth. *Merrill-Palmer Quarterly, 31*, 67–83.

Minuchin, S., Montalvo, B., Guerney, B. G., Rosman, B. L., & Schumer, F. (1967). *Families of the slums: An exploration of their structure and treatment.* New York: Basic Books.

Minuchin, S., & Fishman, H. C. (1981). *Family therapy techniques.* Cambridge, MA: Harvard University Press.

Murrell, S. A. (1974). Relationships of ordinal positions and family size to psychosocial measures of delinquents. *Journal of Abnormal Child Psychology, 2*, 39–46.

Nye, F. I., Carlson, J., & Garrett, G. (1970). Family interaction, affect, and stress. *Journal of Marriage and the Family, 216*, 216–226.

Rutter, M., & Graham, P. (1976). Social circumstances of children with psychiatric disorder. In M. Rutter, J. Tizard, & K. Whitmore (Eds.), *Education, health, and behaviour: Psychological and medical study of childhood development.* New York: John Wiley.

Searcy-Miller, M. L., Cowen, E. L., & Terrell, D. L. (1977). School adjustment problems of children from small vs. large families. *Journal of Community Psychology, 5*, 319–324.

Tolan, P. H., & McGuire, D. (1987). Children and family size. In J. Grimes & A. Thomas (Eds.), *Children's needs: Psychological perspectives.* New York: National Association of School Psychologists.

Touliatos, J., & Lindholm, B. W. (1980). Birth order, family size, and children's mental health. *Psychological Reports, 46*, 1097–1098.

Tuckman, J., & Regan, R. A. (1967). Size of family and behavior problems. *Journal of Genetic Psychology, 111*, 151–161.

Wadsworth, M. (1979). *Roots of delinquency.* Oxford: M. Robertson & Co.

Wagner, M. E., Schubert, H. J. P., & Schubert, D. S. P. (1979). Sibship-constellation effects on psychosocial development, creativity, and health. In H. W. Reese & L. P. Libsitt (Eds.), *Advances in child development and behavior, Vol. 14,* (pp. 58–155). New York: Academic Press.

Wagner, M. E., Schubert, H. J. P., & Schubert, D. S. P. (1985). Family size effects: A review. *The Journal of Genetic Psychology, 146,* 65–78.

Zajonc, R. (1976). Family configuration and intelligence. *Science, 192,* 227–236.

Zuk, G. H. (1966). The go-between process in family therapy. *Family Process, 5,* 162–178.

7

Untangling Incestuous Bonds:
The Treatment of Sibling Incest

Marsha L. Heiman

Through a shared history and common bonds, siblings have the potential to provide each other with support, guidance, and information. What happens when the bond goes beyond the expected boundaries and becomes sexual and exploitative in nature? With the notable exception of a handful of writings (Bank and Kahn, 1982; Cole, 1982; Finkelhor, 1980; Loredo, 1982; Santiago, 1973), the topic of sibling incest has been virtually ignored, or at best minimized, despite reports which estimate that sibling incest may be the most common but underreported form of incest.

The same lack of attention within psychological writings to sibling problems in general, and incest in particular, is not true within the fields of history, literature, and mythology, where examples of sibling incest abound. One such example of sibling love is the creation myth of the sun-sister and moon-brother legend of the Pacific Coast Indians. As described by Santiago (1973):

> The sister paints her hands to discover her nocturnal paramour. Upon seeing the paint on her brother's back the next morning, she flees to the sky; he tries to chase her; but they are eternally separated as the sun and the moon. (p. 8)

Given different cultural norms and diverse familial atmospheres, what yardstick is one to use to differentiate normative, sexual exploration and curiosity between children within a family from more incestuous sibling behavior? Finkelhor (1980) has defined typical sexual play as "activities of young children of the same age, engaged in mutuality, that are limited to the showing and touching of genitals, and that goes on for short periods of time" (p. 172). According to Finkelhor's definition, key elements which distinguish natural sexual play between siblings from incest would be age proximity and developmentally appropriate activities which are limited and transitory in nature. Excluded from typical sexual play would be "sex engaged in by force, among older children or among children of a large age difference, attempts at intercourse or compulsive activity that goes on too long" (p. 172). Using Finkelhor's characterization as a guidepost, sexual contact between siblings is considered to be incestuous when either there is a large age difference between partners (regardless of the form of the sexual activities) and/or the activities go beyond normal exploration to include oral-genital contact or intercourse. Although this definition provides a useful, theoretical framework for gauging normative sexual play among children, a phenomenological experience which feels exploitative, frightening, or unusual and confusing should not be ignored, regardless of the age of the participants or activity involved. As Santiago (1973) notes, "Any form of seduction between siblings, if not dealt with properly, may lead to serious emotional problems in childhood or later in adulthood" (p. 170).

Meiselman (1978) suggests that the taboo against sibling incest has always been the weakest, since the act is often viewed as "child's play" and does not cross generational lines. Furthermore when the brother initiates the sibling incest, it does not violate social expectations of male dominance. Interpreting sexual contact between siblings as trivial, natural, or unimportant has resulted in many parents dismissing a child's report of being sexually exploited by another sibling. The unfortunate aspect of failing to question whether the sexuality between siblings really falls within normal bounds is that a transitory event, if not corrected and redirected, can become integrated into a pattern of responding. Although not addressing sibling incest in particular, Groth (1977) reports that many male sexual offenders committed their first offense as juveniles. As such, Groth cautions against viewing inappropriate juvenile sexual behavior as mere child's play or uncontrollable adolescent hormonal urges.

As more attention has been focused on the prevalence of incest in general, others have begun to question the "myth of benign sibling incest" (Cole, 1982). Bank and Kahn (1982) have noted:

> . . . the breaking of the incest taboo by siblings is special, and its greater frequency does not mean its ramifications are any less significant. . . . sibling incest has profound implications for personality development because it is a basic attack on social custom and taboo and often involves such contradictory feelings as guilt, love, shame, empathy, and anger, as well as the processes of identification. (p. 169)

UNDERSTANDING SIBLING INCEST

How is one to understand the occurrence of sibling incest and the motivations underlying breaking the taboo? Freud originally hypothesized that brother-sister incest was a result of unresolved oedipal issues, such that incestuous longings for the parent were displaced onto a sibling. In reviewing the literature, Bank and Kahn (1982) note that at the heart of the psychoanalytic theory of sibling relationships was the belief that "if siblings are of the same sex they are rivals for parent love; if of the opposite sex, they are the natural outlet for displaced oedipal desires" (p. 162).

However, displacement of unresolved oedipal love as a motivator of sibling incest ignores the conditions which are necessary to overcome the incest barrier. Frances and Frances (1976) remind us that the incest barrier is a universal phenomenon observed in all "bonding-motivated animal species." Certain species-specific behaviors were selected to minimize the likelihood of incest. These authors argue that "much of what seems most human in our family structure has evolved in response to a biological imperative (enforced by natural selection) that incest be avoided" (p. 236). Therefore, any explanation of sibling incest must examine the family environment, which has the power to relax or enforce the incest taboo, thereby fostering or restraining sexual impulses.

Expanding psychoanalytic insights, Santiago (1973) observed:

> When either or both parents are not available physically or emotionally, the siblings lacking an object for rivalry may turn to each other instead to meet dependency and erotic demands. What initially appears to be the 'second best' love may turn out to be 'even better' than the original. The absence of authority and the greater chances of

concealment (out of mutual need and fear) enhances the eventual per-
petuation of the sexual relationship. (p. 7)

Recognizing the importance of "contextual circumstances," Bank and
Kahn (1982) have emphasized the high accessibility of siblings to
each other and the inability of parents to meet the needs of their
children as preconditions for the incestuous sibling relationship.
They explain that "incest is more likely to occur if there is parental
neglect or abandonment so that brothers and sisters begin to need
each other for solace, nurturance, and identity, or as a vehicle to
express rage and hurt" (p. 195). Or, as stated by Twitchell (1987),
"The romantic orphan looking for a parent finds his sister" (p. 120).

The familial environment thus becomes a critical factor in explaining sibling incest and the breakdown of incest barrier. Only one
demographic study to date has explored the patterns and characteristics of families where sibling incest occurred. In examining 25 families of sibling incest, Smith and Israel (1987) found three consistent,
distinctive family dynamics: "(1) distant, inaccessible parents; (2)
parental stimulation of sexual climate in the home; and (3) family
secrets and extramarital affairs" (p. 103).

While the importance of the familial environment cannot be
underestimated, neither can such dynamics totally account for the
phenomenon of sibling incest. Not all siblings become incestuously
involved when their parents are unavailable or absent. Rather, sibling
incest is multidetermined by a combination of intrapsychic and interpersonal factors. Finkelhor (1984) explains that all forms of sexual
abuse by definition require: (1) a motivation to sexually abuse; (2) an
overcoming of internal inhibitions against acting on the motivation; (3) an overcoming of external impediments to committing sexual abuse; and (4) an overcoming of the victim's resistance to the
sexual abuse. Finkelhor's preconditions applied specifically to sibling
sexual abuse appear in Table 1.

Although the specific motivation underlying sibling incest may
vary, as can the duration and configuration of the incestuous relationship, Bank and Kahn (1982) have described two general types of
sibling incest: "power-oriented, phallic, aggressive incest and nurturing, erotic, loving incest" (p. 178). Power-oriented incest is exploitative and coercive with one sibling, usually an older brother, initiating the incest. By contrast, nurture-oriented incest is maintained by

TABLE 1
Preconditions for Sibling Incest*

Preconditions	Factors Related to Each Precondition
Precondition 1: Motivations to sexually abuse	
Emotional congruence	Arrested emotional development
	Need to feel powerful and controlling
	To fulfill dependency needs
	To bind anxiety
	Revenge toward absent parental figure(s)
	To prevent disintegration of ego or family
	Re-enactment of childhood trauma
	Provides nurturance and object constancy
Sexual arousal	Modeling of sexual behavior present in the home
	Normal, exploratory sexual behavior arouses further desires
	Awakening and awareness of sexuality
Blockage	Inadequate social skills
	Inadequate understanding of sexuality
	Unresolved oedipal conflict
	Mixed messages within environment, such as repressive norms and permissive attitudes
	Inability to relate to opposite sex peers similar in age
Precondition 2: Overcoming Internal Inhibitions	Drugs/alcohol
	Psychosis
	Inadequate impulse control
	Failure of incest inhibition mechanism in family
	Inability to take another's perspective
	Sexuality between siblings is minimized as child's play
	Lack of defined boundaries placed on sexual behavior
	Modeling

(*continued*)

TABLE 1
(*Continued*)

Precondition 3: Overcoming External Inhibitors	Absent parents Lack of supervision of siblings High access of siblings to one another Unusual sleeping or rooming conditions
Precondition 4: Overcoming Victim's Resistance	Victim is emotionally insecure or deprived Victim is dependent on offending sibling Reports of sexual contact have been dismissed Victim lacks knowledge about sexual abuse Victim enters relationship as a way of maintaining family integrity Coercion

*Adapted from the work of David Finkelhor (1984). *Child sexual abuse: New theory and research*. New York: Free Press.

mutual consent, with siblings holding onto one another as a defense against an empty or troubled family environment. The eroticism of the sibling relationship, whether in an aggressive or nurturing form, appears to be motivated by different needs and a result of different sibling characteristics. The sources of such motivation to sexually abuse another can be the fulfillment of some emotional need, the result of sexual arousal, or the gratification of sexual needs which have been blocked by alternative paths.

Motivation, in and of itself, is not sufficient, however, to account for abuse. Certain internal inhibitions must be overcome if the motivation to abuse is to be realized. Factors predisposing an individual to override this internal barrier include drugs or alcohol, psychosis, poor impulse control, or lack of defined sexual boundaries. In sibling incest the development of impulse control and the establishment of norms for sexual behavior are strongly influenced by the structure and dynamics of the nuclear family.

Even when the motivation to abuse is strong, and even if internal inhibitions are diminished, certain external conditions must also be present for abuse to occur. Various environmental factors, by their very presence may foster or inhibit the opportunity for enacting the abuse. Absent parents and high accessibility between unsupervised siblings contributes to an atmosphere of maximal opportunity and minimal constraint.

Once both internal inhibitions and external inhibitions prohibiting incest have been reduced, then the resistance of the victim must be overcome. Often victims are lured, tricked, confused, or physically coerced into the sibling sexual relationship. Some siblings, however, may cross the barrier out of a misguided need to maintain a sense of family. When sibling incest does occur, it is rarely initiated simultaneously by both partners (Bank and Kahn, 1982; James and Nasjleti, 1983). Usually one sibling by virtue of age, size, or role within the family, pushes the relationship over the boundary of normal sexual interaction. By way of example, the following case scenario of sibling incest examines each of the four preconditions of sexual abuse.

Precondition 1: Motivation

A 14-year-old boy, Steve, is living with his parents, paternal grand-mother, and his younger sister who is 6 years old. Both parents work long hours and are often away on business trips. Recently Steve's father's business suffered a crisis and came close to bankruptcy. The paternal grandmother is often left in charge of the children, however, her health has deteriorated and she is less available to the children. As a result, Steve has been given increasing responsibility for his younger sister. Steve has a growing resentfulness toward his new role in the family which often interferes with his social life. Feeling angry and burdened by his responsibilities for his sister, and the lack of avail-ability of his parents, Steve acts out his sexual impulses with his sister.

Precondition 2: Overcoming Internal Inhibitions

Steve is able to overcome his inhibitions by rationalizing that no harm can come from brothers and sisters exploring each other's bodies. Steve's sexual advances toward his sister are also fueled by his suspicions and subsequent rage that his mother is having an extramarital affair. By having little time to socialize with peers his own age, as well as lacking confidence in his ability to attract a peer, Steve turns to his sister who is viewed as a safer vehicle for experimentation.

Precondition 3: Overcoming External Inhibitors

External inhibitions are overcome due to the high accessibility between siblings and the unchaperoned home environment. Both parents are often out of town on business or working at the office late hours. The paternal grandmother is ill and spends most of her time in bed, depending on her grandchildren for support.

Precondition 4: Overcoming Victim's Resistance

Sally's resistance to her brother's advances is tempered by her trust and dependence on him. Initially she is confused by the sexual contact. Steve, however, spends more time with her than her parents and has been her primary source of support and affection in the last year. Her parents always appear preoccupied with their financial difficulties, and Sally does not want to burden them further by revealing Steve's advances.

Both individual dynamics and system factors contributing to sibling incest must be sufficiently accounted for in any treatment model. If, for example, one restructures the family system so that siblings are more carefully supervised and less accessible to one another, but ignores the individual characteristics which have motivated the offending sibling, then there is a possibility that the abuser may find another victim (Finkelhor, 1984). By considering the multidetermined factors and motivational realities which foster the development of sibling incest, the therapeutic needs of all family members can be more carefully addressed.

TREATMENT PHASES AND THERAPEUTIC TASKS*

It is not the experience of today that drives us mad, it is remorse or bitterness for something which happened yesterday and the dread of what tomorrow may bring. (karen marie christa minns, 1982, p. 23)

In many families where sibling incest has come to light, the family

---

*The treatment model presented is based on cases referred from the county juvenile detention center, the state's protective care agency, and an adolescent psychiatric hospital. All of the cases referred reflected Bank and Kahn's "power-oriented" types of sibling incest; therefore, all aspects of the model may not generalize to the more "nuture-oriented" form of sibling incest.

alone decides the course of action, whether to ignore or minimize the activities, reprimand the siblings, place stronger sanctions against further involvement, or seek help from outside professionals. When families do come for help they are often confused, outraged, and overwhelmed, clinging to defenses of denial and secrecy. As with all forms of incest, the shock of disclosure sets a crisis into motion (Solin, 1986). Such a crisis holds the potential for change despite the regressive pull to remain the same.

In this section, treatment issues and guidelines for intervening with families in which the incest has occurred between siblings living at home will be considered. Although many of the issues remain the same with adult survivors, the therapeutic maneuvers must change, since key participants may be geographically or emotionally inaccessible.

With intact systems, reinstating the incest barrier is a major goal of treatment. The therapeutic phases and tasks to be accomplished within the treatment process are presented in Table 2. Using Finkelhor's model as a general framework for explaining abuse, therapeutic tasks are formulated on the theoretical basis that: (1) the breakdown in the structure and function of the family has produced a climate which fosters the acting out of sexual impulses; (2) the offending sibling's internal inhibitions against committing incest are ineffective; and (3) the victimized sibling's resistance to the incest has been overcome.*

Treatment Phase 1: Assessment

The initial task in treating sibling incest is to engage and to assess the family on a number of critical variables which will have direct ramifications for later intervention. The assessment phase can be overwhelming for the clinician, since many agendas and individual needs must be considered. Following disclosure of the incest, not only is the family system in shock, but every member of the family experiences intense emotional reactions. The parents may be disgusted by

---

*The terms *offending sibling* and *victimized sibling* are chosen to reflect issues of responsibility. The convention of referring to the offending sibling as male and the victimized sibling as female is used to reflect the most commonly reported form of sibling incest. It should be noted, however, that sisters can sexually abuse brothers, and that incest can also occur between siblings of the same sex.

TABLE 2
Treatment Phases and Therapeutic Tasks

Treatment Phase	Therapeutic Tasks
I. Assessment	Assessment of victim's safety
	Assessment of family structure
	Assessment of offending sibling's motivations and perceptions of events
II. Reorganization of the Family Structure	Parents are reinforced as a strong executive unit
	Parents are put in charge of monitoring offending sibling's actions/impulses and other sibling's safety
	Stronger alliance between each parent and child is fostered
III. Healing the Incest Wound	Victimized sibling discloses abuse to parents
	Parents give clear message about the unacceptability of offending sibling's behavior
	Offending sibling, with family present, apologizes to victimized sibling and takes responsibility for actions
	Offending sibling learns alternative ways of coping with needs and impulses

the incest. The victimized sibling may be angry yet worried about the ensuing consequences. The offending sibling may be frightened about what lies ahead, while also ashamed and remorseful. In families with a history of incest, defensive silence, stifling secrecy, and desperate denial frequently make the assessment phase difficult. Even in the most supportive situations, it is not uncommon for victims to retract their allegations or for the parents, under the guise of protecting family members from the painful past, to discourage talking about the incest. Consequently, in the assessment phase family members should be separated, with individual sessions held to gather basic information about what has occurred and to gauge the impact of events on the family.

Within the assessment phase, three areas must be probed: (1) the victimized sibling's safety; (2) the family structure; and (3) the offending sibling's motivations and perceptions of events. With information about the preconditions which fostered the sexual abuse, the therapist will be better able to make interventions to ensure that the incest stops and that the family moves toward healing.

Interviewing the Victimized Sibling Of immediate priority is an interview with the victimized sibling. She often holds the key to understanding exactly what transpired. Shortly after the incest disclosure, defenses rigidify and a tendency to protect the family, instead of the self, may ensue. This pattern is particularly prevalent amidst family pressures calling for the victimized sibling to "forgive and forget." The interviewer needs to persistently inquire about: the nature and duration of the incest; how the incest began and was maintained; how access and eventually silence was achieved; what feelings exist toward the offending sibling and toward the parents; and what concerns remain about safety. Repeated reference to the sexual abuse and the use of specific sexual terms and language will help to open up the secret while detoxifying talking about such a taboo topic. The interviewer might ask:

- What occurred between your brother and you? When did your brother first approach you? How often did the sexual abuse occur?
- Where were your parents when your brother sexually abused you? Are you and your brother left alone often?
- Has anyone else within or outside the family touched you in a way that made you uncomfortable?
- Did your brother ever threaten you about what might happen if you told? What made it difficult for you to tell your parents or some other adult about the incest?
- What did you think when your brother first approached you? How did the sexual contact feel?
- How do you feel about your brother now? What would you like to see happen to him? Do you think he would try anything now?
- How did your parents react when they learned about the abuse? Prior to this disclosure did you ever try to tell your parents about the abuse?

Such direct questions are needed to begin breaking a silence which has immobilized the family and distorted its development. Making the unspeakable speakable has therapeutic value for the victim who most likely has struggled alone with the hurt, pain, and confusion of the abuse. Knowing how, when, and where the incest occurred can later be used to help the offending sibling acknowledge the abuse, thereby lessening denial and repression.

Unless the victimized sibling feels safe within the home, treatment cannot be effective. The victim's safety will depend on the degree to which: (1) the parents treat the abuse seriously and are willing to make specific accommodations to protect the child; (2) the victim is given support by the family; (3) the offending sibling acknowledges his role and takes responsibility for the incest; and (4) family members can handle stress without resorting to violence and/or alcohol. The critical step in ensuring the victim's safety is removing the opportunity for access. If stringent supervision arrangements cannot be made, then removal of the offending sibling from the home should be considered, until changes within the family have occurred.

Interviewing the Parents   As with the victimized sibling, very specific information should be elicited from the parents regarding their knowledge of the incest. Typical questions would be:

- What have you been told about the incest? Do you believe your daughter?
- Did you ever suspect that the incest was occurring?
- Who else in the family knows about what occurred?
- How do you understand the incest?
- Have you or anyone in your extended family been sexually abused?
- Do you think that your son could have learned this behavior from anyone else in the family? Do you think your daughter has been abused by anyone else in the family?
- What are your feelings toward both children?

How the parents respond to the disclosure and how they are feeling toward each of their children is of particular diagnostic importance. The degree to which the parents believe that the incest is a serious event requiring special accommodations is an important barometer of the family's ability to move forward and resolve their crisis.

It is not uncommon for parents to be angry at the offending sibling and yet want the victimized sibling to quickly drop the issue. When sibling incest is discovered, the family homeostasis is disturbed. The embarrassment and shame attached to breaking the incest taboo cause many parents to want to minimize events, bury the incest in the past, and quickly return the family to a state of pseudo harmony. Parents must be assured that, if they want to help their children resolve this trauma, attitudes towards the incest must be unveiled and processed.

In the parent interview, family organization and structure should be assessed. Specific areas for structural interventions will be highlighted by knowledge of parental availability to the children, accessibility of the siblings to one another, and the degree of boundaries drawn between the generations. A genogram can provide a non-threatening way to gather this information. McGoldrick and Gerson (1985, p. 2) explain that genograms "enable an interviewer to reframe, detoxify, and normalize emotion-laden issues, creating a systemic perspective which helps to track family issues through space and time."

Eliciting a history of past sexual abuse within both the nuclear and extended families, as well as questioning sexual norms, attitudes, values, and boundaries, provides information about patterns that may have promoted the abuse. It is especially critical to ascertain whether any other form of abuse is occurring within the family. It is not uncommon for sibling incest to occur simultaneously with father-daughter incest. The sexual atmosphere in these families varies from overly repressive environments which stimulate promiscuity to sexually overstimulating environments which enhance arousal. Smith and Israel (1987) note:

> In its most restrictive form, covert sexuality simmers below the surface, encouraged by provocative play, nudity, or teasing circumstances. In its least restrictive environment, sexual contact between siblings is stimulated by overt sexuality. . . . To account for sexualized behavior among children within the family, an explanation unfolds more completely when we view their behavior as imitative, as stimulated, and as reactive to actions performed by adults. (p. 106)

Interviewing the Offending Sibling   After both the victimized sibling and parents have been evaluated, then the offending sibling is seen. By seeing the offending sibling last, a comparison can be made between the facts supplied by other family members and those provided by the offending sibling. The degree to which the offending sibling is able to honestly and openly disclose relevant details reflects his strength of character and readiness for treatment. Interviewed last, the offending sibling wonders what will be revealed. As anxiety builds, defenses are lowered and urges toward denial and secrecy are broken.

The same questions asked of the victim need to be directed to the offending sibling. The onset of the incest, its extent and duration, as well as the techniques used to engage and silence the victim, must be probed. Equally important are the motivations for the abuse and how the offending sibling overcame internal inhibitions to commit the incest. Sample questions include:

- How do you understand what occurred between you and your sister?
- How did the incest begin? What was the nature of the sexual contact? How often did you have sexual contact with your sister?
- What did you tell your sister to get her involvement? Did you ever tell your sister that she must keep the contact a secret? Did you ever threaten her?
- How did it feel when you were with your sister?
- How do you think your sister felt about the contact?
- How did you feel after having sexual contact with your sister? Did you ever think you should stop?
- What was your previous sexual experience?
- Has anyone within or outside the family ever touched you in a way that made you uncomfortable?
- How are you feeling now that your family knows?

An important prognostic indicator is the degree to which the offending sibling can recognize that his behavior was inappropriate and take responsibility for what has occurred.

The assessment phase encompasses a series of individual interviews with each family member. The severity of the abuse and the question of safety dictate whether these interviews must be accomplished in one day or can be spaced over the first several weeks of treatment. For example, if the sibling incest included both sexual and physical abuse, it is critical to see each family member within the same day to determine the best way to protect the victimized sibling. The goal of the assessment phase is to obtain a general picture, to be elaborated over time, of the preconditions which fostered the abuse. In and of itself, the assessment phase can have a powerful therapeutic effect. As information is uncovered, emotions are released within the family. Unveiling the secret paves the way for rebuilding the family and addressing the emotional needs of each member.

Treatment Phase 2: Reorganization of the Family Structure

Once all family members have been questioned about their knowledge of the abuse, the treatment enters the intervention phase. Based on the information collected from each family member, hypotheses can be made about why the incest barrier failed. Unless the family can be restructured to protect its members and restrain the acting-out of sexual impulses, then all other therapeutic moves will be ineffective. This phase sets the stage not only for change but also for healing, as the therapist actively works to develop a context shift in the family's structure and organization (Friesen, 1985).

Whatever the particular individual motivations to abuse or the unique family patterns, all forms of sibling incest may be conceptualized as problems of control — control of impulses, control of distance within relationships, and control of information and communication shared within the family. Minuchin and Fishman (1981) remind us:

> In families where one of the members presents symptoms related to control, the therapist assumes problems in one or all of certain areas: the hierarchical organization of the family, the implementation of executive functions in the parental system, and the proximity of family members. (p. 58)

Therefore, the tasks for this stage of treatment become: (1) reinforcing the parents as a strong executive unit; (2) making specific accommodations to reduce sibling access, with the parents put in charge of monitoring the children's activities; and (3) fostering alliances between each parent and child, with special emphasis on the relationship between the same-sex parent and child.

Boundaries between the parents and children need to be reinforced, and the parents elevated to a position of strong control. By virtue of their absenteeism, many of these parents have little power or control over the family. The parents must come together to provide a united front, to reconstruct the incest barrier, and to monitor sibling access.

In the course of normal development, impulse control moves from an external to an internal locus of control. Thus, the infant's impulses are first restrained by parents, who serve as a "collective ego" until their teachings can be internalized. Similarly, in the beginning of treatment specific accommodations must be made so that the siblings are never left alone to act out their impulses. The parents are assigned the task of monitoring the offending sibling's actions. Once external inhibitions have been reinstituted within the family, the parents can work to help the offending sibling develop internal controls.

Even if the parents are separated or divorced, attempts should be made to involve both parents in this process. When however, father-daughter incest has occurred, then issues of control become even more poignant. Fathers who sexually abuse their daughters have inappropriate amounts of control. These fathers misuse their power and generally control the family by threatening, authoritarian methods. In such cases, work needs to occur with the marital couple to reorganize the power imbalance, before parents can be placed in charge of monitoring sibling behavior.

Next, the sexual atmosphere within the home must be examined. If the environment is overstimulating, then changes must be made to reduce the overt sexuality displayed within the family. Smith and Israel (1987) report that 48% of the siblings within their study had witnessed provocative behavior on the part of their parents, while 32% of the sibling incest cases were actually preceded by father-daughter incest. On the other hand, if the atmosphere is too sexually restrictive, open discussion of sexuality can appropriately educate children about sex. In all cases parents should strive to help children separate sexual from emotional needs.

Commonly in these families, the parents are physically and/or emotionally unavailable. Fostering alliances between each parent and each child helps to reverse the pattern of abandonment and unavailability while providing children with stronger role models. Strengthening the relationship between the same-sex parent and child encourages the identification process, a critical ingredient in resolving any outstanding oedipal issues. If the offending sibling has more power than the parent or acts like a spouse to replace the parent, then shifts in the hierarchy are needed to restore the proper sense of role balance. Having the same-sex parent and child spend more time together is a simple but effective way to begin shifting coalitions and power hierarchies. Reinvolving the distant or absent parent can help to resolve unmet needs, which may have encouraged or fostered dependence between the siblings.

In general, the parents will need considerable support in dealing effectively with the incest. Reorganizing the structure within the family may be easier than establishing closer alliances. The unavailability and distance of parents from their children may be due to their own lack of internal resources or external supports or may reflect their own inadequate parental models. These longstanding factors are not easily changed. The therapist will need to work carefully with the parents, so that neither the tendency to minimize the abuse nor the tendency to be overpunitive is reinforced. Working through feelings of denial, blame, rage, disgust, and shock is necessary prior to encouraging new alliances. To accomplish these tasks, the family is often broken down into various dyads. Reorganizing the family structure and fostering alliances can take several months, depending on the degree to which the family is able to acknowledge the abuse and accept the need for changing their patterns of relating.

Treatment Phase 3: Healing the Wound

Once a context for change has been developed, the therapist can move to the last treatment phase, where dysfunctional patterns are confronted, growth alternatives promoted, and wounds healed. Working through the incest involves a combination of individual and family sessions. The therapeutic issues and treatment goals to be accomplished for both the victim and the offender are outlined in Table 3. For the victim, there are several core issues which must be addressed. These include: (1) feelings of worthlessness and "the damaged goods syndrome" (Porter, Blick, and Sgroi, 1982); (2) betrayal; (3) helplessness and powerlessness; and (4) isolation and stigmatization of being abused (Finkelhor and Browne, 1985). While encouraging the expression and ventilation of diverse feelings attached to the abuse, the therapist must actively educate and provide the victim with corrective feedback. It is critical to normalize that the victim is not

TABLE 3
Therapeutic Issues and Treatment Goals
for Sexual Abuse Victims and Offenders

INCEST VICTIMS

Therapeutic Issues	*Treatment Goals*
I. Worthlessness/damaged goods	Valuing self Resolving guilt Promoting strengths Developing age appropriate behavior Developing a positive body image Separating sexual from emotional needs
II. Betrayal	Development of trust Ventilation of feelings
III. Helplessness	Asserting self Developing sense of entitlement Developing sense of control/power Defining self and needs
IV. Isolation/stimatization	Building supports Speaking the unspeakable Asking of others Development of nonabusive relationships

SIBLING INCEST OFFENDERS

Therapeutic Issues	*Treatment Goals*
I. Responsibility	Accepting responsibility and apologizing Developing ability to take another's perspective Connecting feelings with behaviors
II. Power/control	Developing impulse control Appropriately asserting self Developing sense of power and masculinity without using exploitation or force Management of anger
III. Sexuality	Defining sexual needs Finding appropriate channels for expressing sexuality Separating sexual and emotional needs
IV. Identity/Self-Esteem	Valuing self Defining self and needs Expression of feelings Development of social skills Building supports

alone, but that other children have been abused. Likewise, the victim needs to be reassured that she is believed and is not blamed for the abuse. Lastly, the therapist needs to help the victim develop a sense of her internal resources, positive qualities, and strength. Individual therapy involves a process of supporting the victim, normalizing and validating feelings, and helping her build a more positive self-image.

Too often victims have lived alone with the abuse, feeling that they were to blame or that they must have deserved the abuse. Exposing the secrets within the context where they have been held and guarded reduces their power, thereby breaking through codes of silence, isolation, and denial. Thus, working within the family opposed to a strictly individual model holds the potential for resolving the pain with those who were part of the pain, those directly responsible. With the stage set by individual therapy, a session is arranged in which the victim shares the details of the abuse with her parents. In turn, the parents need to reassure their child that the abuse is not her fault and that the abuse will never occur again. It is clear that if the preliminary work has not been accomplished, family defenses of silencing the victim will be invoked, along with attempts to minimize the abuse and block further therapeutic interventions. If, however, the victim has been supported and protected and sees that the family is coping with the abuse, then she will be able to discuss with her parents what has transpired. For parents who need to deny the abuse, it is best to postpone family sessions and continue to work with family members individually, to avoid further blaming of the victim.

When a victimized sibling can share the secret and directly express her feelings about the abuse to each family member, she no longer continues in an exploited and victimized role. Furthermore, family sessions in combination with individual therapy for the victim help to place the abuse in its proper context. The abuse moves from an intrapsychic conflict to an interpersonal event. Discussing the incest with the parents also has a corrective value for the victimized sibling, who can receive retrospectively the protection and support that were missing when the abuse occurred. In this sharing process, images of the family's ability to respond to the needs of its members are reshaped, relationships are transformed, and victims are empowered to move beyond the abuse. Despite the pain involved in sharing the details of the abuse, the process of letting go of the secret, along with all the associated feelings of guilt, shame, anger, and depression, contains a powerful potential for healing. Once the silence is broken, the journey towards recovery begins.

Simultaneously, individual work with the offending sibling must occur. For the offending sibling, target areas of intervention revolve around issues of (1) responsibility; (2) power/control; (3) sexuality; and (4) identity (Groth, Hobson, Lucey, and St. Pierre, 1981). Needs fulfilled by the incest must be identified, internal resources that will restrain further inappropriate sexual behavior built, and issues of responsibility clarified. Assuming responsibility for the incest is a critical parameter in the offending sibling's treatment. When the incest barrier has been crossed, there is often an abdication of responsibility so that feelings about the abuse are distanced and isolated from behavior. Once the offending sibling can examine the consequences of his behavior, as well as take another's perspective, he gains the tools necessary to inhibit further inappropriate impulses. As the denial is broken and the offending sibling comes to recognize the hurt felt by the victimized sibling, anxiety, overwhelming guilt, and depression may appear. Having the offending sibling apologize to the victimized sibling provides the vehicle for binding the anxiety and moving toward self-forgiveness. If not resolved, the offending sibling's guilt can become crippling and impair interpersonal relationships, as well as sexual functioning. Whenever possible, it is advisable for one therapist to work with the victim and family while another therapist of the same sex as the offender, meets with the offending sibling. This therapist can provide the offending sibling with needed support and serve as another role model.

Once the offending and victimized sibling feel psychologically ready, a full family session should occur. The purpose of the family meeting is to have the parents take control of the family and help members discuss their feelings about the abuse. Having the offending sibling take responsibility for the incest and apologize in public helps to restore trust and paves the way toward rebuilding the sibling relationship. It is critical that the parents be present when the siblings discuss the incest, so as not to replicate the structure which fostered the abuse in the first place. A public family discussion symbolically reinstates the incest barrier. This family session needs to be framed as a ritual which will help heal and repair relationships. The process of healing cannot proceed, however, with undue speed. Too often the family wants the crisis to be resolved quickly, so that business can go on as usual. The offending sibling may be only too ready to apologize as a manipulation to appease the family and end "all the fuss."

After the incest has been acknowledged and discussed within the family, the individual needs of both the siblings must be reexamined. The offending sibling usually will require an extended course of individual treatment, rebuilding his self-esteem and helping him to further understand the underlying motivations and unfulfilled needs that led him to abuse his sister. Often sex education is a necessary part of this process. The victimized sibling may have some residual feelings about the incest that can best be addressed through individual or group therapy. Continued feelings of blame, guilt, and shame must be resolved for wounds to heal.

CASE EXAMPLE

Denise, a pretty, dark-haired, mature 11-year-old was talking with her mother one evening. Her mother, Pat, a single parent raising two sons and a daughter, was exhausted from working two jobs and thus barely conscious of the message her daughter was desperately trying to deliver. Determined to be heard this time, Denise persevered with all the courage she could muster. Each time the words, "*Mom, Jim bothers me*" came forth, they were misinterpreted by her mother, who absently agreed that her son could be a problem. Denise repeated the phrase, an octave higher in volume. The emphasis and strangeness of her daughter's voice finally struck a chord. Turning to her daughter, Pat finally questioned, "*What do you mean, he bothers you?*" In a wave of relief mixed with trepidation, the incest secret of a year's standing came tumbling out. Explaining to her mother that Jim had been touching her and doing other "naughty" things, Denise took the first step toward freeing herself from the secret hurt and the pain.

In a state of shock, Pat questioned the truth of such allegations. Searching for an alternative explanation, she asked whether Denise had misunderstood her brother's affectionate overtures. Knowing that her daughter rarely lied and seldom gave her a moment of trouble, Pat reached for the phone and called her sister for advice. After a lengthy discussion, the two sisters decided that Pat should seek professional help for her family. The following day Pat made an individual appointment, stating that she needed to talk with someone about problems she was having with her children. She explained, "They just aren't getting along the way they should."

Telling only the limited facts she knew, Pat nervously recounted the events of the last 24 hours to the therapist. When asked if she believed her daughter, Pat despairingly nodded her head affirmatively. The family history revealed that Pat and her husband, Dave, had been apart for eight years. The couple separated and subsequently divorced after Dave suffered a stroke. Despite the fact that his illness left him with some cognitive impairments, Dave held down a steady job. He lived with his sister and her husband some two hours away, and his contact with the children had been irregular and sporadic.

To make ends meet, Pat worked as a waitress during the day at one restaurant and had in the last year acquired a part-time job working weekend evenings at another restaurant. Her older son, Jim, 15, was often left responsible for his brother, Rick, a year his junior, and Denise. Many evenings Rick was out of the home working at a pizza parlor or visiting friends.

Neither Pat nor Jim had much control over Rick who was constantly getting into trouble. Rick had severe school problems, often acting in an angry and aggressive manner. Prior to the disclosure of the incest, Rick had been expelled from school and arrangements were being made to send him to a special school for emotionally disturbed adolescents.

As the oldest and firstborn child, Jim, a tall, slender, and quiet youth, had always been mother's helper and confidant. It had only been in the last year, since his entry into high school, that Jim had also developed some school problems. His grades had taken a downward spiral, and he had begun skipping classes.

When questioned about her knowledge of the incest, Pat reported her surprise. She had never suspected anything improper between her children. It was hard for her to believe that Jim, whom she described as such a "mild mannered" child, would touch his sister. Pat denied any history of abuse within her family of origin, and painfully wondered where she had "gone wrong" in raising her children. Pat's questioning of her role as a parent demonstrated a strength that could be used to help her children.

Before a treatment plan could be suggested by the therapist, Pat needed to be prepared for the course of action that lay ahead. She was informed that by law allegations of abuse had to be reported to the

State's child protective care agency. Most therapists would prefer to avoid reporting abuse, given the chaos and emotional upheaval that ultimately results once an agency with legal authority becomes involved. However, reporting is a legal and ethical mandate which ultimately may provide the leverage necessary to keep a family in treatment.

Pat's initial reaction to learning about the reporting requirement was anger and betrayal, "I came here for help. I never would have come if I had known this would happen." The imminent exposure of this family secret precipitated a strong need to defend her son and minimize the incest, "I assure you it won't happen again." After incest is disclosed, anger and hurt are often displaced onto helping professionals (Solin, 1986). This serves to buffer the strong negative affect, which if expressed directly to the children or to the spouse would threaten the family unity. It is critical that therapists do not react defensively to this posturing and instead align themselves with the part of the parent(s) wanting to help the family. The need to report must be stated in a matter-of-fact way that simultaneously responds to and addresses the parent's concerns and fears. In this case the therapist said, "Pat, I understand what a shock all of this must be for you. Within a few short hours, the vision of your family has been turned upside down. What I really respect is that in the face of such a trauma, you were able to listen to your daughter and take strong positive action to stop what has been occurring. Your inner strength allowed you to recognize that your family would need some support in facing the incest. You turned here for help. I want to be able to give you that help. The purpose of reporting the abuse, which is mandated by law, is not to hurt your son. This agency will talk to your family, as I have been doing, and try to assess everyone's needs."

With support Pat was able to overcome her anxieties and was present when a call was placed to the state agency. After contacting the state protective care agency, the therapist decided that the children should be brought in for a session that afternoon. A worker from the state agreed to be on hand to talk with the mother while the therapist spoke with the children.

With little preparation or explanation about why they were being seen, Denise and Jim were brought into the office. Rick was at work and therefore unavailable for the initial session. The interviews began with Denise alone, to ascertain the details of the abuse and to assess issues of safety. Denise was initially reluctant to talk with the therapist. Encouragement and acknowledgment that many children have experienced similar problems in their families helped break the ice and assist Denise in sharing the details of her abuse.

She revealed that the abuse had been occurring on a weekly basis for the past year, while her mother was out working. It began one evening when Denise and Jim were watching TV on the pull out sofa in the living room. This living room space doubled as a bedroom for Denise and her mother. Due to her brothers' fighting, Pat had given each boy a bedroom in their two-bedroom apartment. There was little organization and little opportunity for privacy in the home.

Trusting Jim, who had always been her ally, Denise was at first confused by the touching. Touching soon progressed to more extensive sexual contact, in which Jim masturbated on her, made her touch his penis, and attempted intercourse. Denise also revealed that Jim often smoked marijuana and seemed high when the abuse occurred. "I always knew when he was going to try something because he would get this funny look in his eyes and make my friends go home." Although Denise often wanted to tell her mother, she was fearful about Jim's response, since he had threatened to hurt her physically if she told. Of late he had become more aggressive in trying to get her to comply with his requests. Further inhibiting disclosure was Denise's concern that her mother would not be able to cope with "more trouble from the boys." Jim's more frequent attempts at intercourse, however, had been the catalyst to expose the incest. Although the secret was now out in the open, Denise remained fearful that her mother would not be able to control her brother's actions, since she and Jim were left alone so often.

After speaking with Denise, the next move was to tell Pat that her daughter's allegations appeared to be true and to plan with Pat how to approach Jim. It was suggested that Pat speak with her son about what she had learned. Having the parent confront the child in an authoritative but nonpunitive manner helps to reinstate the appropriate power balance within the family and elevates the parent to a position of control. For parents who do not believe the victim and support the offending sibling, extra steps must be taken to work through the parent's denial before a confrontation can occur. Pat's behavior, however, suggested that with clear guidelines she would be able to handle the task of talking with her son. The close relationship between mother and son also mitigated against Jim's denying his actions.

Pat was coached to state what she had learned from her daughter and to give her son the opportunity to explain his view of the events. The possibility that Jim might deny his sister's allegations was discussed. To break through her son's denial, Pat was encouraged to tell him that she believed his sister's report. Jim, when presented with Denise's statements and his mother's belief, acknowledged the abuse. In the presence of his mother, Jim was not able to give any details about the incest or explain his actions. Pat was able to compliment her son on his honesty while expressing her concern about what had occurred. She stressed the need for everyone in the family to receive help.

Now it was time to make plans about the supervision of the children and decisions about who else within the family should be made aware of the circumstances. Although Pat recognized the seriousness of her son's actions, she could not financially afford to stop working evenings. As a temporary solution, it was decided that Jim would stay with his maternal aunt, who was already aware of the situation. In the meantime, Pat agreed to contact her former husband and enlist his help. So as not to encourage further secrets within the family, Rick was informed by his mother about the incest. Additionally an individual session was scheduled with Jim for the following day.

When seen individually, Jim admitted to the range of sexual activities described by his sister. He felt unsure about his motivations for initiating or continuing the incest. He described the first incident of sexual abuse as a spontaneous occurrence. He and Denise were lying on the couch watching a movie when they began to wrestle. At some point the playful, spontaneous wrestling became sexually arousing and led to more explicit touching. From that point on Jim began to initiate more planful and purposeful sexual contact. Jim did admit to some concomitant drug use, although he minimized its importance. Within this initial individual session, Jim expressed remorse for hurting his sister and asked for help in convincing her that he would not molest her again. He had attempted to phone her the previous evening from his aunt's house, but she refused his call.

Jim's own history revealed that he was a passive child with few friends. By contrast Rick was a popular child, who ran with a rough crowd in search of reckless fun. Jim presented the mixed picture of a child who seemed to be mature, serving as mother's close companion and working hard to replace his father and restore order in the home. Yet on the outside, he was socially immature and lacking peer skills.

It was clear from the discussion with Jim that the abuse fulfilled many emotional needs for him and provided a sense of power and control. Exploring his sexuality with his sister was safer than coping with the possible rejection from girls his own age. Although drugs were not responsible for the abuse, they did play a role in reducing his inhibitions. These individual factors, combined with the lack of supervision in the home due to his mother's work schedule and his father's absence, probably accounted for the abuse.

Jim needed help in developing a more positive and confident image of himself as a male, which would enable him to move outside of the home and develop a social network. He particularly needed assistance in identifying his feelings and connecting them with his subsequent behavior. Helping him be more assertive, instead of acting either passively or aggressively, became a focal point of every therapeutic intervention.

The next several weeks of the therapy were aimed at making structural accommodations within the home, while Jim continued to live with his aunt. Jim's remaining outside the home acted as a catalyst for change, since his absence stood as a constant reminder of the problem. Pat, who was emotionally dependent on her son, was forced to assume a more independent role. Initially her dependence was transferred to the therapy situation, where she obediently carried out every directive and sought the therapist's approval and support. At her own initiative Pat began spending more time with Denise, and in fact became more cognizant of all of the children's whereabouts. So as not to place Rick with primary care for Denise, which would only replicate previous conditions, arrangements were made for Denise to stay with a neighbor while Pat worked evenings. Around this issue Pat needed constant support from the therapist to assert her parental power and stand her ground, since Denise insisted that she was old enough to stay home alone.

Once contacted, Dave, Pat's ex-husband, responded quickly and an appointment with both parents was scheduled. The importance of Dave's spending time with all of the children was discussed. Particularly poignant was Dave's explanation that he often stayed away because he thought the children would be better off without him. His rationale revolved around his sense of shame and inadequacy, a result of the illness which left him with some cognitive deficits. As Dave was helped to see the important role he could play within the family, he readily committed himself to helping the children. Both parents were able to avow the importance of being united with respect to the children, while putting aside former differences. Plans were made for Dave to take both sons for the weekend, so he could begin building a stronger father-son relationship.

As the reality set in, both parents began to confront their feelings about the incest. Pat found herself vacillating between understanding the seriousness of what occurred and feeling angry toward her son, on the one hand, and wanting to minimize the abuse and rationalize that Jim did not understand his actions, on the other. Typically, both parents blamed Denise for not coming forth sooner. They needed to be educated about the dynamics of incest so that they could understand their children's behaviors.

Pat also questioned how she could deal with Rick, who was blaming his sister for getting his brother "in trouble." As often happens, other siblings in the family begin to feel resentful about the chaos and the changes that occur once the incest is disclosed. Rick could not understand why Denise did not disclose the abuse immediately, and he therefore blamed her for allowing it to continue. The therapist encouraged Dave to take a supportive and parenting role with his younger son. He was given the task of talking with Rick and helping him gain a better understanding of what occurred. Dave was encouraged to ask Rick why he blamed his sister, how he felt toward his brother, and more importantly what effect this event was having on him. It was particularly important that Rick not be ignored during this crisis period, for he held the potential of being a valuable resource for both siblings. The danger of disregarding other siblings' impact on the family system is that they have the power to pressure the family to dismiss the abuse, thus sabotaging treatment efforts.

Moreover following the incest disclosure, Rick who formerly had been identified as the troubled child, began to make a positive shift in his behavior. With Jim outside the home, Rick became more responsible and less aggressive. No longer having to compete with his brother Jim for his mother's attention and sensing the need for the family to pull together during this crisis, Rick began to assume a more helpful role within the family.

Following these structural changes and Dave's efforts to help Rick understand the incest, Rick was invited to a sibling session with his brother Jim. The purpose of the sibling session was to foster a more positive relationship between the brothers, as well as to enlist Rick's help in Jim's move to establish a social network outside the family. When seen together, both brothers admitted to drug involvement and after some forceful persuasion by the therapist, both agreed to attend a group for adolescents with drug problems. Also as a result of the sibling session, Rick was successful in helping Jim obtain an after school job.

While shifts occurred within the family structure, contact between Jim and Denise remained minimal. In individual therapy, Denise was exploring the myriad of feelings she had about the incestuous experience. She was acutely aware of the intense anger she felt toward Jim. At one point she had vehemently insisted, "*I don't have an older brother.*" Denise's anger was frightening to the family and often resulted in attempts to soften her position, a tack which only intensified her negative feelings. Often the desire to have a united family, in which the siblings have a positive relationship, results in the family's prematurely pushing the victim to let go of her rage. The victim, however, must be given permission to feel the intensity and full extent of her anger; otherwise she will again feel invalidated and further victimized. Therefore, Denise's family was coached to allow the anger as a way of helping Denise to heal, while encouraging her to trust that the family could be empathically supportive of her. In sibling incest, the victimized sibling also needs to test the parents, to see if they will continue to protect and support her once the initial crisis situation is over.

Along with the anger she felt toward her brother, there was a personal sense of blame and guilt. Denise was struggling with her own sense of responsibility for not stopping the incest. As with most victims, there was a part of her that believed she must have deserved the abuse—otherwise it would not have occurred. Her feelings were further confused by the playful and pleasurable nature of the initial touching experience. Once the touching occurred more consistently and progressed to other activities, Denise felt alarmed and uncomfortable. It was important for Denise to resolve the confusing feelings of what was and was not her responsibility. As Denise explored all of these ambivalent feelings, both the therapist and her parents gave her clear and consistent messages that she was not responsible for the abuse. As she began to recognize her brother's responsibility and role as the older sibling, which he inappropriately used in a coercive and threatening manner to maintain the incest, Denise examined what she could have done differently in the interaction. Denise came to realize that her inability to reveal the abuse at an earlier stage was tied to her need to protect her mother and win her mother's approval by always being the "problem-free" child.

As individual work with Denise progressed and she gained more confidence in herself and her right to express her feelings, sessions with her mother were initiated. In a mother-daughter session, Pat was instructed to get her daughter to talk about the incest. Denise was encouraged to share not only details but feelings about the abuse. As Denise described the pain and helplessness of being abused, Pat supported her daughter and apologized for not being aware of the abuse. Pat also gave critical messages about her ability to help Denise deal with her problems. In other mother-daughter sessions, Pat was assisted in teaching her daughter to be more assertive and helping Denise to develop a better sense of her own power and competence.

As Denise strived to resolve feelings of worthlessness, betrayal, and guilt, discussions with Jim centered on helping him understand his sister's perspective. To help Jim deal with his guilt, particularly since his sister refused all phone calls, he was coached to write Denise a letter. Three months into the treatment process, with coaching and encouragement from the therapist, Jim composed the following letter:

> Dear Denise,
>
> I am sorry for what I did to you. It's not your fault. I won't do it to you again. I know what I did was wrong. Please forgive me. Please don't be scared of me. I hope you still love me. I understand that you are angry at me for what I did and I know that it will take time for us to be friends again. I don't blame you for hating me now. I'm not angry at you for telling. It really was best. I want to call and talk to you and see how you are doing. I hope one day you will forgive me.
>
> Love, Jim

After some individual work with Denise and Jim, which helped each sibling sort out some primary feelings about the incestuous experience, a full family session was scheduled. Except for brief encounters, this would be the first time that Jim and Denise had been together since the disclosure of the incest, four months earlier. Although Jim had apologized by letter and both parents had spent much time reassuring Denise, symbolically this session was critical to the life of the family. While offenders and other family members may insist that they have already apologized and talked about events, a family meeting in which the incest is reviewed and the offender apologizes publicly is a powerful ritual by which the incest barrier is reinstated. Furthermore, when the offending sibling takes responsibility for the act, the victim is able to put her own feelings into a more appropriate context. The apology also allows the offending sibling a mechanism for actively resolving his own guilt feelings and attaining forgiveness.

Prior to the meeting each family member was seen alone to discuss what he or she would like to say and see accomplished. Preparation for the family session ensures that everyone is psychologically ready for the encounter while setting a constructive tone which will allow the family to experience itself differently. Within this session both parents assured Denise that the abuse would never happen again and reinforced the importance of her disclosure. Rick was very supportive of both his brother and his sister, offering to help each of them. Jim explained to Denise that he never wanted to harm her, "I didn't mean to hurt you. I guess I didn't think about your feelings. I still don't really understand why I did it, but I promise it will never happen again. I hope one day you will forgive me. I'm really sorry." Jim's apology touched a chord in Denise and although she was not ready to totally forgive him, her quiet nod and soft tears indicated that the door toward healing had been opened.

Following this pivotal session, which occurred during the fourth month of treatment, plans were made to reintegrate Jim into the family. Prior to his return, structural changes in the physical organization of the home had been made. Jim and Rick were to share one bedroom, while mother and Denise shared the other, leaving the living room open as public domain. Adjustments were made in Pat's work schedule so that she would work some extra weekday evenings, instead of weekend nights. When she was at work Denise would stay with a neighbor, while both boys worked in the local pizza parlor.

Dave agreed to take the children consistently for one weekend a month. Since he lived with his sister and her husband, more frequent visitation was not possible. Dave did begin phoning the children weekly so that he could be more involved in their lives.

After these interventions within the family, treatment focused on working with Jim individually. Denise, who was not displaying any signs of distress and had resolved her anger and hurt following the family session and several subsequent individual sessions, was not in need of further treatment. However, the option for treatment was left open for her. Resolving the incest wound is often a process that occurs over time. Certain issues are put to rest while others may remain dormant. Therefore, it is not unusual for victims to find themselves struggling with different and perhaps new feelings about the abuse at different developmental points.

The family was monitored and seen monthly for the following year. Family sessions were supportive for Pat, dealing primarily with normal parenting issues. In individual therapy lasting six more months, Jim continued to gain confidence in himself and to explore his sexuality and masculinity. When asked how he felt at the end of therapy, Jim shared, "I'm glad Denise forgives me. I didn't know it then, but I could have lost a sister. The day she said that she didn't have a brother was the first time I knew how much I had hurt her. I couldn't pretend anymore."

CONCLUSION

The sibling bond can become an anxiety-ridden and guilt-producing bind when boundaries are crossed and the incest taboo broken. The treatment of sibling incest involves reinstating the incest barrier by reorganizing the family structure, reducing unsupervised sibling access, fostering the parent-child bond, helping the victimized sibling resolve feelings of hurt, betrayal, anger, and guilt, and teaching the offending sibling alternative ways of coping with needs and impulses. As incestuous bonds are untangled, the therapeutic process becomes one of restoring the sibling relationship so that the family can heal and all of the siblings can move forward in their development—free of pain, confusion, and shame.

REFERENCES

Bank, S., & Kahn, M. (1982). *The sibling bond*. New York: Basic Books.

Cole, E. (1982). Sibling incest: The myth of benign sibling incest. *Women and Therapy, 1*, 79–89.

Finkelhor, D. (1980). Sex among siblings: A survey on prevalence, variety, and effects. *Archives of Sexual Behavior, 9*, 171–197.

Finkelhor, D. (1984). *Child sexual abuse: New theory & research*. New York: Free Press.

Finkelhor, D., & Browne, A. (1985). The traumatic impact of sexual abuse: A conceptualization. *American Journal of Orthopsychiatry, 55*, 530–541.

Frances, V., & Frances, A. (1976). The incest taboo and family structure. *Family Process, 15*, 235–244.

Friesen, J. D. (1985). *Structural-strategic marriage and family therapy*. New York: Gardner Press.

Groth, N. (1977). The adolescent sexual offender and his prey. *International Journal of Offender Therapy and Comparative Criminology, 21*, 249–254.

Groth, N., Hobson, W., Lucey, K. & St. Pierre, J. (1981). Juvenile sex offenders: Guidelines for treatment. *International Journal of Offender Therapy and Criminology, 25*, 265–272.

James, B., & Nasjleti, M. (1983). *Treating sexually abused children and their families*. Palo Alto, CA: Consulting Psychologists Press.

Loredo, C. (1982). Sibling incest. In S. Sgroi, (Ed.), *Handbook of Clinical Intervention in Child Sexual Abuse*. Lexington, MA: D.C. Heath.

McGoldrick, M., & Gerson, R. (1985). *Genograms in Family Assessment*. New York: W.W. Norton.

Meiselman, K. (1978). *Incest: A psychological study of cause and effects with treatment recommendations*. San Francisco: Jossey-Bass.

Minns, k. m. c. (1982). Et cum spiritu tuo. In T. McNaron & Y. Morgan (Eds.), *Voices in the night: Women speaking about incest*. Pittsburgh, PA: Cleis Press.

Minuchin, S., & Fishman, H. (1981). *Family therapy techniques*. Cambridge, MA: Harvard University Press.

Porter, F., Blick, L., & Sgroi, S. (1982). Treatment of the sexually abused child. In S. Sgroi, (Ed.), *Handbook of clinical intervention in child sexual abuse*. Lexington, MA: D.C. Heath.

Santiago, L. (1973). *The children of Oedipus: Brother-sister incest in psychiatry, literature, history, and mythology*. Roslyn Heights, NY: Libra.

Smith, H., & Israel, E. (1987). Sibling incest: A study of the dynamics of 25 cases. *Child Abuse & Neglect, 11*, 101–108.

Solin, C. (1986). Displacement of affect in families following incest disclosure. *American Journal of Orthopsychiatry, 56*, 570–576.

Twitchell, J. (1987). *Forbidden partners: The incest taboo in modern culture*. New York: Columbia University Press.

8

Psychotherapy With Siblings of Disabled Children

Milton Seligman

The conduct of psychotherapy with a child who has a disabled brother or sister may not proceed differently from therapy with any other sibling subgroup. However, living with a chronically disabled family member changes the familial environment significantly. The special circumstances surrounding the sibling's experience must be understood by the therapist. For example, the family's response to a handicapped family member provides the backdrop against which one can best understand siblings. The specific character of the mother's, father's, extended family's and other siblings' reactions to a chronic disability influences the extent to which a sibling may be scarred by the experience. Other factors, such as socioeconomic status, family size, and the availability of medical, psychological and other social support, affect the family's, and thus the sibling's, ability to cope.

In the past we have not sufficiently acknowledged the intense, long-term, and complex nature of sibling relationships. Now that we have begun to focus our intellectual and clinical lenses on this subset of the family (Bank and Kahn, 1982; Seligman, 1983; Simeonsson and Bailey, 1986), we are beginning to comprehend the immense value of understanding sibling relationships and fostering their positive growth. In families where a disabled child resides we need to be particularly sensitive to the sibling's experience. It is worth noting from the admittedly limited research available that some siblings simply do not fare well; that is, they feel neglected, unloved, and angry, sometimes into their adult lives (Trevino, 1979).

A friend of the author's, in her late sixties, mentioned recently that she still harbors angry and resentful feelings about her youth due to the attention her diabetic sister received from her parents. In our conversation the friend expressed surprise about the intensity of her memories, which felt very distant in time yet continued to evoke strong negative feelings.

In another instance, a professional colleague of the author's, in her late fifties, revealed that she has only recently become aware in therapy of the profound effect her sister with cerebral palsy has had on her life. She attributes her earlier symptoms of excessive and debilitating anxiety to the close bond with and subsequently agonizing separation from her sister. With her parents and her younger brothers now deceased, she has once again been pressed into duty as her sister's overseer and caretaker.

The remainder of this chapter will examine some pertinent factors in sibling adjustment to a disabled brother or sister. Implications for therapy will be noted where applicable.

THE NEED FOR INFORMATION

Siblings often have limited understanding of their afflicted brother's or sister's condition. In her review of studies regarding siblings, Wasserman (1983) noted that there is a startling lack of information about the handicap, its manifestations, and its consequences. Ambiguity about chronic afflictions promotes the formulation of notions that have little basis in fact. The lack of information or distortions of fact may confuse siblings in several ways:

1. They may feel responsible for a particular condition.
2. They may wonder whether it can be transmitted or "caught" and whether they are susceptible to the same disorder.
3. They are confused about how they should communicate to family and friends about the handicap.
4. They wonder what implications a brother's or sister's handicap has for their future.
5. They may feel perplexed and overwhelmed by such discomforting feelings as anger, hurt, and guilt.

The informational needs of siblings have been addressed by Meyer, Vadasy, and Fewell (1985) in *Living With a Brother or Sister With Special Needs: A Book for Siblings*. Their sensitive and down-to-earth contribution addresses the many emotions and questions siblings have about their lives. The authors' insights come primarily from their interviews with siblings. The book conveys what it is like to have a sibling who is handicapped and how siblings typically feel about the future. In addition, the authors provide short, readable, and accurate explanations of the etiology, manifestations, and prognosis of a number of handicapping conditions.

Sometimes the most natural resources available, the parents, are not able or willing to share information or provide emotional support for their non-disabled sons or daughters. For instance, the professional colleague mentioned earlier had been told by her parents that her sister suffered from asthma, even though her sister had cerebral palsy. The parents were attempting to "hide" from the stigma cerebral palsy held for them. Asthma was a more acceptable condition in their view.

Parents may feel overwhelmed by the needs of their handicapped son or daughter. They may be exhausted by the time and attention this child needs and deserves, thereby neglecting other family members. On the other hand, they may not have come to grips with the emotional impact the handicapped child has on them. Parents continue to struggle with how the child will influence the goals and expectations they have had for themselves and for the family. And, as noted above, they may feel deeply the social stigma the handicapped child represents to them.

Other reasons for the parents' lack of communication regarding the disabled child may be: (1) the parents' ignorance about their handicapped child's condition; (2) their wish to spare their normal son(s) or daughter(s) information that may upset them; (3) their lack of understanding of their well* children's need and wish to understand their afflicted sibling's condition; (4) their confusion based on contradictory information from professionals; and (5) denial of their child's condition and its prognosis.

---

*Terminology regarding disabled and non-disabled children differs markedly. In this chapter "normal" children are frequently referred to as "well" or "non-disabled" children and "handicapped" and "disabled" are used interchangeably in reference to a child who has a physical or mental impairment.

All siblings want information. The *type* of information requested appears to be related to age, as Murphy, Paeschel, Duffy, and Brady (1976) observed in their discussion groups with siblings of Down's syndrome children. In their study six- to nine-year-old children asked questions about motor development and speech, discussed what their brothers and sisters could and could not do, and were interested in the medical and biological information presented to them. Concerns about the future became evident among the 10–12-year-old children, while the older adolescents showed concern about their own chances of bearing a handicapped child.

Recently siblings have "come out of the closet," becoming more open about their circumstances, their feelings, and their need to be better informed. Siblings have found that they are not alone and that their concerns are shared by siblings in their own family and in other families. Buoyed by the psychological comfort attendant to knowing that others share this life situation, siblings are speaking out to parents and professionals about their special plight. And finally, older siblings, aided by the newly established Sibling Information Network,* are encouraging a wider dissemination of basic information about handicapping conditions, so that siblings, parents, and professionals will be better informed.

Only with accurate and fairly complete knowledge can professionals move comfortably toward stated treatment goals. Likewise, siblings armed with this knowledge will be in a better position to perceive their situation unambiguously and with less fear. Service providers need to understand that siblings will respond with reduced anxiety when they are presented with accurate information in a compassionate and understanding manner.

This brings us to a potential psychotherapy dilemma. Some schools of psychotherapy actively discourage the therapist from giving advice, thereby placing the burden of responsibility on the client. For siblings—young siblings especially—therapists must temporarily

*The address for the Sibling Information Network is 249 Glenbrook Road, Box U-64, Department of Educational Psychology, University of Connecticut, Storrs, CT 06268. Another resource is *The Sibling Bond*, the newsletter of the National Sibling Network, is published by the National Alliance of the Mentally Ill. This publication is for siblings and other interested persons with concerns about a mentally ill family member. The address for *The Sibling Bond*: National Sibling Network, P.O. Box 3000040, Minneapolis, MN 55403.

abandon this stance and assume a more educative role. Furthermore, it is important for the therapist to feel comfortable providing the sibling with needed information about a brother or sister's condition—or at least referring the sibling to appropriate reading sources. For therapists who plan to work with siblings, it is a good idea to be conversant about the major handicapping conditions children face. After information is communicated to a sibling, a more conventional therapeutic stance is both appropriate and perhaps necessary as the sibling reflects on and begins to integrate the information.

CARETAKING RESPONSIBILITY

Another important issue is the excessive responsibility children (especially girls) feel for their handicapped sibling. This is related to their development of anger, resentment, guilt, and quite possibly subsequent psychological disturbance (San Martino and Newman, 1974; Seligman, 1983; Trevino, 1979).

A handicapped child in the family absorbs a great deal of time, energy, and emotional resources. Therapists need to be alert to the fact that children may be pressed into parental roles they are ill-prepared to assume. As Myers (1978) notes, such youngsters may move too rapidly through developmental stages so necessary for normal growth:

> From the time Roger began going to physicians and consultants, it seems to me that I carried a five-hundred-pound lead weight around in the front of my brain. Never out of my mind was the idea that my brother was retarded, needed special attention, needed special care, and that I had to provide some of it.
>
> My role in those days was someone who was always around to help care for Roger. That was my mother's phrase. My father called me his "good right arm." Roger himself called me "Dad" before he corrected himself and called me "Bobby."
>
> I never felt I dressed like a kid, never felt comfortable with the clothes I wore, never felt I knew how to act as a boy or a teenager. I was a little man. (p. 36)

The tremendous burden visited upon such children as they assume responsibility of a handicapped sibling is vividly expressed by Hayden (1974):

The responsibility I felt for Mindy was tremendous. One year, when my "babysitting" duties involved periodic checking on my sister, Mindy wandered away between checks. After a thorough but fruitless search of the neighborhood, my mother hysterically told me that if anything happened to Mindy, I would be to blame. I felt terrified and guilty. I was seven. (p. 27)

It is often difficult for adults to accept their circumstances when they compare their lot to others who appear to be more successful. Children find their life with a handicapped sibling even less comprehensible when they compare their family to families with normal children.

The whole situation is profoundly unfair. It is unfair that the family must live with schizophrenia, autism, blindness, or retardation while others do not. It is unfair that some children must function as adjunct parents even before they go to school, while others successfully avoid responsibilities of all sorts well into their second decade. The brothers and sisters of the handicapped child learn to cope with this unfairness, and with their own response to it, the sorrow and the anger. (Featherstone, 1980, p. 162)

Siblings may experience a sense of "survivor guilt" due to their healthy/normal lives, which stand in sharp contrast to the potential life of an ill or retarded sibling (Bank and Kahn, 1982). The application of the concept to well siblings is apt because, as Solnit and Stark (1961) remind us, the birth of a handicapped child is often viewed as the death of the expected normal one. Siblings may experience considerable guilt over their advantages, which can be compounded by parents who imply that: "You should feel grateful that you have normal intelligence, can speak clearly, and are able to run and walk. We only wish that your brother had been so fortunate." Such statements can have a binding effect, in that the sibling's only recourse to expiate guilt is to take care of the ill sibling. The danger comes when the well sibling remains in the "service" of the brother or sister through much of his or her life because of guilt and forced obligation.

Socioeconomic status is related to the amount of responsibility a sibling might assume for a handicapped brother and sister (Grossman, 1972). The better off a family is financially, the better prepared the parents are to obtain necessary help from sources outside the family, such as respite care, babysitters, and other professional and recreational services. Families that are less secure financially must rely on resources within the family. Financial problems produce additional stress and can detract from general stability when excessive and unreasonable demands are placed on family members. In financially struggling families the handicapped child may even be scapegoated as the source of the financial woes. In such instances clinicians must be alert to the potential for abuse of the handicapped child.

Research has indicated that sisters assume caregiving roles with greater frequency than brothers. This rather general observation is supported by Farber's (1959) finding that sisters tend to be better adjusted when the retarded child is institutionalized than when the retarded child is at home. An exception to Farber's findings is where a disabled sibling has been "taken away" to a residential school; this resulted in severe separation anxiety for the well sibling due to the bond between the sisters. Therefore, institutional versus non-institutional status of the handicapped child is another factor that cannot be ignored.

According to Travis (1976), burdening siblings with the care of chronically physically ill children seems to be common. Travis reports that siblings who have been excessively burdened may leave home prematurely during their adolescence. She observes that signs of mounting resentment among siblings can be seen in hasty or unkind physical care. Travis further notes that in close-knit families the care of a handicapped child is viewed as a shared responsibility; school-age siblings as a group are expected to help with the physical care of their chronically ill brother or sister.

Travis points out that some chronically ill children enslave their physically normal siblings—"Hand me this, pick up that." Chronically ill children have been observed to be verbally abusive toward their normal siblings, presumably because of envy and confusion. In an informal study by Holt (1958), normal children were reported to have suffered repeatedly from unexpected physical attacks by their afflicted siblings.

Responsibility for the physical well-being of a chronically ill child can be taken to great lengths. Travis reported that in instances where the sick child must be guarded from infection—say, in chronic heart disease—mothers sometimes warn their normal children to avoid crowds for fear of bringing home infections. Guarding the welfare of one's ill brother or sister places an inordinate burden on well siblings, with possible implications for their subsequent adjustment. Siblings in a hemophiliac family, for example, may bear an enormous amount of responsibility in helping to prevent their brother's or sister's "bleeds." These normal siblings are living an abnormal reality as they must restrain their natural tendency to physically interact with their ill brother or sister.

To compensate for their disappointments and frustrations about a handicapped child parents may burden their other children with excessively high aspirations. These normal siblings may be intellectually or psychologically unable to match parental expectations.

All parents are concerned about the future of their children — their education, marriage, careers. The extent to which parents attempt to direct (or guide) a youngster's future depends on numerous factors — their own history of parental interaction, status factors, and financial security, among others. Parents of handicapped children worry even more about the future, as they fret about many of the same issues parents of normal children do, in addition to concerns about the extent to which their child will be able to achieve independence, how they will be able to care for their handicapped offspring in their twilight years, and who will care for the child once one or both parents are deceased (Seligman, 1979).

In instances where a disabled sibling needs lifelong care or supervision, brothers and sisters experience anxiety about the future. They wonder whether the responsibility their parents now assume will later fall on them. They wonder whether they can cope with the decisions that need to be made in the future, and whether they can physically or psychologically manage to care for their handicapped sibling. Another related concern is the doubt a well sibling may have about a future or present spouse's acceptance of or ability to cope with the handicapped brother or sister.

Sibling responsibility for an ill or developmentally delayed brother or sister should be a major source of concern for the clinician. Investigating the extent to which siblings feel or expect to assume responsibility for a handicapped family member is vitally important. How siblings envision the way they will manage life's future demands depends in part on whether there are vestiges of resentment and anger toward the parents and the handicapped sibling from earlier interactions.

If, for example, a sibling is distraught about future care, the therapist must facilitate the expression of anger and anxiety yet also be cognizant that viewing the future in such bleak terms might lead to a sense of overwhelming helplessness. Therefore, while allowing the expression of anger, the clinician must help the sibling identify available community resources that can be of support as responsibility increases. For some siblings there will be rich supply of available community services, while for others (especially those in small towns and in rural settings) there may be meager resources to aid handicapped persons and their families.

One source of emotional support that the clinican ought to keep in mind is other siblings. The therapist ought to help the sibling consider how much responsibility she should assume if there are other able family members. For some siblings the issue will not be the availability of community support but whether they can, without guilt, abandon the powerful burden of responsibility their parents placed upon them out of their own anxieties about the future care of their handicapped child.

CATCHING THE DISABILITY AND IDENTITY CONCERNS

Correcting irrational beliefs requires vigilance on the part of the therapist. Some young children may be concerned about "catching" the sibling's disability (Featherstone, 1980). In a videotape where parents talk about the effects cancer has had on their families, one concern voiced was the well children's fear that they too would be stricken with cancer. Anxiety is exacerbated when normal siblings learn that the disability was caused by a contagious disease like rubella or meningitis.

Marion (1981) observed that younger normal siblings may have anxieties that they too will become blind or deaf in the future. Siblings may believe that if a disability can happen to a brother or sister, then it can happen to them. Believing this, a child may choose to "leave" the family, which is facilitated by the parents' preoccupation with the disabled sibling (Bank and Kahn, 1982). Other well children have been known to develop somatic complaints in their attempt to gain attention from their parents. Some siblings of hearing-impaired children develop a pseudosensory deficit as an attention-getting behavior (Luterman, 1979).

As a consequence of strong identification, normal siblings may feel

overly responsible to the disabled child, thereby justifying psychologically the fact that they are not afflicted. Moreover, siblings have been
known to feel responsible for the disability, particularly when a newborn is deeply resented and they have experienced fleeting thoughts
about a brother's or sister's demise. Trevino (1979) relates that young
children are more likely to be adversely affected by the presence of an
afflicted sibling of the same sex because of the fear of also becoming
disabled, especially if there is no other sibling in the family with
whom to identify.

As Grossman (1972), Schreiber and Feeley (1965), Bank and Kahn
(1982), and Wasserman (1983) note, the development of an identity
separate from that of a handicapped sibling is of considerable
importance:

> The issue of being similar to or different from a retarded sibling
> permeated many of the meetings and seemed to be a source of enor-
> mous concern for all of the group members—In fact the experience
> with this group suggests that the main task of siblings of defective
> children is to avoid identifying with them. (Grossman, 1972, p. 34)

In a related observation, Bank and Kahn (1982) note that relatively
undifferentiated siblings may share symptoms with their disabled
brother or sister, whereas siblings who have successfully separated
tend to act more independently.

Siblings who are ill informed about the nature and consequences of
their brother's or sister's affliction may be confused regarding their
own identity. If adolescents are ignorant of the nature of the handicap, identity issues are sure to arise, since this period of development
is marked by considerable struggle over self-worth and self-identity.
Feigon (1981) observed in her sibling support groups a strong identification with the handicapped sibling that resulted in feelings that one
is or will be handicapped. This again reinforces the need to provide
accurate information to the sibling.

The disease characteristics of chronically ill children may bear a
relationship to identity problems (Bank and Kahn, 1982), although
the nature of the relationship is unclear. Tew and Lawrence (1975)
concluded from their study that siblings of slightly handicapped children were most disturbed, followed by siblings of severely and moder-
ately handicapped children. It may be that identity confusion and an

inability to differentiate oneself from a handicapped sibling are consequences of the perceived "likeness" of the other. In other words, the less abnormal-appearing the sibling, the more likely issues of identity may surface. However, Lobato (1983) and Kirkman (1985) point out that the research consistently supports the position that there is no simple linear relationship between severity and sibling adjustment. The same conclusion holds when one considers the type of impairment (Lobato, 1983). For siblings of the seriously emotionally disturbed, Bank and Kahn (1982) comment that:

> Every well sibling that we have interviewed has, at one time or another, feared the possibility of becoming like a seriously disturbed brother or sister. Some siblings do not dwell on this fear, while others allow themselves to be haunted and dominated by the possibility that they could wind up in serious trouble or in a mental hospital. (p. 253)

In instances of childhood death, healthy children fear contamination by the disease that killed a brother or sister. Childhood fears in healthy children of siblings who have congenital heart disease include concerns that they too may have holes in their hearts or that they are defective in some manner (Binger, 1973; Travis, 1976). And the increased risk of developing mental illness due to heredity places an additional burden on well siblings of schizophrenics (Bank and Kahn, 1982).

Powell and Ogle (1985) note that siblings may become confused regarding their role in the family. One source of confusion is their dual role as sibling and as surrogate parent. As noted previously, caretaking responsibility may promote one's self-view as a parent surrogate, while one is in reality a brother or sister (and a child/adolescent).

Siblings experience confusion over treatment priorities for their brother or sister and their own needs for attention and affection. Indeed, the real or perceived lack of parental attention may be a source of considerable resentment. With young siblings in particular, the therapist should help parents understand the non-afflicted siblings' need for attention. Overwhelmed themselves, parents are often unaware of the burdens on their well siblings. In a recent study, Wallinga, Paguio, and Skeen (1987) discovered that parents thought that their healthy children were coping considerably better than the children thought they were. The study enabled the parents to realize for the first time how much they had neglected their healthy children.

There are times, then, when family therapy may be necessary. At the least an extra session or two with just the parents may be indicated. With this in mind, therapists need to feel comfortable conducting couples and family therapy. Other sources of confusion can arise when parents disagree about child-rearing practices, treat the handicapped child differently, and/or are not at the same stage in accepting the handicapped child.

As therapists help siblings express their identity concerns and their worries about contamination, support groups of similarly aged youngsters may be a useful adjunct to individual treatment. Siblings who may feel different or odd are comforted when they learn in a group context that others share their feelings.

ANGER AND GUILT

Siblings of handicapped children may experience anger in larger doses than siblings of normal brothers and sisters. Whether siblings harbor or openly express their feelings of anger and resentment depends on a number of factors, some of which have been mentioned above:

1. the extent to which a sibling is held responsible for a handicapped brother or sister;
2. the extent to which a handicapped sibling takes advantage of (manipulates) a normal brother or sister;
3. the extent to which the handicapped sibling restricts social life or is the source of embarrassment;
4. the extent to which a handicapped child requires excessive time and attention from the parents;
5. the extent to which the family's financial resources are drained by the handicapped child's medical and other needs;
6. the number and sex of siblings;
7. the overall accommodation parents have made to their special life situation.

Anger may arise in relation to numerous conditions in a home with a handicapped child:

Children feel angry: at parents, at the disabled child, at the wider world, at God or fate, perhaps at all four. Some blame their mother and father for the disability itself (just as they blame them for any new baby). A handicap creates unusual needs; many children envy their brother or sister this special attention. And older children may rage secretly about the sometimes colossal sums of money spent on diagnosis and therapy—resources that might otherwise finance family comforts and college tuition. (Featherstone, 1980, p. 143)

Reactions from acquaintances or strangers to a handicapped brother or sister may lead to open expressions of hositility, as illustrated in the following comments from a college student:

I heard some guy talking in the back about Mark and how stupid he was, and you could make him do anything and he is so gullible, and all this kind of stuff. I walked back to the kid and slugged him in the face. . . . I always felt that I had to protect him from someone, from teasing, from fights, and any other kids trying to put things over on kids who are at a disadvantage to them. If you love somebody you cannot help but get emotionally involved in that. (Klein, 1972, pp. 12, 13)

Normal siblings may be placed in an insufferable triple bind. Parental demands to care for and protect the disabled sibling clash with those of playmates who encourage shunning; then one's own confused feelings of anger, guilt, love and protectiveness toward the handicapped child and resentment toward the parents for demanding that one love and take care of a handicapped brother or sister result in a most untenable and conflict-ridden situation.

Wherever I went, Mindy went too. . . . I was often excluded from neighborhood games because of a sidekick. And then there was the unwritten family rule that I just leave with Mindy whenever my playmates made fun of her. They often did mock her, of course, and we would leave—except for one time which to this day gives my conscience no rest, when I joined in. I lost many playmates by having to side with Mindy. I felt neglected by my family and shunned by my peers. I was a very lonely little girl. (Hayden, 1974, p. 27)

Feeling ignored and unappreciated for one's achievements leaves lifelong scars on normal siblings. Hayden (1974) continues:

Mindy's achievements always met with animated enthusiasm from our parents. In contrast it seemed, mother and daddy's response to my accomplishments was on the pat-on-the-back level. I was expected to perform well in every circumstance. I wanted my parents to be enthusiastic about my accomplishments, too. I didn't want to have to beg for praise. I didn't want to be taken for granted. I wanted to be noticed. (p. 27)

Reading these quotes, one cannot ignore the parental insensitivity to the plight of Mindy's normal sister. Anger, resentment, guilt, and competition for the parents' attention could have been largely averted by parents who shared their time and affection with both of their children. Parents sometimes embrace the myth that their handicapped child is the only needy one; in some families the nonhandicapped sibling is the most needy.

There are many reasons for normal siblings to experience anger, as well as the guilt that often follows in anger's wake. Even so, in the literature dealing with exceptional families helping siblings understand, tolerate, or accept and express the anger they so often feel is hardly mentioned. Therapists need to help siblings understand the source of their anger, the universality of angry feelings, and the relationship of anger to guilt. For siblings of emotionally disturbed brothers and sisters, Bank and Kahn (1982) note that:

> . . . aggressiveness is one natural way through which siblings communicate. But when one sibling is defective, or is *seen* as defective and needs special treatment by parents, the well child must learn to inhibit, to refrain from aggressive taunts and actions. To establish himself as "well," he must give up and suppress these vital angry parts of himself, or submerge or hide them, lest he further injure his vulnerable sibling. Further, the well sibling learns not to rock the parents' boat, not to roil already troubled waters. Inhibition of anger also means that other forms of spontaneity—such as kidding, humor and "messing around"—get squelched. The relationship between disturbed and rigidly avoidant siblings is serious and drab and lacks playfulness. (pp. 259-60)

While psychotherapists can help parents facilitate the expression of anger by their nondisabled children, they need to be sensitive to the parents' reasons for discouraging the open expression of feelings. When parents are made anxious by their child's feelings, couples or family therapy may be indicated. Also, as noted earlier, sibling support groups are an excellent setting for the expression and acceptance of angry feelings, among others. Perhaps more useful at times than individual therapy, group therapy (or a support group experience) helps siblings vent their feelings and express their guilt and sadness in the presence of others who can empathize with these feelings. One must not ignore the powerful healing powers that a group of peers can have on a child or adolescent.

COMMUNICATION

The presence of a disabled child in the family inhibits communication. This lack of communication within a family over a child's disabling condition contributes to the loneliness normal siblings experience. Siblings may sense that certain topics are taboo and that "ugly" feelings should remain hidden; they are thereby forced into a peculiar kind of loneliness — a sense of detachment from those to whom they typically feel closest. Family secrets or implicit rules forbidding the discussion of a problem force normal siblings constantly to pretend that circumstances are other than they seem. For some parents, discussing their handicapped child with a nonhandicapped son or daughter is as threatening as discussing sex.

Siblings may also avoid asking questions of their parents because of a misguided wish to protect them. Children fear that their parents may lack the capacity to tolerate the illness and that their questions may precipitate a breakdown or a rejection of themselves. Such a pattern of diminished communication may spread to other aspects of family life, producing a generalized "web of silence."

Some parents "teach" their well children that aggression toward a disabled child is bad, disloyal and rebellious (Bank and Kahn, 1982). As a result, angry feelings are kept hidden or discharged in the parents' absence.

> Rather than invigorating the relationship with the give-and-take of insults and punches, easily dished out and quickly forgotten, the well sibling must be wary of hostile impulses toward a sick brother or sister, or risk being charged with kicking the crippled and hurting the handicapped. The well sibling, being presumed to have many riches and advantages, is expected to show restraint, charity, kindness, and loyalty. Being a true-blue Boy Scout is, of course, impossible; and well siblings may vent their dammed-up anger in sneaky and violent ways. (Bank and Kahn, 1982, pp. 260–61)

Children sense parents' underlying feelings, regardless of the actual words used; therefore, open and honest communication is important within the family. Therapists should help parents become aware of certain key words in their communication with children. For example, the words "better" and "worse" invite comparisons, whereas "different" and "cannot" convey that limitations are not due to anything anyone did or did not do. Finally, therapists may wish to urge parents to begin a dialogue with their children as soon as possible.

Insofar as schoolwork is concerned, Michaelis (1980) notes that siblings may be resentful when the handicapped child plays while they themselves must work so hard. Communicating the educational methods used with the handicapped child and the skills that are being taught will help make it possible for the sibling to be supportive rather than critical and resentful. Also, young siblings may not understand that their brother or sister has certain cognitive limitations and as a result spends less time studying and in other learning activities.

PARENTAL ATTITUDES

Because children's views are often extensions of their parents', their ability to accept the handicap and cope with the hardship is largely influenced by parental attitudes (Trevino, 1979). Parental attitudes of authoritarianism and overindulgence, augmented by such feelings as anxiety, depression, guilt, and uncontrolled hostility, help color the views, feelings, and behaviors of normal siblings. Some parents react so negatively to a handicapped child that normal siblings will accordingly be adversely affected (Lobato, 1983), while other parents unconsciously structure the roles well siblings assume vis-à-vis their ill brothers and sisters (Bank and Kahn, 1982). For example, a sibling may learn that to be appreciated and loved one must assume a caretaking role within the family. Such behavior will garner the desired reaction from one's parents and also solidify one's position within the family.

Parental response and adaptation are highly individualistic and result from numerous factors. The author and Darling (in press) cite studies that demonstrate *both* negative and positive reactions. Religious and cultural factors help shape parental attitudes, but unfortunately have been largely ignored in the literature. Some preliminary research tends to support the view that Catholic parents may perceive the birth of a handicapped child as a gift, a blessing that God would bestow only on the most deserving. Such positive sentiments surely influence sibling attitudes. Culturally acquired attitudes can also influence the quality of friendship and professional relationships outside the family.

In her study of brothers and sisters of mentally retarded children, Grossman (1972) concluded that among lower- and upper-socioeconomic status families there was a positive relationship between open and comfortable family discussion of retardation and the sibling's own acceptance of the retarded child. The degree of open communication about the afflicted child in families appears to be a useful barometer of parental attitudes.

Most parents are at some level aware of their influence on their non-disabled children. Parents often experience this "influence" with pride, yet some parents of handicapped children consider this an added burden. Depressed, anxious, and guilty parents, aware of their psychological state, worry about the effect they have on other members of the family. Parental concern about their normal children is an added drain on their available psychological resources.

Although depressed and anxious parents may have a negative impact on their children, their awareness of their psychological state often leads them to seek help so that they can better cope with their circumstances. On the other hand, emotionally disturbed parents who are insensitive to the needs of their non-disabled children and largely deny the circumstances that confront them inflict considerable harm. In therapy with denying parents it is important to move slowly lest their anxiety becomes too severe for them to continue. It would be a therapeutic error to force reality on such parents until they are able to tolerate intensive exploration.

For some parents (and siblings also) denial is an expected stage following the disclosure that one's child has a chronic affliction. With parents who have recently been informed about their child's handicap, support, understanding and concrete guidance are all that is expected of the therapist. Parents who continue to deny far beyond a reasonable adjustment period cause considerable distress to their families and to the professionals who try to help. Denying families tend to "shop" for professionals they feel will lessen their anxiety by agreeing with *their* views of their handicapped child. The therapist can help these parents best by exploring with them the numerous impasses they experience as they interact with professionals, family members, and other families. Therapy can include examining the genesis of the denial, which indirectly helps the non-disabled sibling in the family. As parents examine their behavior and feelings more freely, siblings will also profit from a more open environment.

EFFECTS ON SIBLINGS

The presence of a handicapped sibling changes the experience of each other child in the family. A family with a handicapped child offers well siblings unusual opportunities for growth but also provides fertile ground for the development of problems. A number of potential areas of difficulty have been noted. How these factors interact to culminate in adjustment problems is difficult to determine, yet an examination of potential contributing factors should prove useful to the practitioner.

Researchers and clinicians view the potential for psychological harm differently. Poznanski (1969) reports that psychiatrists treat more siblings of handicapped children than handicapped children themselves. Trevino (1979) believes that non-disabled siblings of handicapped children often have a combination of certain characteristics and are, indeed, children at risk requiring psychological intervention. For San Martino and Newman (1974) guilt provides the foundation for subsequent difficulties non-disabled siblings are likely to experience. From their interviews of 239 families, Breslau, Weitzman, and Messenger (1981) found a marked trend toward aggressive behavior and confused thinking in normal siblings.

Featherstone (1980), drawing upon personal experience as a parent and recounting the experience of others, Grossman (1972), and Kibert (1987), citing research on college-age brothers and sisters of retarded children, take a more cautious view of the effects on non-disabled children. They believe that a handicapped child in the family may have different outcomes: little, negative, or positive impact on subsequent adjustment and coping. Farber's (1959, 1960) early research tends to support the same conclusion, which is further reinforced by Klein (1972) and Schreiber and Feeley (1965). Grakliker, Fishler, and Koch (1962) found no adverse effects reported by the siblings interviewed in their study. And Simeonsson and Bailey

(1986), in their review of 19 studies, conclude that both negative and positive effects have been found. In explaining these mixed findings, one must conclude that the richness of human experiences, personal characteristics, and contexts prohibits firm conclusion. Major research weaknesses also contribute to this state of affairs. What this means for the practitioner is that effective therapy can proceed only when an adequate assessment is performed; that means that the sibling should be viewed within the context of the many variables that influence him or her.

Bank and Kahn (1982) observe that a sibling's adjustment can be affected by the age and developmental stage of the well sibling, since a sibling's ability to comprehend a brother's or sister's illness and what it means for the family changes over time. Another factor, chronicity, determines whether the sibling must cope with a time-limited or more lasting and perhaps more devastating situation. Bank and Kahn also note that the rate of onset, especially with a mentally ill sibling, can be the source of some confusion for the well sibling. And finally, the stigmatizing aspects of a disabled sibling's condition can cause considerable consternation. In a public situation, a well-behaved mildly retarded youngster will most likely go unnoticed, while a drooling, bent figure in a wheelchair will draw considerable attention.

While some contributors to the professional literature are uncompromisingly pessimistic about the effects of a handicapped child on family members, others are remarkably optimistic, especially parents who have written about their experiences. In reviewing the research and commentary about siblings one may be left with the impression that largely negative effects are to be expected. This is simply not true. Illes (1979) reported that siblings of cancer victims are compassionate, tolerant, empathic to parents, and appreciative of their own health. Such positive sentiments underscore both the capacity of children to function under stress and the important contributions they make to their families. Glendinning's (1983) British study, in which she interviewed in depth 17 parents (mostly mothers of severely handicapped children), revealed that siblings were seen to face life optimistically. Drotar (quoted in Wallinga et al., 1987) argues that a child's chronic disability brings family members together, mobilizing positive efforts on behalf of the child which actually benefit the family. Simeonsson and Bailey (1986) note that siblings who have been actively involved in the management of their handicapped family member tend to be well adjusted. It is difficult to integrate this finding with the studies that caution against excessive caretaking. It may be that the critical variable is how the parents interact with their handicapped and nonhandicapped offspring, for example, by providing ample time and by communicating their love and concern to *all* of their children.

In their research Grossman (1972) and Kibert (1987) report that some college students appeared to have benefitted from growing up with a retarded sibling. "The ones who benefitted appeared to us to be more tolerant, more compassionate, more knowing about prejudice" (Grossman, 1972, p. 84). In support of Grossman's findings, Miller (1974) found a number of non-disabled siblings who expressed involvement in the growth and development of their retarded sibling and exhibited a sense of pride that they had been a part of it. Diane, a normal sibling, said the following in her interview with Klein (1972):

> I always felt there was something very different about our family. Of course, you know, Cathy being that difference, Because of her difference there was a degree of specialness or closeness about us that, I do not know, it was sort of a bond that made us all very, very close. We all pitched in and helped each other out. (p. 25)

Another sister, this one of a mentally retarded, cerebral palsied, and epileptic boy, has put her retrospective thoughts as follows:

> I do not mean to imply that life with Robin has been all goodness and light. I have seen the strain that the responsibility of his constant care has placed upon my parents. I worry about the increasing frequency of his seizures and about what would happen to him should my parents become unable to care for him. Robin, himself, like all brothers I suppose, can be truly aggravating. It makes me angry to see him try to weasel his way out of doing things that I know he is capable of doing. Just the other day, I was scolding him for not clearing his place at the table. I guess my sisterly bossing was too much for him. He pointed at me and angrily made the sign for handcuffs—his way of indicating that I should be put in jail.
>
> All in all, I feel that Robin has brought much good into the lives of my family. He has taught us a great deal about acceptance, patience, individual worth, but most of all about love. (Helsel, 1978, pp. 112, 113)

And after a lengthy discussion of brothers and sisters of handicapped youngsters and their adaptation to this special circumstance, Featherstone (1980) remarks:

> I have focused, up until now, on the difficulties that the able bodied child faces. These problems are real enough, and assume major importance in the lives of some children. Nonetheless, the sheer length of my discussion creates a misleading gloomy impression. It may suggest that for the brothers and sisters of the disabled the developmental path is strewn with frightful hazards, that all but the most skillful parents can expect to see their "normal" children bruised irreparably by the experience of family living. The truth is quite otherwise. (p. 163)

From this chapter one realizes that our knowledge of siblings is still in its infancy. However, we are not without some guidance for practitioners who should heed the admonition that sibling adjustment is dependent on numerous intertwined variables and that a simple etiological explanation is impossible. The impact of a handicapped child may be "for better or for worse" and may depend on various mediating variables. However, when a sibling is troubled, his or her improvement may depend in large part on the knowledge and skill of the therapist. We have the opportunity to make a difference.

REFERENCES

Bank, S. P., & Kahn, M. D. (1982). *The sibling bond*. New York: Basic Books.

Binger, C. M. (1973). Childhood leukemia: Emotional impact on siblings. In J. Anthony & C. Koupernik (Eds.), *The child in his family*. New York: John Wiley.

Breslau, N., Weitzman, M., & Messinger, K. (1981). Psychologic functioning of siblings of disabled children. *Pediatrics, 67*, 344–353.

Farber, B. (1959). Effect of severely retarded child on family integration. *Monographs of the Society for Research in Child Development, 24* (Whole No. 71).

Farber, B. (1960). Family organization and crisis: Maintenance of integration in families with a severely mentally retarded child. *Monographs of the Society for Research in Child Development, 25* (Whole No. 75).

Featherstone, H. (1980). *A difference in the family*. New York: Basic Books.

Feigon, J. (1981). A sibling group program. *Sibling Information Network Newsletter, 1*, 2–3.

Glendinning, C. (1983). *Unshared care*. London: Routledge and Kegan Paul.

Grakliker, B. V., Fishler, K., & Koch, R. (1962). Teenage reactions to a mentally retarded sibling. *American Journal of Mental Deficiency, 66*, 838–843.

Grossman, F. K. (1972). *Brothers and sisters of retarded children*. Syracuse: Syracuse University Press.

Hayden, V. (1974). The other children. *The Exceptional Parent, 4*, 26–29.

Helsel, E. (1978). The Helsels' story of Robin. In A. P. Turnbull & H. R. Turnbull (Eds.), *Parents speak out*. Columbus, OH: Charles Merrill.

Holt, K. S. (1958). The home care of severely retarded children. *Pediatrics, 22*, 746–775.

Illes, J. (1979). Children with cancer: Healthy siblings' perceptions during the illness experience. *Cancer Nursing, 2*(5), 371–377.

Kibert, R. (1987). *College aged siblings' perceptions of their retarded brothers and sisters*. Unpublished doctoral dissertation. University of Pittsburgh.

Kirkman, M. (1985). The perceived impact of a sibling with a disability on family relationships: A survey of adult siblings in Victoria, Australia. *Sibling Information Network Newsletter, 4*, 2–5.

Klein, S. D. (1972). Brother to sister: Sister to brother. *The Exceptional Parent, 2*, 10–15.

Lobato, D. (1983). Siblings of handicapped children: A review. *Journal of Autism and Developmental Disorders, 13*, 347–364.

Luterman, D. (1979). *Counseling parents of hearing-impaired children*. Boston: Little, Brown.

Marion, R. L. (1981). *Educators, parents, and exceptual children*. Rockville, MD: Aspen.

Meyer, D. J., Vadasy, P. F., & Fewell, R. R. (1985). *Living with a brother or sister with special needs*. Seattle: University of Washington Press.

Michaelis, C. T. (1980). *Home and school partnership in exceptional children*. Rockville, MD: Aspen.

Miller, S. (1974). *An exploratory study of sibling relationships in families with retarded children*. Unpublished doctoral dissertation, Columbia University.

Murphy, A., Paeschel, S., Duffy, T., & Brady, E. (1976). Meeting with brothers and sisters of children with Down's Syndrome. *Children Today, 5*, 20–23.

Myers, R. (1978). *Like normal people*. New York: McGraw-Hill.

Powell, T. H., & Ogle, P. A. (1985). *Brothers and sisters: A special part of exceptional families*. Baltimore: Brookes.

Poznanski, E. (1969). Psychiatric difficulties in siblings of handicapped children. *Pediatrics, 8*, 232–234.

San Martino, M., & Newman, M. B. (1974). Siblings of retarded children: A population at risk. *Child Psychiatry and Human Development, 4*, 168–177.

Schreiber, M., & Feeley, M. (1965). A guided group experience. *Children, 12*, 221–225.

Seligman, M. (Ed.). (1983). *The family with a handicapped child: Understanding and treatment*. Orlando, FL: Grune & Stratton.

Seligman, M. (1979). *Strategies for helping parents of exceptional children*. New York: Free Press.

Seligman, M., & Darling, R. (in press). *Ordinary families, special children: A systems approach to childhood disability*. New York: Guilford.

Simeonsson, R. J., & Bailey, D. B. (1986). Siblings of handicapped children. In J. J. Gallagher & P. M. Vietze, *Families of handicapped persons*. Baltimore: Brookes.

Solnit, A. J., & Stark, M. H. (1961). Mourning and the birth of a defective child. *Psychoanalytic Study of the Child, 16*, 523–537.

Tew, B., & Lawrence, K. (1975). Mothers, brothers, and sisters of patients with spina bifida. *Developmental Medical Child Neurology, 15*, (Supp. 29) 69–76.

Travis, G. (1976). *Chronic illness in children: Its impact on child and family*. Stanford, CA: Stanford University Press.

Trevino, F. (1979). Siblings of handicapped children: Identifying those at risk. *Social Casework, 60,* 488–493.

Wallinga, C., Paguio, L., & Skeen, P. (1987). When a brother or sister is ill. *Psychology Today, 8*(42), 43.

Wasserman, R. (1983). Identifying the counseling needs of the siblings of mentally retarded children. *Personnel and Guidance Journal,* 622–627.

9

When Parents Separate or Divorce: The Sibling System

Lee Combrinck-Graham

It was 1945. The children were young, the boy, seven, the girl, four. They hurried next to their mother up the platform at Union Station. At last they found a car with empty seats. She settled them down and kissed them goodbye with reminders to the boy, "take care of your sister." Then she left to count the cars up to the engine so she could phone the father's family and tell them exactly where the children were located.

The children, Peter and Midge, were two-year veterans of divorce. It was the first time they were traveling by themselves, but the trip was not new, nor was the train. Between Washington and New York there would be the lunch they had brought, then dixie cups of ice cream, and finally their aunt would get on the train at Newark to help them on the final leg of the trip to Pennsylvania Station.

The children were very different from each other. Peter, introverted and intellectual, could already read and liked to draw. Midge couldn't read yet, and though Peter would have read to her, she was too proud to let him. She was gregarious and curious about people. She whiled away the hours staring at the other passengers, first from her seat, later walking up and down the aisle scrutinizing them.

SEPARATION AND DIVORCE AND THE CHILDREN

Divorce is not for children; it is for adults. Divorce is neither good nor bad for children. It is an event, one of many, that changes children's lives. It is an event, one of many, to which they must, and do,

190

adapt. Divorce spells a change in the child's relationship system. Generations of children have successfully adapted to such changes, and despite the numerous studies detailing the hazards to children of the divorce situation, this current generation of children will probably survive the very high divorce rate of their parents.

That is, they will survive if they are allowed to by a very pathologizing mental health system! Growing up in a single-parent-headed household is not, in itself, detrimental to children, even to little boys whose mothers are the custodial parents. If the fathers have abandoned the children, and there is no sustained bitterness or claim upon the father's involvement, the children do fine, as they can do when their father has died. What is detrimental is fostering the child's entitlement to a relationship to an absent father while other more available relationships are suspended. Problems come, too, through continuing to explain the family's misfortunes by the absence of or abandonment by the father, or because of the marital breakup. Clinging to the facts of separation and divorce as if they explain later developments tends to interfere with getting on with the business of living.

There are other hazards to children of divorce detailed in the research literature: young boys in mother custody, as we have described; teenaged girls when mother remarries. Again, it is not the fact of the divorce and remarriage that causes the problem. It is the atmosphere of withheld entitlements to the child, the unfulfilled promise of birthright, that seems to keep everyone believing that these children's lives are not normal, that they are missing an essential part of childhood, that they are, ultimately, defective.

We now know some aspects of the divorce process that make it easier for children to adjust to the changes: parents' clarity about their distaste for each other combined with recognition of the validity of the children's relationships with each; acceptance of differences in parenting styles, so mother can say, for instance, "That's how Daddy does it at his house, but this is how we do it here"; a responsible means of addressing and resolving issues about the children without involving the children.

Most approaches to assessing the effects on children of parental divorce and separation view the parents' conduct as the indicator of whether the family system is failing or succeeding in its adjustment. While parental functioning is a critical component of child development, it is not the only one. Assessing the children's passage through these difficult times solely in terms of parental functioning (or dysfunctioning) ignores the significant contributions of the children themselves, as individuals and together, as resources to each other.

The situation of Peter and Midge described above could have produced a lot of handwringing. They were so young! He was in the midst of his oedipal period when his father left! They were too young to travel alone for more than five hours on a train! The poor things, from a broken home! And so on. The fact is, they didn't mind the train trip. They thought it was an adventure. They did mind the tug of war for their affections between their father's family and their mother. How did they deal with it? Despite their great differences in personality, they had each other. They entertained each other, and when they grew older, they consulted each other on family matters. Together they were able to shrug off some of the conflict raging around them.

SIBLINGS

Family therapy has hardly touched on the extraordinary family-binding functions of the child subsystem in a nuclear family. Thus Bank and Kahn's 1982 work enters the literature as a belated, but long needed, recognition of this important family subsystem. Only with the present volume is there a systematic effort to present how the sibling system can (indeed, should) be engaged in family therapy.

Some work has looked at the effects of birth order on sibling relationships (Toman, 1969) and of a complementary relationship between siblings in the carrying of family burdens (Boszormenyi-Nagy and Spark, 1984). These glimpses of sibling patterns emphasize explanation rather than examining how siblings arrange things with each other to contribute to the family functioning or suggesting how these relationships can be worked with in family therapy. Indeed, Toman's birth order model has developed into an individual typology, similar, in some respects, to the kinds of characteristics described by astrologers!

An interesting notion about sibling subsystem effect on family functioning comes from an analysis of census data (Koo, Sachindran, and Griffith, 1984). They make the following observations:

1. The probability that mothers of more than two children will divorce after separation is significantly lower than for childless women.
2. Among white women, mothers of more than three children

are at a disadvantage regarding chances of remarriage (this is not true among black women).

3. Among white women, the presence of a youngest child between the ages of two and five years at separation decreased the probability of divorce after separation.

These observations could be interpreted in a variety of ways, but generally they confirm the important effect of the children on how their parents negotiate relationships. Some explanations for the findings could be: parents who stay together to have more than two children may be more committed to each other and more ambivalent about leaving their relationship; the financial burdens of more children prohibit divorce; or religious beliefs that lead to large families also prohibit divorce. It is also possible, though, that the sibship itself has a binding power that gives these families a stronger center of gravity.

Even recognizing the importance of these sibling relationships, family therapy, especially with young children, has focused on primarily the parents as the major change agents in the family. Often the identified patient is the only child seen in ongoing therapy sessions, and when all the children are included, it is not unusual for the "noninvolved" siblings to sit patiently by while therapist and parents talk to and about the problem child.

Bank and Kahn (1975) suggest five autonomous functions of the sibling subsystem within the family: identification and differentiation, direct service to each other, mutual regulation, translating to and for each other, and dealing with parents. This focus on the functions of the sibling subsystem within the family can lead to more practical recognition of how children shape and affect their family environments (the parents are not totally responsible). Furthermore, recognizing the functions of the sibling system can direct therapists to consider how this subsystem might be called upon to effect change in family systems. Lewis (1986) describes how siblings can be cultivated as resources to each other even when their families deteriorate and they are placed in separate foster homes. Lewis translates her recognition of sibling functions into healing action.

SIBLINGS AND PARENTAL SEPARATION AND DIVORCE

For a child whose parents are separating or divorcing, there is no doubt that the transitions are easier to manage if there are siblings.

Few would argue with this yet very few writing on the divorce process and children have actually addressed the sibling system. Strikingly, Steinman (1981), reviewing the effects of joint custody, reports the children's responses as if there were only single-child families, though her sample of 24 families included some with two and three children. In a follow-up study of parents' satisfaction with joint custody, whether there is one or more than one child is not a factor that Steinman and colleagues consider (Steinman, Zemmelman, and Knoblaugh, 1985). Other reports of children's reactions to divorce do not address siblings or possible differences in reaction if there are siblings. Wallerstein (1985) mentions siblings as a kind of after-thought, quoting several young people in their ten-year post-divorce follow-up as reporting closeness with their siblings. She observes, "It seems that when the relationship between the parents weakens and disrupts that (sic) siblings can turn toward each other to huddle together, to protect each other, to remain intimate with each other, and perhaps most of all to remain faithful to each other" (Wallerstein, 1985, p. 553).

Eno (1985) specifically addresses sibling relationships in divorcing families. She notes that the sibling relationship, which is usually the subsystem that stays intact during and after the separation and divorce, is often seen in stark relief. Eno observes that siblings relation-ships are often tampered with by changes in the parent system, how-ever, as when parents involve the children in parent-child coalitions. On the other hand, she reports that the strength of the sibling system can protect the children from parents' attempts to involve them in their struggles with each other.

Isaacs, Montalvo, and Abelsohn (1986) have also discussed the sibling subsystem in families of divorce. Like Eno, they focus on the sibling management of the situation in the absence of strong, effective parenting. Thus, they look at the sibling system primarily from the point of view of helping the parents regain executive control of the children and helping the children help the parents to do this.

I take a different point of view. I see the child subsystem as making a significant contribution to the way things happen in the family. I hold children responsible for their actions, which I take to be proac-tive and adaptive as well as reactive to their parents. Taking this position does not mean that I blame children for what happens to them; but neither do I blame the parents. Things happen; people deal with them. It is important to study how they do, in order to expand the repertoire of experiences that the therapist can pass on to others.

A SAMPLE OF FAMILIES SURVIVING
SEPARATION AND DIVORCE

Over the past 15 years I have studied more than 80 families in which there has been separation or divorce. Many of these families were referred for help with the process of divorce and settling custody disputes. Many others come to work on post-divorce adjustment. Others came for treatment around issues unrelated to divorce. And still others were families of friends. Some of the families came early for consultation and have continued to keep in touch. Some of the children were seen only a few times for evaluation, following which contacts ceased.

Seventy-two families (82%) were clinical cases. Thirty-two (44%) of these had only one child involved in the current divorce.* Forty (55%) families had more than one child, and of these, eight had three children. Not one of the families in my clinical practice had more than three children, a finding in keeping with Koo et al.'s (1984) observations about family size and divorce.** The children's ages ranged from 18 months to 21 years at the time I first saw them, with most of the children between 5 and 11 years of age.

Twenty-three (72%) of the only children and 25 (63%) of the sibling families were in custody of the mother (66% of the clinical families). Six (17%) of the only children and five (13%) of the sibling groups were in custody of the father (15% of the clinical sample). Three of the only children and eight of the sibling groups were in joint custody at the time of the initial contact (also 15%). In three families (4%), siblings were living in different households.

In attempting to make a gross assessment about the degree of bitterness or the ease of managing the post-separation adjustment, I found that there were no differences between families with only one child and those with more than one child. That is, the presence of siblings alone did not protect the family from bitter custody battles or

---

*Seven families had children by other marriages. These children are not referred to here even though they were often involved in evaluations.
**Isaacs et al. (1986) describe a divorcing family with four children. Clearly it is not unheard of. It is much more likely to occur, however, when the children are older—that is, in adolescence or young adulthood.

make the post-separation adjustment easier. There did seem to be differences in the way the children handled the problems. The children who had siblings were healthier, more age-appropriate, and showed better social adjustment than only children, despite continuing senseless struggles between their parents. How do they manage? Let's let the children teach us.

LET THE CHILDREN TEACH US

There are three areas in which children must continue to function during a parental separation and divorce: taking care of the parents, taking care of themselves, and getting on with their own developmental tasks.

Taking Care of Parents

Perhaps the most important task for children whose parents are separating or divorcing is to manage the parents' relationships, both to each other and to the children. This is a task that children do without help, since no one in their system is likely to recognize it as a legitimate function for them or to accept that they should be coached on how to do it better. More commonly it is thought that the children should be protected from these "parentifying" tasks. Children always assume responsibility for their parents' feelings and well-being. This, in itself, is not parentification, but a part of being in a family and a fundamental way that children learn to care for others. Thus, trying to protect children from caring for the parents not only is unrealistic but actually interferes with basic functions of children in families. Furthermore, protecting children from these functions makes it necessary for them to manage these tasks on their own without help and often surreptitiously. In our efforts to protect these youngsters, we may actually add to their difficulties.

Children take care of parents in a variety of ways. In the cases of single children the task appears to be most difficult. If the parents have undergone a bitter separation, and bitterness continues, the child may choose one parent, spurning the other. A common complaint brought by primary custodial parents of only children is, "Donnie screams and makes such a fuss when his father comes to pick him up. I just can't see how this won't warp his feelings towards all men." The message is, visits with the father should be terminated to protect the child from developing a warped attitude toward men! The likelihood that the child is taking care of the mother by making such a scene is very difficult for the mother to contemplate. The father will usually say that as soon as they drive away the child is perfectly happy. A variant of this is when the mother accuses the father of sexual abuse, and the child gives ambiguous responses to direct questions, but screams, dutifully, when the father comes for visitation, thus confirming the mother's viewpoint.

Another single child variation is suddenly wanting to live with the noncustodial parent. This occurs most often when the noncustodial parent has been away or has appeared erratically in the child's life, or when that parent has formed a relationship which may lead to remarriage, or when that parent has remarried and is forming a new family. Children who testify in court that they want to live with the long estranged father are taking a terrible gamble, one that can only be taken in the confidence that the mother will understand and stand by the child anyway. Taking care of your separated parents is not easy for a single child.

For siblings, however, the tasks are considerably lighter. Often it becomes a non-issue, particularly when the separation is comparatively amicable and the living and visiting arrangements are fairly stable. For the Bachs, a mother custody family with three siblings, the children usually visited their father together, though each enjoyed special time with him. If there were tensions between the parents, the children usually balanced things out between them. For example, when their father and future stepmother announced their intention to marry, the children covered the range of reactions. Generally they were pleased and interested. The youngest child worried about whether there would be more children. The older boy worried about his mother. Thus they encouraged the father, supported the mother, and looked out for their own interests in what looked like a well coordinated response.

> Peter and Midge's father joined the Navy right after his divorce, so it was his mother and sister who had the children for regular visits. The visits were fun, in some ways. Their grandmother liked to play games and to dress up in costumes. She brought them presents and took them places. But she was very critical of their mother. She told them that Washington was full of "lice" and compared her generosity

to their mother's meager circumstances. It made them very uncomfortable. Midge stood up for her mother, declaring that she hadn't seen any lice. Peter withdrew.

At home the children overheard a telephone conversation between their mother and paternal grandmother. Their mother explained to them that Grandmother had complained that they hadn't polished their shoes, cleaned their fingernails, or written to her often enough. Their mother was upset, feeling criticized. The children didn't feel that she was criticizing them, but they wanted to do something for her. To take the pressure off his mother, Peter wrote a letter to their grandmother, and, following his example, Midge dictated one for her mother to write.

When children try to ignore the stress from their parents, their siblings can help. One girl commented: "It's not going to get any better. You know, it's really ridiculous when an 11-year-old can think more clearly than two grownups." The sadness reflected in this comment did not pervade her life and her functioning, partly because of her relationship with her siblings. This 11-year-old had two sisters, one older, one younger. They were all excellent students and socially successful. They took care of each other, explained things to each other, and took what they could from each of their parents, expecting that there would probably not be any more. When Dad became involved with a girlfriend, it made life a bit easier, because now the girlfriend could take care of their father. This allowed them to devote themselves more to their mother, who did not have a significant other.

Siblings often care for their parents by dividing the tasks between them. One example was when Alan, aged 11, sided with his mother, got very indignant with Dad's alleged cheating on Mom, and refused to see him. Joel, aged eight, thought it was very unfair for Mom to have his brother and Dad to have no one, so he moved in with Dad and refused to see his mother. Both parents commented that "the boys have always been so close." But because they had chosen these roles, they did not get to see each other. In my office, with no parents present, the boys were thrilled to get together, but when Alan broached the subject of Joel's coming "home," Joel said that he would not even visit until Alan agreed to visit with the father, and the entire quarrel began again. It was tempting to believe that the parents had bound their sons into these polarized positions, but when the boys were seen alone, their own contribution was obvious. With his mother and father present, Joel represented his decision to move in with Dad on the grounds of fairness, and he held Alan just as accountable as his parents. Though in no way willing to come to the bargaining table about their relationship, the parents were willing to let the boys get together, and finally agreed to drop them once a week at the mall with enough money to buy a pizza.

Alan and Joel had a most dramatic method of dividing up the tasks of managing parents. One might argue that by polarizing themselves they contributed to the standoff between their parents. After having met their parents and found no topic on which a conversation could be held, except their agreement that the boys were fond of each other, I believed that Alan and Joel had accurately assessed the reality of their parents' situation and had balanced things out as best they could. On the face of it, it is neither a constructive or destructive solution. It is a way that the family members manage, and with two siblings to divide up the tasks, it is less stressful than if only one child were being torn in this very bitter dispute.

The way Joel and Alan took sides was not unique. In fact, in families where there are two children, each child taking the side of a different parent is not uncommon. It is also not uncommon to switch sides, depending on the issue or upon which parent seems to need more attention. The youngsters, who usually travel together back and forth between their parents, seem to be willing to have their own conflicts about it. In one instance where the parents separated and didn't divorce for at least 12 years, the boys took turns, Eddie sometimes being on Mom's side with Marty on Dad's and then switching. They also took turns sympathizing with one parent or the other. When Dad broke up with his girlfriend they gave him extra time and attention. When Mom was in graduate school, they gave her extra. When Mom moved to the suburbs so they could go to a better high school, they arranged to spend more weekends with Dad. When Dad moved to another city, they were relieved of some of the balancing while he was gone, but when he moved back they knew they owed him a little extra. Putting all this energy into their parents detracted from their own interests and distracted them from some of the normal tasks of growing up. Eddie, the older, flunked out of school in 11th grade, and when he began to get his life together two years later Marty began to have academic troubles. In this family the parents had an informal joint custody agreement. But there was little question who was managing the custody arrangement: Eddie and Marty.

In the Clark family with two boys, Ron and Teddy, Mr. Clark had custody, and rancor was persistent between the two parents. It meant that all of the boys' contacts with their very available mother were fraught with uncertainty and bitterness—the difficulty getting away from the father's home, and the mother's sadness that she had lost custody of them. In this case, Ron, the older, had chronic underachievement and social problems. He finally went off to a second-rate college and flunked out in his first semester. On leaving college, he got a job and his own apartment, kept his distance from both father and mother, and had a better relationship with both. Subsequently he started college again, one of his own choosing and for which he paid himself. Teddy, the younger brother, quietly overdosed on his stepmother's sleeping pills and spent nine months in a psychiatric hospital, where he finished his senior year in high school. Ironically, being in the hospital changed the access that each parent had to him, though Mr. Clark paid the bills. It was a more neutral territory than his father's house. Ron, too, could be more involved with Teddy on this neutral ground without unbalancing the parents' relationships. A superb student, Teddy was discharged in time for his graduation from high school, and he left for college two months later.

The extraordinary measures these three sibling pairs took to manage their parents' relationships appeared, in each pair, to have been at a price: for Alan and Joel, of their relationship with each other, for Marty and Eddie, of their involvement in their social and academic lives, and for Ron and Teddy, the threat of suicide. Alan and Joel were seen at only one point in the family's working out of the divorce. If the stalemate between their parents were to continue, the boys could either continue their chosen positions or give up on their parents entirely. Marty and Eddie each had a period of social and academic failure in their high school years which appeared to be directly related to their jobs of parent managing. But Eddie, the older, recovered and went on to college after taking a year off. Marty, who was bright and talented, will undoubtedly recover too, as he moves into a more autonomous phase of his own life. Ron is an example of this. His successes came when he had established himself on neutral territory. And while the desperate gesture of Teddy was very alarming, the removal to the hospital changed his relationship with both his brother and his mother. His first year in college was highly successful.

We can judge the parents of these youngsters for placing them in these compromising positions, and we can concern ourselves with the "pathological" methods employed by the youngsters in managing the situation. Yet it is important to see that these patterns evolved in an effort to solve complex relationship problems, an effort that was much more coordinated and less burdensome on any one individual when siblings participated in the process.

Taking Care of Each Other

Apparently taking care of the parents is the first priority for most children of separated or divorced parents. Taking care of each other is second. Looking after one another can be a strong, positive experience, maintaining a continuity of caring in a relationship system otherwise undergoing major changes.

Single children usually have only one or both parents with whom to relate. They may become intensely involved with one or both parents, which makes it difficult for the parents to become involved with new partners and for the child to accept these partners. Indeed, often when one parent does get a boy- or girlfriend, it is seen by the child as a betrayal. Or, alternatively, the parents' new relationships revolve around these single children. When Sara O'Brian's mother remarried, she sought sole custody of Sara. Her reputation, veracity, and integrity as a person and spouse appeared to be at stake in a bitter custody suit. She would be vindicated in her husband's eyes if the judge ruled in her favor. Sara's father, too, had centered his relationship around her. In this case, he and his fiancé, having had nearly full custody of the child in the early stages of their relationship, had simply organized their lives around Sara. She was increasingly confused, lured on the one hand by the familiarity of her Daddy, and seduced on the other hand by the exotic promises made by her Mommy.

When grandparents are not too partisan in these relationships they can offer some relational continuity to their grandchildren, and occasionally another set of relatives does, too. Thus grandparents and other relatives can take some of the intensity off of the single child, but usually the child alone is the object of the fights and that experience cannot be shared with the other well-meaning relatives.

Siblings, on the other hand, have each other. Older siblings help their younger ones in a myriad of ways: reminding them of the schedule of when they will be with which parent, helping them pack, helping them dress and fixing their hair, guiding them through first days at school, and explaining things to them. The children in the Warren family interacted like this in my office: Six-year-old Ellen sat on the lap of 15-year-old Kate, often even when the mother or father was present. While offering this physical nurturance, Kate also supervised Ellen's play in the office, corrected her spelling, and chided her when she got chalk on her clothes or when she interrupted.

Far from being an interfering burden, this relationship between Kate and Ellen was mutually beneficial. Ellen was also affectionate with her parents, and the emotional ties between the sisters did not interfere with Kate's peer relationships. Furthermore, Ellen's naivete and innocence often freed Kate to see her situation differently.

The Kelly children seemed to have taken an oath of silence about whether they would prefer to live with their mother or father. But seven-year-old Sally kept revealing her preference for the mother. She said she laughed more at her mother's and cried more at her father's. Karen, aged nine, countered by saying she laughed more at her father's and cried more at her mother's. My asking questions such as, "At whose house do you do this or that more?" developed into a kind of game where if Sally said one thing, Karen would say the opposite. So I tried it the other way around, asking Karen first. "At whose house do you play with your friends more?" "At Mom's." When I asked Sally, she said, "At Mom's," and the game was over with much laughter and teasing. Later, after more than a year of custody probing, Sally again led the way for Karen. She said, "I don't care who I live with. It's not my decision. I'm just a kid. I just want to live with my Mom." "Not me," said Karen, resuming the old game. "So, I should tell the judge that you don't really care, but you want to live with your Mom?" I said to Sally. "Yes," she said, feeling satisfied that she had both hedged and delivered her message. "That goes for me too," Karen spoke softly, finally given the courage to express her choice by her sister's logical illogic.

In families with three children, a pattern of babying the youngest seemed consistent. In many of the families I dealt with, the youngest usually encouraged this by being unaware of what was going on and asking the naive and innocent questions that framed the situation in a special way for the older ones. In the Warren family, for instance, six-year-old Ellen provided comic relief from tense moments in a session where Kate and Annie, her 15- and 11-year-old sisters, were trying to explain a sensitive position to their difficult father. Ellen would bounce over with a drawing she was making, plop onto her father's lap or sit down next to Kate, offering Kate the opportunity to fuss over her hair or the chalk on her fingers. She would then say, seriously, demonstrating that she was tuned in all the time: "Well, Dad, you just should't yell all the time," and then she'd be off, back to playing. The older girls would pick up, "You don't yell as much as you used to, but we just don't feel as comfortable at your house." Ellen had managed to rearrange everyone's mood and attention.

Five-year-old Michael's questions about the visiting arrangements with his father would elicit elaborate explanations from his six- and seven-year-old siblings, Patty and David. Often even David, the acknowledged oldest and wisest, would falter in his understanding and then turn to his parents, "Why do we have to wait until afternoon to go to Dad's?" The parents then realized that they had just negotiated something nonsensical, and they had to revise it.

In a third family with three children, the Roberts family, the younger two children were ten-year-old twins, Randy and Omar. Despite the fact that they were veterans of conflict between their parents, and now a two-year bitter and unresolved custody dispute, the twins functioned in apparent oblivion, depending on the 15-year-old sister, Kathy, to interpret life for them. Kathy, whose own allegiances were clear to her and whose own future social life and career goals were already developing, was grounded in the family through her concern for her brothers. This was not a position she appeared to resent; it was a responsibility that she welcomed. It required the boys, however, to continue to be naive.

Thus, single children have to take care of themselves or rely on adults to do so. Sibling pairs can balance relationships between them; when there are three sibs, the youngest often functions as a baby, eliciting caretaking and explanatory functions from his or her older siblings. These are some of the patterns of taking care of each other.

Taking Care of Themselves

For many single children in a divorce situation, taking care of themselves is almost synonymous with taking care of the family. These children are often overdressed, overindulged, and overstimulated. They are precocious, cute, and often extremely socially precocious with adults. Harry, at three years old, is a special example. A perfectly adorable child, Harry was verbal, articulate, and, without being a genius, able to do many things with the skill of a five- or six-year-old. He could write his name, draw a person with all body parts, and play such games as checkers. An interesting contextual experiment demonstrated that Harry's highest skill level was entirely in relationship to his mother. Even in his mother's presence, Harry could not perform at the same level of excellence for his father or for me that he had for her. Thus, the single child's accomplishments in many cases are tied to the relationship with a parent or both parents.

Lest it be thought that I am deriving my opinion only from Harry, let me mention Tom, aged 11, who was socially gauche, an outcast with his peers, but a computer genius. He enjoyed the rather terrible relationship with both of his parents of pretending to dominate them with his superior intellect. Or, how about Richard, who at 12 had been living with his mother for 11 years and who despite his superior intelligence did extremely poorly in school and had poor social relationships. The overall effect was that he had an almost exclusive relationship with his mother and his maternal grandparents. When there is only one child, as we have said, the attention of the family and concern is focused on this one and the child is likely to be so drawn into the family struggles that there is little energy left over for relating to school and friends. Harry, the angelic three-year-old, was a concern to his daycare teachers because he did not socialize, a fact that both bothered his mother and gladdened her heart, assuring her she was the only one he really needed.

Siblings have a very different pattern of personal development. They may be indulged and attempts may be made to "buy" their affections for one side or the other. But because of the built-in system of checking things out with one another, and perhaps because of having each other to interpret the world outside the family, they usually appear to be less tied to their parents than their only child counterparts.

Cathy, aged 13, was living with her father, while her older brother Joe lived with their mother in another state. Cathy stated that she stayed with her father because she felt sorry for him. On the other hand, she maintained frequent telephone contact with Joe. Joe had gotten into some legal trouble and was on very bad terms with the father. Cathy, on the other hand, was on good terms with the father.

Nevertheless, the contact with Joe seemed to help Cathy evaluate herself in relation to her peers, something her father could not help her to do. Her conversations with Joe also helped her to focus more on her friends as a source of interest and support, helping to move her out of the rather still environment of her home.

Sally Kelly, mentioned above, first came to my office when she was just under five years old. In our first visit, she sat in my office with older sister Karen and her mother. She paid no apparent attention to our conversation, but concentrated on forming colorful, neat rows of letters and writing the words she knew. Later, when I saw her in my office alone, she asked me how to spell certain words, which she then wrote. She absolutely refused to discuss her family situation, but enjoyed a drawing game that allowed her to demonstrate her competence in this area. Two years later it was reported that Sally had, in a moment of upset, confessed to her father than she had to save money to buy herself a house, because no one was going to take care of her. This story confirmed my impression of Sally's way of coping with the discord in her family. She was trying to make herself self-sufficient. Sally's relationship with her sister was both differentiated and close; her school performance was exemplary, and she had many friends.

Of course, having siblings does not protect a child from difficulty. Megan, aged seven, had some serious learning and coordination problems which seemed to exaggerate the differences between herself and her perfect adopted brother, Paul, aged four. The learning problems were the focus of a custody battle, and the proper intervention was delayed in the competition between the parents to do the right thing. Nevertheless, when there are siblings, children are usually freer to take care of themselves in areas outside the family.

CHILDREN OF DIVORCE GROWN UP: WHAT CAN HAPPEN

I have followed some of the families in my informal sample for almost 15 years. Many of the children have grown up and, as they have moved into a more differentiated phase of their own lives, have left the divorce and custody bitterness behind. Wallerstein (1985) comments on the pervasive sadness and persistent dysfunction in the children of divorce on ten-year follow-up. She also comments that in a subgroup of families the most enduring relationships were among siblings, and that these relationships survived the pulls of adolescence and young adulthood. I did not find either pervasive sadness or an unusually persistent sibling attachment with the young adults whose families had undergone a divorce. One youngster, Marcy, told her stepmother than she felt relieved that her parents had divorced, because both of them were more bearable, especially after they had remarried. Marcy, the oldest of three, married in her mid-twenties and appears to have a very solid start on her adult life. She is still close to both of her parents and her two siblings, in spite of the fact that all three have gone their own ways in their adult lives. Marcy's family fortunately did not have continuing bitterness after the divorce.

Of the clinical sample, two pairs of brothers discussed previously, Eddie and Marty, and Ron and Teddy, have both grown up. Despite the rocky adolescence of the boys, which did seem to have been exacerbated by ongoing conflict between their parents, their young adult years found them settling down, finding direction for themselves and making their own separate relationships with their parents. This same period found Ron and Teddy, who were temperamentally very different, drifting apart into their own kinds of lives.

> When Peter and Midge grew up they grew apart from one another into their own relationships. When they reflect back on their lives, the divorce of their parents more than 40 years ago was one event in their lives whose ultimate significance was to expand the numbers of significant family members in their system and to increase the amount of travel they had done and their sense of confidence and autonomy. The effects of the divorce itself are indistinguishable from effects of moves, relationships with different teachers, the ultimate interaction of personality, style, and skills with each of their environments.
>
> While Peter and Midge had been so close and mutually dependent as young children, and while this mutual dependence increased each time the family moved, as adults they were so different that people were often surprised to learn that they were siblings. One might imagine that having gone through an experience like divorce together, they would be exceptionally close, but they weren't.
>
> Peter and Midge were very different kinds of people. It is not surprising that their lives took divergent courses. Their relationships with family members were different. Peter was exceptionally close to his mother and to his paternal grandmother, while Midge made a separate truce with their father. Peter continued to be scholarly and intellectual, and while he had many friends, he remained single and led a somewhat

monastic life. Midge married, had children, and expressed her gregarious curiosity in people through her work in human services.

When they spent time together, they were pleased by the familiarity of each other, but were often surprised at their very different views of their own family and their history. Indeed, more than 40 years after their parents' divorce, Midge and Peter were not unlike most adult siblings with a sector of shared experience but the largest portions of their lives being mutually independent.

THERAPEUTIC IMPLICATIONS

In describing some of the ways that children manage in divorce, I have taken the position that often mental health professionals intervene because they have made a judgment about the effectiveness of family members' ability to manage the family relationships and get on with their own personal business. Many parents seek counseling for their children simply because there is a divorce. There is no question that the changes involved in the process of divorce are challenging for all family members, but that does not mean that they will fail to meet the challenge. In most cases they do not. We have seen some of the ways that children, especially those with siblings, even siblings of entirely different temperament, cope. We have also seen some of the outcomes of these coping mechanisms. This information should encourage therapists who consult to divorcing families to pause before making a judgment. Ask the kids how they are doing, rather than how they are failing. Ask them what kinds of arrangements they've made, what works, and if they have any complaints they think anyone can do something about. Build on the kinds of solutions the children have already put into place. Work from the direction of children influencing parents as well as parents influencing children. These are the things that I have learned from the children of divorce so far. As I continue to see them, I will learn more — there is no doubt about it.

REFERENCES

Bank, S., & Kahn, M. (1975). Sisterhood-brotherhood is powerful: Sibling subsystems and family therapy. *Family Process, 14*, 311–337.
Boszormenyi-Nagy, I., & Spark, G. (1984). *Invisible loyalties*. New York: Brunner/Mazel.

Eno, M. (1985). Sibling relationships in families of divorce. *Divorce Therapy*, 139–156.

Isaacs, M. B., Montalvo, B., & Abelsohn, D. (1986). *The difficult divorce*. New York: Basic Books.

Koo, H. P., Sachindran, C. M., & Griffith, J. D. (1984). The effects of children on divorce and re-marriage: A multivariate analysis. *Population Studies, 38*(3), 451–471.

Lewis, K. G. (1986). Sibling therapy with children in foster homes. In L. Combrinck-Graham (Ed.), *Treating young children in family therapy*. Rockville, MD: Aspen.

Steinman, S. (1981). The experience of children in a joint-custody arrangement: A report of a study. *American Journal of Orthopsychiatry, 51*(3), 403–414.

Steinman, S., Zemmelman, S. E., & Knoblaugh, T. M. (1985). A study of parents who sought joint custody following divorce: Who reaches agreement and sustains joint custody and who returns to court. *Journal of the American Academy of Child Psychiatry, 24*(5), 554–562.

Toman, W. (1969). *Family constellation* (2nd ed). New York: Springer.

Wallerstein, J. S. (1985). Children of divorce: Preliminary report of a ten-year follow-up of older children and adolescents. *Journal of the American Academy of Child Psychiatry, 24*(5), 545–553.

10

Stepsiblings in Therapy

Elinor Rosenberg

THE REMARRIED FAMILY CONTEXT

The growing population of remarried families and their highly tenuous nature have contributed to the increasing recognition of the ambiguousness of steprelationships and of the lack of universally agreed-upon norms governing them. Clinicians are now aware that the developmental tasks of remarried family members differ from those of the intact family; however, it is not yet possible to define what the "normal" remarried family should be. How are stepparents different from biological parents? What feelings and responsibilities should they have for their stepchildren? What is a "normal" stepsibling relationship? Is the goal to be just like a biological brother or sister or is it to be more like a friend or a cousin?

Cherlin (1978) claims that such ambiguity and confusion arise from an "incomplete institution," that is, one that does not have agreed-upon typical behavior and guidelines for solving common problems of family life. He sees the remarried family as struggling without norms embedded in the law and culture of society. Cherlin gives as an example the fact that in all states there are laws governing marriage and sexual relationships between blood relatives, but many states do not have legal barriers to such relationships between stepparents and stepchildren or between stepsiblings. Even language is inadequate, as the "step" prefix originally referred to a replacement for a dead parent, not for the more common divorced one (Bohannan, 1963).

Each family struggles with this ambiguity in its own way. The struggle is aggravated by popular mythology. At one extreme is the wicked stepmother of the fairy tales (e.g., Cinderella's misfortune). At the other extreme is the idealized television family ("The Brady Bunch"). In the absence of clear norms, expectations, and guidelines, and in the face of such mythology, members of the remarried family operate with the hope that they will achieve a happy, healthy family the second time around. The fear of "failing" once again haunts many remarried families as they struggle to achieve a satisfactory cohesiveness.

The remarried family differs from the intact family in its structure and in its developmental course. The shift in structure evolves, for example, from two intact two-parent households, to separate one-parent households with a wide range of contact and quality of relationships, and then to a remarried family. Wallerstein (1983) describes tasks for children during the first shift as unfolding in a sequence: (1) acknowledging the reality of the marital rupture; (2) disengaging from parental conflict and distress and resuming customary pursuits; (3) accepting the permanence of divorce; and (4) achieving realistic hope regarding future relationships. Similarly, divorcing adults go through phases related to responsibilities for the decision to divorce—mourning the loss of the intact family and rebuilding family structure and relationships.

McGoldrick and Carter (1980) delineate four developmental issues for the second shift to the remarried family: (1) restructuring family boundaries to allow for inclusion of the new spouse-stepparent; (2) realigning and interweaving relationships in the various subsystems; (3) making room for relationships of all children with noncustodial parents, grandparents, and other extended family; and (4) sharing memories and histories to enhance stepfamily integration. Thus, for all family members, entering into a remarried family requires revisiting the "old business" of the original family, opening to new relationships and new traditions, and ultimately accepting a different model of family with permeable boundaries allowing for the preservation of the old bonds while making room for new ones (Kleinman, Rosenberg, and Whiteside, 1979).

Since divorce and remarriage can occur at any of the stages of the life cycle after marriage, the tasks of divorce and remarriage will interact with the expected and normal tasks of the existing life cycle phase and will have varying effects. A divorce occurring at the stage of "family with young children" will create very different issues than will divorce at the stage of "the family in later life." Similarly, the issues in a remarriage involving young children will be very different from those in a family with adolescents, where joining a family and being "harmonious" may be contrary to the adolescents' need to begin separating from parents. The wide variation of circumstances and the complexity of stepfamily issues, coupled with the ambiguity of roles, functions and boundaries, make each family's struggle a unique one.

Crises in remarried families emerge at various stages of family life, from the premarital stage to later years. Occasionally the family refers itself with a complaint, "we are having trouble bringing two families together." More commonly, one or more children are referred as identified patients, with the feeling that this child or these children are causing the family "trouble," i.e., they are threatening the stability of the new family. Remarried families cite problems with children as their primary difficulty, while intact families rate financial stress as their most difficult problem (Duberman, 1975). The major works on remarried families (Sager et al., 1983; Visher and Visher, 1979; Wald, 1981) have delineated a number of dimensions to help us understand the remarried family. They have examined the biological, structural, legal, cultural, and developmental aspects of remarriage and have noted that "pseudomutuality" and detouring of conflict often occur. Because the new spouses are usually afraid of marital turmoil and a second failure, their conflicts can go underground and be detoured to an available child. There is also considerable discussion in the literature of the relationship between stepparent (particularly stepmother) and child and alliances along biological lines. While fighting among sibling groups is frequently cited as a significant family problem in the remarried family, the literature pays almost no attention to the stepsibling subgroup per se, and there is little available literature on therapy with the stepsibling subgroup (Rosenberg, 1980). This is consistent with the traditional omission of the sibling subgroup in clinical literature (Bank and Kahn, 1982).

CHARACTERISTICS OF STEPSIBLING RELATIONSHIPS

Children approach the new marriage of their parents with a wide range of needs and expectations. At one extreme are those who look to the new family to fill unmet needs, hoping it will be a source of increased gratification. At the other extreme are those who are concerned about losing what they already have, who fear the effects of replacement, and who see the new family as an interference with their health and welfare. They do not look forward to becoming a stepsibling.

Stepsibling relationships: (1) are instantaneous, (2) lack a shared family history, (3) bring into the new family common experience of loss of the original family, (4) are bound to face complex sets of conflicting loyalties, (5) have fluid boundaries, (6) may involve shifts in sibling position roles and functions, (7) will inevitably be part of an abrupt change in family size, (8) may have to deal with complicated sexual boundary issues, and (9) may have to confront incongruity between the individual life cycle and the family life cycle. Let's look at some of the issues in each of these areas.

(1) *Instantaneous relationships:* While stepsibs may have had an opportunity to meet and get to know each other while their parents courted, they have not had the experience of adapting and accommodating to each other over years of individual and family development. "How should I know she didn't like to be tickled?" asked one girl about her stepsister. Tickling had been an affectionate way of interacting with her own biological sister. Previous experience with siblings may help or hinder new stepsibling relationships. In families where the parents had secretly or only briefly dated, the stepsibs may be strangers to one another. Or, as happens in small towns, the stepsibs may know each all too well—as classmates, even as class enemies.

(2) *Lack of shared family history:* Stepsiblings do not have years of family history to anchor their family life. Customs, values, and family styles differ, requiring tolerance and accommodation. One young girl was irate to find that her new stepmother used cake mixes; in her original family cakes were made only "from scratch" and she found this new practice totally unacceptable. Standbys and features of the old family, once taken for granted, often become obsolete. Their loss may be colored by longings for the past.

(3) *Common experiences of loss of the original family:* A commonality shared by stepsiblings is loss of the original family. The children struggle with feelings about the past—real and idealized. They process the loss in their own way, looking to relieve themselves of the sense of guilt and responsibility accompanying the divorce or death of a parent. One common defense is to turn guilt into blame; a

stepsibling subsystem then becomes a potential arena for conflict. "If you hadn't spilled your milk he wouldn't have left." "You made me spill my milk." In metaphorical forms this dialogue continued for years following the breakup of one family. When the mother remarried, the siblings carried the argument into the remarried family. Stepsiblings then became new objects responsible for "spilled milk." Children may also fear yet another loss if this new family does not survive, sometimes blaming Mom or Dad for having made a "botch" of it once again.

(4) *Conflicting loyalties:* In every remarried household there are at least three families—his old family, her old family, and the new family with its various extensions. Stepsiblings are asked to make room for each other's heritage and loyalties to the past while at the same time making room for the present. "We open Christmas presents on Christmas Eve"—"Well, we open ours on Christmas day" is an exchange which reflects the conflict of family traditions and loyalties. Children may find it very difficult to compromise to meet the needs of the new family. In addition, family members living outside the household continue to exert a strong pull, which sometimes stresses the bonds developing within the household.

(5) *Fluid boundaries:* Depending on custody and visitation agreements, there may be frequent shifts in household memberships, sleeping arrangements, mealtimes, rituals, and accommodations. Stepsiblings can find themselves spending more time with each other than with biological siblings living in another household. Relationships can be interrupted on a daily, weekly, monthly, or yearly basis. "I never know who's going to be sharing my bedroom or who will show up at dinner," complained one eight-year-old in a family where siblings and stepsiblings visited on staggered schedules. Flexibility is required for the many entrances and exits common in the stepsibling group.

(6) *Shifts in sibling position, role and functions:* After years in particular positions and roles in the sibling group, children may find themselves confronted with a new gender ratio or ordinal position in the stepsibling group. The oldest, youngest or only child can be displaced. One may no longer be the only girl or boy. It's hard to predict which changes will be experienced as good or bad, as each spot has its privileges and burdens. "I used to be in charge of the trash," complained a formerly oldest boy now relegated to "inside

work." A previously parentified child may find it particularly difficult to surrender that position to an older stepsibling, even if the attendant responsibilities had been burdensome.

(7) *Abrupt change in family size:* Remarriage means consolidating and sharing common economic and emotional resources. In some families the event may improve the standard of living; in others there may be a sense of giving up already meager resources. Frequently one family moves into the other family's house, requiring an adjustment of space allotment and of turf. "She never forgave me for taking up half of her room," said one young woman of her stepsister years after she had left home. Others might welcome the companionship. Issues of fairness so universal in sibling relationships can be even more sensitive in the stepsibling group.

(8) *Sexual issues:* The trustworthiness of intact families are guided by incest taboos, as members deal with feelings of attraction towards each other. Remarried families do not have this advantage; moreover, what is legally considered incestuous is ambiguous. At one extreme are stepsiblings who have been raised together from early childhood and whose experience closely replicates that of biological siblings. At the other extreme may be an 18-year-old boy and an 18-year-old girl whose parents marry. Are they then forbidden from being boyfriend and girlfriend? One 15-year-old girl became very involved in her girlfriends' crushes on her stepbrother and served as an excited messenger with their love notes and phone calls. This was a thinly disguised expression of her own attraction to him. Combining unrelated children of the opposite sex is likely to stir up sexual conflicts, particularly during adolescence. Ambiguity and lack of guidelines can loosen sexual boundaries and make things uncomfortable for all family members.

(9) *Incongruity between individual life cycle tasks and family life cycle tasks:* In the life cycle of the intact family, there are natural patterns of attachment and separation. The remarried family may represent attachment at a time in a child's life when the task is to separate. While the remarried family needs its members to pull together, an adolescent needs to establish an identity apart from the family. One father was very angry at his 17-year-old son for "never being home" (and thus not helping this new family blend), when the boy's activities would have been totally accepted and supported in an

intact family. With help, the parents recognized the regressive pull and readjusted their expectations so that the family's developmental needs no longer interfered with the adolescent's.

THERAPEUTIC APPROACHES

Family therapists generally agree on the principles of interventions with remarried families (McGoldrick and Carter, 1980; Sager et al., 1983; Visher and Visher, 1979; Wald, 1981): The dynamics of the individual and the family system must be understood; interventions should focus on blending two original families into one remarried family; and issues should be framed in a context of normal (non-pathological) tasks that are different from the life cycle tasks of the intact family. Realistic goals should be set to confront such common myths as instant love, wicked stepmother, "step is the same" or "step is less"; attachments to the past and differences between step and biological relationships must be validated. Although literature shows support for the marital and parental subgroup, the needs of the sibling subgroup are seldom addressed.

The structure and function of the stepsibling subgroup will reflect the ways the above described characteristics interact and become organized. If conflict and tension about the new marriage are intense, the stepsibling group can functionally collude to sabotage the new relationship. If the new arrangement meets the stepsibling's needs, the group can organize to support the new union—with the hope of permanency. What becomes apparent is that there are significant issues around being a stepsibling that need to be dealt with in any remarried family and that the sibling subgroup—whether supportive or sabotaging—is a potentially powerful force with a significant influence on the new family's stability. There are times when therapy with this stepsibling subgroup is a crucial systems intervention.

The indications for stepsibling therapy are similar to those described by Bank and Kahn (1982) in recommending sibling therapy: (1) when the stepsibling relationship hinders development; (2) when it creates conflict and difficulty; (3) when it destabilizes the family; and/or (4) when it causes psychological damage. Seeing the children from the two original families—without parents—supports structural change and promotes blending. It is a move away from "his children" and "her children," underscoring "we children." Excluding the parents from the stepsibling subgroup emphasizes the commonality of problems for children of a remarried family. This can become a potential support group; for adolescents the group gives them a way to join the family while they separate from parents.

THE PARKERS:
A FAMILY WITH LATENCY AGED CHILDREN

Mrs. Parker referred her ten-year-old stepson, Tommy, for evaluation two months after her marriage to Mr. Parker. She hoped that treatment would be as useful to him as it had been to her own ten-year-old daughter following her divorce five years earlier. This was a second marriage for both Mr. and Mrs. Parker. Mrs. Parker's first husband had remarried and lived within walking distance. Mr. Parker's first wife had abandoned the family when the youngest child was an infant and had not been heard from since. The remarried household now included Mrs. Parker and her three daughters, ages six, seven, and ten, and Mr. Parker and his three sons, ages five, ten, and eleven (see Figure 1).

The couple had met through Tommy's friendship with Mrs. Parker's daughter Susie; they had been sweethearts and were still "going together" when Mr. and Mrs. Parker married. While the nature of the relationship of these ten-year-olds generally seemed age-appropriate, there may have been an overdetermined quality to it as they modeled a wish for parents to "get together." At the time of referral Mr. and Mrs. Parker complained that Tommy's behavior at home and school was disruptive and was ruining the family. He reportedly provoked a great deal of fighting in the stepsibling group. There already was a tendency for Mr. Parker to defend "his boys" and for Mrs. Parker to defend "her girls."

After an individual evaluation of Tommy and a family evaluation, the therapist reframed Tommy's problem as difficulty in bringing two families together, suggesting that the family could use help in forming a new unit. The interpretation itself seemed to have a therapeutic effect. That is, the evaluator's statement that it was natural for families to have difficulty coming together seemed to have the effect of legitimizing the struggle and allowing them to work on it overtly.

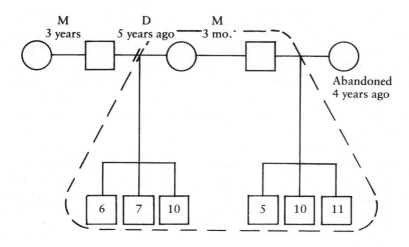

FIGURE 1
Parker Family

The family accepted a recommendation for weekly stepsibling sessions and weekly parental sessions to be reassessed after 20 weeks. An agreement was made that the stepsibling group sessions would require confidentiality of all its members. The therapists, however, were not confined by confidentiality and could share information at their own discretion. The family was treated by a male-female cotherapy team. It was hoped that the cotherapy relationship would be used as a model of conflict resolution without "divorce" and would provide family members with gender-related identity figures.

The criteria for sibling therapy were met: Tommy's and Susie's relationship, now as stepsiblings, was hindering their development; it was creating conflict and destabilizing the family and was in danger of causing psychological damage. The new family was splitting down original family lines, with Mrs. Parker and her girls on one side and Mr. Parker and his boys on the other side. Each subgroup was hanging on to old family traditions and alliances and seeing the new family as a threat to the integrity of the old family.

In the beginning of therapy the stepsibling group focused on past losses, the absent parents, and fantasies about the good old days.

Mrs. Parker's daughters spoke of how much better it had been, that is, how many more privileges they had had when they lived in the single-parent household before the boys moved in and new rules had been established to incorporate more people. Mr. Parker's sons expressed discomfort at living in "her" house and longings for their old neighborhood. Ghosts of absent parents flickered in and out. A common experience for each sibling group was resolution of conflict through separation and loss.

The issue of loss was a particularly poignant one for the boys, as their mother had abandoned them when the youngest was an infant. It is likely that Tommy's strong attachment to Susie as a girlfriend at such a young age was his way of holding onto a female (Bowlby, 1969). The primary theme of these early weeks was "Tommy is ruining our family and we all know that when families are ruined they break up."

The stepsibling subgroups were encouraged to describe their past history to each other. Photograph albums were shared. This process helped the boys discover that they all felt a similar pain around their mother's abandonment and feared that they would drive this stepmother away as well. Each worried he was the one who had driven her off and defended against that fear by blaming another. Over two to three months, they stopped blaming and decided it was no one's fault. The girls were empathic with the boys' pain and were willing to allow their mother to also mother the boys.

With some resolution of issues related to the past, the children began to focus on the present. One issue was the family's nameplate. The oldest boy was planning to make a signpost in his shop class, and there was intense discussion about which name would be used and where it would be placed in the house. Would it replace Mrs. Parker's sign with the previous family name her girls retained, or would there be two name signs instead? By the fifteenth week of treatment the sign problem had been solved. There would be two signs—each with an original family name. One would be hung on the front porch; one would be hung on the inner porch. The names would alternate each year. There was notable unity among the children on this resolution. Their ability to agree was an indication that the house was beginning to be seen as a home for everyone.

Tommy and Susie's relationship was an ongoing issue in the family.

They still considered themselves boyfriend and girlfriend, but living together in the same house was complicated. This dilemma was regularly validated by the therapist's saying such things as, "It's hard to be boyfriend and girlfriend as well as stepsiblings." "It's also hard to have a mom and dad whom you first knew as boyfriend and girlfriend rather than the readymade parents one has upon birth." Overt validation and discussion seemed to cool things to a more comfortable and tolerable level.

Work with the parents focused on similar issues from the past and on learning to be stepparents. The cotherapists supported the parents as they struggled with the ambiguities facing them. For example, they wondered how much "romantic" behavior they should allow between Tommy and Susie: holding hands watching TV? kissing at bedtime? The therapists raised the parallel issue of the newly married parents' romantic relationship. What affectionate behavior between them was appropriate in the family? Exploration of the issues supported the parents in the kind of trial-and-error process common in any new family form.

After 20 weeks of therapy, behavior in the stepsibling sessions reflected alliances across the original family lines. "His kids" and "her kids" were now feeling more like "the kids." The family was now seen altogether for several sessions, during which there were the typical struggles between parents and children — children seeking more favors and privileges, parents encouraging more responsibility and maturity. They seemed to be coping with the problems seen in all families. The belief that conflict leads to breakup had been disproved. Tommy's idea that he was a bad kid who drives mothers away was also disproved. Termination was completed. A follow-up session several months later found the family continuing to do well and enthusiastic about an upcoming family camping trip.

Over the course of the next eight years Mr. and Mrs. Parker consulted with the therapists at different developmental bumps in the family's life. Different children were seen for brief interventions. At age 17, Tommy reflected to the therapist, "Boy, that was weird. One day she was my girlfriend, the next day she was my sister."

This case illustrates the characteristics common in stepsibling relationships described above, as well as the group dynamics and the way the sibling subgroup can be focused upon as part of a therapeutic intervention.

Before Mr. and Mrs. Parker married, Tommy and Susie had been managing an appropriate boyfriend/girlfriend relationship with parents offering effective limits. They were known at school as "liking each other," became partners in organized activities, and visited each other's supervised homes occasionally on weekends. With the marriage the family was confronted with the ambiguity of what was now a stepsibling relationship. The parents became worried and unsure of themselves. Tommy and Susie struggled with the tensions—sometimes with unified provocativeness and sometimes by fighting with each other, which functionally served to cool things off. The therapists worked with the siblings and with the parents to validate the difficulties of the family's ambiguity and to coach and support both parents and children to find more adaptive solutions.

In the meantime, all the children were struggling to make peace with their families of the past and their present family. The boys were in varying ways hungry for the affections of a stepmother yet fearful of another disappointment. Early fights between the boys and girls about the way things "should be" were handled by the therapists' accentuating the value of their differences and indicating how much they had to offer each other. The children eventually concluded that in spite of their differences they had many common interests. Time also played an important role, as the shock of being an instantaneous family gave way to the delights of getting to know each other and feeling more familiar and comfortable.

The girls' loyalty to their father sometimes conflicted with the sense of the new family and the way they treated Mr. Parker. At birthdays and holidays, for example, there was much tension around who would be where and what they would do. Holidays were also a time when the boys fantasized about their mother's return. Surely she would remember them on Christmas and at least call. Their disappointment at not having their fantasies realized was often displaced onto their stepmother, as they blamed her for not being the right kind of mother. They were angry, for example, when she was not available to give them a ride downtown—this *proved* she did not care about them. The therapists encouraged them to keep the right feelings with the right people and empathized with their understandable disappointment.

The abrupt change in family size from four to eight people meant a significant adjustment of resources. In some ways there was more and in some ways there was less. They had a mother home fulltime, rather than Mrs. Parker at work fulltime as she had been when single and the boys in charge of a string of questionable babysitters. They also had more income, as Mr. Parker worked overtime and Mrs. Parker received child support. On the other hand, they had less household space and a good deal of irritability about sharing. The therapists labeled this as a natural problem for all remarried families and encouraged their pioneering efforts to work it out through trial and error. Sometimes the female therapist served as a coach to the girls and the male therapist as a coach to the boys in negotiating space and boundaries. Coaches conferences were also held within the session to allow the children to observe a reasonable negotiation of significant differences between two non-quarreling adults. Mr. and Mrs. Parker began to model the cotherapists' way of negotiating.

Seeing the stepsibling subgroup separately facilitated the changes as the children worked on their own issues with each other without having to deal with or worry about their parents' reactions. The changes, however, could not have been made without concomitant parental work.

THE SMITHS—A FAMILY WITH ADOLESCENT CHILDREN

The Smith family is a dramatic example of an instantaneously formed remarried family. Mrs. Smith had been divorced for four years; Mr. Smith had been divorced for five years. Three years ago they married, forming a household with Mrs. Smith's son and two daughters. Mr. Smith's three boys remained with their mother in another city. There had been periodic phone calls with them but no visits of Mr. Smith's boys to father's new family as the new couple approached their third anniversary. At that time there emerged a crisis between Mr. Smith's boys and their mother. The boys were pushing curfew limits and their mother felt helpless in sustaining discipline. She decided that they needed the firm hand of their father. Quite precipitously a plan was made for all the boys to join the household. The household then became Mr. and Mrs. Smith, Michael Smith, 17, Sandy Ryan, 16, Robert Smith, 16, Jennie Ryan,

15, David Smith, 14, Daniel Ryan, 13, and Johnny Smith, 15 months (an "ours" child) (see Figure 2).

A few months after the boys had moved in Mrs. Smith sought help. At first she wanted most everyone to receive individual treatment, as each child seemed to be symptomatic. Michael was staying out late, Jennie was smoking with Robert in impermissible places, David had quit football, a longtime love; first report cards had arrived and none of the children was doing well. In addition, there was serious fighting among the siblings and stepsiblings. Everyone complained that belongings and privacy were not respected and there was a universal cry that parents were unfair in their demands and expectations.

In a full family evaluation session there appeared to be a number of battle lines drawn. Mr. and Mrs. Smith were finding themselves unable to manage a large group of children and alternately unified together against all the children and then aligned with their own biological children. Mr. Smith's boys joined forces and vented anger at their father, seemingly related to old hurts and disappointments. The children engaged in constant bickering, with overt hostility towards each other. Sometimes it was his kids against hers. At other times it was boys against girls. Only the "ours" child remained free of

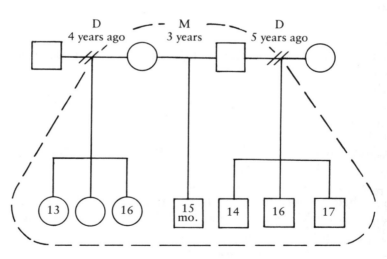

FIGURE 2
Smith Family

battalion assignment. As he wandered among the group, Johnny approached every family member and was responded to with caregiving play and/or affectionate gestures. He was the one person in the room biologically related to everyone and seemed to be the symbol of hope for the future of the family.

While the content of the assessment session was primarily complaints and disapproval, what also became apparent was the sexual tension and excitement in the room. There were coquettish looks, "footsies," and vague references to mischievous behavior. One early hypothesis was that the passionate fighting between the stepsiblings was a thinly disguised attraction. The teenagers did not know how to handle this attraction; the parents did not know how to handle the attraction.

The overall treatment plan presented to the family was for the family to meet together with a male and female cotherapy team and in various subgroups, in order to help the family come together and to manage its volatility. After three full family sessions where issues were labeled, it was decided to schedule meetings which paralleled the family's development. The original family groups met weekly back to back. Mrs. Smith and her children went over their past history, dealing with such issues as the causes of the divorce and her children's ongoing relationship with their father. Her two older daughters expressed resentment that their housekeeping and babysitting responsibilities had increased since the boys arrived; mother seemed reluctant to ask the boys to do their proper share.

Mr. Smith's boys were exploding with resentment towards their father for his past sins in their own home and for his distance since his new marriage. They called him to task for hurting their mother and for neglecting them. They were particularly hurt that he had not informed them that he was expecting a new child. Through these sessions Mr. Smith became aware of how much his sons wanted him. He realized that he had behaved like his own absent alcoholic father and that the past was being replayed unconsciously and powerfully.

After six weeks of therapy tensions between parents and children diminished, but conflict between the parents and within the stepsibling group persisted. A shift was made to weekly meetings with the couple and weekly meetings with the stepsibling group.

The stepsibling group was visibly vibrating with excitement and tension. There were the usual issues of remarried family adjustment—turf, allotment of space, and shifts in position and roles. These were labeled and validated. Problem-solving was similar to that described for the Parker family. The process of making the issues overt and normalizing them as part of remarried life seemed to reduce tension.

There was, however, still a palpable excitement in the group that would climax with little provocation. Finally the therapist spoke the unspeakable, "It must be hard to be living with people you might be dating if your parents hadn't married." This observation was at first responded to universally as the height of absurdity, producing gales of laughter and rolled eyes. Undaunted, the therapist acknowledged that they were all very attractive young men and women, close in age, with similar interests and activities. Why wouldn't they be attracted to each other? Effort was made again to label and validate their issues, but care was taken not to further stimulate the teenagers' sexual feelings towards each other. For example, they were not encouraged to describe the extent of their attractive feelings toward each other or to express their fantasies (which might have had the effect of heating up rather than cooling down the atmosphere of the group). Displacement was also used by describing other stepsiblings the therapists had worked with and how they had managed their attraction towards each other.

These issues were also discussed with the parents, so that they could provide as much support and structure as possible. For example, guidelines about modesty and bedroom and bathroom privacy were established. In the process, the parents too came to acknowledge and accept the sexual issues around unrelated people living together.

As the sexual issues in the group were addressed, the earlier tension and fighting seemed to diminish. After 20 weeks of therapy the boys reported that the girls did not "bother them" anymore; that was understood as a metaphor for their feeling in control of their impulses.

Another major issue in this family concerned joining and belonging. Once the initial shock of the instant family was past, the parents—in particular—became committed to the development of a more cohesive family. This commitment came at a time when the 16- and 17-year-olds were working towards separation. The oldest boy, for example, was spending many of his waking hours away from home, working and visiting with friends. The parents experienced this as his resistance to the new family and persistently expressed their dissatisfaction. The other teenagers supported him as he paved the way for them. The therapists commented to both siblings and parents, "It is hard to be asked to join a new family when you are feeling ready to leave all families and be on your own." This intervention appeared to help the children feel more comfortable with age-appropriate behavior and to help the parents see the pulling away as normal and healthy rather than resistant and oppositional.

The final month of treatment included weekly full family sessions. The therapists began to feel obsolete as the parents assumed more of the executive functions and the family dealt more effectively with its own business.

This case illustrates many of the issues related to a remarried family with adolescents and the way work with the sibling group can be crucial to the individual and family functioning. It is unlikely that the conflicts common to the stepsiblings could have been dealt with as effectively in full family meetings. The separate group provided a safer context in which to explore touchy subjects. The process and structure also contributed to a more positive cohesion across original family lines, allowing the family to come together appropriately as a remarried family with adolescent children.

SUMMARY AND CONCLUSIONS

Clinicians are becoming increasingly aware of the ambiguities with which remarried families must struggle. Each family must make its own relationships rules. Stepsibling relationships have tended to be an overlooked aspect of remarried family life. With closer attention to these relationships we see some particular ways in which stepsiblings may present difficulties—individually and as a subgroup—in forming a remarried family. The stepsibling subgroup is a logical focus of therapeutic intervention. In this group common issues can be identified, validated, and worked with without the complications of having to deal with parental reactions.

The two clinical examples illustrate how these issues are related to ages and stages of development. Younger children are more likely to be struggling with attachment. As they try to relate to two households, they tend to fear that having one means losing the other. If they accept (and attach to) a stepparent, does this mean they will lose a biological parent? If they become friends with a stepsibling, will they lose their own biological sibling? Adolescents struggle with issues of identity, sexuality and separation. The formation of a remarried family can complicate these struggles. To the question of "Who am I?" is added "Who am I now in this new family?" Sexuality can be overstimulated by the presence of unrelated people in the household. Also, an adolescent "on his way out" can find it difficult to be asked to join a new family.

While there is a clear structural advantage to separating the family across the generational boundary and thus encouraging a blending of the original families, it must be emphasized that work with the stepsibling subgroup, even when it is only a temporary part of the total treatment plan, must always be accompanied by work with the parents. While parents think their children will speak more freely when they are not present, they may also worry about what is being said about them. There may also be a concern, particularly with a cotherapy couple, that the therapists will become the "good parents" to the sibling group. Separate ongoing work with parents provides an opportunity for these concerns to surface and for the therapists to offer support to the parents. Therapists may act as coaches to this new (and usually insecure) parental partnership.

As clinicians work with remarried families, they increase their awareness of the special tasks facing stepsiblings and the potential power of the stepsibling subgroup. In doing so, they add to their resources for understanding and helping remarried families in the development of a happier, healthier family the second time around.

REFERENCES

Bank, S., & Kahn, M. (1982). *The sibling bond*. New York: Basic Books.
Bohannan, P. (1963). *Social anthropology*. New York: Holt, Rinehart & Winston.
Bowlby, J. (1969). *Attachment and loss*. New York: Basic Books.
Cherlin, A. (1981). *Marriage, divorce, remarriage*. Cambridge: Harvard University Press.
Cherlin, A. (1978). Remarriage as an incomplete institution. *American Journal of Sociology, 84*, 634–650.
Duberman, L. (1975). *The reconstituted family*. Chicago: Nelson-Hall.
Kleinman, J., Rosenberg, E., & Whiteside, M. (1979). Common developmental tasks of forming reconstituted families. *Journal of Marital and Family Therapy, 4*, 79–88.

McGoldrick, M., & Carter, E. (1980). Forming a remarried family. In E. A. Carter & M. McGoldrick (Eds.), *The Family Life Cycle*. New York: Gardner Press.

Rosenberg, E. (1980). Therapy with siblings in reorganizing families. *International Journal of Family Therapy*, 2(3), 139–150.

Rosenberg, E., & Hajal, F. (1985). Stepsibling relationships in remarried families. *Social Casework*, 5, 287–292.

Sager, C., Brown, H., Crohn, H., Engel, T., Rodstein, E., & Walker, L. (1983). *Treating the remarried family*. New York: Brunner/Mazel.

Visher, E., & Visher, J. (1979). *Stepfamilies*. New York: Brunner/Mazel.

Wald, E. (1981). *The remarried family*. New York: Family Service Association of America.

Wallerstein, J. (1983). Children of divorce: The psychological tasks of the child. *American Journal of Orthopsychiatry*, 58, 2.

11

Children of Alcoholics: Their Sibling World

Rosalie C. Jesse

Alcoholism presents a special blend of intrapersonal and familial contradictions. We are scarcely beginning to sort through these, let alone accurately apportion causal relationships. For years, individuals afflicted by alcoholism were viewed rather disdainfully by mental health treatment professionals. Influenced by the psychoanalytic explanation of the alcoholic's primitive oral character structure, prognosticators were pessimistic. Finally, during the 1970s, the family systems thinkers began to announce the fact that, in most instances—before an alcoholic landed on skidrow—there were *other people* who affected and were affected by the alcoholic.

Voila! In alcoholism treatment circles, at least, the age of systemic thinking had begun. As the spouse of the alcoholic was introduced to treatment, there were vague rumblings in the background. But few treatment facilities then accepted the notion that a mere child could make the kind of noise that should be taken seriously. (The Children of Alcoholics (COA) movement was not even launched until the 1980s!)

Today it is difficult to imagine back to the time when there was no COA influence upon our thinking. Perhaps no other mental health effort has spread so quickly and so pervasively. This is largely attributable to such crusading groups as the National Association of Children of Alcoholics, who have drawn attention to themselves and to the plight of other still suffering COA's. Let us note, with interest, that with all this talk about and from children of alcoholics, we hear very little about their *siblings*. . . .

EVOLVING THOUGHTS ON SIBLING RELATIONSHIPS
IN ALCOHOLIC FAMILIES

One of the first observers to write about sibling *relationships* in the alcoholic family was Canadian social worker, Margaret Cork (1969). Although Cork is not very often cited by COA commentators, she really is, in my opinion, *the* pioneer in the field. She was the first to call attention to the poignancy of younger children in her book, *The Forgotten Children*. In this seminal little work, Cork reports data from her unstructured interviews of 115 Toronto children from alcoholic families who were between the ages of 10 and 16 years. These children reported *intense sibling rivalries*: "In all age groups there was a keen awareness of family disunity and dissension and separation among brothers and sisters" (p. 27).

Older children who, of necessity, had assumed parental roles were resented by their juniors. Conversely, the apparent need of older children to dominate their juniors appeared to have arisen from deep feelings of frustration associated with their conflicting roles. Older children were jealous of the amount of attention their parents paid to younger siblings. Children who had formed an alliance with one parent against another also felt divided against their siblings.

What about a sibling *bond*?

Much earlier than Cork was Newell (1953), who claimed that exposure to parental alcoholism during the formative years of childhood presented the child with bewildering inconsistencies, antagonisms, and *interpersonal ambivalence*. Did this ambivalence which characterized the sibling relationships in the alcoholic home differ from so-called "normal" sibling rivalry and dissension?

From what I could observe among the alcoholic families with whom I worked during the early 1970s, children of alcoholics bore a resemblance in their sibling patterns to those described by Cork. Initially I had begun to see these children in a conjoint therapy modality. While viewing the alcoholic family from a systems perspective, the tendency was to disregard the child's intrapsychic functioning. However, I began to suspect that an exclusive systems approach was obscuring rather than clarifying the problem. After the alcoholic parent had been sober several months, a formerly quiescent child would begin to demonstrate increased behavioral and psychological problems. This phenomenon, which was later demonstrated empirically (Jesse, 1977), was stated, "The mere fact of parental abstinence does not seem to improve the life of the child." In some cases, the life of the child appeared to actually worsen with the parent's sobriety. These youngsters showed sudden, abrupt changes which were accompanied by bold, dramatic, acting-out behavior that frankly baffled their parents.

What was the child trying to communicate through such troubled conduct? If the recovery of the alcoholic parent did not significantly improve the life of the child, the disturbance in the child also increased family stress and thereby threatened the alcoholic parent's sobriety. The other siblings in the family, although showing less overt problems, were undoubtedly suffering inwardly, albeit silently.

My growing questions and concerns about the problems of these children and their siblings led to a gradual shift in therapeutic emphasis. I began to see problem children from different families together in small peer groups. When a child was admitted to a group, the sibling was admitted to the next group. The basic group intervention was to let the child find his place among his peers while the group process was used as the material of therapy. The influence of the group, rather than the dominance of the adult therapist, was believed important in facilitating behavior change and emotional development. Because the alcoholic families with whom I had been working had inherent problems with power and leadership, the assumption was that the children would function more adaptively in a group which did not emphasize adult authority.

Leader interventions were directed towards changing behaviors. It was believed that aggressive tendencies could be suppressed by evoking incompatible responses other than those directly based on fear and discomfort. By eliciting shared emotional responses within the group, a frustrated, aggressive child, for example, would become aware that other group members had had a comparable fate and were having similar emotional reactions. Thus, an increased affiliative mode was expected to develop.

The emphasis in group procedure was to leave group rules to the decision-making process of its members. The group work was based on talking rather than activity as a way of increasing the verbal rather than acting-out potential of the children. Although periodically special activities, such as group outings, were planned, the emphasis within the groups was always on group discussion. Particularly relevant to these group discussions was the clarification of a child's attitudes and values towards alcohol use. Thus, one important aspect of the leader's role was to serve as an educator, presenting basic information about the effects and consequences of alcohol abuse, exploring the child's attitudes towards alcohol and his parent's alcoholism and clearing up any misconceptions. A part of this focus was to help the child better understand the afflicted parent, as well as to alleviate the child's irrational guilt — "the bad me" incurred from parental abuse and derogation. Sibling relationships were expected to be strengthened as children became more self-accepting from the peer group culture. Children and their siblings would thereby derive greater benefit from their concurrent involvement in family therapy with the alcoholic parent, the co-alcoholic parent, and the siblings.

However, the problem within the groups was that the children had a tremendous amount of difficulty listening to each other or even showing concern for one another's problems. Problems in bondedness to peers as well as to siblings were apparent. From observation, sibling relationships appeared to be overflowing with aggression and a "me first" attitude.

The group was expected to serve as the psychotherapist, helping the child evaluate himself on critical attributes and offering a place among peers for interpersonal support and alliance. However, the group did *not* act as a psychotherapist. First, group cohesion simply did not develop. The children behaved as social isolates, and a great deal of acting-out occurred.

Contrary to expectation, the children seemed to derive the most observable benefit from planned outings where there were organized sports and games. These play activities seemed to provide the children with much needed tension reduction. Positive stimulation led to expressions of competence that increased self-esteem. The group discussions, on the other hand, seemed to arouse feelings of restlessness, boredom, and rivalry. Group rules were rarely heeded. Silliness and aggression were favorite mechanisms for gaining attention. The problems of these children of alcoholics did not appear amenable to peer group intervention. The children's reactions were not unlike those of siblings of drug-addicted adolescents who were treated in a group modality by Coleman (1978): "It is felt that the behavior of the group represents a microcosm of the youngster's internal environment the roots of which lie within the families' historical milieu. These developmentally produced defenses are still too rigid to penetrate. . . . It is still questionable if any internal pathology has been altered." (p. 125)

From the early peer groups of children of alcoholics, I was formulating questions, just as I had in the earlier family therapy experiences. In either context, I still did not understand a particular child's problems from the unique vantage point of that child. At the time, I did not fully understand the direction I was heading in terms of a therapeutic redefinition for children of alcoholics. But the developmental reality of the middle years of childhood — the psychological separateness of the world of children and the world of adults — seemed to be guiding my concern to the inner, personal world of the child.

To reach the child's inner, personal world it became necessary to traverse the psychological structure of latency. This structure is built upon cognitive skills which have to do with the consolidation of self-image and the manipulation of symbols. "Cognitive," according to Sarnoff (1987), is used in this context to mean "the way an individual organizes his perceptions of the world." This inner, personal world of the latency-aged child could best be understood by studying the child's cognitive perceptions.

As I began my early studies with symptomatic children of alcoholics and their siblings (Jesse, 1977), I interviewed parents and siblings, as well as the child, and obtained psychometric data from each child. Basic to the research was a developmental perspective which considered the child as the primary source of data. Although alcoholism was believed to generate a special type of interactional system where each individual was molded in subtle ways and the system itself became dynamic and self-perpetuating, the research interest was solely on the child within the matrix of that system. I believed that, even after the alcoholic parent has gained sobriety, the child's perception of alcoholic family roles and relationships would remain ubiquitous. The guiding theory for this position had been derived from George Kelly (1955), whose fundamental postulate was that a person's psychological processes are channeled by the ways in which he anticipates events. On the basis of the child's interpretations of past events, he was expected to develop a set of predictions about how he and others would behave in the future. Although these expectations might have little to do with the way the alcoholic parent was actually behaving during recovery, the child would continue to persist in a conceptualization of this parent as deviant.

Moreover, the child would continue to play a role in relation to each parent and sibling according to an already established understanding of interpersonal functioning derived from the period of active alcoholism. Even though this understanding might be minimal, fragmentary or misguided, the family equilibrium would thus be maintained during recovery while any change was resisted. An assessment of the child's responses to alcoholic family life thus became an assessment of the ways in which a child anticipated events and construed relationships.

The selection criteria for these children, ages seven to twelve, included that the child had lived with the alcoholic parent for at least two years prior to the parent's treatment for alcoholism. The impact of the final stage of untreated alcoholism on the child's perception of family relationships was the critical issue of the research.

An unstable family constellation was believed to govern systems functioning. This family configuration was one where the members would be segregated into isolated units rather than presented as an interconnected system of familial role figures.

Elsewhere (Jesse, 1977) I have described the advantages of family relationship analysis from the unique perspective of the child. Succinctly, the psychological separateness of the world of children and adults makes it very difficult to learn about a child's intrapsychic processes unless the appraisal is child-centered. Attempting to understand the immediate damage of alcoholic family life on the vulnerable self of the child should be the aim of treatment, research and prevention efforts. Otherwise, our interventions may have the diabolical effect of perpetuating the firmly established alcoholic system.

As I studied the family relationships of these children of alcoholics and their siblings, I was able to gather data for both empirical and projective analyses. The statistical method provided a quantitative measure which could be converted to a schematic mapping of each child's familial relationships and interpersonal attachments.

When the statistical analyses of the multiple role relationship clusterings for a particular child were completed, an aggregate data analysis was performed. Two important characteristics of an unstable family constellation were demonstrated: The child displayed a faulty self-identification and was either isolated from or in opposition to his parents. In the most disturbed families, the ability of the child to cognitively isolate the alcoholic parent from all other role figures was profound. This finding supports object relations views which see problems in parent-child bonding as interfering with a child's psychological development. This finding also attests to the stability of the child's perceptions of parental deviance even after the parent has gained sobriety.

Similar conclusions were drawn about the child's perception of deviance in both parents when the parents were presented as a dyadic cluster, as was the case in one-half of the children. When the parents were not clustered, there was no alignment of the child with the non-alcoholic parent. Or, in the separated families, none of the children was allied with the parent remaining in the home. Such dramatic findings stress the caveat that parental abstinence as a single factor does not strengthen the child's relatedness to parental role figures.

However, the unexpected finding of the study was evidence of a perceived *common bond* among siblings. Despite prominent evidence of isolation of certain siblings or opposition to other siblings, the unstable family constellation did not reflect a complete lack of sibling relatedness.

How can we better understand this sibling bond of the latency years in children of alcoholics?

At least during the middle years of childhood, children of alcoholics tend to develop a compensatory relationship with their siblings. Alienated by the threatening and bewildering interactions of their parents, children of alcoholics appear to derive at least some fragmentary support from their siblings. The implication for an only child within the alcoholic family is especially poignant. These lonely, confused youngsters have no type of compensatory support within the nuclear family. Siblings, however, are able to develop a system for coping. This compensatory system-within-a-system appears to be a direct outgrowth of, but does not completely satisfy the requirements for, the parent-child relationship.

To understand the relationship between lack of parental support and stress experienced by children of alcoholics, I examined the *actu-*

al and *preferred* support perceived by youngsters in the aforementioned subject pool (Jesse, 1977). A Stress Situation Test, adapted from Kelly (1955), was administered to the child as a card-sorting procedure. As the child discussed different stressful life situations, the cards were sorted from an array of family helpers, to include parents and siblings, as well as other societal helpers, into supportive and nonsupportive relationships. As these helpers were considered again, the child was asked to determine whom he might have preferred to provide support for each of the described stressful events.

An individual child's *actual* and *preferred* helpers were converted to a matrix of interassociations, and a cluster analysis performed. The statistical results demonstrated that children preferred significantly more assistance overall than they had received. When help had been provided by siblings, it was most often the case that older siblings provided assistance for younger siblings. Rarely did an older sibling report receiving or desiring assistance from a younger child during the instances when the older was experiencing stress. The only exception to this was the older's need for the younger to be compliant when the older had been acting in a parentified role. When younger children misbehaved, the older sibling seemed to experience considerable stress.

Of all societal helpers available to provide support, such as other relatives, teachers, clergy, physicians, counselors, etc., only the parents were preferred over siblings to provide that support for both older and younger siblings.

Content analysis of the stressful situations of children of alcoholics indicated that firstborn siblings often felt overwhelmed by their parenting responsibilities. Alongside their feelings of being overburdened was resentment towards younger siblings, who posed a threat of parental retribution. Often the firstborns encountered punishment for the infractions of their younger brothers and sisters.

Although younger siblings appeared to derive support from the older child-caretakers, there also were reports of harshness in discipline which amounted to physical abuse by the older siblings. Other forms of psychological abuse, such as vicious teasing, taunting, and harassing were reported. These interactions seemed to be a reflection of the type of sadistic interactions which were reported as having been observed in parental interactions.

For example, one child, an incest victim, aged 11, produced an assessment protocol filled with sadomasochistic themes. Her self-identification was most strongly associated with the "pitied" role figure of her dog. She explained this:

> My dog learned how to get over the back fence. One day when my Dad was drunk, the dog got out. My Dad went over and got her back and picked her up by the hair and threw her back over the fence so hard that she laid there and cried all day.

This same child, a firstborn, also reported her own intense feelings of rage, which were displaced onto her relationship with her younger sister, aged eight:

> One day when my sister kept on buggin' me, I grabbed her by the neck and almost choked her to death.

The younger sister, who had been a member of another sibling group, had reported the same incident as being the most distressing of her sibling interactions.

> One day my sister almost strangled me for not getting out of her room. I cried and cried all day because my neck hurt so bad.

Throughout the assessment of stressful situations in the lives of these children, there was a preponderance of reports of failures in parental empathy. Often, these failures seemed to induce as much — or more — stress and confusion in the children as actual physical abuse. Psychological cruelty among siblings during periods of family tension was a common report. Although the children seemed to rely on each other for support during family conflicts, these sibling helpers were not effective in assuaging the distress of their brothers and sisters.

SIBLING PREDICAMENTS IN LATENCY

Children of alcoholics appear particularly vulnerable to the effects of stress during the middle years of childhood. We are reminded by Sarnoff (1976) that the structure of latency is inadequate for dealing with intense stimulation from parental interactions. At such times, a child tends to become disorganized and excited in his behavior. Parental mistreatment of a child divests the child of his mature potential and infantilizes him. The more stress which is faced by the child, the more likely he is to display regressive and aggressive behavior. This regression to an oppositional, aggressive mode often masks the wish for further regression to a passive, dependent mode. These intrapsychic dynamics of a child have profound implications for family systems functioning.

During the last 10 years, as I have continued to work with children of alcoholics and their families, I have come to better understand their sibling predicament. While the perceived commonality among siblings seems to occur during the years of middle childhood, this relationship bond is tenuous. Adolescence often involves the rupture of that bond, which is not repaired, not even during adulthood. Many adult children of alcoholics report estrangement from the sibling attachments of their youth. The following retrospective account from a woman in her thirties describes the changes of the sibling relationship over time.

> Before the alcoholism of my parents got so bad, my brother and I would be arguing and fighting. But, after my mother left home and my Dad started coming home drunk every night on a tirade, my brother and I really clung to each other. We were only eight and ten, but we didn't have anyone else but each other. A lot of times I felt like I was his Mom. Except when our Dad would come home and start picking on him and beating him up, I'd just stand there and watch. I didn't dare open my mouth to even tell him to stop, or else I might be next. Finally, during my teens, when my Dad started molesting me, I couldn't take it anymore, so I split. My brother and I never got close again. I don't think we ever will. My brother drinks heavily now, and I guess he's an alcoholic, too. I can't stand to be around him. He reminds me of my Dad.

While these children seemed to rely on each other for support during times of stress, the majority of these sibling interactions were based on survival needs. It is questionable whether siblings from an alcoholic family are capable of providing each other with true empathy. Most often it is the crisis nature of parental interactions which brings the siblings together in supportive relating. Coleman (1978) has reported this same pattern among siblings of drug-addicted adolescents: "Except for their collusion in impulse expulsion and on rare occasions when severe trauma strikes, the sibs are still emotionally distant from each other."

How a given child will function within the sibling system appears to be strongly associated with a birth order factor. Children do not adopt family or social roles independent of other members' functioning within that system. The ordinal position of a child strongly influences his or her sibling experience.

The classic description of alcoholic family dynamics involves delegation of a parentified role to one of the children, often the firstborn. With the parents' increasing psychological and physical unavailability, the child comes to function with a pseudo-maturity that belies unmet dependency needs. These firstborns begin to assume caretaking functions at an early age through what is perceived as necessity. The child's *perception* is emphasized here, because often there is a disparity between the actual and perceived necessity. The parents may have been unresponsive to the child's phase-appropriate depencency needs in early childhood, which is tantamount to abandonment. At the first sign of crises, these firstborns often react to family stress by using a compensatory mechanism for covering over their emotions. As the needs for parental support and nurturance are unmet, this child uses responsible, organized, caretaking behaviors to provide the illusion of safety and security. Essentially, the child abandons her own inner, needy child-self as she pursues her caretaking role with a vengeance. It is no surprise, then, that these children take on the responsibility for their siblings, usually performing effectively, however joylessly.

Common among the recollections of female firstborn children of alcoholics is a feeling of being "special" in some way to their alcoholic fathers. These girls maintain the secret belief that they are favored by the father over the other siblings and even the mother. Fantasies of growing up to become president or a benevolent queen are the type of narcissistic visions which conceal deep hurt over early parental neglect. Such grandiosity is often fueled by the perceived inadequacy of the non-alcoholic mother. One little girl, aged 12, confided:

> I have to run the house because my mother is a wimp. She can't stand up to my Dad, and she can't take care of me—or my little brother—or my Dad. Sometimes I think I'm my mommy's mommy. That doesn't seem fair because she won't listen to me when I tell her what to do.

The child admitted that she and her younger brother, aged nine, "begged and begged" the mother to leave the alcoholic father so as to avoid continued family violence. However, she reported her mother's passivity in the face of the father's physical and psychological abuse of the children:

> Once he came home and saw that my kitten had gone to the bathroom on the front porch, so he made me scrub the whole porch — with a toothbrush. My mom stood there and watched. I felt mad and ashamed.

In addition to physical abuse from fathers, these firstborn daughters are also at high risk for incest. Often the "special" position which they perceive with their alcoholic fathers is seductive in nature, although the child may not fully understand this until a sexual act has been committed. If there is no overt sexual abuse, these firstborn daughters may be grappling with a type of emotional incest. Used by either the mother or father and sometimes both, the daughter may be the recipient of intimate details of the parents' actual and imagined sexual relationship. These inappropriate revelations are confusing to the child, who uses dissociation as a way of coping when she becomes psychologically disorganized. The 12-year-old daughter in the previous vignette described nightly rituals when her drunken father would make her sit and listen to his paranoid ravings about her mother.

> When he was talking to me, I'd just sit there and freeze my body and my mind. He thought I was there listening to him tell me that my mother was sleeping with other men, but I wasn't hearing very much at all. I'd keep nodding my head, pretending to be listening, but my mind would be asleep. When he stopped talking to me, I made him take me out to get some ice cream.

Firstborn daughters of alcoholics are the siblings least likely to receive treatment in their childhood. Unless they are the victims of reported sexual and physical abuse, these dutiful children maintain a level of adaptation that camouflages their problems. They may fake their way through life until adulthood, when their problems finally lead them to seek treatment. During the latency period, they tend to excel academically and often shine socially. In contrast to their more troubled siblings, these oldest daughters are not usually singled out by their parents as being in need of intervention. However, the astute therapist will be able to see beyond the false-self adaptation of control and competence. The inner self of the lonely, unmirrored child screams for attention through her driven, compulsive strivings. This child will require sibling therapy.

When the firstborn is a son of an alcoholic father, the child is more likely to incur the parent's anger and derogation. The father's expectations may be unrealistically high for this son, who can never quite measure up to the parent's perfectionistic standards. These firstborn sons also may be involved in an unhealthy alliance with the co-alcoholic mother. Used by the mother as protector and confidante, the boy derives a feeling of competence which offsets his father's belittlement. Although these boys take on chores and caretaking responsibilities at an early age, they usually have not received adequate caretaking themselves. The adaptation as "dutiful son" keeps the youngster relatively problem-free during middle childhood. However, these boys, too, require sibling therapy. Unless the youngster receives professional assistance during the childhood years, his inner conflicts push for expression with the onset of puberty. Diffuse anger is expressed through passive-aggressive stratagems while the social facade of "dutiful son" is preserved. Problems with teenage substance abuse are likely to occur.

When the mother is alcoholic, the family distortion results in a firstborn daughter who tends to be allied with the father, at times functioning in a wife role to him, and also performing as the mother to her siblings. While the alcoholic mother may not pose a severe threat to her firstborn son in terms of overt incestuous acts, her relating is likely to be seductive or grossly inappropriate. The son may be exposed to the mother's belittlement through verbal abuse. Or the mother may flaunt numerous lovers before the boy, with the covert message that he is not and can never be enough for her. The son's helpless rage, confusion, and overstimulation often lead him to repeat the cycle of addiction.

THE PARENT/SIB

Another aberration of alcoholic family life which has not been described in the literature is the parent/sib. This parent, who may be either the alcoholic or co-alcoholic spouse, comes to form a sibling-type relationship with his or her own children. Although this parent-child role reversal is another accommodation which the family makes to the progression of alcoholism, there appear to be potent intrapsychic factors which also explain the regressive nature of the parent/sib dynamics. Often the parent/sib is a product of intergenerational alcoholism, a middle child or a youngest child who grew up being cared for by siblings. Although in the family of origin this child may have been resented by the sibling caretaker, the parent/sib begins to repeat this pattern with her own firstborn. The dysfunction of the parent/sib seems to lead to the overfunction of the child-caretaker, and the coalition thus formed is extremely powerful and resilient.

The parent/sib-child relationship, despite its imperviousness to change, may be viewed by the child-caretaker with resentment during adolescence. As the child begins to pull away from the parent, the teenager and parent engage in rivalrous, bitter sibling-type interactions. These young people try to escape the oppressive family milieu by marrying prematurely. All too soon, they repeat the cycle of parent/sib-child involvement with their own offspring. As adult children of alcoholics, when they do begin to make strides in growth and individuation, they express outrage at their parents' narcissistic use of them in childhood.

During family treatment, when the parent/sib and children appear, the therapist will be struck by a style of family relating which most nearly resembles a leaderless group of siblings. Bickering among the parent/sib and the children is a common feature of family interactions. Typically, the parent/sib is mistakenly assumed to hold a position of power in the family. However, the actual source of power must be identified from within the child sibling system. Initially, family interventions are designed to neutralize this power. Coleman (1985) has discussed failures in family therapy as a result of the surreptitious power of the sibling cohort. Elsewhere (Jesse, in press), I have described family interventions which are directed at facilitating the parent/sib's rightful assumption of a leadership role.

CASE ILLUSTRATION: THE CANDY CANE KIDS

Mrs. Cane, a diminutive woman in her late twenties, sought assistance because of the serious acting-out behavior of her sons, ages seven and nine. Although the boys were described as good students in school, they had literally been tearing the house apart since their father departed from the family environment at the mother's insistence several months earlier. While in the care of their babysitter, the youngsters had knocked holes in the walls, broken windows, set fire to the carport and a neighbor's lawn, and ripped shrubs from the front yard. Mrs. Cane, who preferred to be called by her given name, Candace, or better yet, by her nickname, Candy, approached the therapy situation in a state of anxiety and helplessness with an urgency for the therapist to stop the destructive acting out of her sons, NOW! Candy, who was employed as a secretary, intimated that she was going to have to quit her job and go on welfare unless the therapist could remedy the home situation at once. During the initial interview, Candy also expressed a great deal of frustration and bewilderment at the giggling, secretive bond which had developed between her two sons. "Just look at them!" She exclaimed as the boys stole furtive glances at each other and broke into laughter. "They act like this is all a *big joke*. It's just like they know some kind of big secret joke, but I don't get it."

By the end of the evaluation phase, the big family secret appeared to be Candy Cane's denial of her own alcoholism. Through the process of assessing her substance abuse history, including intergenerational alcoholism in both her parents, Candy's denial began to weaken. She admitted to an increasingly serious problem with alcohol, which had led to the breakup of her marriage. She was also using alcohol as a way of coping with the stress imposed by her sons. She admitted that since their severe acting-out she frequently withdrew to her bedroom to drink and talk on the telephone to one of her many new boyfriends. Sometimes she passed out in drunkenness only to awaken hours later and find the house in shambles. Except for the teenage babysitter who came while Candy was away working or dating, the boys often had no supervision.

Indeed, Candace Cane admitted that she had come to rely heavily on her older son, Teddy, to perform many of the routine household tasks and caretaking functions of his brother, Tommy. Candy expressed a preference for her youngest son and disclosed a parent/sib attachment to Tommy. She turned to him for emotional support in her husband's absence. An overidentification with Tommy led Candy to favor the boy with her time, when she was sober, and to deny the older boy her attention or affection.

During the time that Candy was away from home on dating and drinking escapades, or when she withdrew during hangovers, Teddy and Tommy clung together and destructively acted out their confusion and anger.

After a brief inpatient detoxification, Candy began her recovery through frequent attendance at Alcoholics Anonymous meetings. She was mystified about the continuation of her children's severe acting-out behavior during her early recovery. However, she became more realistic about her expectations of the therapist, and no longer demanded an immediate solution to the problems in her children. As she learned experientially about the process of her own recovery, she began to understand that her youngsters, too, required time to heal from the neglect and psychological unavailability which she had imposed during her active alcoholism.

On those occasions when Candy would arrive for appointments with her sons, the air would be charged with an undercurrent of energy as they waited in the lobby. Incessant talking or giggling by the two boys was no less dramatic than Candy's helpless, childlike demeanor. She would come into the sessions, shaking her head, telling the therapist that she felt "off balance," and looking to the therapist to provide leadership and clarification. During these shifts in family homeostasis, it became apparent that Candy was resisting moving into the position of power in the family as much as she was being thwarted in this effort by her sons. Although the boys' destructive behavior had been reduced considerably as the therapist became directive with limit-setting, Teddy, the older boy, continued to exercise tyrannical behavior in the household. The more Candy attempted to assume a position of dominance, the more Teddy resisted. Much of his anger was displaced onto Tommy. Teddy was bullying with his brother, and Tommy was retreating into clingy, whiny, regressive behavior. A new coalition was formed as Candy began to protect Tommy from Teddy. An intense sibling rivalry ensued between the two boys, but this dynamic seemed to strengthen Candy's influence in the family. As she progressed in her recovery from alcoholism, she developed new feelings of confidence that made her more willing to be the parent in the home.

The final test of Candy's parenting came in the second year of her recovery. By now, she had gained sufficient physical and emotional sobriety to function as a full-time parent. Candy's dominance had resulted in changes in Teddy, who, when he could not win in a power struggle, became a sobbing, needy little boy who cried for Candy's support and nurturance. Sessions with this parent-child dyad strengthened Candy's ability to provide Teddy with much of the mothering he now required and accepted. Individual sessions with Tommy decreased his regressive swings, and continued family therapy greatly improved his relationship with Teddy.

Candy's psychological growth resulted in a renewed conviction that she wanted to provide her children with better parenting than she had received. As the middle child in an alcoholic family, Candy had been ill-prepared for the mature responsibilities which child-rearing had demanded of her. With faulty role models, she had no one to emulate except her own alcoholic parents and her sister, whose parenting of Candy was reminiscent of Teddy's subjugation of Tommy. Candy had not followed in the footsteps of her achievement-oriented sister. Rather, she had escaped into a romantic involvement with her high school sweetheart, whom she married abruptly after becoming pregnant with Teddy.

Near the end of her two years of treatment, Candace, as she was now referring to herself, regretted that she had been too immature to be a success in the marital relationship with her ex-husband. But she looked ahead hopefully to the college courses she wanted to take to upgrade her career. Candace was finally able to admit that she had been too filled with bitterness and resentment to ever be an equal partner in marriage. Not surprisingly, she had escaped into alcohol and eventually divorce.

In summary, it is likely that a parent/sib dynamic is operative within an alcoholic family when the family presents with (1) a bickering, sibling-like quality to the children's interactions with the parent; (2) a parent's expression to the therapist of utter helplessness; and (3) an almost immediate elevation of the therapist to the role of family messiah. For the family therapist, the importance of an early detection of this dynamic is to uncover the covert source of power within the sibling system.

Middle siblings, such as Candy, who are from an alcoholic home will slip very easily into adult parent/sib relationship patterns. These siblings frequently demonstrate severe problems in identity formation. With no consistent, same-sex, parental role figure, these middle children experience identity diffusion and blurred ego boundaries. When they become parents, they tend to reexperience the traumas of the family of origin and to recreate the scene of the family crime with their own children.

BIRTH ORDER VARIATIONS

The middle child in an alcoholic family begins life as the target of resentment. It is this child whose legitimate demands for maternal care and attention present a developmental crisis for the firstborn. A still photograph of the alcoholic family nursery would most likely depict a sulking, whiny firstborn tugging at the leg of a preoccupied mother holding the new infant. Now, if we add sound to our picture, we would also hear the mother's discounting of the older child's emotional crisis. "Stop your whining! You're a big boy now. Can't you see I've got to take care of your baby sister?"

As the child is given a clear directive to grow up overnight, pseudo-maturity develops alongside resentment. Every older sibling experiences this to some extent:

> A child who has been put into second place by the birth of a brother or sister and who is now for the first time almost isolated from his mother, does not easily forgive her this loss of place; feelings which in an adult would be described as greatly embittered arise in him and are often the basis of a permanent estrangement. (Freud, 1917)

Is the previous scene any different from that of other non-alcoholic families when a firstborn resents the new baby's presence? Yes. It is likely that the alcoholic environment is marked by early caretaking interactions that are less empathic than those in most chemical-free families. Indeed, the use of excessive alcohol can be viewed as evidence of a self-disorder in the parent (Kohut, 1977). But alcohol is simply the more obvious rejoinder. An insecure sense of self is frequently present in the non-alcoholic parent as well. Depending on the quality of interactions between these parents and the child, a self emerges which is either a firm, healthy structure or more-or-less seriously damaged.

An inadequate self-development usually marks the psychological picture of these middle siblings from alcoholic families. Without consistent affirming responses from the parents, the child's self development tends to be chameleon-like in structure. Changeable, moody, dependent, these youngsters are typically fighting back an empty depression most of their lives.

A middle child who is displaced from maternal care by a younger brother or sister suffers from the same feelings of resentment as a firstborn. However, she does not have to attempt sudden maturity, for there is the older sibling available as an attachment figure. As the precocious firstborn is encouraged by the parent to assume care for the middle child, the middle begins to experience intense resentment and rejection. The effect of the mother's rejection is potentiated by the unbuffered resentment from the older sibling. "Leave me alone. Go play by yourself." Such a common form of firstborn revenge can be even more cruelly articulated: "Stay by yourself. I don't like you. I hate you."

A miserable, lonely middle child in an alcoholic family is fearful of the older's domination and resentful of the youngest who has replaced her. Without parental support to assuage her bitterness, her rage is turned back upon herself into self-hating and self-destructive inner tensions. These youngsters often engage in autistic-like acts, such as self-rocking or masturbation, as a way of trying to achieve inner soothing and comfort. The middle child from an alcoholic family may be a prime candidate for driven, compulsive substance abuse behaviors such as chemical dependency, eating disorders, and other forms of addiction.

When an alcoholic family crisis precipitates the systems imbalance which leads to sibling clinging, the middle child may experience care and quasi-affection from her brother and sister. In this way she also becomes addicted to crises situations and may, throughout her life, seek harmful, destructive relationships as a way of achieving the brief interlude of contact which she has come to believe is love.

When the firstborn sibling is a brother, the middle sister may also be a victim of sibling incest. However, if the firstborn is a sister, it is more likely that the middle child will escape father-daughter incest until the older leaves home. A middle child who does not suspect that her father is molesting her older sister will actually resent the close bond between them.

The youngest sibling among children of alcoholics usually begins life in a family which has become increasingly more disorganized and chaotic from the parent's drinking. Parental responsibility for this child may be abrogated early on to the care of the firstborn sibling.

As the alcoholic parent's drinking progresses, the co-alcoholic becomes more obsessively preoccupied with the spouse, to the exclusion of all the children.

The firstborn sibling typically forms a close bond with the youngest child, attempting to protect him from the destructiveness of the alcoholic as well as from the resentment of the middle child. These youngsters may actually be overprotected and coddled by the firstborn. Often, one or both of the parents uses the child for emotional comfort, thereby encouraging the child's immaturity. Immature behavior may be tolerated and even encouraged as a way of keeping the child symbiotically attached to a parent. Silly, irrelevant behavior is similarly encouraged as the only form of comic relief in the family tragedy.

When these youngest children begin school, they often have problems adjusting behaviorally and academically. Poor impulse control, aggression, immaturity, and difficulties with attention and concentration all lead to problems in learning. Academic difficulties often lead to the child's being identified as learning-disabled in some way. School phobias and unrealistic fears may lead to problems with truancy.

In a study which compared later born sons and firstborn sons of alcoholic fathers to their peers, Michalik (1981) found that later born sons of alcoholic fathers appeared to be at greater risk for the development of adolescent adjustment problems, to include alcohol problems. These later born sons were distinguished from their adolescent peers by problems of communication, interpersonal skills, persistence, and the inability to use rational decision-making. The sons of alcoholic fathers also tended to become disorganized under stress.

Youngest daughters of alcoholics have similar problems in adjustment. However, these little girls seem to fare better than youngest sons during the latency period. The youngest daughters draw less negative attention to themselves with less observable conduct problems until their adolescence. Then, by the age of 13, problems which seem to have been crystallizing during the preteen years suddenly erupt.

SIBLING THERAPY FOR CHILDREN OF ALCOHOLICS

Most children of alcoholics who are referred for professional assistance during the latency years are either youngest or middle siblings. Regardless of which child is identified as needing help, the remaining siblings in an alcoholic family also require assistance. As can be seen from the preceding discussion, there are intricate patterns of sibling alignments and transactions which govern a child's position in the family. A focused-on child is the one who has been delegated to carry the message about the family pathology, but that child will never be extricated from the pathology until there is an alteration of the sibling subsystem and the alcoholic family culture.

After 15 years of ongoing work with alcoholics, I am convinced that their families must be comprehended from the mind's-eye view of their children, as well as in the more global, systemic frame. This twofold method of investigation has been summarized by Kahn (1986): "It is necessary to have (1) a high-intensity, small-focused lens by which each individual's process of structuralization, history, and affect, cognition, and feeling can be experienced and 'known' and (2) a large lens through which relational patterns, context, group rules and small group culture can be experienced and 'known'."

The small group culture of the alcoholic family will begin to change slowly during recovery, although the sibling system will strongly resist that change. The first experience of change is a shift in family membership. While the family may consist of the same people, usually some kind of regrouping occurs. Recovery frequently portends separation and divorce, particularly in the case of the alcoholic mother. These women are often abandoned by their mates just at the point of entering treatment. Even a parent's removal from the home during inpatient rehabilitation constitutes a mini-regrouping of the family. Also, the recovering parent who returns home after several weeks at a treatment facility will not be the same parent who left home in drunken desperation. Similarly, the parent who is away at daily A.A. meetings has forsaken the preexisting culture of the family for the larger community of recovery and its culture.

Independent of the parents' comings and goings, the sibling system will continue to function to maintain the status quo. This subsystem proceeds during recovery exactly as it did during active alcoholism, largely because the siblings within that system continue to perceive and behave as if the parent is deviant.

"Remember that we deal with alcohol—cunning, baffling, powerful." This exhortation of Alcoholics Anonymous (1976) to its members warns of the compelling, negative force around which their lives have been organized. When alcohol has been removed from a family system, there occurs a power vacuum. As the family is thrown into the midst of this vacuum, the sibling system reacts to reestablish the preexisting balance.

Elsewhere (Jesse, in press), I describe in detail the Children's PACT (Parents as Co-Therapists) Model for training parents to work with their own referred child and siblings. This treatment approach has evolved over the years as I have treated alcoholic families and their youngsters, often treating a particular family off and on over long periods of time. The PACT Model recognizes three major aspects of alcoholic family recovery.

1. The alcoholic parent's recovery proceeds *slowly* in distinct phases of physiological, psychological, and social growth. The importance of a slow and gradual rate of change for the alcoholic and the family is emphasized. (Ask any recovering A.A. member, who knows at an experiential level that recovery does not stabilize until after several years. This view is consistent with the literature on relapse (Gorski and Miller, 1983), which states that the alcoholic is prone to relapse under stress until neuropsychological functioning has been strengthened by 24 to 48 months of continuous sobriety.) This biopsychosocial model emphasizes different levels of a parent's ability and readiness to assume leadership functions within the family. Also emphasized is an awareness of an underfunction or overfunction of the co-alcoholic parent, and a need to interrupt this dysfunction gradually. Both parents will require training to see, hear, and know each other in recovery, as well as to begin the process of helping to heal their children. The therapist assumes the role of leader in the family until the parents gradually move into leadership functioning. The therapist also serves as translator between siblings and parents.
2. Children of alcoholics also require recovery, which must be long-term and consistent with the developmental position of the middle years of childhood.
3. Sibling recovery is required as a part of child and parent recovery, as well as to assist the siblings, regardless of whether or not the siblings are showing overt symptoms.

Treatment is intended to support the alcoholic family during the first two years of recovery, with periodic monitoring thereafter.

Sibling treatment commences after an initial family evaluation. Each sibling is then seen individually by the same therapist, who begins the process of joining. The early phase of treatment is intended to decrease regression or compensatory behavior by reconstituting the structure of latency. This is accomplished through play therapy procedures, which facilitate self-regulation by fostering soothing and calm internal states. Interventions to be avoided are those which increase agitation or tension, such as family therapy sessions around the issue of the parent's drinking or sibling group meetings. Ego-strengthening continues for several months while the family proceeds through the *inclusion* phase of treatment.

The inclusion phase of the PACT model is derived from the conception of three fundamental issues which govern human relatedness: *inclusion*, *control*, and *affection* (Schutz, 1958). These issues are preeminent in the dynamics of the alcoholic family in recovery. *Inclusion* concerns who is *in* the family and who is *out*, and whether one is among the "in" crowd or excluded. This phase of treatment for the siblings and parents usually will last through the first year of a parent's abstinence from alcohol.

The middle phase of sibling therapy is intended to disrupt the dysfunctional power dynamics of the sibling system and to develop new, positive bonding among siblings. Techniques such as rallying and rehearsing, which have been described by Bank and Kahn (1982), are invaluable for fostering new patterns of relating. It is during this time that the siblings are brought into family therapy sessions with their parents, or parent-child dyads used to strengthen parenting behavior. This *control* phase of therapy concerns issues of dominance and power, and who will be in charge of the family. The sibling system still seeks to resume previous power dynamics, but these are easily interrupted by the therapist, who continues to model leadership for the family. As the parents gradually assume leadership functioning, the power of the sibling subsystem decreases proportionately. By the end of this phase of treatment, usually after the family has been seen for one and a half years, the parents are functioning effectively as leaders and a new, healthier bond of sibling relating has developed.

The final phase of therapy, which has to do with issues of intimacy among family members, is known as the *affection* phase. Alcoholism has been called "the disease of intimacy," and parents as well as children have difficulties expressing positive attitudes, let alone loving comments, to each other. This phase is intended to strengthen the positive aspects of sibling relating, as well as to increase parent-child bondedness. This treatment phase is usually completed by the time the parent has accomplished two years of continuous abstinence.

One final thought about the nature of therapeutic work with siblings from an alcoholic family has been borrowed from the lyrics sung by Gilbert and Sullivan's Buttercup, who, during *H. M. S. Pinafore*, warns, "Things are seldom what they seem, skim milk masquerades as cream. . . . "

The sibling subsystem in an alcoholic family has developed out of the survival needs of children. Survival is the most powerful motive to govern the family history. It is unlikely that this subsystem will relinquish its power easily without the guarantee that the new family leadership will offer a superior way of life.

REFERENCES

Alcoholics Anonymous. (1976). New York: Alcoholics Anonymous World Services, Inc., p. 58.

Bank, S. P., & Kahn, M. D. (1982). *The sibling bond*. New York: Basic Books.

Coleman, S. B. (1978). Sib group therapy: a prevention program for siblings from drug-addicted families. *International Journal of the Addictions, 13*, 115–127.

Coleman, S. B. (1985). The surreptitious power of the sibling cohort. In S. B. Coleman (Ed.), *Failures in family therapy* (pp. 27–72). New York: Guilford.

Cork, R. M. (1969). *The forgotten children*. Toronto: Addiction Research Foundation.

Freud, S. (1917). Introductory lectures on psycho-analysis. In *The standard edition of the complete psychological works of Sigmund Freud*, Vol. XV. New York: Norton.

Gorski, T., & Miller, M. (1983). Relapse: The family's involvement. *Focus on Family, 10/11*, 17–18.

Jesse, R. C. (1977). Children of alcoholics: A clinical investigation of familial role relationships. Doctoral dissertation, California School of Professional Psychology, San Diego.

Jesse, R. C. (1987). The child in recovery. *Alcoholism and addiction, 8*(2), 19.

Jesse, R. C. (in press). *Children in recovery*. New York: Norton.

Jesse, R. C., McFadd, A., Gray, G., & Bucky, S. (1978). Interpersonal effects of alcohol abuse. In S. F. Bucky (Ed.), *The Impact of Alcoholism*. Center City, Minnesota: Hazelden.

Kahn, M. D. (1986). The self and the system: Integrating Kohut and Milan. In S. Sugarman (Ed.), *The interface of individual and family therapy*. Rockville, MD: Aspen.

Kelly, G. A. (1955). *The psychology of personal constructs: A theory of personality*. New York: Norton.

Kohut, H. (1977). *The restoration of the self*. New York: International Universities Press.

Michalik, M. (1981). The impact of an alcoholic father on the adjustment of adolescent sons. Doctoral dissertation. California School of Professional Psychology, San Diego.

Newell, N. (1953). Alcoholism and the father image. *Quarterly Journal of Studies on Alcohol, 11*, 92–96.

Sarnoff, C. (1976). *Latency*. Northvale, NJ: Jason Aronson.

Sarnoff, C. (1987). *Psychotherapeutic strategies in the latency years*. Northvale, NJ: Jason Aronson.

Schutz, W. C. (1958). *FIRO: A three-dimensional theory of interpersonal behavior*. New York: Holt, Rinehart & Winston.

III

Balancing Closeness and Separateness

LATE ADOLESCENCE AND
EARLY ADULT YEARS

During late adolescence and the early twenties siblings begin to spend more time away from each other as their peer world takes on greater significance. They continue consciously and unconsciously to deal with the conflicts and pressures of becoming more self-sufficient, experimenting with different styles of relating to the world. This is a time when siblings have a great impact on each other, as they explore identities that will be similar or different.

One main developmental task of this period is for each child to determine how much of the collective identity of the family to take with him or her into adulthood. Leaving the family can be frightening and many young adults have difficulty doing it, choosing instead to stay enmeshed. The converse is also true: Some young adults deal with separation by making a sharp break. Both extreme styles cause difficulties in the long run. While the authors in this section deal with different problems, they share the conviction that it is often useful to help young adults with the separation process by reconnecting them with their siblings, so they can renegotiate a less destructive means of leaving.

Lewis starts off with a look at the messages communicated to siblings through symptoms. Siblings may be a part of the immediate precipitant that led to a symptom, they may be connected to the secondary benefits of the symptom, and they may be connected to the symptom during the recovery process. Seven functions of symptoms are identified: connecting, equalizing, protecting, peacemaking, dirty fighting, flagging, and separating. While symptoms may play an important role in sibling relationships throughout the life span, seemingly sharp differences between siblings around symptomatic behavior are often a direct expression of the conflicts over separating and still being connected.

The next chapter by Falconer and Ross presents a new concept that has been overlooked in the literature. The tilted family refers to a family with children of only one sex. While gender tilting does not in itself cause problems, it often presents the family with unique issues. Falconer and Ross describe their research findings on nonclinic families and compare them with a study of tilting in families where the identified patient was schizophrenic, manic depressive, anorexic, or behaviorally disordered. They give clinical examples where tilting is a factor in family development around the issues of puberty and leaving home, with unresolved family crises, and in families with a psychotic child.

The last two chapters in this section address specific clinical issues—eating disorders and schizophrenia. Anorexia and bulimia are not uncommon among today's families. Working from a transgenerational and symbolic-experiential orientation, Roberto describes the eating-disordered family as one with developmental deficits but with a veneer of competence. Transgenerational family loyalties bind the family together into a vortex. Despite the usual symmetrical relationship between siblings close in age, eating-disordered siblings attempt to de-identify with each other. Change requires "destroying the vortex." Three goals of her treatment are to give the "well" siblings more attention, to use adolescent experimentation to challenge the family's rigid belief system and legacies, and to develop a sibling alliance so brothers and sisters can help each other separate from the family.

Working from a Milan-style systemic approach, Harris addresses the importance of the sibling in helping the chronic client. After describing his work setting he outlines four key systemic terms: positive connotation, neutrality, rituals, and circular questioning. Harris demonstrates his use of systemic therapy in his work with a 27-year-old man with a seven-year history of hospitalizations. He looks at the family's wish to exclude the siblings while describing his utilization of them as a therapeutic resource.

12

Symptoms as Sibling Messages

Karen Gail Lewis

When a family or individual comes to therapy, family therapists make assessments that help them understand the meaning of the presenting problem. A symptom has a meaning; a therapist understands it as either overt (a cigar can also be just a cigar) or as covert, unconscious, or metaphoric. In an attempt to understand the symptom, family therapists hone in on the significance of the symptom, asking questions that reflect their own theoretical perspective. Many therapists wonder about the life stage of the family and of the individual with the problem. Some therapists focus on major changes or losses or on alliances and triangles. Some look for the symptom's meaning in relationship to marital conflict. And many family therapists try to understand how the symptom fits into the nuclear family's systemic patterns and into multigenerational patterns.

Here I present another area for consideration in understanding the meaning of the symptom—the sibling relationships. This is not a new form of therapy; no new techniques or skills are needed. I am suggesting only that we look at the symptom as having specific meaning to one or more siblings. Clearly symptoms can serve many functions within the family system; the possibility of a sibling connection to the problem should not be overlooked (Lewis, 1987, 1988).

SIBLING RELATIONSHIP TO SYMPTOMS

Symptoms may carry conscious or unconscious messages to one or more siblings. One rarely wakes up and says, "Today I will have a problem in order to send a message to my sister." Yet there are many people who are overtly aware that their problem is a form of communication to a brother or sister or that the problem will have an impact on that sibling. The message may be an affectionate one ("I know Mom and Dad are on your case, so I will divert their attention for a while, to give you some space") or an angry one ("I am tired of you always getting all the attention; it's my turn now"). A person may develop a symptom for some other reason and then see its benefit to the sibling relationship; at that point the symptom sends a message — again, affectionate or angry — to a sibling. Another person may discover that old sibling issues interfere with recovery from a symptom. Siblings, then, may be involved in the identified patient's symptom in at least three ways: (1) They may be a part of the immediate precipitant that led to the symptom; (2) they may be connected to the secondary benefits of the already developed symptom; or (3) they may become fused with the symptom during the recovery process.

Immediate Precipitant

Many family therapists initially ask: Why did this problem occur at this particular time? In trying to identify the immediate precipitant, family therapists look for an imbalancing factor or significant change in the symptomatic person's life. They may investigate the whole family system, family roles, concrete life events, or life-cycle transitions for hints as to the source of distress. Frequently, the immediate precipitant is directly related to a sibling, e.g., a brother just went off to college, a sister just got engaged, a sister just had an irreconcilable argument with the parents and was kicked out of the house, a brother was just diagnosed with a serious illness. Therapists may recognize the importance of these problems but see them only as a part of the whole family dynamic. The importance of the sibling relationship itself is often overlooked. While an event involving the sibling may have an imbalancing effect on the whole family, among the siblings it may have distinct significance. Further, some problems are related just to the siblings and have nothing to do with the whole family.

In February the Waltons bring their 16-year-old daughter, Ann, for therapy. She has been a champion cross country runner, but her performance has slipped this past year. If she were just no longer interested, they would not be concerned, but Ann says she still wants to run and does not understand what is happening to her. The immediate precipitant for the referral was a conference with Ann's coach, who has been worried about her sagging performance and recommended therapy.

Ann is the youngest of three girls; all are blond and relatively attractive, and all have excelled in sports. Both Clair, 19, and Donna, 18, were high school volley ball champions. In September Clair started college, where there was no volley ball team, and Donna had a knee injury that required surgery. Mrs. Walton says she has adjusted to her first daughter's going away: "I have to get used to it; Donna goes next year. Fortunately, I'll still have Ann for a while."

Ann is described as the family peacemaker. She tries to cheer everyone up and hates to hear her two sisters fight. A repeated family statement about Ann is that "She hates to stand out from the others."

There is no doubt that the family is reacting to a life-cycle change. Ann, as the family peacemaker, is probably tuned in to her mother's loss, as well as to the changed marital relationship now that father's "Cutie Clair" is gone. However, Ann has a separate issue with her sisters. She does not like to stand out, and with both sisters now out of competitive sports she is in a dilemma—excel alone or stop. By doing poorly in sports, she sends a message to both Clair and Donna: As the baby of the family, I will not outshine you. Since this message is not a conscious one, she is unable to directly talk about her discomfort in being more successful than her older sisters. Her decreased running speed sends that message.

Secondary Benefit

A symptom may arise for a variety of reasons, not particularly having to do with a sibling. Once the problem exists, the identified patient realizes, often consciously, the added benefit it has in the sibling relationship. It can serve as an annoyance to a sibling, hence becoming a form of dirty fighting; it can serve a protective function, distracting attention from a troubled sibling; it can serve a peacemaking function, bringing the family closer or bringing an ousted sibling back into the family. Once a secondary benefit is recognized, the original precipitant, clouded by the new benefit of the symptom, may be hard to find. And, in fact, in solving the problem and preventing a relapse, knowledge of the original precipitant may be less important than an awareness of the secondary benefits.

The immediate precipitant to Susie's emotional withdrawal was her going to college. She became overwhelmed by having to make life choices without mother and worried about her mother not needing her since mother returned to work. Yet at the same time Susie felt smothered by her mother's control over her life. After one semester Susie's grades began dropping; she stopped going out with the other students and spent hours on the phone crying to mother. She went home frequently.

Susie had always been jealous of her sister Joyce, who was smart, a champion athlete, and an overachiever. Susie was the cute and funny child. What became apparent to Susie during her therapy was her glee that mother was spending so much time worrying about her. Joyce was starting a new business, but mother had little time to visit her; often, when Susie was home for the weekend, mother would get off the phone with Joyce when Susie "needed to talk." It was a chance to finally get back at Joyce, to "get the upper hand." Although Susie had been angry and jealous of Joyce for years, her withdrawal at school was not directly related to Joyce. However, as a secondary benefit, the symptom put Susie in a powerful position; she had finally gotten more than Joyce — her mother's full attention.

Recovery

Sometimes the sibling becomes involved only when the identified patient tries to give up the symptom. The family issues may have been addressed, and the original need for the symptom may no longer exist. But as the treatment progresses the patient gets in touch with fears about the effects recovery may have on one or more siblings.

If a sibling has been having difficulty in some area of life, the patient may feel disloyal about getting better and worry about leaving the sibling behind. Perhaps the patient developed the symptom to equalize the sibling relationship; now, despite having gained insight or having outlived the need for the problem, the patient feels unable to let go until the sibling also gets better. Frequently I hear, "If I get better I will be leaving my brother behind," or "My problem is the only thing that keeps my sister interested in me. If I get better, we will have nothing in common."

Leanne, 27, is the youngest of four children. For years she was the only child without serious problems: Two of the older siblings were alcoholic and one was anorexic. Both parents were recovered alcoholics. Leanne developed bulimia four years before entering therapy. She was aware that the bulimia numbed her feelings about her brother's molesting her years ago, as well as her sadness about the family's disintegration. She also recognized that the bulimia had become a means of staying connected with her anorexic sister and her other weight-obsessed sister. Their major contact for years had been around dieting. As Leanne stopped bingeing and purging, she lost her food and weight obsession and began to eat normally. She then became very depressed and returned to the bulimia. After a few weeks she raised what she called the "final issue." She said, "I've always felt different from my sisters and my brother. If I get better, what do I have in common with them? I will be the only normal one, and then I will *really* feel like an outsider."

MESSAGES INHERENT IN THE SYMPTOM

The function or message hidden in a symptom is either an attempt at healing or a covert attack. The intent can be conscious or preconscious — accessible to awareness through directed discussion. A frequently heard comment is "I never thought about it before, but. . . . "

Usually the message in the symptom is kept secret from the sibling. This allows the patient to disown responsibility for the feelings behind the message. It is a sheltered way to hurt a sibling, to avenge a past grievance, to protect or connect with a sibling, or to facilitate bringing an excluded (scapegoated) brother or sister back into the family. I have identified at least seven different functions served by symptoms in a sibling relationship (Lewis, 1987, 1988). While there is some overlap, for simplicity's sake I will describe them separately.

Connecting

If as children the siblings had what Bank and Kahn (1982) call low access — little emotional influence on each other — as adults they may feel isolated and want to get closer. This is especially likely to occur when there is a large age difference between the identified patient and the other siblings. The isolation also may stem from the rigidified roles they had as children, such as the "baby," the "troublemaker," the "favorite," which kept them cut off from each other.

On the other hand, siblings with high access — those close in age who shared toys, friends, clothes, and dreams — sometimes grow apart over the years. For some, their lives have gone in different directions and they have not found successful ways to reconnect. Others do not like the way their siblings have chosen to live as adults. Even though they do not socialize with each other or do not like each other as people, they often miss the old warmth and camaraderie.

Some symptoms, then, serve the function of connecting or reconnecting with a sibling. Whether it is positive or negative, the siblings are now talking. Siblings who have been distant or even hostile now offer advice; they call to see how the brother or sister is doing. Sometimes they spend hours talking about the sibling's problems. While for some the time spent together is filled with support and caring, even arguing or complaining is a form of connection. "You should," "if only you would," are signs that the sibling is in the other's presence or thoughts. And some sibs are willing to accept quantity over quality.

Equalizing

Equalizing often occurs when the identified patient has stood out from the others, has not been equal or has had more than a fair share of parental favoritism, natural abilities or talents, physical attributes, or social skills. While there are benefits to this specialness, the sibling may be the target of sibling jealousy or ostracism. At some point, the benefits are no longer worth the tension, anger, or exclusion.

A symptom may be activated when, as an adult, the identified patient feels guilty about again being more successful, happier, having better adjusted children, etc., than a less fortunate sibling. The symptom can deter success. A secret symptom, such as bulimia, allows the person to maintain the image of success while secretly being unsuccessful like a sibling (or less successful than a sibling). It should be noted, however, that often the siblings do not see the inequality between themselves and the patient or, if they do, they are not bothered by it.

Protecting

The protecting function has several facets. The symptom can rescue a sibling from parental scrutiny or overinvolvement. This may happen when the identified patient feels the other sibling needs some space from the parents in order to grow and change. It can also protect parents from problems that the patient feels will be too upsetting or overwhelming. On the other hand, by developing a problem requiring family therapy, the identified patient can get professional help for another sibling. (This is often an accidental benefit, since most people do not know a therapist will ask for the whole family to attend the therapy.)

Peacemaking

When there is a break in family relationships, often one person's having a problem can function overtly or covertly to make peace. When an older sister has always been the troublemaker, or a brother has been estranged from the family, little sister's developing a serious problem sometimes has the effect of pulling the whole family together. In this sense, the symptom provides the family with an opportunity to repair old grievances or to at least reestablish contact with the disengaged child. Sometimes the symptom provides an opportunity for a shift in roles so that the former troublemaker or "sick" sibling is elevated to "helper."

Dirty Fighting

A symptom may be a weapon in a secret battle with a sibling. This often occurs when the identified patient is not acknowledging anger at or competition with a sibling. The covert battle may be about a current issue or a leftover gripe from childhood. When siblings have not learned to have clean, productive fights, symptoms can become a form of dirty fighting. There are several ways in which this can develop: when parents interfere with children's finding their own solutions to fights, when parents teach their children that arguing is bad or will hurt someone's feelings, when competition is stridently avoided and children do not learn how to deal openly with negative feelings. Another precursor for dirty fighting is rigidity of family roles, with the symptomatic sibling trapped in a role that does not allow expression of anger. Dirty fighting may also be attention-grabbing when the identified patient feels unnoticed, such as when another sibling demands much of parents' time and energy.

Flagging

The flagging function of a symptom occurs when one person in the family sees a problem that other family members are ignoring. By developing a symptom, the patient says to the family, "Hey, look, there is a serious problem here that we must attend to." The problem can be within the identified patient or within one or more family members. By flagging the siblings' attention, the patient is enlisting their help in getting the family to pay attention.

Separating

The development of a symptom can provide a person with an escape, a means of separating from an enmeshed family or an entrenched role. Through involvement in the symptom, the person can escape — emotionally or physically — from the family or the role. This function often occurs when a person has played a major role within the family and needs a "vacation." The role may have been the overresponsible child, or it may have been one complementary to another sibling, such as the serious one vs. the comic. The symptom allows the person simultaneously to remain with the family and maintain distance.

MIXTURE OF MESSAGES

The presenting problem may include more than one message to more than one sibling, and the same or different messages may be sent to each sibling. It is also possible that when more than one sibling is having a serious problem at the same time, they may be sending mutual messages to each other. For example, Betty's agoraphobia serves the purpose of keeping her from going to law school, which equalizes her with Steve, her older brother, who flunked out of law school a year earlier. For his part, Steve, since flunking out, has become suicidally depressed. After the therapist worked with the two siblings together for a few weeks, the brother told Betty he felt she had cut him off when he entered law school. He said his depression was in part a reaction to feeling the loss of their former closeness.

AWARENESS OF SIBLING CONNECTION TO SYMPTOM

It never ceases to surprise me how aware the identified patient is of the connection between the problem and a sibling. When I ask what seems a simple question about a sibling, the responses are frequently to the point:

"What is your sister like?"

An anorexic responds, "I was always the cute, popular one; she was always fat and unliked as a child. I know my being skinny won't make her happier, but. . . . "

An underachieving professional woman is asked, "What does your brother do for a living?"

Without looking directly at her therapist, she responds, "He's having a hard time finding himself, and he's almost 40. I'm embarrassed that I make more money than he, and *I* make so little."

Not only are these patients aware of the sibling connection to the development of the problem, but they also seem aware of its relationship to stopping it. Not wanting to get better while a brother or sister is still troubled is a frequently mentioned concern. Further, many patients are aware of being stuck in their roles relative to their siblings:

An unassertive woman complains about a situation at work. The therapist asks, "What would your brother do in that case?"

She clearly asserts, "Oh, he would speak up right away. But I'm not supposed to be able to do that."

SIBLING ISSUES ACROSS THE LIFE SPAN

A sibling's involvement in a person's symptom can cut across the life cycle. With children, the importance of their mutual effect is well documented (Bank and Kahn, 1982; Dunn and Kendrick, 1982; Faber and Mazlish, 1987; Minuchin, Montalvo, Guerney, Rosman, and Schumer, 1967). Their identity is built in part upon being just like or totally different from their brothers and sisters (Schachter, 1982). In adolescence the peer world takes precedence over the family, but the quality of the sibling relationship is still reflected to some extent in one's style of friendship.

In adulthood relationships are influenced by parental introjects and transferences, as well as sibling ones. While brothers and sisters often drift apart as they develop their personal and professional lives, their internalized siblings stay with them. For instance, a woman who is the youngest of her siblings may relate to people in authority positions, or even to her own peers, as older siblings. A man who had been looked up to as the "brain" among his siblings may expect colleagues and friends to treat him with the same esteem.

Over the years siblings grow, develop, and change. However, their images of each other may remain frozen in early childhood. Some become stuck in behaviors or interactional patterns that are then recreated in new relationships, without ever recognizing the sibling origin. These "frozen images" (Bank and Kahn, 1982) may become the bases of sibling transferences which carry over into dating and marital relationships, friendships, and employment. They may also influence people's relationships with their children, and of course they may be transmitted so that siblings in successive generations replicate the same frozen or mythical projections.

Elsewhere I have described types of presenting problems that can be sibling-related throughout the life cycle (Lewis, 1985). Here I will just summarize the issues for adulthood and old age. In adulthood, a common symptom of people in therapy is loneliness or a sense of isolation from others. Family loyalty and established family roles can interfere with one's freedom to connect with peers. When siblings are not close or are not friends, a person can feel disloyal becoming close to a nonfamily friend. In addition, establishing new roles with siblings can free the adult for healthier roles with peers.

Employment problems are frequently seen as related to parental transferences. However, I believe it is more useful to focus on the sibling transferences, since it is easier to make changes in a lateral relationship than in a hierarchical one. When a client complains about perpetual job dissatisfaction or is underachieving at work, I always inquire about their siblings' work status. I am struck by the frequency of responses that reflect an equalizing message—discomfort at possibly outperforming a sibling.

Unless working directly with the aged, therapists may not be aware of the importance of siblings to a troubled old person. It is not uncommon for an old person to deteriorate when worried about a brother or a sister or just after the death of a sibling, even if estranged. I once met with a 35-year-old unmarried woman who struggled with depression. She was an only child and her mother had died many years before. When she brought her father into a therapy session, I inquired about his siblings. He said his last sibling, a sister, had gone into a coma six months earlier. He cried as he talked about his family's coming to an end. He said he had never shared any of these feelings with his daughter; "That's life, you just got to keep going." The daughter said she had not known about her aunt's condition, since her father and his sister had never been close. Her depression had started shortly after the hospitalization. Most likely the connection would not have been made if I had not asked about his siblings.

LOOKING FOR THE SIBLING CONNECTION

Most of my adult clients do not mention their siblings during therapy. Unless there is a particular reason, I do not ask about them. However, in listening to the presenting problem I may hear a sibling message. Sometimes, when a client is stuck, out of the blue I will ask about the brothers and sisters. I may ask general questions, such as, "Tell me something about your two brothers," or more pointed ones, such as, "What would your sister do in the same situation?" Not uncommonly, in telling me about a sibling clients make their own connections between the problem and the sibling.

No fancy treatment strategies are necessary in looking for the sibling connection. The therapist just needs to be aware of the potential for the symptom to be related to a sibling. De Shazer (1985) says a therapist does not need to know the exact cause of a symptom, for a number of therapeutic "skeleton keys" can unlock different problems. Since many factors go into symptom development, it seems reasonable to focus on one where there is a good chance of success. Entering through sibling messages may lead to quick resolution of the problem, particularly with people who have had extensive prior therapy. A change of focus has the same effect as a reframe—"to change the conceptual and/or emotional setting or viewpoint" (Watzlawick, Weakland, and Fisch, 1974, p. 95).

> Dana had had ten years of psychodynamic therapy before she was married, and then she and her husband began systemic marital therapy. Always the symptom was her depression. The marital therapy focused on the multigenerational patterns that were being replayed and

the complementarity of the spouses' relationship—she the patient, he the helper. They found it interesting but not particularly relevant.

In a first interview with them (after a referral from the frustrated marital therapist), I asked about their siblings. Dana said she has 2 sisters, one is mildly retarded. I asked if Dana's life was turning out similar to her retarded sister's. Dana looked shocked and cried. She spoke of her guilt at having a college education, being married, and now planning for children, when her sister could not do any of those things. I asked her if walking on bent knees would make her sister any taller and said she was making herself incompetent so her sister would not feel so inadequate. Dana looked horrified and said, "My depression isn't helping Lucy at all. This has nothing to do with her." Two weeks later Dana was looking for a new (more appropriate) job and talking with her husband about things they could do together during their spare time so she would not be so depressed.

CLINICAL EXAMPLES

Most often a symptom has multiple meanings, and the message to the sibling is only a small part of the entire communication. In the examples below the sibling aspect is highlighted, not to indicate special significance but to spotlight its existence. The first example shows the multiple sibling transferences and messages that exist within a family. The second demonstrates how understanding the sibling message allows for direct access to a potentially complicated problem.

Example 1

The Gordons—parents Stan and Tracy, their daughters Mickie, 19, and Brigid, 17, and son, Billy 12,—come to therapy after Brigid threatens suicide. In the first family session, it quickly becomes clear that Brigid feels caught in her parents' dilemma about whether to stay together or to divorce. A year ago Stan took a job in a town two hours away; he now comes home only on weekends. Two months ago he said a decision had to be made—either Tracy moves or they divorce. Tracy does not want to move since she plans to start college in the fall and there is no college in the new town. She adds, "Besides, Brigid wants to finish high school here; she doesn't want to move."

Brigid identifies two reasons for her depression: She feels responsible for mother's not moving and her father does everything with her younger brother, Billy—"he never spends any time with me." With that, Billy becomes teary. I ask, "Are you aware that she feels that way?" "Yeah. That's why I always feel guilty when Dad and I are out playing soccer. I wouldn't mind if she joined us sometimes, but I know she wouldn't like it."

The other major issue that arises during the first session is Tracy's anxiety about Mickie, her older daughter, who dropped out of college a few months ago. Mickie says nothing as Tracy says how angry she has been at Mickie. As an afterthought, Tracy adds, "I guess I haven't said as much since I found Brigid's note mentioning suicide."

By the end of the first session, the couple's marital dilemma has been identified as a major factor causing tension within the family. Tracy and Stan ask to meet with me alone to talk about how to resolve this problem. Brigid is referred to one of my adolescent therapy groups.

During the couple's meeting, Stan and Tracy talk about their having to get married when Tracy became pregnant with Mickie just after their high school graduation. Clearly these 20-year-old wounds are still raw. Each parent asks for an individual appointment.

Stan's meeting is first. He says his parents had wanted him to get married when Tracy became pregnant. He had been against it, but his brother had gotten married two months before, and Stan had never seen his father so happy. He hoped his marriage would have the same effect. Stan had always been in the losing end of the competition with his older brother for father's affection and approval. Although he played sports and was very bright in high school, he felt his father never appreciated or valued him. Father admired the brother's mechanical skills and thought Stan was just a playboy. Eighteen years later, Stan is a successful attorney, while his brother Mike is stuck in a routine engineering job. Unfortunately, although Stan finally won father's respect in his career, he lost his brother, because Mike is terribly jealous of Stan. One thing Stan had always had over Mike was a stable marriage. That was underscored last year when Mike divorced his wife. Their parents never liked Mike's wife. Stan says that, if he and Tracy separate, he no longer has that over Mike; further his parents would be very upset with him, since they are very fond of Tracy.

As Stan talks about his marriage, he describes Tracy's doing all the right things but his never feeling she really appreciates or values him. I note the similarity to his feelings about his father. Stan looks surprised and then says "Tracy and Dad are very different . . . [pause] . . . well, maybe they really are alike." He does feel that nothing he could ever do would please her. I ask why he would want to stay with a woman with whom he does not get what he needs. The session ends with this rhetorical question.

The next week Tracy comes in and immediately begins to talk about how she does not want to move. She wants to go to school. She has always been the perfect daughter, doing whatever her parents expect of her. But she has spent her whole life waiting — waiting for her father to come home from work, waiting for him not to be too tired to notice her, waiting for her turn. When Tracy was 12 years old, her mother gave birth to a son and became deeply depressed. Although Tracy did much of the mothering of her younger brother, she did not mind, for she knew her brother loved all she did for him. She gained value from giving and attending to him. She gave numerous examples of how she always put her brother first.

The summer before she entered college, Tracy became pregnant by Stan. Both sets of parents encouraged the marriage, "So, college had to wait." When Brigid was four years old, Tracy was planning to go to college when she became pregnant again. Again she had to wait. She gave many more examples of how she put her own plans aside for Stan's professional advancement. This time she wants to go ahead with college. "I'm turning 37 and I feel my life is just passing me by." She had not been brave enough to tell Stan "no," so she blamed not moving on Brigid. She does not know if she loves Stan anymore; they have grown so apart over the years and she has been so angry for so long. And besides, "He always shuts me out; he never talks with me." The therapist points out that she has recreated her sibling relationship in her marriage. She keeps putting others before herself — first her brother and now Stan.

The couple's session scheduled for the following week is canceled. Stan calls to say he has the day off and would rather take Tracy out on their boat; they never have time to spend together. He says he will call again soon for another appointment.

The first week Brigid is in the therapy group she talks about her anger at her father for ignoring her and at her mother for invading her privacy by reading her diary. The group is supportive. The next week, after her father's individual appointment, Brigid reports that father and she are really talking together. He told her about his growing up and that he realized he was treating her in some way like his older brother (that had never even been mentioned in the therapy sessions).

In a meeting three months later, the parents report that Brigid has improved considerably: She is no longer depressed, has found a part-time job, and is dating. She is also doing things with her older sister—something that has not happened for two years. Mickie has found an interesting job and Tracy seems to accept the fact that Mickie is not ready to be in college yet.

Stan and Tracy both say things are much better between them but they do not know why, "except that we are talking together more than ever." As an aside, and as if by coincidence, Stan adds that he called his brother and they spent a whole day out on the boat, "talking about all kinds of things, and about growing up, too." They are scared, they say, for now that they feel better about each other it is harder to think about divorcing. The living situation is still a very serious problem: Stan does not want to commute and Tracy does not want to move.

Without the sibling distortions and projections, Stan and Tracy are faced with the very real fact that they are in different places in their lives—he is looking ahead to an early retirement and she is just beginning. At this point the major question in therapy is whether their marriage can survive these differences.

Therapists never really know what causes change in families. Maybe it is my wishful thinking that Tracy and Stan recognized the sibling transferences and chose to stop repeating the patterns. Stan and Tracy had both recreated their sibling relationships; when the sibling transferences were identified, perhaps they were freed then to meet each other anew. Brigid's suicidal ideation, intentionally or not, served the purpose of distracting (a protecting message) Tracy from harping on Mickie about dropping out of college; it also allowed her to hear from Billy that he not only noticed how she felt but cared about her feelings (a connecting message). Brigid's suicidal thoughts did not seem to be a conscious precipitant for helping her parents get unstuck, for her connecting with her siblings and for her father's connecting with his brother, nor for supporting Mickie's decision to leave college. But they did in fact serve those purposes.

Example 2

Six years ago I saw Mrs. Zee and her three children for about six months when her son, at age 15, had run away from home. Mrs. Zee now wants help for Alicia, 16, her youngest, who has just joined a cult and is "dating" the 27-year-old cult leader. Mrs. Zee cannot understand why her easiest child, the one she was the closest to, should now cause her such trouble. Alicia tells her mother she knows what she is doing. Since Alicia has always spoken warmly of me, Mrs. Zee asks her to meet with me once; then she will let Alicia make her own decision.

Mrs. Zee catches me up on the past six years. Bobby, now 21, disappeared for a few years, during which time he stole some of mother's jewelry. He now lives in the same town and works at odd jobs. He is not allowed in the house, but he can see his brother and sister elsewhere. Mother will only talk to him by telephone. Timmy, 18, is a senior in high school, but doing very poorly. He has no plans for next year. He seems not to have many friends and spends almost all his free time in his bedroom.

When I meet with Alicia she recalls her earlier visits with me when she was "such a young kid." We reminisce about things we did together in therapy. I ask her about her brothers. Alicia is delighted that Bobby has returned to their home town, but she is sad that he and mother cannot get along. Alicia tells me she is worried about Bobby, who is "heavy into drug dealing. . . . Do you remember how Timmy and I used to fight? Well, during the past few years we got real close. Maybe it had something to do with Bobby being gone. Now, though, he stays stoned most of the time. Since I got in the cult, I can't do drugs, it's not allowed. I really worry about him; I don't know if he'll be able to graduate this year."

I ask her how she went from being "the perfect kid and Mommy's favorite," to getting involved with this crazy cult. She talks in circles for a few sentences and then says, "You know, it's about time I stopped being so good." I add, "It sounds like it is a way to keep you off drugs too." She looks surprised and says, "I guess that's true."

Later I ask her what Bobby says about her being in the cult. Alicia smiles, "Last weekend, I took off and Mommy called Bobby to see if I was over there. They started talking about the cult, and Bobby suggested Mommy hire a deprogrammer. He is coming over on Saturday to talk with me and Mommy about this." I ask, "I bet you're glad to have Bobby talking to your Mom, to say nothing of having him back in the house." I ask her what Timmy says about the cult. He is real scared for her. In fact, "Last night he said he'd even stop drugs if I would get out." "What did you say to that?" I ask. Alicia gets silent for a few minutes and then says, "I had been thinking of making that offer to him recently. It's odd, isn't it?" I ask, "Isn't that a form of blackmail, Alicia?" "Yes, but if it'll get him straight . . . " She cries softly, "I don't want him to get as bad as Bobby. It hurt so much when I lost him when he was gone; I couldn't stand it if I lost Timmy, now."

Alicia's brothers agree to come with her to meet with me. For a while treatment was complicated with each of them going back and forth on the blackmail pact. Whatever the multiple reasons for Alicia's involvement with the cult, the more powerful aspects seemed to be related to her brothers. Joining the cult served at least four functions: equalizing, protecting, peacemaking, and dirty fighting.

By joining the cult, Alicia was equalizing her role with her brothers. She had always been the best behaved child, mother's favorite, the one who did no wrong. Now she too had a serious problem, and Mother was angry at her. As she hinted, she found a way to escape drugs and yet be like her two brothers. The cult was a convenient way to protect her from drugs *and* equalize her with her siblings.

The result of the protecting function was to get Bobby and Timmy into treatment, where they could get help for their drug problems. The blackmail scheme suggests that on some level Alicia was aware of her wish to get them help. The peacemaking function is best demonstrated by her setting the stage for reuniting Bobby and their mother, putting him back in his rightful position as helpful oldest child. Further, by participating in something so much worse than just running away, Alicia took the focus off Bobby's earlier behavior.

The fourth function of the cult was covert dirty fighting. Alicia was very angry at both of her siblings, but she was not in a secure enough position to tell either of them. Bobby had been her idol, and he had deserted her without notice. Timmy then became her good friend, and he deserted her for drugs. She had worried so much about each of them; she may have felt it was their turn to worry about her.

There is no way to know for sure how much of this was conscious, how much coincidentally fell into place. It is likely that at least one immediate precipitant to Alicia's joining the cult was her anxiety about the heavy sibling drug use. It is also possible to see how she set up her recovery in such a way that her siblings had to get better, too.

SUMMARY

Looking within the family for an inherent message is not a new idea to family therapists. Some family therapists see the symptom as an analogy for another family member's problems (Madanes, 1984), as a way to detour marital problems (Minuchin, 1974), or as a means of resolving family-of-origin issues (Boszormenyi-Nagy and Spark, 1984; Bowen, 1978). Considering a sibling function does not detract from any of these ideas. Instead, it adds to a therapist's resources when looking for hypotheses and effective means of intervention.

REFERENCES

Bank, S., & Kahn, M. (1982). *The sibling bond*. New York: Basic Books.

Boszormenyi-Nagy, I., & Spark, G. (1984). *Invisible loyalties: Reciprocity in intergenerational family therapy*. New York: Brunner/Mazel.

Bowen, M. (1978). *Family therapy in clinical practice*. New York: Jason Aronson.

de Shazer, S. (1985). *Keys to solution in brief therapy*. New York: Norton.

Dunn, J., & Kendrick, C. (1982). Siblings and their mothers: Developing relationships within the family. In M. Lamb & B. Sutton-Smith (Eds.), *Sibling relationships: Their nature and significance across the life span*. New Jersey: Lawrence Erlbaum.

Faber, A., & Mazlish, E. (1987). *Siblings without rivalry*. New York: Norton.

Lewis, K. G. (1985). Involving siblings in therapy at different life stages. Presentation for American Family Therapy Association, San Diego, CA.

Lewis, K. G. (1987). Bulimia as a communication to siblings. *Psychotherapy, 24*, 640–645.

Lewis, K. G. (1988). The sibling relationships of bulimic women. Doctoral dissertation, University of Massachusetts.

Madanes, C. (1984). *Behind the one-way mirror: Advances in the practice of strategic therapy*. San Francisco: Jossey-Bass.

Minuchin, S. (1974). *Families and family therapy*. Cambridge: Harvard University Press.

Minuchin, S., Montalvo, B., Guerney, B. G., Jr., Rosman, B. L., & Schumer, F. (1967). *Families of the slums: An exploration of their structure and treatment*. New York: Basic Books.

Schachter, F. (1982). Sibling deidentification and split-parent identification: A family tetrad. In M. Lamb & B. Sutton-Smith (Eds.), *Sibling relationships: Their nature and significance across the life span*. New Jersey: Lawrence Erlbaum.

Watzlawick, P., Weakland, J., & Fisch, R. (1974). *Change: Principles of problem formation and problem resolution*. New York: Norton.

13

The Tilted Family

Clark W. Falconer and Colin A. Ross

In the movie *Crimes of the Heart* from Beth Henley's award-winning play, we are introduced to a family of three sisters. The oldest sister, nicknamed Lenny, is portrayed as a somewhat neutered woman with a shriveled ovary. She has never had a relationship with a man and sees her only hope for creativity in her grandmother's garden. The middle sister, Meg, Lenny's opposite, is a caricature of a woman overinvolved in female sexuality. She is portrayed as the failed Hollywood songstress who lives off her sexual charms. She has just left yet another in a long series of men. The youngest sister, Babe, has just shot her husband. Babe likes to play the saxophone in cowboy boots. The father of the family was, or became, an alcoholic, and after he left the family his wife, the three sisters' mother, killed herself. Babe, following in her mother's footsteps, is chronically suicidal.

The many reviews and discussions of this movie, which garnered almost unanimous acclaim, considered various aspects of these three women's relationships to each other, to men, and to the community and society as a whole. However, to our knowledge no one focused on a central aspect of this family — the fact that the sibship was of one gender. In our work both as clinicians and as researchers we have found that family structure in its most real aspects, that is, number of children, gender and sibship spacing, has a great influence on the development of both children and parents. In particular, we have been struck by the importance of the type of sibship portrayed in Henley's play — all boys or all girls. We have come to call families with such sibling configurations "tilted" families. (Families with only one child are also considered "tilted.")

In recent decades as the number of children per family has dropped to 2.2 or even lower in industrialized countries, the chances of having children of both sexes in a family have decreased. This demographic fact may increase the impact of our work, since there are now many more tilted families. As we will show, tilting has both theoretical and practical implications.

RESEARCH STUDY AND FINDINGS

Based on an extensive review of family structure studies and his own survey of over 3,000 families, Toman (1976) concluded that family constellations do influence personality traits and behavioral styles. Given this background and our clinical hypothesis, our work was undertaken to investigate the relationship of sibling sex configurations to normal development and to specific psychiatric disorders.

The structural dimensions of the family have long been considered important determinants of the family's social environment. Such structural factors as father-absence (Kagel, White, and Coyne, 1978) and family size and birth order (Toman, 1976) have been the focus of considerable research interest. The influence of the gender composition of the family's children, in contrast, has been relatively neglected. In addition, most of the relevant work conducted to date has taken the perspective of child development. Elder and Bowerman (1963), for example, examined the relationship of sibling gender configurations and perceptions of parental involvement in child-rearing among a large group of seventh-grade children. Rosenberg (1965) and Nystul (1981) studied the effects of different sibling gender constellations on the self-concepts of university students.

Quite by accident we noticed in our unit* that a number of families contained only children of one gender. We have observed clinically that the *parents* of gender-tilting families frequently present in family therapy with a unique set of issues, including feelings of isolation, difficulties in role behavior, and a sense of loss about not having children of the other sex. We therefore began to ask certain questions of these parents:

*Family Therapy Unit, Health Sciences Centre, Winnipeg, Manitoba, Canada.

- Why did you decide to have only one child? Who decided there would be no more?
- What was it like when the first child was a boy/girl? How did this influence your deciding to have another?
- Where is mom's little girl? Where is dad's little boy?
- After you had two girls/boys why did you decide not to have more?

The responses to these questions led to our clinical hypothesis that living in a tilted family is associated with unique developmental issues that affect the family members and family functioning, especially in role behavior, sexual identity, acting-out, and loss. We then set out to test this clinical hypothesis with research in both normal and abnormal situations.

First we compared, with a number of research instruments, two large groups of families with all-boy and all-girl sibships. Second, we completed a study of 200 families: 50 families with a schizophrenic child, 50 with a manic-depressive child, 50 with an anorexic child, and 50 diagnostically nonspecific clinic families (most showing nonpsychotic disorders of a crisis or behavioral nature). We compared the family sibling structure of each group and then looked at whether there were any significant differences in the number of tilted families in each group.

Research with Normal Families

In the study of normal families the subjects were the husbands and wives of 40 volunteer families who were recruited through personal contacts, discussions at workshops and community seminars, and referral by other participants. In order to match the male-tilted and female-tilted families as closely as possible, eligibility for participation required that: (1) there be two or more children in the home, at least one of whom was of school age (i.e., between the ages of 6 and 18 years); (2) the family members be related biologically, rather than through remarriage; and (3) all the children be of the same sex. The final sample included both spouses from 20 male-tilted and 20 female-tilted families.

Each couple was given a set of questionnaires including a brief review of demographic information, a set of standardized inventories, and a group of questions prepared by the authors to address the specific influences of gender tilting.

Family functioning and satisfaction were examined with Moos and Moos' (1986) Family Environment Scale (FES) and Olson and Wilson's (1985) Family Satisfaction Scale (FSS), respectively. Family interaction questions asked the subject to estimate the amount of time, in hours per week, that he or she spent engaging in eight particular activities.

Two standardized personality assessment instruments were also employed: the Bem Sex Role Inventory (BSRI) (Bem, 1981), which provides reliable estimates of masculinity and femininity, and the Personality Research Form (Jackson, 1984), a true/false questionnaire that has been constructed to tap 14 of the basic attributes of personality outlined by Murray (1938).

Ten additional questions probed our specific hypothesis (Falconer and Ross, 1986) regarding gender-tilting. These items asked the subject to indicate on 5-point scales (-2 to $+2$) the extent of agreement with a series of statements. The statements addressed such themes as: feeling left out or isolated in the family; having a sense of the uniqueness of the family structure; expressing a sense of loss or guilt about not having children of the opposite sex; and communication of sex roles within the family.

The different family types were well-matched with regard to demographic characteristics. Thirty-nine families came from socioeconomic classes I–III according to the Hollingshead (1975) four-factor index, while one family was of class IV. Both spouses were employed in 21 (52.5%) of the families, with the numbers of one-income and two-income families being comparable for both the male-tilted and female-tilted groups. The average number of children (2.65 per family) was identical for the two family types, and the age range of the children was very similar (age of oldest to age of youngest=4.08 years for male-tilted families and 4.04 years for female-tilted families). In addition on average husbands were significantly older than their wives (M=41.85 vs. 39.40 years for husbands and wives respectively).

Table 1 summarizes the responses to the survey of family activities. For each item on the list, the subject was asked to estimate the number of hours that would be spent pursuing that activity "in an average week." Since almost half the wives were not employed outside the

TABLE 1
Means and SDs for Estimates of Hours
Spent per Week in Different Activities

Activity	Male-Tilted		Female-Tilted		Results
	Husbands	Wives	Husbands	Wives	
Working outside the home	52.10	15.05	46.15	18.70	b
	(12.02)	(11.75)	(16.19)	(17.12)	
Alone with spouse	15.75	13.70	16.15	15.90	n.s.
	(17.30)	(7.52)	(13.90)	(13.13)	
Engaged in conversation with children	8.95	16.25	8.60	14.65	b
	(9.98)	(9.37)	(5.89)	(12.48)	
Engaged in recreational activity with children	8.70	8.55	5.55	7.15	a
	(4.90)	(4.59)	(3.80)	(6.83)	
Engaged in social activities with only other members of same sex	3.45	3.75	4.20	3.35	n.s.
	(4.37)	(2.49)	(4.16)	(2.25)	
Engaged in social activities with mixed-sex company	4.75	4.30	5.15	4.20	n.s.
	(3.81)	(1.56)	(4.70)	(2.38)	
Helping children with school work	1.45	3.10	1.25	2.40	b
	(1.39)	(2.02)	(1.02)	(2.41)	
Engaged in a recreational activity alone	3.05	4.85	6.90	2.95	a×b
	(2.82)	(4.58)	(5.76)	(2.86)	

Note: The *Results* column indicates the comparisons that are statistically significant.
  a=Main effect of family type.
  b=Main effect of sex of respondent.
  a×b=Interaction effect of family type×sex of respondent.
  n.s.=not significant.

home, they reported spending fewer hours engaged in that activity. The female spouses also indicated that they spent more time in the average week talking with their children and helping their children with homework.

One activity rating showed a significant effect for the gender-tilting dimension. The parents in male-tilted families reported that they spent more time engaged in recreational activities with their children.

In addition, a reliable interaction of family type and sex of respondent was observed in the estimates of time spent in recreational activity by oneself. As can be seen in Table 1, both wives in male-tilted families and the husbands in female-tilted families reported that they spent more time engaged in solitary recreational activities.

In order to limit the risk of Type I error due to multiple comparisons, the 10 FES scales were collapsed into their three major dimensions prior to analysis. The average scores observed in each of the FES dimensions are presented in Table 2. The relationship dimension of the FES showed a significant main effect of family type, with overall higher scores being obtained by the female-tilted families. A closer look at the component subscale scores indicated that this finding was primarily due to higher levels of conflict being reported by the spouses of the male-tilted families. No other significant findings emerged from the FES.

Olson and Wilson (1985) recommended the use of the FSS total score as an index of family satisfaction. In the present study a 2×2 (family type $\times$ sex of respondent) ANOVA of the FSS total scores revealed a significant main effect of family type, with members of female-tilted families expressing higher levels of satisfaction overall. In addition, wives in both male-tilted and female-tilted families tended to express higher levels of satisfaction than husbands. When these effects were probed with separate analyses of the component subscales, it was evident that the higher satisfaction scores of the female-tilted families were related to contributions of both Cohesion and Adaptability. The main effect of sex of respondent was attributable to the tendency for wives to give higher satisfaction ratings on the Cohesion dimension, but not on the Adaptability subscale.

Table 3 presents the 10 attitudinal statements pertaining to gender-tilting. The mean scores for most of the items are negative in direction, indicating an overall tendency to *disagree* with these statements. Nevertheless, there was still substantial variation in the ratings, which were in a series of 2×2 (family type $\times$ sex of respondent) ANOVAs. Two statements dealt with the respondent's sense of being the "odd person out" (item 2) or feeling "isolated" (item 5) in the family. Each of these items resulted in significant family type $\times$ sex of respondent interactions. Wives in male-tilted families and husbands in female-tilted families expressed lower levels of disagreement in each case. Statements addressing a possible sense of loss or guilt

TABLE 2
Means and SDS of Scores on Family and
Personality Self-Report Inventories

Inventory	Male-Tilted		Female-Tilted		Results
	Husbands	Wives	Husbands	Wives	
Family Environment Scale					
Relationship Dimensions	17.00	18.25	20.25	20.05	a
	(4.30)	(3.51)	(3.54)	(4.75)	
Personal Development	28.85	30.40	30.85	30.60	n.s.
Dimensions	(5.34)	(4.66)	(4.40)	(5.83)	
System Maintenance	11.45	11.00	10.60	11.10	n.s.
Dimensions	(3.52)	(3.55)	(3.28)	(2.90)	
Family Satisfaction Scale					
Cohesion	26.85	28.60	28.65	30.55	a,b*
	(4.36)	(3.97)	(4.61)	(4.32)	
Adaptability	19.85	21.00	22.05	22.25	a
	(3.31)	(2.90)	(3.39)	(3.35)	
Total	46.70	49.60	50.20	52.80	a,b*
	(7.08)	(5.90)	(7.27)	(7.37)	
Bem Sex Role Inventory					
Masculinity	5.16	4.82	4.97	4.39	a,b
	(0.75)	(0.64)	(0.73)	(0.68)	
Femininity	4.52	4.97	4.75	4.99	b
	(0.51)	(0.46)	(0.53)	(0.40)	
Personality Research Form					
Impulse Expression &	29.20	23.35	21.85	21.10	a,b
Control	(9.82)	(7.04)	(6.95)	(6.36)	
Orientation to Work &	38.50	33.20	37.75	34.35	b
Play	(4.65)	(6.13)	(5.85)	(8.96)	
Interpersonal Orientation	62.00	66.60	62.65	66.20	b
	(10.41)	(9.08)	(6.09)	(9.67)	
Dominance	11.30	10.65	10.80	9.35	n.s.
	(4.28)	(4.32)	(4.83)	(5.55)	
Autonomy	8.55	6.10	6.85	6.20	b
	(2.54)	(3.74)	(2.23)	(2.98)	
Understanding	12.25	12.80	11.70	13.75	n.s.
	(5.18)	(3.79)	(3.24)	(3.15)	
Infrequency	0.30	0.30	0.45	0.15	n.s.
	(0.57)	(0.57)	(0.76)	(0.37)	

Note: The *Results* column indicates the comparisons that are statistically significant.
a = Main effect of family type.   b = Main effect of sex of respondent.
b* = Main effect of sex of respondent: $.10 < p < .05$.   n.s. = not significant.

279

TABLE 3

Means and SDs for Ratings of Attitudes Towards Gender-Tilting

	Male-Tilted		Female-Tilted		Results
	Husbands	Wives	Husbands	Wives	
1. I feel like I've missed out on something important by having children of only one sex.	0.00 (1.17)	+0.15 (1.50)	−0.40 (1.43)	−0.40 (1.35)	n.s.
2. Sometimes I feel like the "odd person out" because of the gender composition of my family.	−1.50 (1.10)	−0.60 (1.67)	−0.55 (1.43)	−1.70 (0.66)	a×b
3. Since most of the people in my family are of one sex, I find myself expressing more "masculine" values as a result.	+0.05 (1.10)	−0.85 (1.31)	−0.45 (1.28)	−1.80 (0.62)	a,b
4. Since most of the people in my family are of one sex, I find myself expressing more "feminine" values as a result.	−1.00 (1.08)	−0.75 (1.45)	−0.45 (1.23)	−0.65 (1.57)	n.s.
5. I occasionally feel isolated in my family because of my gender.	−1.65 (0.75)	−0.70 (1.63)	−0.85 (1.35)	−1.90 (0.45)	a×b
6. Deep down, I must admit that I feel a bit guilty about not having children of the other sex.	−1.32 (1.05)	−1.55 (1.54)	−1.50 (1.05)	−1.38 (1.10)	n.s.
7. I really have a sense of my family being unique because of its gender composition.	−0.15 (1.14)	+0.15 (1.60)	−0.25 (1.45)	0.00 (1.30)	n.s.
8. Since most of the people in our family are of one sex, I find that my spouse expresses more "masculine" values as a result.	−0.80 (1.20)	−0.60 (1.57)	−1.45 (1.10)	−1.20 (0.95)	a
9. Since most of the people in our family are of one sex, I find that my spouse expresses more "feminine" values as a result.	−0.75 (1.07)	−1.50 (1.05)	−0.60 (1.39)	−1.05 (1.32)	b

Note: The *Results* column indicates the comparisons that are statistically significant.
a = Main effect of family type.   a×b = Interaction effect of family type×sex of respondent.
b = Main effect of sex of respondent.   n.s. = not significant.

about not having a mixed-sex family (items 1 and 6) did not produce any significant difference between the male-tilted and female-tilted family members or between husbands and wives. Similarly, there were no significant findings associated with the statements regarding the perceived uniqueness of the family structure (items 7 and 10).

The remaining statements pertained to the expression of masculine and feminine values, both by the respondent him/herself (items 3 and 4) and by the respondent's spouse (items 8 and 9). Female spouses showed stronger disagreement than males with the idea that gender-tilting affected their own expression of "masculine" values. However, husbands and wives did not differ when asked whether gender-tilting affected their *spouse's* expression of these values. With both self and spouse ratings of masculine values, couples from female-tilted families had stronger disagreement than couples from male-tilted families. For the items dealing with the expression of "feminine values," no significant effects of gender-tilting were evident in either the self-ratings or the spouse ratings. However, the spouse ratings did show a significant main effect of sex of respondent, with the wives acknowledging stronger disagreement that their spouses were expressing more feminine values as a result of gender-tilting in their families.

The BSRI masculinity and femininity scales were scored as the average ratings given to the masculine and feminine descriptors. The results were largely complementary to those of the attitudinal items discussed above. One should bear in mind that both spouses in each family filled out the BSRI. Predictably, husbands achieved higher scores than wives on the masculinity scores. In addition, the couples from male-tilted families achieved higher scores on the masculinity dimension, but not on the femininity items.

The 14 PRF scales were reduced to six dimensions prior to statistical analysis, according to guidelines suggested by Jackson (1984). As with the FES, the component subscales were examined post hoc when significant comparisons emerged on the combined measures. The three remaining scales of the PRF (Autonomy, Understanding, and Dominance) were examined individually.

Four of the six ANOVAs produced significant main effects for the sex of respondent factor. The female spouses achieved lower scores for Impulse Expression, Work Orientation, and Autonomy, but scored higher on the dimension of Interpersonal Orientation. The Impulse Expression dimension also yielded a significant main effect of family type, with the male-tilted families obtaining higher scores. When this dimension was broken down into its component subscales it was observed that parents in male-tilted families expressed greater personal Impulsivity, and a lower need for Order. Wives achieved higher scores on Harm Avoidance than did husbands, but this scale was unrelated to gender tilting. The analyses of the remaining PRF dimensions did not produce statistically reliable findings with respect to family type.

In sum, the normal families could be classified as traditional, intact middle-class families which were comparable in all important respects except for the gender composition of the children. Nevertheless, it was evident that this one area of difference had a number of important ramifications, with regard both to the respondents' perceptions of their families and to their perceptions of themselves.

The parents in the male-tilted families reported higher levels of conflict in their homes, and they also expressed lower levels of satisfaction with their families. In contrast, the behavioral estimates of the amount of time spent engaged in particular family activities indicated that the parents of male-tilted families actually spend *more* time involved in recreational activities with their children. Apparently, the overall *amount* of interaction between family members is higher in male-tilted families, but the *quality* of the family relationships is more conflictual and less satisfying than in female-tilted family environments.

It should be noted, however, that the "outlying" spouses did not actually report that they spent *less* time in family activities. Rather, they reported that they spent *more* time by themselves. Hence, they may not be getting excluded from family activities that are sex-role inappropriate for them; they may be choosing to spend more time alone. In either case, there is some verification of the hypothesis that outlying spouses in tilted families are sensitive to their unique roles in their families. We suspect that there is a potential in tilted families for coalitions to form along gender lines, with alienation of the outlying spouse.

Overall, a consistent pattern emerges that indicates higher conflict in the male-tilted families, with a lower level of expressed satisfaction. The social environment imposed by the family structure leads to the parents making personal adaptations. The parents of all-boys, for example, may alter their own concerns for organization and order since they have learned that these are, in fact, difficult to achieve in male-tilted families. Their more masculine sex roles, as well as the more rash, reckless, and spontaneous styles suggested by the PRF Impulsivity scale, may also reflect personal changes engendered as an adaptation to their male-tilted family environments.

Research with Clinical Families

Family structure information was obtained from 200 patients, divided into three psychiatric diagnostic groups (schizophrenic, manic-depressive, and anorexic) and one group of diagnostically nonspecific family therapy clinic patients. All schizophrenic patients were interviewed individually regarding their families of origin. Approximately half of the bipolar patients were interviewed individually while half were contacted by telephone. The data for the anorexic/bulimic and family clinic patients were extracted from clinic charts.

The four diagnostic groups differed on a number of demographic characteristics. The eating disordered patients were all female, while the sex distributions of the identified patients in the other groups were mixed (affective disorders: 30 females; schizophrenics: 23 females; clinic families: 24 females). The average ages of the identified patients with eating disorders (M=22.2 years) and in the clinic families (M=24.7 years) were also significantly lower than those of the schizophrenic (M=42.8 years) and the affective disorders (M=46.1 years) patients.

The bipolar and schizophrenic patients came from families larger than those of either the eating disorders or clinic patients. In addition, the spacing in years between successive children in the families of the former groups was greater. However, since the schizophrenic and affective disorders patients were older, it may be that their larger, more widely-spaced families of origin reflect differences between the generational cohorts rather than factors specifically associated with these diagnoses. This caution does not extend to the examination of the sex configurations of the families of the different patient groups. Regardless of the overall size of the families, it would be expected that there would be an equal distribution of males and females for conditions in which gender-tilting is irrelevant.

When we narrowly define gender-tilting, we include as tilted only those families with children of a single gender. In all, 47 of the 200 families (23.5%) could be classified as tilted according to this strict criterion. For the affective disorders, schizophrenic, and clinic families, the number of male-tilted and female-tilted families did not vary significantly. Among families of eating disordered patients, it was observed that 16 contained female-only children, while none was male only. Using a more lenient criterion to define tilting (i.e., families in which there may be children of both sexes, but with more children of one sex) underscored the robustness of this finding. Twenty-one families of eating disordered patients (42%) were tilted in a female direction by two or more children, while only one was tilted to this extent in a male direction. In addition, significantly more patients with affective disorders came from families which were female-tilted by two or more children ($N=16$) than came from male-tilted families ($N=6$).

The major finding in this research was that patients with eating disorders have a higher likelihood of coming from female-tilted families. Female-tilting was also more prevalent among bipolar patients, although to a lesser degree.

Several other investigators have observed that the families of patients with eating disorders are predominantly female in their sibling structures (Bruch, 1973; Dally, 1969; Hall, 1978). However, the significance of this finding and even its reliability have been questioned (Garfinkel and Garner, 1982; Gowers, Kadambari, and Crisp, 1985). The arguments for and against female-tilting in the families of this patient group appear to be more methodological than substantive. Table 4 summarizes the findings of six studies of the families of patients with eating disorders in which the sex distributions of the children were considered. As is evident from the table, the results have been very consistent, although the interpretations have differed. Gowers, Kadambari, and Crisp (1985), for example, focused on the sex of the siblings and found that the numbers of brothers and sisters were about equal. Bruch (1973), on the other hand, examined the *families* as the relevant units of analysis, thus including the patients themselves when considering the sex composition. As is well-known, the patients are overwhelmingly female; hence their inclusion or exclusion is an important factor in determining gender-tilting. Table 4 indicates that the tendency for eating disorder patients to have more female than male siblings is small and only approaches statistical

TABLE 4
Gender Compositions in the Families of Patients with Eating Disorders

STUDY	N of PATIENTS	N of SISTERS	N of BROTHERS	SISTER BROTHER RATIO	N of GIRLS IN FAMILY	N of BOYS IN FAMILY	GIRL/ BOY RATIO
Bruch (1973)	70	69	68	1.01:1	139	68	2.04:1
Dally (1969)	140	137	117	1.17:1	277	117	2.37:1
Gowers, Kadambari & Crisp (1985)	252	228	216	1.06:1	456	240	1.90:1
Hall (1978)	50	62	48	1.29:1	112	48	2.33:1
Theander (1970)	94	114	102	1.12:1	208	114	1.82:1
Falconer & Ross	50	60	51	1.17:1	110	51	2.16:1
TOTAL	656	670	602	1.11:1	1302	638	2.04:1

significance. The *families*, however, are female-tilted by a ratio of about 2:1.

Many investigators consider the dynamics of the family system to be a central etiological factor in the eating disorders (Minuchin, 1978; Palazzoli, 1974). Others have suggested that these patients overidentify with traditionally feminine sex-role stereotypes (Bruch, 1973). The present findings suggest that these two influences may be related. The prominent female-tilting in the families of patients with eating disorders can be seen as providing a social environment that is more likely to promote the expression of traditionally feminine values. Given the importance of the family in the developmental socialization of the children into appropriate role behavior, the feminine influence inherent in the structure of the patients' families may lead to identification with more extreme gender roles.

The similar finding observed with the bipolar patients is more difficult to explain. Unipolar major depression is known to have a higher prevalence among women (Weissman and Klerman, 1977), which may also be related to feminine social roles (Amenson and Lewinsohn, 1981) learned initially in the families of origin. Bipolar affective disorder, on the other hand, is thought to have a more equal rate of incidence among males and females. Furthermore, the importance of family social and cultural influences on the etiology of bipolar disorder has not been emphasized to the same extent as with the eating disorders. The present results should be viewed as preliminary evidence related to family factors in bipolar disorder, which are in need of replication.

It appears that the sibling structure of the family represents an important determinant of the social environment in normal development and this, in turn, appears to be related to certain forms of psychiatric disturbance. Although there was no evidence that male-tilting plays a role in the development of any of the disorders investigated, female-tilting clearly emerges as a characteristic of the families of patients with eating disorders.

The present findings correspond well with those reported by Fishbein (1981) concerning families requesting therapy at the Philadelphia Child Guidance Clinic. Fishbein's review of family structural variables indicated that all-girl family constellations showed the lowest likelihood of treatment-seeking of any sibling configuration. Our study of normal families found lower levels of family conflict reported by the parents of female-tilted families. Fishbein suggested that female children tend to be more supportive and involved with family traditions, thus strengthening interpersonal commitments and family norms. An extensive body of sex-role research has also demonstrated that females are less likely than males to behave aggressively in a variety of situations and more likely to respond to challenges with cooperative rather than competitive interpersonal strategies (Deaux, 1976). Many of these findings appear to hold true for male and female children as well as for adults, with the trends becoming increasingly apparent with age (Cook and Stingle, 1974; Stingle and Cook, 1985). As our study suggests, this type of sex-role behavior may have important consequences for the family in general, both in normal development and in the development of certain psychiatric disorders.

Not only do the parents in all-boy and all-girl families have different perceptions of their families, but their self-concepts appear to be affected as well. In keeping with views expressed by Erikson (1963), Fishbein (1981) and systems theorists (Minuchin, 1978; Palazzoli, 1974), socialization into parent and child roles is a reciprocal process. The structure of the family emerges as one determinant of that process, with "gender-tilting" representing a central aspect of that structure.

FINDINGS AND BELIEFS ABOUT GENDER TILTING

Tilting might be important in family development and may even play a role in the development of psychopathology for several reasons. First, in a family with an imbalance of children of one gender we believe there may be strong feelings associated with this imbalance and a parallel wish for rebalancing. These feelings, we postulate, have to be directed somewhere. It makes sense to us to assume that one child in a family may collude with the parents and other siblings to take on their projections of these feelings. The finding in the eating disordered families is conceptually consistent with this idea. In these families uncertainty about femininity and sex role (Boskind-Lodahl, 1976) and about whether to take on more masculine characteristics (Cantelon, Leichner, and Harper, 1986) or to be more feminine (Squires and Kagan, 1985) is thought to contribute to the development of an eating disorder. One would expect an increased frequency of eating disorders with smaller families and more tilting, as we have observed. Second, the pressures of socialization of children into appropriate role behavior may lead to more extreme gender role identification in tilted families, which have stronger masculine or feminine influence. Third, the biological bisexuality of all humans may be differently expressed in families where the gender is imbalanced. Fourth, we believe that regardless of how much a parent loves and wishes for an opposite-sex child, he or she still also wishes for a child of the same sex. Because of this wish, when the first child does not fit the fantasy, the hope for the second and third child to fit the wish grows, i.e., he/she should be the opposite of the first child. Before we give our clinic examples it is worth reiterating that no family structure is inherently pathological and our research results and clinical hypotheses do not in any way imply that different structures are more or less likely to lead to health and happiness.

CASE EXAMPLES

The Johnson Family — Tilting as a Factor in Family Development Around Puberty

Bank and Kahn (1982) state that, "a parent's influence on a child's sexual identity is primary," but "a sibling can tip the scales and seriously influence how an individual completed the resolution of his or her sexual unfolding." This sibling influence is evident with the Johnson family, which consisted of mother, father, and three daughters aged 18, 15, and 13. The family came to see us because the 13-year-old daughter, "Bobby," was staying home from school. What struck us was the father's depression and lack of involvement and mother's overinvolvement. When the therapist commented on the fact that this family had no sons, the father became more animated, smiled, and said, "I guess I'm overrun by females. We even have a female cat and a female dog."

Of interest was Bobby's unisex name. Although she had been christened Roberta, she had been called Bobby almost from the day she was brought home from the hospital. Father said, "I don't know — she just looked more like a Bobby than a Roberta." Father mentioned that this youngest daughter, as she grew up, had trouble deciding whether she was a boy or a girl. We postulated that Bobby carried the family's projected wish for a son. The exploration of this idea seemed to increase father's involvement with the family and to strengthen the parent-child boundaries, thereby facilitating the structural change necessary to resolve the presenting problem. The idea was explored by looking at how the daughters were named, how the decisions were made to get female animals, how the parents decided to have no further children, and what effect the gender distribution had on both the parents' and siblings' hopes and expectations.

Father had always fantasized about being an athlete and had looked forward to playing games with "his boys." One after another the older girls had rejected this role as they passed through puberty and it had fallen to Bobby. Until puberty she had eagerly played games and attended sporting events with her father. Mother was involved with her two older girls and seemed not to have room in her life for another. However, when Bobby refused to attend school she became the center of the whole family's attention; in particular, her mother and sisters suddenly focused on her. Bobby's fear of going to school seemed directly related to her entering puberty and having to deal with her femaleness.

Our exploration seemed to give to all family members a real sense of father's uniqueness and his loss in not having a longed-for son. At the same time the exploration freed family members from guilt. Before they all seemed to feel that they had done something wrong; they were relieved to discuss openly the impact of their family structure on all of them. This case highlights several important dynamics: (1) the affective issues in the parental dyad around having and naming children; (2) the father's sense of too much femaleness; (3) the exaggeration of the problem by bringing animals into the family; and (4) the attempt at resolution by giving the last daughter the ambiguous name.

The Wilhe Family—Tilting as Part of an Unresolved Family Crisis

This family, consisting of father, mother, and two boys 13 and 10, came to therapy because the mother was depressed and increasingly suspicious that her husband was having an affair. Exploration revealed that in fact this was not the case; however, father had been spending more time away from home coaching a girls softball team.

Both parents stated that the second son was like the "girl" in the family, noting that he did not seem to be interested in the games and ideas of his peers. Mother in particular said that she thought he should be playing with his friends more and complained that whenever his father was at home he spent inordinate amounts of time hugging him and following him around.

Although this dynamic might easily be explained as part of the boy's fear of parental separation, our exploration discovered that after the birth of the second child the wife had still wanted to "try for or even adopt a girl," but father felt they couldn't afford a third child. Shortly after the birth of his second son he had an affair and then proceeded to have a vasectomy without telling his wife in advance. The vasectomy and the affair ended any further discussion of their having a little girl.

It was our distinct impression that this family had never fully dealt with its feelings about not having a girl. Our work with the couple showed quite clearly that both parents had had strong wishes for a little girl and that mother felt she had failed by not giving birth to one. She then overtly encouraged her husband to have an affair by withdrawing from him sexually and telling him that as he was no longer fertile he might as well have another "girl." The husband himself recognized the affair as an attempt to "have a girl" and restore his place and balance in the family.

Initially the family atmosphere was tense and clouded with unresolved anger. Mother was curt and accusatory while father was "so nice" and "loved his family." He was able to see how his work with the girls softball team was increasingly isolating him from his family. Exploring what they were both lacking and missing seemed to help resolve the presenting problem and decrease the blaming, defending sequences.

This work was done by first carefully looking at how the family structure had affected all members. This provided a more neutral, less conflicted area to work on and introduced new patterns of relating and new ways of seeing one another. Mother came to identify how her grief had been disguised in the pattern of blaming her husband. The father became able to talk about his loss and the pain he had felt in having a vasectomy "for the family."

In this case exploration of a buried developmental dilemma around tilting and gender expectation provided a new pattern of understanding that was consistent with the family's reality. We do not mean to imply, however, that present behavioral sequences are unimportant; rather, we contend only that tilting is one of many dynamics that can provide leverage for a therapist to help change current behavior. Tilting might be seen as both personal and interpersonal failure. For the Wilhes the "failure" to create a female child led to both personal loss and interpersonal distress reverberating throughout the family.

The Green Family — Tilting in a Family with a Psychotic Child

Mr. and Mrs. Green and their two sons, John, 21, and Tom, 20, came to our clinic after John had had a psychotic break and presented to our emergency team. Tom was bisexual and John was grossly overinvolved with his parents; in fact, his social life consisted only of going out with them. Father spent time each night washing John's back.

As we routinely do, usually in the first session, we asked the family members about the nature of their family structure and what possible feelings they had about it. This quite naturally led to the exploration of their wishes for a girl. Mrs. Green said she didn't worry about not having a little girl and knew her sons would give her a granddaughter. "Besides," she said, "the boys aren't leaving for a long time." Father laughed. Both parents seemed isolated, ineffective, and uncertain of their own sexuality. The parents had not slept together for many years, both dressed in neutral-color, baggy slacks and shirts, and mother wore no makeup; together they effectively hid any evidence of gender differentiation.

We hypothesized that not having a girl was very significant in this family and spent what seemed to be productive time exploring this issue. For example, Tom seemed surprised and relieved at the opportunity to use the discussion of the missing daughter to share many previously unspoken feelings about his own sexuality. Listening to his brother, John was most appropriate and attentive. This exploration allowed the family to develop a wider sense of its possibilities, to look at what it had been missing, and to take the focus off John. Both sons were very animated during the discussion.

Over the next several months, John was involved in individual sessions and pharmacotherapy, Mr. and Mrs. Green engaged in couple therapy, and in family therapy the four of them continued to explore this issue of not having a daughter and its relation to gender identity, role behavior, rules, boundary, and hierarchy. During this time Tom left home and John recovered from psychosis.

We are not proposing a cause-and-effect relationship between tilting and serious mental disorder or between exploration of family structure and recovery. However, this case does demonstrate how the tilting dynamic may have far reaching effects in stabilizing family dynamics in a pathological manner. In families in which both parents have major problems with gender and other identity issues, the loading of the family with children of all one gender may heighten these conflicts. In this case we speculate that Tom's bisexuality and John's psychosis were reflections of family and parental identity issues magnified in a tilted unit. If there had been a daughter, we speculate that this might have given Tom more freedom to be male, mother a person to project her wishes onto, father another female to love and be loved by thereby heightening his own secure sense of masculinity, and overall a different outcome for the family.

ROLE CONFUSION IN TILTED FAMILIES

In all families tasks are assigned according to roles and family members are responsible for completing them. The tilting process can have an important and insidious effect on this process. For instance, when a family tilts with three or more sons, mother may find her role behavior constricted through the gender imbalance, in the sense of having few female friends and participating in traditionally "male" activities to the exclusion of "female" interests. For instance, in one family we saw, the wife/mother with three sons had given up almost all interests other than hockey. We should make it clear that we are not endorsing these traditional roles and values as correct or desirable. Spouses may become isolated in their tilted family, uncertain of who they are or how they should behave. Fathers with two or more daughters may become depressed, isolated, demasculinized, and uncertain about how to deal with a world of women that both attracts and repels them. Gender confusion may develop when parents are not able to turn their wishes for a child of one gender or the other into reality. These wishes may then be displaced, denied or projected onto someone or something else, or a child may be treated as a member of the opposite gender or allowed to run wild, expressing the family's frustration.

PROBLEMS OF AUTONOMY IN TILTED FAMILIES

Autonomy is the ability to make independent choices and to take responsibility for those choices. In tilted families there is potential for fusion among the same gender members, with an odd person out. Without a clear sense of self, one's ability to make autonomous choices is hampered, as is one's ability to distinguish who is responsible for incorrect choices. A father may give up part of his masculinity in a female world and become increasingly uncertain of what choices are his. He may deal with this issue by becoming rigid and authoritarian, not allowing choice among the females. The reciprocal case applies for mothers. Children living in this fusion may be conflicted and have difficulty making emotionally-laden choices. In particular, we have noted that parents in heavily tilted families tend to choose the word "we" over the word "I." When parents do use the word "I," they often do so in a rigid manner. One father said, "We always decide together what's best for the boys." When asked to differentiate and use the word "I," he replied, "We do what my wife thinks is best for the boys."

PROBLEMS WITH BEHAVIOR CONTROL IN TILTED FAMILIES

Each family must set up rules and methods for dealing with needs, socialization, and danger to self and others. The clarity of these rules, whether they are spoken or unspoken, is a measure of the family's rigidity or flexibility. We believe that when a family tilts parents have greater difficulty in defining a clear hierarchy and boundary. In a family with a balanced sibship there is less tendency for distortion. The clinician needs to be aware of this potential underlying structural problem in order to help the family create clear, flexible rules.

Another fruitful area for exploration is each spouse's family of origin. As Toman (1976), (see Chapter 3), has shown, certain sib rank order matchings have a greater chance of marital and family success. According to Toman, an older sister marrying a younger brother is the best combination. We have found that exploration with each parent of the nature of his or her sibling structure enhances understanding of self and spouse and of relationships with their children. An interesting research question is whether children coming from tilted families have more marital problems later in life than those coming from families with balanced sibships.

SENSE OF LOSS IN TILTED FAMILIES

Whenever there are hopes and expectations, there is the possibility of disappointment. When two people marry, they bring with them personal, family, and cultural expectations; loss is almost inevitable. Families without children of both genders have to deal with such loss. They may seek to rebalance by looking outside of their own family. The mother may look for a little girl in her niece, her own mother or grandmother. The father may become involved in Big Brothers, spend more time with "the boys," or become a zealous hockey coach. Each of these and myriad other possibilities, such as the development of symptoms in a family member, has the potential for sickness or renewed health. The degree of resolution of these problems is a measure of the family's strength. We believe that a tilted family rebalances one way or the other regardless. We predict that tilted families are more likely than non-tilted ones to adopt children, and that they often adopt to rebalance their gender distribution. It is not so important whether parents rebalance inside or outside the family but it is crucial that they deal with their feelings about not having children of both sexes.

SUMMARY

There is an important place for the role of research on the role of sibling structure in the etiology, treatment, and prevention of mental disorder. Our research has confirmed that there are differences in family structure in major mental disorders and that families of anorexics are female-tilted. The ground-breaking works of Toman (1976) and Bank and Kahn (1982) have opened up a whole new field of possibilities for understanding family life; looking at the effect of gender tilting is another new possibility. The tilted family is a particular family structure which may carry with it increased risks of certain problems. Although Beth Henley did not say so overtly, and critics did not discuss it, we believe that, for Lenny, Meg, and Babe, as for many others, living in a tilted family was associated with subtle but unrecognized "crimes of the heart."

REFERENCES

Amenson, C. S., & Lewinsohn, P. M. (1981). An investigation into the observed sex difference in prevalence of unipolar depression. *Journal of Abnormal Psychology, 90*, 1–13.

Bank, S. P., & Kahn, M. D. (1982). *The sibling bond.* New York: Basic Books.

Bem, S. L. (1981). *Bem sex-role inventory professional manual.* Palo Alto: Consulting Psychologists Press.

Boskind-Lodahl, M. (1976). Cinderella's stepsisters: A feminist perspective on anorexia nervosa and bulimia. *Signs: Journal of Women in Culture and Society, 2*(2): 342–356.

Bruch, H. (1973). *Eating disorders: Obesity, anorexia and the person within.* New York: Basic Books.

Cantelon, L. J., Leichner, P. P., & Harper, D. W. (1986). Sex-role conflict in women with eating disorders. *International Journal of Eating Disorders, 5*, 317–323.

Cook, H., & Stingle, S. F. (1974). Cooperative behavior in children. *Psychological Bulletin, 81*, 918–934.

Dally, P. (1969). *Anorexia nervosa.* London: William Heinemann Medical Books.

Deaux, K. (1976). *The behavior of women and men.* Monterey: Brooks/Cole.

Elder, G. H., & Bowerman, C. E. (1963). Family structure and child-rearing patterns: The effect of family size and sex composition. *American Sociological Review, 28*, 891–905.

Erikson, E. H. (1963). *Childhood and society.* (2nd ed.). New York: Norton.

Falconer, C. W., & Ross, C. A. (1986). The tilted family. *Canadian Journal of Psychiatry, 31*, 649–652.

Fishbein, H. D. (1981). Sibling set configuration and family dysfunction. *Family Process, 20*, 311–318.

Garfinkel, P. E., & Garner, D. M. (1982). *Anorexia nervosa: A multidimensional perspective.* New York: Brunner/Mazel.

Gowers, S., Kadambari, S. R., & Crisp, A. H. (1985). Family structure and birth order of patients with anorexia nervosa. *Journal of Psychiatric Research, 19*, 247–251.

Hall, A. (1978). Family structure and relationship of 50 female anorexia patients. *Australia and New Zealand Journal of Psychiatry, 12*, 263–268.

Hollingshead, A. B. (1975). Hollingshead four-factor index. Unpublished manuscript, Yale University.

Jackson, D. N. (1984). *Personality research form manual.* (3rd ed.). Port Huron: Research Psychologists Press.

Kagel, G. H., White, R. M., & Coyne, J. C. (1978). Father-absent and father-present families of disturbed and non-disturbed adolescents. *American Journal of Orthopsychiatry, 48*, 342–352.

Minuchin, S. (1978). *Psychosomatic Families.* Cambridge: Harvard University Press.

Moos, R. H., & Moos, B. S. (1986). *Family environment scale manual.* (2nd ed.). Palo Alto: Consulting Psychologists Press.

Murray, H. A. (1938). *Explorations in personality.* Cambridge: Harvard University Press.

Nystul, M. S. (1981). Effects of siblings' sex composition on self-concept. *Journal of Psychology, 108,* 133–136.

Olson, D. H., & Wilson, M. (1985). Family satisfaction. In D. H. Olson, H. I. McCubbin, H. Barnes, A. Larsen, M. Muxen, & M. Wilson (Eds.), *Family Inventories* (rev. ed.). St. Paul: Family Social Sciences, University of Minnesota.

Palazzoli, M. S. (1974). *Self starvation.* London: Human Context Books.

Rosenberg, M. (1965). *Society and the adolescent self-image.* Princeton: Princeton University Press.

Squires, R. L., & Kagan, D. M. (1985). Sex-role and eating behavior among college women. *International Journal of Eating Disorders, 4,* 539–548.

Stingle, S. F., & Cook, H. (1985). Age and sex differences in the cooperative and noncooperative behavior of pairs of American children. *Journal of Psychology, 119,* 335–345.

Theander, S. (1981). Anorexia nervosa—a psychiatric investigation of 94 female patients. *Acta Psychiatrica Scandinavia, 214* (suppl), 1+.

Toman, W. (1976). *Family constellation.* (3rd ed.). New York: Springer.

Weissman, M. M., & Klerman, F. L. (1977). Sex differences and the epidemiology of depression. *Archives of General Psychiatry, 34,* 98–111.

14

The Vortex:
Siblings in the Eating Disordered Family

Laura Giat Roberto

Psychosomatic families, especially those with an anorexic or bulimic adolescent, suffer from overly rich emotional connectedness between members. "Enmeshed," "centripetal," and "too richly cross-joined" are some of the terms used to describe this connectedness (Hoffman, 1975; Minuchin, Rosman, and Baker, 1978; Stierlin, 1972). In the Eating Disorders Program at Eastern Virginia Medical School we have been following eating disordered families since 1982 in an effort to find new and more powerful interventions for the affected young women, their parents, and their siblings.

Anorexia nervosa and bulimia are usually seen in teenagers and young adults; 85% of them are female, and they commonly present between 14 and 20 years of age, the younger being starvers and the older binge-purgers. That is, families tend to notice self-starvation early, near its onset, and bring their daughter to the doctor or therapist at around age 14. The parents and siblings of a bulimic girl are less aware of her secretive binge-eating and purging and are slower to mobilize around her. Bulimics, who usually begin purging in mid to late adolescence, usually hide their behavior successfully until young adulthood. Compared to young adolescent patients, these young adults are more likely to be chronically symptomatic (Halmi, Casper,

The author wishes to acknowledge Paul Dell and Robert Marshall Smith, colleagues at the Eastern Virginia Family Therapy Institute, for their commentary on earlier presentations of this material; and Janet Smyer for her clerical assistance.

Eckert, Goldberg, and Davis, 1979). The frequency of relapse with anorexia attests to a low success rate over the long term with traditional models of psychotherapy (Garfinkel and Garner, 1982).

Anorexia nervosa is a disorder which tends to mobilize therapists quickly around the identified patient. Self-starvation produces a young woman who looks emaciated and skeletal. She is dehydrated and has hypothermia; the clinician may see amenorrhea and endocrinologic changes, gastric ulceration and thinning, spinal deterioration and neurological, cognitive, and affective impairments (depression) (Spack, 1985). Kidney and liver failure can occur.

Bulimia does not always elicit the same level of familial or professional alarm, since it often occurs in women of normal weight who are living away from the parental home. However, complications of bulimia include tooth loss and gum disease, menstrual irregularities, functional hypoglycemia, enlarged colon, esophogeal damage, hiatal hernia, hypokalemia, dehydration, and cardiac arrest (Boskind-White and White, 1987). While such severe symptoms necessitate immediate medical intervention (and at times hospitalization), behavioral change requires intervention in the entire understructure of interactions and ascribed meanings ("legacy") in the extended family system of grandparents, parents, symptomatic daughter, and siblings, as well as spouses and children if they are present (Roberto, 1987).

THE NATURE OF EATING DISORDERED FAMILIES

Families with an anorexic or bulimic daughter present with a peculiar veneer of competence overlaying severe deficits. Characteristic defects include: lack of sustained conflict and conflict resolution; disqualification of messages using rejection, confusion, or denial; triangulation of the symptomatic daughter into parental distress; enmeshment with isolation from the outside community; overprotection; detouring of family conflict into psychosomatic symptoms; tenacious loyalty to old patterns of behavior; and a spirit of self-sacrifice (Minuchin et al., 1978; Selvini Palazzoli, 1978). These "process" characteristics make it difficult for family members to talk about affect-laden personal differences or to make space for consideration of individual and dyadic (e.g., husband-wife) needs.

In addition to these "process" problems, eating disordered families show specific developmental deficits. The parents do not encourage and teach their children a process of individuation which should rightly culminate in moderate attention to hygiene and self-grooming, a sense of self-respect, and pursuit of autonomous social and emotional strivings. The sons and daughters become unwilling to conduct their lives away from the family in a deep and satisfying manner, and instead channel their need for independence into efforts to control weight, body contours, and appearance.

Life within the "vortex" of the psychosomatic family thus contains few options for each member as he or she attempts to cope with internal needs and differences. Strivings for intimacy, for mastery or achievement, for acceptance, and for independence may only be realized in specific ways, since there are strong transgenerational values and belief systems or "legacies" that dictate which choices will generate approval (Roberto, 1986). These "family legacies" interfere not only with maturation in the identified patient, but also intimacy between her parents and among her siblings. In such a rigid, binding family structure sons and daughters grow up emotionally guarded, self-punitive, and nonsupportive, while appearing superficially competent, self-confident, and attractive.

The family legacies in eating disordered families focus heavily on symbolic meanings of food and eating (e.g., starving to express anger); achievement of perfection and success; fitness and appearance-consciousness; preservation of harmony and sameness; and a demand for loyalty and cohesion (Roberto, 1987; Schwartz, Barrett, and Saba, 1985; White, 1983). There is a strong implicit demand for compliance with these legacies in order to be considered a "good son" or a "good daughter." Family members carry a sense of obligation toward one another, particularly the children toward the parents: This involves the determination to make the parents proud, to guard their happiness, to avoid disappointing their expectations, and to protect them from emotional loss.

Often one or both parents, most visibly the mother, tend to exert control over sibling intimacy and conflict as the children grow more verbal and more differentiated with age. Each child is thus encouraged to bond primarily with the adults and only nominally with the siblings. Sibling bonding is experienced as challenging by the parents. This focus produces siblings who do not know each other intimately, who relate on a partial level of appearances, and who do not perceive one another's needs or distress (Bank and Kahn, 1982).

In families of anorexics, the bonding between siblings usually is total-ly compromised. Bulimic offspring, who periodically make explosive efforts to separate, may turn to a sibling despite parental pressure.

By preadolescence, the sibling who will later become anorexic or bulimic becomes the identified patient while the others are perceived (and may perceive themselves) as unblemished. The potentially symp-tomatic sibling is seen as a sensitive or easily distressed child. She may begin to express her distress by starving or overeating and then move on to long-term patterns of self-starvation, binge eating and fasting, or binge-eating and purging. As she persists in using food, starvation, and/or purging to express emotional turmoil, she becomes ill with medical symptoms. These may include exhaustion and collapse, di-gestive problems, dehydration and systemic dysregulation, cardiac complications, or organ failure. She appears increasingly confused, distractible, withdrawn, hypersensitive, and clouded in her judg-ment. As the "well" siblings are enlisted or volunteer to monitor her health, the "vortex" of family demands and self-denial threatens to engulf them also.

LIFE IN THE VORTEX: SIBLING DEIDENTIFICATION

Since the identified patient is in adolescence when the eating disor-der appears, the brothers and sisters are likely to be preadolescents or adolescents themselves. The adolescent family of the 1980s tends to be small, with a narrow age span from oldest to youngest child. Further, the disintegration of extended family networks into small, mobile, nuclear family units has removed cousins and other peers from the household or neighborhood (Bank and Kahn, 1982). There-fore, the "well" siblings, like their ill sister, are engaged in a process of separation and individuation from the distressed family.

On the surface the therapist sees many similarities in appearance and values among brothers and sisters, an image evoked in Selvini Palazzoli's case of the "all for one and one for all" family (Palazzoli, Boscolo, Cecchin, and Prata, 1978). Little is known about the con-cordance rate of anorexia or bulimia in siblings; however, cross-ad-dictions to drugs and/or alcohol are common (Schwartz et al., 1985), as is obesity.

The eating disordered teen can be considered in a "high-access" relationship with her siblings (Bank and Kahn, 1982). High-access relationships are characterized by areas of similarity, such as being close in age, being of the same gender, attending school during the same time period, attending schools homogeneous in their academic emphasis, sharing friendship circles, sharing a room and possessions (and often clothing), and forming similar identifications. High-access relationships are generally characterized by reciprocity between the siblings (Dunn, 1983), where brothers and sisters interact on a symmetrical level, sharing in play and emotional interchange, mimicking each other, and stimulating each other to action and fantasy. However, what ought to develop into highly attached, empathic relationships between the symptomatic sister and her siblings is stunted by the rigid and affectively suppressed structure of the family. Because the children hold themselves in check, siblings form alliances based primarily on responsibility and family loyalty. They rarely engage in the emotional, conflictual give-and-take that produces mature understanding and intimacy.

The centripetal structure of the anorexic or bulimic family includes parental overprotection but not support. The overprotective stance often seems to emanate from the mother, who appears intrusive into the emotions and decisions of the children. However, this focus on the children meets the dependency needs of *both* parents and is expressed either as compliant dependency ("we need you to be like us") or oppressive dependency ("we demand that you be like us"). In this context of dependency, one daughter is pulled into a "three-way marriage" with her parents, which the siblings readily perceive. As she becomes the bearer of her parents' projections and needs, she is separated from her siblings and communication on a deep personal level is interrupted. The anorexic or bulimic daughter is invariably described as "always having been such a good girl"—better than her brothers and sisters. This view prevails until her compliance, passivity, and self-destructive behavior begins to take on bizarre proportions: starving; throwing tantrums at the dinner table; engaging in food rituals (e.g., peeling grapes); leaving evidence of self-induced purging; or showing confusion, amnesia, or disorientation. Then panic occurs; the affected daughter is labeled as "ill" or "bad" and another sibling is perceived as "the good one" or "the well one."

Despite these "high-access" conditions, the triangulation between mother, father (or a grandparent), and symptomatic daughter interferes with the process of fighting and cooperating that creates sibling closeness. The parents, hypervigilant in their monitoring and emotionally overactive with the children, force the children to "go through" them to communicate with each other. This communication pattern results not from overt demands or authoritarian instructions but from such dependency and reactivity that the siblings (and at times the therapist) cannot help but to direct their communications toward the sensitive parents. The parents, central in the family's affective life, evolve into speaking for their children, interpreting them to one another, mediating and suppressing disagreements, and thus preventing any real interaction between siblings. The child may soon get the message, "You need me because I need you; without your 'goodness' I will become unhappy."

This overinvestment in the life of the children is often an attempt to counteract parental deprivations experienced by mother and/or father in childhood. Or it may represent a response to pressures experienced in highly connected families of origin. The overinvestment also functions as a distraction from marital problems that might threaten family cohesion (Roberto, 1987; Stierlin, 1972). However, despite parental monitoring of *all* the children, the desire to fulfill transgenerational legacies creates a tendency for preference or favoritism to be shown toward the most loyal, compliant, successful, and apparently "perfect" child. Researchers find that favoritism and differential focusing intensify sibling rivalry, conflict, coalitions, and ultimately severe alienation or "deidentification" (Bank and Kahn, 1982; Dunn, 1983; Holmes, 1980; Schachter, 1985).

Deidentification (the state of extreme alienation) and partial identification (the persistent sense of being "different") are usually much more common in families with "low-access" siblings (Bank and Kahn, 1982). In families with an eating disorder, the sense of "differentness" arises from impoverished communications between the siblings, such that sisters (and, even more so, sisters and brothers) come to understand only parts of each other and lack deep knowledge of one another's needs and wishes. The parts which are perceived and understood are those which conform with familial values and legacies: strivings for success, beauty and popularity; self-control; and loyalty to the family. Siblings in a partial identification are likely to support each other only when necessary to protect themselves against a third party (e.g., the therapist!); those who are deidentified are rarely mutually supportive (Bank and Kahn, 1982).

Since interpersonal conflict is threatening to the family, disrupting the surface cohesion, the excessive competition and rivalry for approval cannot surface and be discussed openly and then resolved. Through adolescence and into young adulthood, the sibling roles become "frozen" and rigidified into that of "sick" anorexic or bulimic girl and "well" successful sisters or brothers. As the "sick" sister sinks further into her symptoms and the sibling subsystem disintegrates, former partial identifications are weakened and become deidentifications. Siblings feel different from one another—unrelated, unattached, and unconcerned.

Tragically, this circumstance comes about at precisely the point when the anorexic or bulimic sister is most needy of peer support and the siblings most needy of an alliance to achieve separation from the centripetal, binding family unit. In a pathological dynamic called "the Cain complex" (Schachter, 1982), the "well" siblings either leave home in a state of emotional cutoff from other family members or join a coalition with one or both parents against the "sick" sister. The family's request for treatment often occurs when one of the brothers or sisters has sided with a parent and reported the patient's purging and food restriction. Even this "referring" sibling may be crippled by the struggle for status, fearful of change and loss (Selvini Palazzoli, 1985), and tempted to depart quickly if asked to participate in therapy.

DESTROYING THE VORTEX: THE PROCESS OF CHANGE

Although clinical research clearly shows that transgenerational deficits and conflicts underlie the enmeshed, dysfunctional behavior of the eating disordered family (e.g., Selvini Palazzoli, 1978; Selvini Palazzoli et al., 1978), it is curious to note that most treatment programs stop short of actually focusing on these patterns in therapy. For instance, the family in treatment is required to "bring everyone living at home" (Sargent, Liebman, and Silver, 1985), excluding siblings who have left the family of origin and now reside elsewhere or attend college. Logistically, it is simpler to work with family members residing together than to gather departed siblings; yet the brothers and sisters of a starving or purging woman are affected by precisely the same familial pressures that maintain her illness. Further, these siblings possess the necessary adaptive skills *within the belief system of the closed family unit* to help the identified patient. Although the siblings have succeeded in differentiating themselves enough to physically leave the family home, they are well aware of the covert legacies and demands that burden them and the ill sister. They are also usually aware that family visits are not fun and that there is something wrong. Yet they are not outsiders and have an appreciation for the deep-rooted nature of parental wishes and family traditions. In centripetal, closed family structures, it simply adds to therapeutic potency to involve as many extended family members as is possible.

Our clinical methods in the Eastern Virginia treatment program reflect current transgenerational theory, specifically symbolic-experiential family therapy (Whitaker and Keith, 1981). Although patterns of enmeshment, self-sacrifice, pathological loyalty, drive for success and other family beliefs are clarified and challenged, messages to the family emphasize the here-and-now rather than historical and analytic commentary. The therapist's role is to maintain neutrality and to reframe for the family in metaphorical language the destructive family legacy, using terms experientially familiar to them. Metaphorical language is particularly useful with psychosomatic families because it brings affect and drama into their constricted, avoidant family process. For example, an anorexic daughter can accept that she is "fighting with her body and not with words." Her father can also accept that "fights seem so disrespectful and unpleasant in such a good family." The mother can see that "it must at least preserve decorum if she fights with her body."

Comments in this paradoxical manner challenge the premises underlying the dysfunctional belief system while maintaining the family's tradition of being interconnected and mutually respectful. Messages about the family's covert belief system, values, and mandates also appeal strongly to adolescent and young adult children, since at this point in their lives they are questioning interpersonal rules. As Kahn and Bank (1981) have noted,

> By uniting together in the service of helping one of the siblings, the now adult children can more successfully challenge the usual patterns of defense of one or both parents. (p. 94)

Finally, because there is recurrent cycling of blame between members due to overly rich emotional interconnections, in the early phase of treatment metaphorical reframings are better tolerated than direct challenges (Roberto, 1986).

Unlike structural or strategic interventions, interventions into destructive family legacies do not focus solely on parent-child conflict. We believe that the alienated and rigidified relationship between the anorexic or bulimic daughter and her siblings is as important in symptom maintenance as parent-child, parent-parent, or parent-family-of-origin conflicts. The "sick" sister and "well" brothers and sisters show a number of symptom-maintaining patterns in their relationships. First, there is the destructive "freezing" of the role of the "sick" sister (Bank and Kahn, 1982), so that her communications are disqualified. For example, one anorexic 17-year-old, when attempting to explain to her younger sister that she felt depressed about chronic parental alienation at home, was told, "You'll feel differently when your faith in Christ is improved." Such disqualifications serve only to increase the anorexic's sense of differentness and self-blame.

A second problem is the negativity and mistrust generated by the process of sibling deidentification, such that symptomatic sisters are fearful of provoking rejection with bids for aid. For example, a bulimic 32-year-old woman appealed to her older brothers for help in recalling instances of violent paternal abuse; they replied, "We don't know what you're talking about, and besides, our kids need to be whipped into line too." Finally, even when the affected sister is courageous enough to explore ways of changing the family organization, preferred brothers and sisters may be reluctant to ally with her for fear that they will lose status.

There are three central goals for the eating disordered patient and her siblings in transgenerational family therapy:

1. to create a therapeutic context in which the problems and dilemmas of the "well" brothers and sisters receive more attention, and the disorder of the "sick" sister is less monitored and pathologized;
2. to take advantage of the developmental stage of prepubertal and postpubertal siblings to introduce doubt, questioning, and an experimental attitude toward the rigid, constricted family belief system;
3. to combat the centripetal nature of the family, its "vortex," by

developing the sibling alliance so that younger and older siblings can help each other separate from and leave the family.

In the earliest family sessions, brothers and sisters often resist
being included with the symptomatic sister in therapy. Inclusion disrupts the process of deidentification around which a "well" sibling
has often forged much of his/her identity (Bank and Kahn, 1982). As
mentioned earlier, the "well" siblings have often attained "white
knight" status, compensating for the stress and humiliation of the
defective member by performing and appearing superbly. Because
their efforts have won parental approval and family cohesion, alliance
with the "sick" sister is anxiety-provoking. Secondly, the affective
"vortex" of family expectations can be extremely threatening to these
"well" siblings and motivate them to avoid participation in escalating
conflict.

The therapist who accepts at face value the privileged position of
idealized or referring siblings is in danger of validating it (Selvini
Palazzoli, 1985) and with it the whole underlying family pattern of
favoritism. It is necessary to intervene early to explicitly confirm the
position of the nonsymptomatic siblings as part of a parental coalition, thus exposing the dysfunctional aspects of their position. Yet it
is equally necessary to avoid further burdening them by violating
their loyalties and demanding further self-sacrifice in the name of the
distressed sister (Kahn and Bank, 1981).

With appropriate caution, much can be done to accomplish our
three goals for the sibling group. Below we discuss these separately
and consider the expected effects on the starving or purging of the
eating disordered sister.

Creating a Therapeutic Context
With Attention to "Well" Siblings

To the extent that they have been allowed, the "well" siblings have
shared with their sister in important group functions; forming identifications; differentiating from one another; mutually regulating behavior; providing services to one another when needed; dealing with
the distressed parents through coalitions and alliances; "translating"
and mediating in parental disputes; and forging into formerly unfamiliar adolescent territory (Bank and Kahn, 1976; Rosenberg, 1980).

However, due to the illness ensuing from their sister's starving or purging, one or more siblings have moved beyond serving as potential resources and assumed the role of the "good," nonneedy, and successful ones. It is the therapist's task early in family therapy to diffuse the emotionally fused triangle of parents (or parent and grandparent) and "sick" sister by acknowledging and underscoring the presence of brothers and sisters who have their own developmental tasks to complete, their own internal anxiety and pain, and their own emotional connection to parents and sister.

Whenever possible we arrange this intervention beginning in the second or third session; the first session (and if necessary the second) is devoted to a painstaking review of the eating disordered patient's symptoms, emotional state, physical condition, and relations with each family member. After this initial exhaustive assessment siblings usually have intense emotional reactions to the enmeshed family's problems, ranging from anxiety and caretaking efforts to disgust and refusal to participate further. These responses create fertile ground for exploration of fraternal and sororal needs, identification of symptoms, and discussion of each member's unique position in the family.

When siblings are married or have already left the family home for college, the therapist must attempt to include them at the earliest possible date. Various steps are taken, including messages when the sister is hospitalized or messages requesting a consultation in the form of information about the family. We do not directly communicate to these siblings that they are part of the family problem, since they believe they have escaped the vortex of painful familial needs.

Once siblings have joined the family session we utilize two to three sessions to expand the presenting problem to include the roles and symptoms of the siblings; possible roles are parental confidant, family therapist, "maverick" who dares to be different, guardian to the sister, nonentity who requires nothing from the family, and "white knight" who serves as a model of perfection. The effect of this intervention on the starving or purging sister is to detriangulate her from parental conflict and move her toward a sibling subgroup. At this time, she is likely to make sudden but dramatic decisions and abandon her former passive, reactive stance. Some anorexics decide to enter the hospital for refeeding; others demand immediate cessation of meetings and threaten to grow worse; still others suddenly stop purging or restricting food. Almost all report a nonspecific sense of relief in the first month of sessions, which is attributed to "things being out in the open."

> Kate, an obese 26-year-old college dropout, had since age 19 en-
> gaged in binge-eating followed by self-induced vomiting twice a day.
> Despite individual therapy for 18 months on a twice-weekly basis, she
> had made no progress and was increasingly depressed, hopeless, and
> withdrawn. Although she was paralyzed by her symptoms, she was
> medically stable enough for outpatient treatment. In the first family
> therapy sessions she and her 22-year-old collegiate sister laid out how
> their older brother, Clint, 30, had become a parental stick-in-the-mud
> businessman like Dad, how the 22-year-old worked to keep trim and
> good-looking like their parents, and how Kate secretly worried about
> the 22-year-old's continuous alcohol abuse. By the fifth session Kate
> was quite actively verbal about her frustration; she now binged and
> purged only weekly; she began to lose weight. For the first time she
> approached her brother about the way he distanced himself from her
> and others.

Utilizing Adolescent Experimentation
to Challenge the Family Legacy

The first phase of family therapy of eating disorders includes an evaluation, a medical and nutritional intervention when necessary, and an expansion of the presenting problem to include the responses of the siblings. This phase terminates when the therapist delivers to the family a description of the enmeshed, rigid, appearance-oriented family legacy which has bound them all to strict codes of behavior (Roberto, 1986). The second stage of therapy involves an attempt to challenge and alter this familial pattern, thereby allowing the eating disordered woman and her siblings to separate emotionally and abandon perfectionism without being perceived as deviant and without somatizing stress. The sibling group, developmentally in or close to adolescence, is ideally positioned to issue challenges from inside the centripetal, closed family system.

During the second phase of treatment, many sibling conflicts are reframed as by-products of the competitive, pressured family system. The therapist suggests that they may have hurt each other "unintentionally" in the process of surviving emotionally, e.g., bidding for parental attention while the needs of a brother go unmet (Ranieri and

Pratt, 1978). In these midphase sessions, the symptoms of the identi-fied patient are referred to as self-sacrificial and dutiful in terms of complying with the transgenerational family legacy. The siblings are encouraged to focus on similarly self-sacrificial behavior, such as episodes of superficial compliance when covertly they disagree or are angry, excessive efforts to control and improve their looks and weights, and problems in directly engaging in conflict. Such discus-sion paves the way for later strengthening the sibling generational alliance without demands from or confrontation by the therapist.

Finally, as the patient and her parents battle in the sessions over symptomatic behaviors such as weight loss, excessive exercise, covert binge-eating, and evidence of purging, the siblings are drawn into the battle by the therapist, who may ask a young adult brother or sister instead of the identified patient to respond or may elicit the siblings' position on such matters as intimacy, self-control, and family con-flict. Siblings can provide a questioning stance about alternative methods of coping with overprotection, enmeshment, conflict avoid-ance, rigidity, and perfectionism. In turn, since over the years they have become emotionally constrained by the wish to succeed where she has not, they obtain a degree of spontaneity and freedom by the therapist to "break the rules." Working together under the therapist's orchestration, the siblings can participate in a mutual process of separation and individuation (Bank and Kahn, 1982; Hamlin and Timberlake, 1981).

> In the fifth family session, Kate's elder brother Clint acknowledged that he regretted having lost his personal involvement with her. Kate revealed that, because of her anger and self-consciousness, she had refused to participate in his wedding three years before and had delib-erately avoided him and his wife since then. The siblings agreed that the mutual withdrawal had produced hurt feelings and perceptions of abandonment, and that their surface cordiality belied severe underly-ing alienation and mistrust. Kate and Clint began speaking by tele-phone and meeting between sessions.
>
> During the next month of meetings, Clint revealed that during his elementary school years the children were introduced rapidly to sup-pression of needs and pseudomutual behavior as their father pursued a 12-hour business day and their mother commuted across country to attend to her terminally ill mother. Clint was unwilling to voice dis-agreement with this "responsibility first" legacy; indeed, the father

reported with pride that only through self-sacrificial hard work had their paternal grandfather survived financially while a business partner jumped from an office window during the depression. However, Kate's younger sister, Sylvie, began to take issue over family appearance consciousness with mother. The therapist was then able to reflect to this family their legacy of "responsibility first—cooperate or perish" and to point out that through food compulsions and withdrawal Kate spared her loved ones and herself discord while primarily sacrificing her own development.

Destroying the Vortex: Developing a Sibling Alliance

In the third phase of treatment, the family is viewed as a three-generational grouping with each generation addressed separately. This is a painful period in which family members face what it means to give up their previously enmeshed organization: the adolescent offspring preparing to leave home; the awesome responsibility of pursuing separate lives; and the underlying misery of the unsatisfactory parental marriage. During this time siblings often pull back from their growing knowledge of one another and keep contact to a minimum, and parents may encourage this behavior to protect the siblings from "contamination effects" emanating from the recovering sister's unfamiliar and threatening autonomous behavior (Hamlin and Timberlake, 1981). This phase focuses on strengthening generational boundaries (Roberto, 1987), and appears quite structural in format: At times brothers and sisters are seen together and the marital or parental unit (parent-friend, parent-grandparent, divorced parent) is seen separately.

The siblings are encouraged to develop their newly acquired language regarding important life events, family patterns, and perceptions. Remaining myths regarding the incompetence of the symptomatic sister and the superior strength of her peers are explored and modified. The therapist explicitly supports a mutual alliance among the siblings while acknowledging individual differences. Since siblings often are separated by college responsibilities or distant residency, work continues over the telephone, around prolonged holiday visits, and by planned visits. By this time a fundamental shift will have occurred for the anorexic or bulimic sister—she will no longer automatically think of the parents as the primary resource in her life.

After destruction of the family "vortex" supportive treatment must focus on the parenting subsystem. One or both parents usually become depressed and/or angry at the loss of the comforting family fusion. Careful intervention will help them to experience the new, more differentiated family positively and to restore the marriage or the parental support network.

> In the third month of family sessions, Kate engineered a prolonged and emotional confrontation with both parents at home; afterwards she neither walked out nor purged. Her brother and sister did not schedule any further time together but attended several dinners as a group in the parental home. Their mother subsequently described the paternal grandfather as a tyrannical figure who had hounded and criticized father and his brother into hopelessness and overwork. Kate spontaneously made plans to depart for college; Clint and his wife took their first marital vacation, and Sylvie prepared for a semester abroad. Kate, no longer binge-eating or vomiting and at normal weight, began to speak by telephone to her sister on a weekly basis. Although the parents declined an invitation for marital sessions, the mother asked to view videotapes of the middle phase of therapy and reported that she and her husband were gratified that the therapy had touched on such long-term problems.

CONCLUSION

Eating disordered families suffer from extreme emotional connectedness that binds the offspring to the older parental and grandparental generations. This connectedness is like an emotional vortex drawing all the offspring into a centripetal, interdependent spiral. One consequence of the family vortex is a destructive deidentification process between the anorexic or bulimic daughter and her own siblings, contributing to her self-punitive attitudes, withdrawal, and dependency. Transgenerational family techniques offer a powerful tool for entering into these overconnected families and separating offspring as a group and as individuals. These techniques hinge on formulation and use of each family's unique "legacy" or belief system and its attendant expectations and demands. Adolescent and young adult sons and daughters can make considerable use of this therapeutic metaphor, since it highlights limitations in family functioning and mobilizes developmental interest in individuation and change. When the siblings participate in the therapy process, the anorexic or bulimic sister is strengthened, since overprotection and deidentification by her siblings are blocked. As the sibling group achieves greater mutual empathy and bonding, their cooperation boosts reexamination of the family legacy. And, as sons and daughters reexamine the rigid demands, constricting beliefs, and perfectionism of old family patterns, challenge and change inevitably follow.

REFERENCES

Bank, S., & Kahn, M. D. (1976). Sisterhood-brotherhood is powerful: Sibling subsystems and family therapy. In S. Chess & A. Thomas (Eds.), *Annual progress in child psychiatry and child development* (pp. 493–519). New York: Brunner/Mazel.

Bank, S., & Kahn, M. D. (1982). *The sibling bond*. New York: Basic Books.

Boskind-White, M., & White, W. (1987). *Bulimarexia: The binge-purge cycle*. (2nd edition) New York: Norton.

Dunn, J. (1983). Sibling relationships in early childhood. *Child Development, 54*, 787–811.

Garfinkel, P. E., & Garner, D. M. (1982). *Anorexia nervosa: A multi-dimensional perspective*. New York: Brunner/Mazel.

Halmi, K. A., Casper, R. C., Eckert, E. D., Goldberg, S. C. & Davis, J. M. (1979). Unique features associated with age of onset of anorexia nervosa. *Psychiatry Research, 1*, 209–215.

Hamlin, E. R., & Timberlake, E. M. (1981). Sibling group treatment. *Clinical Social Work Journal, 9*, 101–110.

Hoffman, L. (1975). "Enmeshment" and the too richly cross-joined system. *Family Process, 14*, 457–468.

Holmes, J. (1980). The sibling and psychotherapy: A review with clinical examples. *British Journal of Medical Psychology, 53*, 297–305.

Kahn, M. D., & Bank, S. (1981). In pursuit of sisterhood: Adult siblings as a resource for combined individual and family therapy. *Family Process, 20*, 85–95.

Minuchin, S., Rosman, B., and Baker, L. (1978). *Psychosomatic families: anorexia nervosa in context*. Cambridge, MA: Harvard University Press.

Palazzoli, M. Selvini (1978). *Self-starvation: From individual to family therapy in the treatment of anorexia nervosa*. New York: Jason Aronson.

Palazzoli, M. Selvini (1985). The problem of the sibling as the referring person. *Journal of Marital and Family Therapy, 11*, 21–34.

Palazzoli, M. Selvini, Boscolo, L., Cecchin, G., & Prata, G. (1978). *Paradox and counterparadox*. New York: Jason Aronson.

Ranieri, R. F., & Pratt, T. C. (1978). Sibling therapy. *Social Work, 23*, 418–419.

Roberto, L. (1986). Bulimia: The transgenerational view. *Journal of Marital and Family Therapy, 12*, 231–240.

Roberto, L. (1987). Bulimia: Transgenerational family therapy. In J. E. Harkaway (Ed.), *Eating disorders*. Rockville, MD: Aspen.

Rosenberg, E. B. (1980). Therapy with siblings in reorganizing families. *International Journal of Family Therapy, 2*, 139–150.

Sargent, J., Liebman, R., & Silver, M. (1985). Family therapy for anorexia nervosa. In D. M. Garner & P. E. Garfinkel (Eds.), *Handbook of psychotherapy for anorexia nervosa and bulimia* (pp. 280–311). New York: Guilford.

Schachter, F. F. (1982). Sibling deidentification and split-parent identification: A family tetrad. In M. E. Lamb & B. Sutton-Smith (Eds.), *Sibling relationships: Their nature and significance across the lifespan* (pp. 123–151). Hillsdale, NJ: Lawrence Erlbaum.

Schachter, F. F. (1985). Sibling deidentification in the clinic: Devil vs. angel. *Family Process, 24*, 415–427.

Schwartz, R. C., Barrett, M. J., & Saba, G. (1985). Family therapy of bulimia. In D. M. Garner & P. E. Garfinkel (Eds.), *Handbook of psychotherapy for anorexia nervosa and bulimia* (pp. 280–310). New York: Guilford.

Spack, N. P. (1985). Medical complications of anorexia nervosa and bulimia. In S. W. Emmett (Ed.), *Theory and treatment of anorexia nervosa and bulimia: Biomedical, sociocultural, and psychological perspectives* (pp. 5–19). New York: Brunner/Mazel.

Stierlin, H. (1972). *Separating parents and adolescents: a perspective on running away, schizophrenia, and waywardness*. New York: Quadrangle.

Whitaker, C. A., & Keith, D. (1981). Symbolic-experiential family therapy. In A. S. Gurman & D. Kniskern (Eds.), *Handbook of family therapy*. (pp. 187–224). New York: Brunner/Mazel.

White, M. (1983). Anorexia nervosa: A transgenerational system perspective. *Family Process, 22*, 255–273.

15

My Brother's Keeper:
Siblings of Chronic Patients as Allies in
Family Treatment

Ethan G. Harris

In the not too distant past the term "chronic patient" evoked images of older individuals who displayed the effects of years of continuous hospitalization. Women were seen in faded housecoats with stringy hair, shuffling along hospital corridors or rocking distractedly in a dayroom before real or imaginary television programs. Men typically exhibited a three-day growth of beard, wore oversized pants held up by a worn belt or a cord and an odd-colored shirt hanging out at the waist, and held a cigarette in stained fingers. Showing signs of years of cultural and emotional deprivation, their verbal production was minimal, the glazed eyes focused at a point miles away or deep inside.

Some individuals fitting this description may still be found in the back wards of hospitals, but their numbers are greatly diminished. In the wake of deinstitutionalization, the "chronic clients" of the '80s present in marked contrast to their namesakes of 30 years ago. Despite its bad press, deinstitutionalization has spruced up chronic clients. They are now generally younger in age and indistinguishable in many ways from nonchronic nonclients in demeanor and dress. What does distinguish them are periodic crises. Some (Torrey, 1983) say these are induced by a disruption of the chemical balance in the brain; others (Haley, 1980) say they are brought on by the difficulty in negotiating the developmental stage leading to independence from family; and most claim that there is an interplay between these two factors. When crises do occur, frequently characterized by social withdrawal, lack of desire to work, unclear communication, or occasionally violent outbursts, society's response is to hospitalize these individuals, usually for a period of no more than a month or two, and frequently in a community setting until their behavior can be tolerated again in the community.

In short, chronic clients of the '80s have come to relate to the hospital not as a permanent habitat, but as a temporary solution when the pressures of life become unbearable. The fact that this solution occurs frequently enough to become a fixed pattern in the lives of these individuals is what classifies them as chronic. As a result of their shorter hospital stays, the role of the family assumes far greater importance than it once did.

THE FRAMINGHAM DAY HOSPITAL

Created in 1974 with the purpose of preventing and reducing hospitalizations, the Framingham Day Hospital (FDH) program has addressed itself to the needs of the modern chronic client. No specific criteria for admission were established, so that age, diagnosis, level of functioning, and socioeconomic background vary widely: those who eventually will work and those who won't, those who raise families and those who do not, those who live independently and those who do not all participate meaningfully in the program. Indeed, in keeping with the "new age" definition of chronic, only 25% of 205 clients surveyed in the period from July 1984 to January 1987 had been treated at the local state hospital in the five years prior to their admission to FDH. While the label "chronic client" may be a shorthand way of describing those who have a pattern of periodic debilitating crises in their lives, the term itself is discouraged in this setting because of the danger of afflicting these individuals with a self-fulfilling prophecy.

One crucial factor that determines the program's unique role as a treatment facility is its setting. Because of the name "hospital," visitors might be inclined to expect an institutional building—red brick, fluorescent lights—but instead the facility is located in a former home, with carpeting, natural wood, and fireplaces. The home-like atmosphere is an antidote to the medical environments that many members have experienced and helps members feel they are contributing members of a community rather than patients in a hospital. The attitude of respect and responsibility counters the stigma that many members bear because of their devalued role in society.

Another consideration that helps determine treatment is the "free-standing" nature of the program. Although under the jurisdiction of the Massachusetts Department of Mental Health, the day hospital has relative autonomy in decision-making with regard to program, admissions, discharges, and overall policy. The sense of "determining its own fate" is conveyed from administration to staff and then to members/clients. Decisions made through a mutually negotiated process contribute a spirit of freedom and responsibility.

Perhaps the most significant single feature of the Framingham Day Hospital is its time-limited treatment approach—typically four months. While some program components remain available on an aftercare basis, members understand that they have a limited amount of time to achieve a specific set of goals. Customarily, they accelerate the process of change as they have less time remaining in their stay in the program. In designing the program, it was very important to convey the message that it would not be a "permanent home" but rather a means to an end, that end being enhanced functioning in the community. Actions in the program are continuously seen as metaphors for a member's functioning in a work, family or social setting, and early attempts are made to connect members to community resources.

The Family Component

The family is viewed as a major context in which change can occur. Even before the clients enter the program, families are encouraged to become involved in the treatment process. The family's willingness to alter their pattern of behavior with regard to the identified patient is a primary determinant in fostering that individual's potential for change. In family therapy the therapist offers sameness but not too much sameness, difference but not too much difference (Andersen, 1986). He is empathetic and appreciative of the family's experience but attempts to introduce "news of a difference" that can break unfortunate repetitive behavior patterns (Bateson, 1979).

SIBLINGS OF THE CHRONIC CLIENT

Sibling Needs

Addressing the often neglected needs of siblings can be a crucial intervention in families with chronic clients. Because the family resources tend to be focused on the symptomatic child, it is customary for the needs of his brothers and sisters to go under-attended. Calling the family's attention to the experience of the siblings not only addresses the needs of a deprived element of the system, but also shifts the focus away from the identified patient, who is freed to rely more fully on her own resources. Siblings of chronic clients experience a variety of difficult feelings peculiar to being raised in a family with an unavailable brother or sister. Addressing these feelings can have a salutary effect on the entire family.

Probably the most debilitating of the siblings' feelings is fear. Since questions about the "cause" of mental illness remain unanswered in society as a whole, the family is likely to arrive at an explanation that suits its belief system. The fear of becoming schizophrenic or manic-depressive may be based on either a genetic or environmental belief about causation of mental illness. "Will I suffer from the same behavior pattern as my sister?" "Could this disturbance be transmitted to my children?" Not only are questions such as these likely to go unanswered, but they often are never asked.

Another common feeling that the sibling must contend with it guilt. Sometimes it is survivor's guilt: "Why didn't this happen to me?" Sometimes it is self-blame: "Did I cause this illness by being cruel to him? When I bullied him? Excluded him? Teased him? Thought evil thoughts about him?" As Dearth et al. describe in their compelling book, *Families Helping Families*, "Guilt over his or her own well-being is common. Those whose lives are moving ahead and providing them with some success and satisfaction often silently wonder, 'Why me? Why is my life going well while my sister's is in chaos? Does enjoying my life while she suffers this tragic illness make me a bad person?" (1986, pp. 42–43).

Overresponsible siblings may wonder if there is more they should be doing to help. They are often in conflict between their desire to pursue their own interests and the expressed or covert demands of the family to "babysit" their brother or sister. Their vision of the future may be influenced by expectations to assume responsibility for their sibling after the death of their parents. They may be troubled by guilt for not having observed symptoms earlier or for keeping observations of strange behavior to themselves . . . or for not keeping them to themselves. Is there a certain protective role they should play? Again from Dearth et al: " . . . the well young family members ask themselves or others exactly what is owed to the ill family member. They ask, 'What are my family obligations to my sister?' 'Should I be my brother's keeper?'" (p. 43). Must they be protected from physical or mental abuse by peers? Are there family secrets—deaths of relatives or other family troubles—that must be concealed from the brother or sister who is perceived as emotionally ill-equipped to handle the news?

Whether older or younger, it is not uncommon for well siblings to feel cheated of a "normal" brother or sister. There are fantasies of what might have been. "If it weren't for this problem my brother would have taught me, accompanied me, supported me, or admired me." Feelings of grief and loss are prevalent, yet often not addressed.

Another feeling is related to the sense that "my sibling is a reflection on me." As a result, siblings may restructure their lives so that their friends do not encounter their disturbed brother or sister. They live with a high level of shame. "What will my friends think of me if/when they discover my brother or sister has serious emotional problems?"

And finally, siblings struggle with intense anger: anger at seeing their brother or sister getting attention they are not; anger at the loss of "normal" family life; anger at the rigid roles they may be expected to play in the family.

Sibling Roles

Sibling as Bystander   David Kantor (Kantor and Lehr, 1975) uses the term "bystander" to describe the family member who steers clear of the intense action in the family often to observe it more objectively. Frequently the sibling of a chronic client finds himself somewhat removed from the maelstrom of energy that consumes the parents and his symptomatic brother or sister. His greater distance permits him to have a more dispassionate view of family life. In a therapeutic context, this cooler perspective represents an important contribution to the therapist's understanding of family life and offers other family members the opportunity to see themselves in a different light. For example, the family might be discussing an interaction in which a mother is trying to get her 22-year-old son out of bed on a Saturday morning. The therapist might turn to the younger sister and ask, "What does father do when mother goes upstairs to awaken your brother?" "He goes down to the basement and does woodworking." Embroiled in their struggle, mother and son may not be aware of father's activity in a way the more emotionally distant daughter can be. Her observation may stimulate (1) mother's awareness that she would like father's help, (2) son's awareness that he might respond better to an approach from father than mother, (3) father's awareness that he would like to take more responsibility in the interaction, or (4) all of the above.

Sibling as Ally　Being in the same generation offers the siblings a perspective unavailable to their parents. There exists the potential for a supportive alliance to develop between siblings. The sibling may be able to validate the patient's experience of what it is like to be a child in this particular family. Shared perceptions of parents can serve as a powerful validation to a "crazy child." Uniting around a harsh parental edict, for example, may serve to normalize the patient's reaction and serve as an antidote to being disqualified by other members of the system. The schizophrenic patient may be just as angry, but feel more affirmed and less crazy by the support. "Yeah, that's the way the folks are sometimes," can be a comforting statement to a child who is questioning the validity of her response. Bank and Kahn (1975) have described how sibling coalitions can serve to balance parental power and mutually educate each other about parental behavior. When a "well sibling" allies with a disturbed one, "The effect is to nullify and cancel out some of the parental scapegoating of the sick sibling" (p. 329). Sharing normal activities—sports, hobbies, partying—with a brother or sister is another way to alter the patient's self-image of being defective, incompetent, and needy.

TREATMENT OF THE CHRONIC CLIENT: THE MILAN APPROACH

We have employed several ways of working with chronic families at the Framingham Day Hospital, as we searched for a way to best respond to their needs. After utilizing first an experiential, then structural, then strategic approach, we have found that our version of the Milan approach has been most useful and powerful.

Positive Connotation

One major principle of the Milan approach, positive connotation, has proven highly effective in working with this population. Already demoralized and disillusioned, expecting to be told once again what's wrong or what they should be doing differently, the validation of their current behavior can have a shockingly therapeutic effect on these families. It can be a powerful antidote to the criticism that families direct at themselves and the blame they anticipate from professionals. The longer and more serious the families have experienced their problems, the more effective this approach can be. Rather than being advised that they should ask their dependent 30-year-old son to leave the house, for example, a family might be told that his presence is evidence of the family's caring and devotion to one another. Such a statement frees them to look at their behavior in a new light. Perhaps they will want to prove they can still care for him outside the home. Perhaps once their unexpressed desires to keep him home are acknowledged, they can relinquish their need for a public posture and enjoy his presence without conflict and struggle. Positive connotation respects people's behavioral communication as well as their verbal position. Rather than attempting to resolve a problem in a specific way, it addresses the process of resolution itself by honoring both sides of a dilemma and freeing the family to make an unambivalent choice (Palazzoli, 1978a).

Siblings who are very involved and responsible for the care of their disturbed brother or sister can be described as loyal, helpful and protective and recognized for the sacrifices they are making. Contributions that they have been "asked" to make covertly can now be openly acknowledged. Made overt, unspoken parental messages lose their power, offering siblings a freer choice to continue or discontinue their role as helpers. Alternatively, other family members may encourage them to be less helpful when their roles become explicit. If change does occur, not only will the sibling be relieved of a family burden and feel less resentful, but the chronic client may also be in a position to assume greater responsibility. The message conveyed is, "If I help you less, it means you are less helpless."

Neutrality

The concept of neutrality is another cornerstone of the Milan approach. Each member's position and opinions are given equal weight. The therapist does not favor one therapeutic outcome over another or even advocate that the family change at all. This position can be frustrating to individuals looking outside themselves for guidance, but empowering when they realize that they are best qualified to determine what happens to their own family. The therapist and the family together consider the consequences of change or no change. This removes pressure felt by the family to alter the pattern of functioning. When therapists see chronic families in distress and believe it is "obvious" that their lives would be "better" if they changed, families interpret this attitude as an implication that they are doing something wrong. They are torn between the pressure to change as the therapist advises and the instinct to maintain control over their lives. Since chronic families tend to feel a great sense of failure as they compare themselves to the "normal" families around them, a nonneutral approach is generally counterproductive.

An attitude of neutrality can produce change in a family which has historically given the identified patient's views less credence than those of other family members. His brothers or sisters, who have tended to devalue the patient's statements and behavior, are influenced by the therapist's attitude of giving equal weight to his views. The differentiation between "sick" and "well" becomes blurred as all family members are seen as contributing in their own way. The neutral position also helps to remove the therapist from the bind he is apt to find himself in with families that have struggled with a mentally ill member over the years. Feeling overwhelmed and confused, families turn to helpers for a solution. But for the therapist to offer help might only confirm the family's feeling that they are unable to solve their own problems. The frustrating pattern of moving from one therapist to another without finding satisfaction is a familiar one in these families. The neutral therapist can break this pattern by not proposing a solution, implying that change will come from inside the family system.

The approach is also valuable for therapists who tend to become frustrated by the lack of change ("resistance") with chronic families. By not investing themselves in change, they reduce their sense of the disappointment if it does not occur. (Palazzoli et al., 1980a)

Rituals

As positive connotation can change people's perception of the *meaning* of behavior, rituals, another cornerstone of the Milan approach, allow them to experiment with new *action*. Odd day-even day rituals can allow new behaviors to alternate with the old. Families are asked to behave in their usual way on even numbered days, alternating their behavior with new actions on the odd days (Palazzoli, et al., 1977, 1978b). This approach introduces predictability into a chaotic system. Further, the therapeutic stance of neutrality is underscored in this way. There is nothing inherently better about new behavior, but it can be compared over time with old patterns, permitting family members to choose which they prefer. For example, a sibling dyad might be instructed to alternate roles of who helps whom. On odd days the "healthy" one helps the "sick" one. On even days they reverse roles and the patient becomes the expert. Rigid roles can be unlocked as each experiences both roles. Having experienced both, the participants have a basis for selecting their preference. The therapist is tacitly saying, "You can be more than you are."

Circular Questions

By asking circular questions the therapist enables family members to learn about themselves by encouraging them to think about their behavior in new ways. The therapist proceeds as the explorer engaged in a searching process with the family. By implication the family is encouraged to look internally for solutions rather than externally to the therapist. The therapist is guided by the hypotheses he has formulated and the "feedback" responses from the family. Motivated by his curiosity about the family, his questions address relationship patterns in the family system: "When Ralph stays home from school, what does mother do?" "When parents fight, who among the children gets most upset?"

Utilization of circular questions also allows for the introduction of new ideas into the family system and avoids explicit behavioral demands on the part of the therapist. For example, one could ask, "If, instead of waking Peter up each morning, you bought him an alarm clock, do you think there would be a greater or lesser chance of his getting to work on time?" (Tomm, 1984b).

When siblings are used as an information source, other family members can hear how their behavior is perceived. Parents may be less likely to disqualify observations about their relationship with the identified patient if the source is another child rather than the spouse or the patient. For example, the therapist might ask a sibling, "Is Greg more likely to do his chores if he is reminded or left to do them on his own?" Because the siblings tend to be less emotionally involved, their comments may have more impact. They may also be less protective of their brother or sister and advocate an approach which fosters greater responsibility.

Circular questioning can also be used to shift the family's attention away from the problems of the identified patient, thereby reducing their impact on the family system. A sibling may be used to comment on the parents' relationship, frequently a neglected topic because of the attention devoted to the "illness" in the family: "What do your parents talk about when they aren't discussing Jill?" might be a way of doing this.

Despite the many reasons to involve siblings in family therapy the therapist must contend with strong forces to keep them out. For understandable reasons some parents exhibit a tendency to exclude siblings from treatment. For others the reasons for keeping siblings out of treatment range from practicality to superstition. Families often do not want to burden their successful offspring with the time and emotional energy that involvement with their troubled siblings entails. For the parents to include them in the therapeutic process would be to acknowledge that they had a role in family crises. By excluding them from treatment, they can perpetuate the myth that these "healthy" children can be insulated from the problem which parents perceive as threatening the level of success they may be enjoying in the world.

In addition to this protective motivation, there is a superstitious element at play which contributes to the family's reluctance to include siblings in treatment. Excluding them is like a quarantine from a contagious disease. The family may believe that on some level mere proximity to an "infected" brother or sister might cause the transmission of the disease to a sibling. As Bank and Kahn have described in *The Sibling Bond*, symptom contagion "may not merely be a case of superstition. In cases of highly identified siblings, especially identical twins, it is not unusual for siblings to mirror one another's symptoms, seriously threatening their parents' sense of competence. A not uncommon response is to blame one child for being a bad influence on another and to restrict their contact" (1982).

Siblings, too, have their reasons for not participating in the treatment process. Therapy may be viewed as healing to their symptomatic brother or sister but not to them, since they do not feel in need of healing. Even if they were to acknowledge their own needs, siblings might strive to avoid placing demands on an already overburdened system. They might see their entry into the therapeutic process as shifting attention away from the "real problem" in the family and altering their self-sacrificial role.

Siblings may also remove themselves from the therapeutic process as a self-protective act. They may fear that they will not be able to bear the intense feelings of anger, shame, and hopelessness that might emerge in a family session.

Testimony by families of the mentally ill bears this point out: "The survival-oriented responses siblings often make are to shut down parts of their emotional lives, to become over responsible or to disengage from the ill member or family as a whole. In light of these factors the problems of sisters and brothers have been frequently ignored—and so have their potential contributions to helping the family and the ill person cope with chronic mental illness" (Dearth et al., 1986, pp. 32–33).

Utilizing Siblings:
From Complementarity to Symmetry

Complementarity refers to a dyadic relationship in which two individuals balance each other's parts of an interaction, one occupying the superior ("one-up") position, the other the inferior ("one-down") position: strong-weak, helpful-helpless, introvert-extrovert, sadist-masochist, etc. Such a relationship can continue indefinitely as long as each member is satisfied with the role he or she is playing and can supply what the other is missing. The danger in "escalating complementary" interactions is that each participant adopts an extreme position of differentness, causing their behavior to lack flexibility and richness. When this occurs, the antidote is "symmetry," an interaction which stresses equality and sameness (and in extreme cases can lead to dangerous competitiveness such as the international arms race) (Watzlawick, Beavin, and Jackson, 1967, attributed to Gregory Bateson).

Extreme complementary roles generally exist in chronic families in which one child is perceived as "sick" and the other as "well." If these roles can be altered by introducing greater symmetry or balance, the result can be therapeutic. The "well" sibling may find herself in an overresponsible role, assisting the overwhelmed parents in caring for their disturbed child. Bank and Kahn (1981) describe the role of the overresponsible sibling as a type of "noblesse oblige." This can be stressful for the sibling and demeaning to the identified patient, particularly when the more helpful sibling is younger. When this sibling agrees to be less helpful, the patient can experience herself as less needy. Her increased competence may provide the parents with an opportunity to attend to their own relationship. They may begin to discuss how they are or are not working together as a parental team.

> One family seen recently at the Framingham Day Hospital exemplifies this pattern. Bill C., 19, had been recently discharged from the state hospital. He was perceived as needy, helpless, and incompetent by the parents, who relied on Catherine, his 13-year-old sister, to help him with fundamental activities of daily living. A pattern emerged in which the needier Bill behaved, the more helpful Catherine became. Conversely, as she became more helpful, Bill became less and less competent. A pattern of escalating complementarity had been established.
>
> An example: One day, as Bill was preparing lunch for himself, Catherine was advised by her mother to "check" on him. Knowing he was being observed, Bill stopped stirring the vegetables. Since Catherine was rewarded by her parents for being helpful, she suggested that Bill resume stirring. But Bill, feeling that he was doing something wrong, asked Catherine to do it for him, a request to which she readily complied. Later she was praised by her parents for being helpful to her brother. By forming a coalition with her parents, the "white sheep" can inflate her own identity (Bank and Kahn, 1975).
>
> A way of breaking this pattern of escalating complementarity is to introduce symmetry into the relationship. Tasks should be found in

which both members need to work together, such as moving a bureau to the basement, or in which the complementary roles are reversed. For instance, Bill, who is good in math, could be encouraged to help Catherine with her algebra homework.

Another way siblings can be an asset in treatment is by making a plea for fair treatment in the family. Frequently siblings are in a better position than either parent to make a case for placing more demands on their disturbed brother or sister. They are often passionately committed to the concept of fairness in family life. Their brother or sister should not "get away" with something they cannot. They tend to be vigilant in protesting special treatment. Often the additional attention of therapy has served to perpetuate the problem rather than solve it. A sibling "voice" can help modulate this tendency in the family.

SIBLING GROUPS

Sibling groups can be a useful therapeutic intervention, particularly as an adjunct to family sessions. Groups exist that both include and exclude the identified patient. For siblings of a schizophrenic family member, where feelings run especially high, it may be prudent for them to have an opportunity to express themselves in a group without their brother or sister. It might be difficult for the schizophrenic to tolerate his siblings' intense anger at his unusual behavior, sadness at their loss of a "normal" brother or sister, or fear of becoming mentally ill themselves. "When sadness, anger, or hopelessness are not expressed and confronted, . . . depression can become a constant state of mind for the well sibling" (Dearth et al., 1986, p. 47). In a siblings-only group, they might feel less inhibited and more readily express their special needs. This could be a comforting change, for those who come from families in which the attention is directed primarily to the patient and open discussion of their feelings does not occur. The group provides an opportunity to express themselves and be heard in a nonthreatening environment and realize perhaps for the first time that their experience is shared by others.

However, groups including the identified patient can be effective in removing the distinction between normal and abnormal siblings. Mutual support still can be offered, and in addition identified patients and normal siblings have the opportunity to appreciate each other's experience. Furthermore, in these groups the sibling subsystem can be strengthened, thereby lessening the sense of isolation which is often prevalent in these families. These groups can create an environment in which mutual empathy is fostered. Siblings may appreciate the struggles of the identified patients rather than dismiss with anger their unusual behavior, and the patients might become less self-involved as they perceive their siblings' distress. This new understanding could lead to modification of their behavior, motivated by caring about their brothers and sisters.

A CASE STUDY

The Butler Family

First, let me introduce the members of this family:

Marlene, the 51-year-old mother, works as a part-time medical secretary. She has a boyfriend in a town two hours away. The family is aware of him. Strikingly attractive, she appears ten years younger than her stated age.

Kenneth, the 54-year-old father, is the president of a struggling hi-tech firm. He has boyish, athletic good looks. He also is having an open affair. Despite their financial distress, the couple owns a home in a well-to-do suburb of Boston.

Elizabeth, 30, is a cum laude graduate of a west coast university. Separated from her second husband, by whom she has a son, now 4, she resides in California and has little contact with the family.

George, 27, is the identified patient. He is currently in a day treatment program following his seventh state hospital stay. He is diagnosed as schizophrenic and has a history of alcohol abuse and violent behavior. He was first hospitalized at the age of 17.

David, 23, works in his father's firm. He was treated briefly two years ago for severe depression. He did well academically in high school, but has few friends.

Carolyn, 15, is a model student and popular with classmates. She is shy, quiet, agreeable, appearing younger than her stated age.

Historical Background

George was first hospitalized at the age of 17 for seven months at an expensive private hospital. He completed high school at the hospital, then attended college for a year. He then joined the Air Force but after six weeks became psychotic and was hospitalized. Since that time he has had a series of hospitalizations at the state hospital, often preceded by harassment of women, subsequent violent behavior toward police, and abuse of drugs and alcohol. His work history has been sporadic, peer relationships superficial and fleeting. When not in institutions, he has alternated living between his parents' home, their summer home, his own apartment, and halfway houses. It seems important to him either that he have a girl friend or that people think he does.

George has complained to hospital staff that his parents should have been divorced 15 years ago. He has felt caught in the middle of their constant fighting.

The parents' behavior includes open affairs and a lack of guidance for George. When George's psychiatrist became angry at the parents for not paying their psychiatric bills, George again felt in the middle. The parents enjoy sports and vacations, spend freely, and struggle financially. At one point mother left father following a business failure.

George was referred to the Framingham Day Hospital after spending four weeks in the state hospital. He was simultaneously referred to AA and required to attend three meetings a week as a condition of his attendance at the day treatment program. Mother was opposed to the referral, maintaining that George only needed to get a job. She minimized his drinking and passed off the incidents of sexual harassment as normal youthful sexual impulses. Her opposition was supported by David, who took the position that George was "seeking attention" and needed to grow up and take responsibility for his behavior. Father overtly supported the referral, claiming, "the professionals know more than we do."

Treatment

Engaging the Family   At this day treatment setting, it is routine to engage family members of all clients in family treatment. The team consisted of the family therapist, day hospital counselor, a member of the social work extern program, and a member of the staff at George's residence, a halfway house.

George first agreed to a family meeting in a session with his counselor. She then called to arrange an appointment. Although initially skeptical, mother was agreeable to attending "at least one" meeting and was willing to ask her husband and the other children.

On the day of the appointment, David arrived on time. Mother came with Carolyn 10 minutes late, and father came 20 minutes late, claiming he had just been informed of the meeting the night before and had to make special arrangements to get away from work. Elizabeth, in California, did not attend. The family disorganization was already revealing itself in their approach to treatment: David seemed self-reliant and more organized than his parents. Carolyn presented herself as mother's "good little girl."

Presession #1 The team met to hypothesize on the meaning of George's behavior in the system. It was felt that it could be seen as an organizing force in the family, which was on the verge of disintegrating. When his behavior was viewed as "not mad, not bad, just young" (Coppersmith, 1981), George could be seen as providing the family with an opportunity to tackle its next developmental challenge — leaving home of the children. But certain shifts in the marriage would have to occur for this to take place. At this point George's behavior was a metaphor for the family's ambivalence about taking this step, which might mean control and/or redirection of sexual and aggressive impulses.

The children were seen as a great resource, since in many ways the parents had abandoned their role, creating a family of six children. We decided to ask questions that would connect George's behavior to recurrent behavioral patterns in the family, with the hope of introducing new ideas, and expanding the family's range of behavioral options.

Session #1 Our initial plan was thrown off course when David launched into an attack on the system of helpers. Despite years of hospitalization, his brother was no better than he was ten years ago. Questions which focused on the family's reaction to George's behavior met with little response. For example, Carolyn responded with a shrug when we inquired if she thought her parents were closer or more distant when George was in the hospital.

I took a break and met with the team. We agreed that the family was interpreting the questions as blaming them. The children, particularly Carolyn and David, were protecting their parents by refusing to discuss their role until they were given permission to do so.

After the break I showed more interest in the parents' complaints about the system by asking the children how their parents were disappointed in the system and how they would have wanted different treatment. I was able to highlight differences between the parents by asking David, for example, which parent he thought was less disappointed in the therapeutic system (mother). George, a child of the system, had the hardest time with these questions, as he needed to be loyal both to his parents and his helpers. Nevertheless, by asking his parents and siblings, "From whom does George think he can get the most help, his parents or helpers?" I encouraged the family to think about who they wanted to be responsible for George and, metaphorically, for any family problems.

Comments on Session #1   By both their answers (David) and non-answers (Carolyn), George's siblings provided rich information that would not have been available otherwise. David felt free to voice the family's disappointment in the system. Carolyn's silence was eloquent in revealing where the land mines existed in the family. Her reticence told us to "proceed with caution." A non-answer to a question may reveal discomfort, but that doesn't mean the question should not have been asked. Frequently these questions stimulate internal thought processes which bear fruit later.

Intervention #1   We saw David's attack as his way of protecting his parents from being blamed—by themselves, by each other, by their children, and especially by the therapist. We chose to acknowledge their willingness to become involved in the process despite their previous unhappy experiences with therapy. Frequently therapists tend to focus on the deficiencies in parenting rather than strengths, we said, but in this family the children recognize the contributions of their parents. We recommended that the children get together (including Elizabeth by phone) and produce a report on the contribution their parents have made to their lives.

Comments on Intervention #1   This first intervention employs both positive connotation and a ritual. David's criticism of the therapist was given a meaning other than the one that the family might perceive, and his protective role in the family was emphasized. We also began by focusing on positive parental behavior as a way of helping the parents see their role differently. Their "failures" may be noticed by the therapist, but not emphasized.

The ritual is meant to reinforce the earlier statement. Parents frequently rely quite heavily on their children for an evaluation of their performance. Concurrently, the ritual seeks to reinforce the sibling subsystem, to place each sibling on an equal plane, and to encourage involvement of the absent sibling.

Presession #2 Responding to the feedback in the previous session, we decided to focus on the relationship of the family to the system. The parents felt they were failures, and the energy being directed toward the failures of the system was in anticipation of the therapist's criticism of them. The children could testify as to the value of their parents. We were hopeful that a "going with the flow" approach might increase the family's behavioral options.

Session #2 Once again we were surprised. What dominated the discussion was petty, child-like bickering between the parents in an embarrassingly overt fashion. Children were asked if this went on at home, if they feared parents would split up, and who was affected most by the parental arguing. Carolyn responded that the fighting had been incessant for years, that the children indeed wished that they would split up, and that, while it pained all but Elizabeth, George was most affected. We wondered about how the children dealt with it. Most often they handled their pain individually, so we asked the children if it would be easier or harder if they turned to one another for support, would their parents approve or not, etc. Our questions of the children were repeatedly interrupted by the parents' arguing.

Comment on Session #2 Circular questions can introduce new ideas and new ways of handling a problem. In this case, I asked future-oriented questions with embedded suggestions to introduce the idea that the siblings could be a mutual support group (Kahn and Bank, 1981). As a general rule, when we think about how children can compensate for what may be missing from their parents, we consider the potential of the sibling subsystem. The parents' preoccupation with their own needs to the exclusion of the children's led us in this direction.

Carolyn was surprisingly revealing in this session and seemed quite perceptive. This is an example of the power of her bystander role. Usually we find that the most dispassionate, least involved sibling, often the youngest, can be the most objective.

Intervention #2   We acknowledged the importance of arguing as a way of keeping the family together and giving everyone a job. These spouses did not want to hide their pain from their children. We were not sure if they should give it up, if they wanted to, and if they did, when. Perhaps the children would be in a better position to decide these questions. We suggested planned weekly fights by the parents, during which the children would meet (1) to decide if they should continue or not and (2) if not, to plan together a way to stop them.

Comment on Intervention #2   This intervention is also comprised of both a positive connotation and a ritual. Seeing the fighting in a positive light serves to make family members less defensive and creates a context in which they can think about whether they really want to "keep the family together" and if this is the way they want to do it. The parents might be provoked to wonder if they want to continue to be parents in this way, or the children might examine if they want to be this involved in their parents' lives.

The ritual is designed to reinforce the positive connotation. While a structural approach might attempt to find a way to put the parents in charge, in this case the emphasis is on promoting the evident family strengths as they are demonstrated. The children are being asked, covertly, to be their parents' marriage counselors. This role has principally fallen to George, but since it had been unacknowledged, he has had to struggle with it internally. The rituals serve to (1) bring the hidden roles into the open when there is greater option for behavioral change and (2) spread the responsibility among all the children. In the sibling discussion, George could hear Carolyn's case for remaining removed and present his case for greater involvement in the parents' marriage.

Presession #3   We hypothesized that the parents' fighting was their way of asking to be taken care of by their children. Team members suggested focusing on the previous generation—how the grandparents would/would not have responded to the arguments (three were deceased, one alive).

Session #3   I began by asking the couple questions about what suggestions their parents would have for solving their disputes, but after a while David, who had been contained, exploded: "We are here to talk about George. Why aren't we talking about George?" He was overtly hostile and accused George of laziness and not helping himself. I followed David's lead and began looking for connections between George's problem and the behavior of other family members. I wondered, if George's problems were less, how would it affect the parents' marriage? Would they be closer or more distant? Also, how would it affect the siblings? Would David be more or less involved? More or less depressed? Would Elizabeth be more or less distant? Would she call more or less often? Would Carolyn be more or less outspoken? Would she be more or less aggressive?

All family members present were asked these questions. In addition they were asked what Elizabeth would say were she here (I learned later that after this session David called Elizabeth in California to ask her some of these questions). The replies were often noncommital, but judging from shifts in subsequent behavior the questions stimulated new ways of looking at family patterns.

Comments on Session #3   This interview provides a good example of the use of future-oriented circular questions. The connection between George's problems and other family members is strongly implied. The questions also call upon members to consider their view of the future—how life could be different. Circular questions are also used to "include" an absent member. As the connections are made between George's behavior and his siblings, it is hoped that their awareness will be heightened. Consequently their range of choices will be expanded. They can ask, "Do I want it to be this way?"

Intervention #3   We suggested that, since George was extremely concerned about his parents and their marriage, his drinking and bizarre behavior were his ways of keeping them married. He might worry that without some concern to unify his parents they would fight more and split up. We suggested that the parents continue to plan their weekly fights, that when they began to argue George do something bizarre to distract them, and that David advise his parents on how to handle George. Carolyn is to be quiet, observe all, and report back to the therapist at the next session.

Comment on Intervention #3   This is another example of positive connotation and prescribing rituals that will alter the meaning of behavior from covert and out of control to overt and in control. The family members receive respect from the therapist, who accepts their behavior on their own terms. The responsibility for change then becomes the family's, not the therapist's.

Presession #4   The team met for what was to be our final session, since George would be leaving the program in a week. His day treatment counselors noted that he was attending AA meetings regularly and had been sober for nearly three months. He had stopped complaining about the living conditions at the halfway house and was beginning to socialize. We remained concerned, however, about his stigmatized, defective role in the family and wondered whether his overwhelming needs had prevented his siblings' problems from being addressed and, in turn, whether his siblings had concealed their difficulties for fear they would wind up like their brother.

Session #4   My questions focused on the needs of George's siblings. I asked all family members, "If David were less worried about his brother, who would take his place?" "If Carolyn or David worried less about George, who would they worry about?" "Who was second, third, etc., most in need of help in the family?" "If Elizabeth, David, or Carolyn had a problem, what would it be?"

Comment on Session #4   These future-oriented circular questions introduced the idea that others in the family besides George have needs and stimulated family members to remove the focus from George. This attention had reinforced his problematic behavior. The questions served to shift the focus to others, who very likely have been neglected.

Intervention #4   The family was told that it has proven itself willing and competent to respond to the needs of a member in distress. Since the children were almost all adults now and must more and more learn to rely on each other rather than their parents, each was to think of three needs, one suitable to be responded to by each other sibling and ask him/her to fulfill it. As the oldest child participating in the meetings, George was to call Elizabeth and inform her of this task.

Comment on Intervention #4 The notion of balance is introduced — rigidly complementary roles can be reversed. People can both help without being deprived and be helped without being stigmatized. George is given special status as oldest and care is given to include the absent sibling.

Follow-up The results of a six-month follow-up were encouraging, though not dramatic. Parents had entered marital counseling. David had a girlfriend. Carolyn was fighting more with mother. Elizabeth was in the process of divorcing her second husband. George was hospitalized briefly after a drinking episode following his termination from the day treatment center. Upon discharge, he entered a transitional employment program, and he has now been working part-time for three months. The relationship between David and George has improved to the point where they have arranged a weekly tennis match. George is planning a trip to Los Angeles to visit his sister in two months.

Conclusion

Follow-up demonstrated some moves toward separation in the family on the part of George, Carolyn, and David, who became less concerned with their parents' problems and more with their own. The parents began to take action to resolve their relationship conflict rather than continuing to use it as a way to engage their children. Elizabeth, who protected herself from the demands of the family, felt somewhat safer to re-engage.

Much of this work could not have been achieved without the contributions of the siblings. The family had been in chronic crisis, dealing with both chronic marital conflict and chronic mental illness. Each child dealt with the crisis in his/her own way: Elizabeth withdrew from the family, although there is evidence that her style of avoiding emotional intensity might have cost her the ability to sustain an intimate relationship. David overfunctioned in such a way that he was able to achieve success in the vocational area of his life but had difficulty in social relationships. He lacked the ability to express his own needs and resented others when they expressed theirs. George organized the family with his struggles, which served to protect others from confronting their own pain. Carolyn gained popularity by pleasing others but at the expense of asserting her own rights. Each child's role represented a part of the collective family psyche: George's behavior indicated the extent of family pain; Carolyn's reticence indicated the danger of violating loyalty; David's responsibility pointed to a void in parental responsibility; and even Elizabeth's absence was revealing in demonstrating the difficulty in leaving and the effort required to avoid being pulled back.

Each sibling, by altering his or her role, can create change in the system. When siblings change in concert, orchestrated by an objective outsider, they represent a powerful force for altering family behavior. In this case, Elizabeth, by increasing her contact removed some burden from David, demonstrating that George was not the only vulnerable one in the family, and showed how one could leave without breaking off contact entirely. David, by relaxing his need to be in charge and express needs of his own, allowed room for George to feel more competent. By assuming greater self-reliance, George took the pressure off his siblings, especially David. This reduced the tension between the two boys and allowed them to become closer. And Carolyn's comments on the family system from the bystander position enabled her siblings to see their roles differently. By speaking up for herself, she took some of the heat off George.

It is common to overlook siblings as a potential resource in family treatment, particularly in working with chronic clients where the needs of one member can appear so compelling. But, even the most removed siblings can make a valuable contribution in altering recursive behavioral patterns.

REFERENCES

Andersen, T. (1986). Workshop in Cambridge, Mass. Oct. 18, 1986.

Bateson, G. (1979). *Mind and nature.* New York: Dutton.

Bank, S. & Kahn, M. (1975). Sisterhood and brotherhood is powerful: Sibling subsystems and family therapy. *Family Process.*

Bank, S., & Kahn, M. (1982). *The sibling bond.* New York: Basic Books.

Coppersmith, E. (1981). He's not bad, he's not mad, he's just young. *Journal of Strategic and Systemic Therapies, 1,* 1–8.

Dearth, N., Labenski, B. J., Mott, H. E., & Pellegrini, L. M. (1986). *Families helping families.* New York: Norton.

Haley, J. *Leaving home.* (1980). New York: McGraw-Hill.

Kahn, M., & Bank, S. (1981). In pursuit of sisterhood: Adult siblings as a resource for combined individual and family therapy, *Family Process 20,*(1), 85–95.

Kantor, D., & Lehr, W. (1975). *Inside the family*. San Francisco: Jossey-Bass.

Palazzoli, M. Selvini, Boscolo, L., Cecchin, G., & Prata, G. (1977). Family rituals: A powerful tool in family therapy. *Family Process, 16*(4), 445–453.

Palazzoli, M. Selvini, Boscolo, L., Cecchin, G., & Prata, G. (1978a). *Paradox and Counterparadox: A new model in the therapy of the schizophrenic family in transaction*. New York: Jason Aronson.

Palazzoli, M. Selvini, Boscolo, L., Cecchin, G., & Prata, G. (1978b). A ritualized prescription in family therapy: Odd days and even days. *Journal of Marriage and Family Therapy, 4*(3), 3–9.

Palazzoli, M. Selvini, Boscolo, L., Cecchin, G., & Prata, G. (1980a). Hypothesizing-circularity-neutrality: Three guidelines for the conductor of the session. *Family Process, 19*(1), 3–12.

Palazzoli, M. Selvini, Boscolo, L., Cecchin, G., & Prata, G. (1980b). The Problem of the Referring Person. *Journal of Marital and Family Therapy, 6*(1), 3–9.

Tomm, K. (1984a). One perspective on the Milan systemic approach: Part I, overview of development, theory and practice. *Journal of Marital and Family Therapy, 10*(2), 113–125.

Tomm, K. (1984b). One perspective on the Milan systemic approach: Part II, description of session format interviewing style and intervention. *Journal of Marital and Family Therapy, 10*(3), 253–271.

Torrey, E. F. (1983). *Surviving schizophrenia*. New York: Harper & Row.

Watzlawick, P., Beavin, J., & Jackson, D. (1967). *Pragmatics of human communication*. New York: Norton.

IV

Settling Old Scores

THE MIDDLE YEARS

It is commonly assumed that by the time one reaches adulthood siblings play only a small role in one's life. Adulthood may be a time when siblings have less overt importance, but the residual effects of earlier experiences echo throughout one's adult functioning. Adult choices of friendships, lovers, and marital partners often are a reflection of both positive aspects of the sibling relationship and unresolved issues.

In establishing oneself in a career or as a professional, old sibling ghosts may interfere. The choice of career and quality of work may carry embedded reverberations of idolized sibling wishes or unresolved competition. The chapters in this section look at some aspects of adult functioning—in the individual's personal and professional realms—that may be affected by leftover sibling issues, and the uses of individual and family therapy to resolve those issues.

Bank refers to birthright as a person's "fundamental right to a good relationship" with a sibling. Parents, both in the past and as their children have grown into adulthood, often impair or even destroy that relationship. He describes the role of the therapist in connecting and reframing a patient's anger, guilt, and depression about a sibling as parental neglect, abdication, emptiness, tolerance of sibling abuse, or favoritism. The chapter outlines ways the individual therapist removes the long-term effects of the parents' attitudes.

Not to be confused with a focus on multiple personality disorders, Watanabe's chapter on character work deals with the ways individuals carry the internalized images of real and fantasied siblings with them into adulthood. She presents another perspective of the sibling influence on adult life—the unique role siblings play in shaping the personality as well as the expectations for and patterns of intimacy. Character work focuses on and isolates the individual thread in the tapestry of a personality. Character work helps identify aspects of internalized sibling persona. Knowledge of these voices provide blueprints for understanding where the troublespots are in current adult relationships.

A growing arena for therapists is the family business. Carroll recounts his own experience of growing up in a family's business. He then reexamines the concept of sibling rivalry through the duality of family and business, focusing on three components of the relationship—actual, transferential, and family legacy. Carroll demonstrates his theory using clinical examples from his consultation practice and from legendary American family businesses.

The final chapter of this section addresses an issue often overlooked by professionals—their own transferential sibling issues. Looking at co-therapy and co-authoring, Doherty uses the FIRO model of group stages of development to follow the professional development of collegial pairs. The three stages—inclusion, control and intimacy—are balanced against sibling identification and de-identification concepts.

16

The Stolen Birthright:
The Adult Sibling in Individual Therapy

Stephen P. Bank

Angry and red-faced, a woman begins to weep, wondering aloud why she has been relegated to insignificance by an older brother:

> He acts like I don't exist, like he never knew me. He hasn't called in five years despite my calling him and remembering his kids' birthdays. Not that our relationship ever was that good. He treated me like dirt when we were kids, and he used to beat me up, sometimes badly. I wouldn't tell my parents because they would never believe that Mister Perfect would ever hurt a little kid. I was Miss Nobody, and he was the star, handsome, successful, a complete bastard to me.

Her therapist listens to example after example of her brother's cruelty, his favored position, his disinterest. Then the therapist, who has been trying to teach the patient to assert herself, suggests that she write her brother a letter, communicate her anger, confront him with his abuse and his neglect. Compliantly the woman responds, "Hmm. Uhmm . . . Maybe I should do that . . . Get things out in the open."

This patient (wisely) ignored what the therapist suggested, feeling misunderstood. The therapist makes not one mistake, but several. First he sends her to do battle with a person who has not only defeated her but who has little or no interest in hearing what she has to say. Sensing this, the woman placed the suggestion in the "useless

341

suggestion" file which our patients keep handy when we're off their wavelength.

But there is a more serious error. This therapist has missed the parental context of the tortured sibling connection. The patient's words were loaded with references to her parents' favoritism, and she said that they did not protect her from her brother's abuse. Nevertheless, her therapist ignored this and suggested the problem was anger and miscommunication between brother and sister. Here lies the flaw in the therapist's theory of what went wrong. "Here-and-now" therapy disregards historical context and suggests that the past is interesting but irrelevant. Nothing could be further from the truth in doing psychotherapy with adult siblings. *Sibling conflicts, when extreme, bitter, and prolonged are a significant outgrowth of a disturbing family situation which could not, originally, have been the children's "fault."* A useful first step in therapy with adult siblings shifts the patient's focus from siblings to parents. The injured sib begins to understand the twisted relationship with a brother or sister as the inevitable and tragic outgrowth of parental inadequacy, hatred, narcissism, neglect. "Stolen birthrights" include not only what one sibling steals from another but also the loss of the children's fundamental right to a good relationship—a loss allowed by parental actions and inactions.

It is not the aim of therapy to convince the patient that siblings are good and parents are bad; this would merely substitute one form of blame for another. But helping our patients to see the present threads of a relationship as part of a fabric which was woven *for* the siblings, not just *by* the siblings, can allow them to come to terms with and appreciate the depth of their family's tragedy. Although this chapter focuses largely on the therapist's *first* steps, there are tangible steps that must be taken later to improve the relationship. The therapist's initial attitude simply sets the stage for later actions (see Kahn and Bank's 1981 discussion of "rituals of forgiveness").

Therapists may indirectly blame the adult siblings for a relationship whose destructive course was set for them long ago. Such writers as Jeffrey Masson (1984) and Alice Miller (1984) have pointed out that Freudian drive theory considered children to be the innate carriers and originators of aggressive and sexual urges. Miller warns that therapists, encumbered by their own blind spots about parents, may silently encourage patients to *not* recognize the devastating effect of parental indifference, cruelty, or ineptitude. It is far easier to let the patient lament her brother's cruelty than to help her painfully recognize that father was not ten feet tall, and that mother's "kindness" involved ignoring daily evidence that the patient, as a child, was being beaten and blackmailed by her brother. When patients tell us of the kind of abuse and favoritism shown in the vignette which opened this paper, they are asking if we will be able to help them open a door into a much darker world of parental indifference, cruelty, or ineptitude. We need to be aware of our own blind spots about parents if we are to take them on such a journey.

My own blind spots about the parental origins of sibling conflict were sharply illustrated when a student pointed out that I had just told a class a grossly oversimplified story about Esau and Jacob. The version I gave my students was essentially the same as I had learned from kindly old Mr. Samuels, my fifth grade religious school teacher. This version blamed the kids and emphasized their innate dislike for each other and their rivalrous instincts. Isaac and Rebecca had two sons, Esau the older and Jacob, the younger. Jacob took advantage of his brother and when he found him starving, offered him a bowl of soup in return for his birthright—the inheritance to the kingdom. Jacob then cunningly deceived his nearly blind father and, donning animal skins, pretended that he was the hairy Esau; fooling his father, Jacob illicitly made off with the family fortune. Left out of this telling were the parental influences in the sibling disaster. A closer reading of the story shows that it was really the mother, Rebecca, who set brother against brother, that she secretly arranged for Jacob, her favorite, to slip away to the security of her brother's estate. This second reading emphasized that Jacob paid a heavy price for being his mother's favorite. He realized that Esau might kill him and destroy his entire kingdom. Jacob averted being murdered by begging forgiveness. Groveling before his dispossessed brother, he guiltily realized that his favored position carried with it a heavy price. He had been misguided by a selfish parent who allowed him to commit a crime against his brother. (I had forgotten this important detail, despite having reread the story as a freshman in college.)

Psychotherapists are the audiences for modern sibling legends. Although we do not hear sagas of heroic nomads from great tribal families, we do hear about disconnected modern brothers and sisters living miles apart in distant suburbs who have become alienated and angry. How we listen, react, edit and then retell the patient's story—changing its meaning, reframing its emotions—will determine whether or not the patient can free himself from disabling feelings of anger, overattachment, and guilt about brothers and sisters. The therapist's task is to retell the patient's story focusing on the "frozen misunderstandings" of childhood (Bank and Kahn, 1982; Kahn, 1986; Kahn and Bank, 1981) and to show how parents, *not* the siblings, were originally involved in what went wrong. Later on the therapy broadens, and the patient sees that the parents were victims who allowed injustices to occur, but that, to borrow a phrase from Scott Fitzgerald, they were "boats against the current, borne back ceaselessly into the past." Here lies the art of therapy: to help patients take responsibility for relationships while understanding their family's powerful effects, to help them understand that parents, while responsible, are also victims of a family system. (Our belief that parents are responsible for the outcomes of the relationships between the children is, of course, a simple invention, knowing also that genetics, economics, illness, culture, war, and luck itself can have a far-reaching impact on what happens between brothers and sisters and how they are reared.) Nevertheless focusing on parental default can have a dramatic effect on the patient who has never previously thought that the sibling relationship might be related to problems with a mother or a father.

When meeting with the patient in the first stages, I make it clear that when a sibling relationship has become embittered over many years (a "disowned sibling relationship") there was something unusual, "abnormal," and strange going on in the family as a whole. I use the word "abnormal" with patients because it emphasizes that most people do have satisfactory relationships in adulthood with their brothers and sisters. (Surveys of large groups of people—for example, Cicirelli [1977]—indicate that cordiality and mutual support are the norm in adult sibling relationships.)

Clinical studies such as those which Michael Kahn and I have carried out for the last 15 years repeatedly suggest that extreme disturbances in the sibling relationship are usually associated with serious parental problems. When rivalry becomes abuse, when envy leads to humiliation, when sexual interest becomes incestuous, when identification leads to a loss of boundaries, parents have been unable or unwilling to see what is going on or incapable of monitoring the situation between their children. Or they have used methods which inflamed sibling difficulties rather than resolved them. In other cases, the parents were sick or physically unavailable, while the children's relationship ran amok. With the support of both statistical surveys and clinical impressions, one can confidently say to the sibling who seeks psychotherapy that there must have been something "terribly wrong" in his or her family of origin. The comment about "things being terribly wrong" actually surprises many patients who have located the problem in the sibling. "Fix my sibling problem," they seem to say, "and all will be well." The therapist replies: "First let's talk about your parents."

I believe it is useful to speak to our patients about their "birthright" to a successful sibling relationship because it emphasizes that something precious, warm, natural (and frequent) has failed to flower. This "something" is a sibling bond which allows a flexible, growing relationship characterized both by closeness and a respect for differences — what Michael Kahn has called a "constructive dialectic." Judy Dunn and Carol Kendrick (1982) find that children as young as 15 months show the capacity to show empathy and understanding of a sibling's emotional state. This capacity for kindness (though never completely free of ambivalence) is readily drawn out when the parents "humanize" the arrival of the newborn and refer to the baby as a person with feelings rather than as a strange "it." The parents who made the newborn a real person, these researchers found, allowed the older children to move into the middle years of childhood manifesting far less hostility toward sibs than did children whose parents had not humanized the newborn's personality. Other studies show that the availability of the father in the weeks and months after the birth of the second child markedly reduced outbursts of anxiety and rivalry in the first child (Dunn, 1985). Supported by information such as this, a therapist can speak with certainty about "good" or "not-so-good" parental influences on siblings, realizing that many patients do not know what a "normal family" or a "happy sibling relationship" might be. Here I use the word "normal" not in a statistical sense, but in the sense that there are certain family environments in which relationships thrive and others in which relationships become twisted or disturbed.

The following guidelines flow from some of the points above and provide a framework for speaking to siblings in the *first* stages of individual therapy.

1. Focus on the parental context of disturbed sibling relationships. Go back to the earliest memories of the past. Delve into the subtle aspects of how the parents organized the current relationship between the adult siblings.
2. Do not try family therapy (other than for crisis intervention) until the patient is conversant with the parents' influence on the sibling connection. To conduct a reasonable yet emotional conversation with the siblings, the patient should be free enough of rage, idealization, projections, rationalizations and revenge motives.
3. While it may be necessary to demonstrate that the parents were blind, inept, or even cruel, or that they somehow failed despite good intentions, never do so in an accusatory way.
4. Ally yourself, whenever possible, with *both* siblings' loss of the right to a successful relationship. Both siblings have suffered, not just one. Help the patient be sad about the loss of prior opportunities. *After* these emotions are expressed and understood, the stage is set for tangible action within the family.

EXAMPLES OF THERAPEUTIC CONVERSATIONS WITH ADULT SIBLINGS

Guilt about Sibling Incest
Reframed as Parental Neglect

An Anglican minister, trying to face the fact that he cut off the very people he cared about—his children, his wife, his coworkers—told his therapist that he had not sent birthday cards to his brothers and sisters in many years and that, in particular, he had avoided contact with his youngest sister since adolescence. The therapist asked, "Why *her*?" The patient replied, "There's something about her . . . there's got to be a reason why I brush her off because we used to be very close when we were little."

With embarrassment and shame, he confessed sexual activities with his 14-year-old sister when he was 17. After watching her undress one day, he seduced her. This activity was repeated frequently, resulting in intercourse; then, after several months, she suddenly broke off all contact. Although his sister finally sought him out when he had gone off to college, he was filled with guilt and continued to move away. He felt unworthy and disgusted with himself, even managing to find an excuse not to attend her wedding. He loathed himself, and now he, a cleric, a man of God, was admitting to his therapist, "I'm only one step better than a pervert."

Our job is to retell the patient his own story (Spence, 1982) in terms which are forgiving of the siblings' motives and place the event within the context of the family disturbance. This is how I addressed the guilt-ridden man's self-loathing:

> Sexual contact between teenage siblings isn't all *that* unusual— something like ten percent of all college educated people say that there was *some* sex play—and most teenagers are sexually very curious about each other. Many kids who are scared to get sex outside the family and don't have much self-confidence learn about it at home where it's forbidden, but much safer. So it's not so unusual that a brother gets aroused about his sister.
>
> What you did was wrong and clearly exploitive. What I think made the difference here was that there were a lot of lonely people in your family. Parents didn't reach out to kids, and nobody showed much warmth. It's not normal; it's not natural. When people don't show much warmth and the kids feel so starved, then they forget about what's right, and they use each other sexually. You and your sister were desperately hungry, and I just don't think you are to blame. You're no pervert. When parents can't meet their kids' needs, the kids take care of one another, sometimes in ways involving sexual contact. You must have felt small and inadequate at the time—your dad couldn't model masculinity or strength. You needed to inflate yourself by using her to make you feel good.

The point to be made repeatedly is that the children's actions were the expectable outcome of an abnormal family situation. The minister's self-hatred and fearful feelings about his sister subsided once he could understand this. That Christmas he sent his sister a note asking how she and her family were doing. Making contact "wasn't such a big deal" once his guilt had been reframed in terms of family starvation.

Therapy of the adult sibling tries to unbalance the internal family system carried in the patient's head by reframing the "pat" explanation of sibling guilt as being an inevitable result of parental inadequacy. Later steps are taken by the patient in small and spontaneous ways. Siblings rarely act as if a light has suddenly been turned on illuminating wondrous possibilities. What happens is that they realize a relationship may be possible in small ways; they are willing to experiment more, to take little risks which sometimes can lead to an expanded relationship. Therapists can prompt these changes by asking whether the patient has taken any down-to-earth steps towards the sibling. The later steps in relationship building—conversations, arguments, cards, gifts, planned and spontaneous gestures of caring, phone calls, suggestions to participate in family therapy—are important manifestations of insights gained in the earlier stages of individual therapy.

Anger at a Sibling Redirected to Issues
Involving Parental Abdication

A woman told me that her brother had ruined her life. In addition, he had been the sole cause of the parents' unhappiness. He was an explosive boy who frequently required parental help when he ran into trouble with the law: In adolescence he became a pot-smoking school truant who manipulated his parents into lending him money which he predictably squandered. As an adult he went on spending sprees and drinking binges, was fired from a dozen jobs, and got into trouble with the Internal Revenue Service. The patient, an industrious, self-starting Spartan, in contrast to her debauched brother, had always felt neglected and had been held to a higher standard by the parents. What Frank had done could not be forgiven for he had robbed Sally of her parents' energies, sapped the family's strength, and squandered its resources. She became violently upset when she had to see him and entered therapy the week after an Easter Sunday family dinner, during which she had an argument with him. She left the parents' house fearing that she would physically assault him.

My first aim was to neutralize her violent emotions. I wanted to help this woman achieve a more complex picture of her brother, instead of remaining tied to a simple "life-would-be-nice-if-he-hadn't-messed-us-up" explanation. I retold the story:

You've got a narrow view on this. There are a lot of families whose kids do get help for serious behavior problems when the child is young enough to change. Your parents didn't do this, and no one ever explained to you what his problems were or how you could react. Your parents didn't show leadership and they weren't clearheaded. They kept bailing him out, never obtained advice. They had a choice; they could have acted differently, but they didn't. This didn't have to become the nightmare that it became. Frank didn't cause this alone. I suppose your parents didn't cause it either, but their reactions weren't normal, they weren't helpful. No wonder you became so super-perfect. There wasn't any room for you to be "just a kid" in this family. How terribly sad for you—your parents had money, they had education, and yet nothing was done, no action was taken so you wouldn't have to be hurt and confused.

The tone of such conversations is hard to communicate on the printed page. The tone is compassionate, the style dramatic, as the therapist recreates a broader picture of family tragedy in which all were victims and where the parents' ineptitude is spotlighted. The therapist is not completely evenhanded in laying out the scene: Parents are more responsible than children. Illusions about siblings as the "cause" of misery are replaced with a call to understand the family as a complex and sadly limited group of people. The therapist says "their reactions were not normal" to emphasize that both siblings grew up in a situation where having a good relationship would have been virtually impossible.

Depression Resulting from "My Sister's Not Loving Me" Retold as an Issue of Parental Emptiness

Rejection by a sibling to whom one was attached is very painful, but if adequate supplies of love, comfort, and understanding are supplied by adults it will not be devastating. Lacking adequate parental care, many brothers and sisters fill the emotional vacuum with a sibling who then becomes an object for idealization and disappointment. In the following segment from a psychotherapy session, we see how the patient—a woman of 30—struggles with her sister's neglect.

Patient: I was there for her at her wedding when she was so upset, and when we were kids I always looked out for her. I even took care of her son when he was sick and she had to work. The only time she was ever good to me was when we were little, but even then she seemed to resent me. But the worst was last year when I told her I was thinking about suicide and she acted very concerned, and then didn't call me for a month. Everything in her life has gone so well, she's married to a guy who has a salary in six figures, two great kids, and nothing to complain about, but every time I need something, she's not there.

Therapist: She can't be your parent. How can she? She was robbed too. What makes you think she has so much to give? She had the same alcoholic father that you had and the same depressed mom that you had. How can she give you what her parents never gave her? How could she learn to care about her little sister if her parents never taught her? How could she learn to be giving if she identified with her father's self-centeredness? Are you putting her on a pedestal because she seems so well off? Emotionally she seems so poor.

My message offers the patient a different version of her sibling relationship and emphasizes, with empathy, that a sibling cannot be expected to make reparations for parental neglect. *Both* children — not just the patient — have suffered parental desertion.

Taking responsibility for one's relationships and for one's part in keeping misery alive is the ultimate aim of therapy. Therefore, after this initial step of emphasizing parental inadequacy, I repeatedly pointed out how the patient continued to wait passively for her sister to give to her, how she lightly passed over the fact that the sister had just begun marital therapy because of a failing relationship with her husband, and how she continued to wait, so to speak, hand dependently outstretched, rather than considering her sister an equal person. These later steps had a beneficial effect. Phone calls and humorous birthday cards began flowing between the sisters; the relationship lost some of its deadly serious quality.

A Mother's Overreaction to Her Son's "Sibling Rivalry" Reframed

Bill, an overactive five-year-old boy, enjoyed a tender and playful relationship with his three-year-old sister. A child psychologist had previously told this mother that the children enjoyed a remarkably good relationship; they had only rare outbursts of anger and very little real bullying. Mother, however, was still terrified that Bill might seriously harm Nancy.

I focused on the mother's brother, who, as the parents turned a blind eye, tortured her. At age 19, she finally told him off and ended his physical and verbal abuse. Years later she still feared and hated her brother and could feel herself become anxious and upset when he so much as entered the same room. The treatment emphasized to her the basis for her projections about her own son and daughter. I understood and validated the torment which took place years ago and emphasized the parents' part in originally allowing the abuse. After eliciting the history of her original family, I said:

> Bill isn't your brother, and his reasons for sometimes hitting Nancy are very, very different from your brother's reasons for pounding on you. Look at the difference in your original family versus the one you've created! You and your husband are *very* tuned into the kids' feelings. You're available, and you don't let the fighting get out of hand. Your parents didn't even know what your brother was doing, and you knew you couldn't appeal to them: They had their own problems and wouldn't have thought your worries were serious even if you had spoken up. And there's another difference between your new family and your old one. You and Ted, through your relationship, show that females count for a lot. Your father and mother gave the silent but clear message—men take advantage of women, boys are more important than girls, girls should be seen, not heard. Your brother grew up not valuing you any more than your father and grandfather valued their wives. You've taught your son differently and his behavior shows it.

Parental Favoritism

Parental favoritism (Bank, 1988) requires—in its extreme and chronic form—parental dysfunction and serious marital difficulties. The unending adoration lavished on one child accompanied by the regular devaluation of another says that the disfavored one is worthless or worth less than a brother or sister. The usual reaction to this is serious sibling rivalry accompanied by depression or behavioral problems in the unfavored child. The unfavored sibling often cannot face the parents' dislike and prefers to focus anger at the favored brother or sister. Here I told a young man that the brother who stole the show did so with the direct encouragement of their parents.

> I can see how his cozy relationship with your parents has hurt you for all these years. But when you blame him for playing up to your parents, I think you're only looking at part of the picture. Your parents didn't have to adore him because of his success and they didn't have to ignore you in the process. Your brother didn't *ask* for parents who would split him off from his brother, and it wasn't his fault that your parents couldn't keep him from stealing the show every time you had something to be proud of. No wonder your brother acts insensitively — not just to you, but to other people. He's had the best of it in your family, but your parents also schooled him in how to be self-centered, and they cut you guys out of having a good relationship.

At the opposite end, entitled siblings may be aware that parents favored them, but they haven't the faintest understanding that it was this special privilege with mother and father that has enraged their brothers or sisters. A 25-year-old man reported that his sister, three years older, had always been rivalrous. Upon the mother's death, she completely stopped speaking to him and began currying favor with their father. I had to press hard for the facts, which the patient preferred not to discuss, emphasizing instead how the sister had "been a bitch" and how she was a grudging, angry person. The man finally told me that the family knew that he was the mother's favorite child. She had wanted a boy for her first child, but had conceived one daughter and then another. On her third try she got the boy she had always wanted and visibly withdrew her interest from her three-year-old daughter, who could never again get as close to her mother as the little boy. This classic case of dethronement was accompanied by the father's disinterest in all of the children, leaving the boy with a singular hold on the mother and his two sisters out in the cold.

Here I told the patient:

> Look, Mark, your sister's anger at you is completely understandable. Wouldn't you feel the same way if your mom had suddenly dropped her interest in you? Your sister's attacks come out of a deep sense of rejection, and I think that she was set up for this by your folks. Your mom isn't around to see what favoring you did to your relationship with your sister, and your dad seemed indifferent when it came to the kids. Your mom favored you too much and it ruined things. Your sister's anger *began* for a good reason.

By reframing the reality of their antagonism in language of parental ineptness, the therapist sought to remove blame from the sister and at the same time implied that the patient was not to blame for drawing the sister's attacks. This move exonerates the patient and the sibling for the historic childhood elements which were embedded in their family's way of doing things, but in no way relieves the patient of the need to examine his or her everyday reactions to the sibling. The first step — reframing sibling conflict in a parental context — leads to later moves which allow exploration of the relationship. In some cases, such exploration results in the realization that the sibling doesn't want an "improved relationship." Therapist and patient then have to work towards accepting this as a stark fact. In other instances, such as the present case, exploration led to family therapy and a gradual improvement. When I saw the man and his sister together a year later, the patient admitted to her that he realized their mother neglected her by favoring him. This admission produced a visible warming of the relationship.

Other patients possess the love of one parent but desperately crave the love of the other parent, who has become the close ally of a sibling. One woman told me that she had never been able to stomach the special relationship enjoyed by her father and her sister. Her whole life story revolved around her father's rejection, her sister's nasty attempts to have dad to herself.

When I pointed out that the patient herself had had a special relationship with the mother which *excluded* the sister and father the patient could begin to see the sister's point of view. I described the family situation, carefully pointing out how the parents had arranged for an envious sibling scenario:

> Here's the family scenario as I think it might have occurred. Your parents had a terrible marriage, so each of them picked a different kid as a "best friend." Your mom picked you. Your dad picked Joanne. This really must have hurt her. All you've thought about is how badly you were hurt because you couldn't have what Joanne had with your dad. Think of how Joanne felt when you came along! No more mother! It's not your fault that this happened! But think — your mom would take you for long walks, you'd chat, have milk and cookies after school and Joanne got left out. While you and your mom might have imagined that she was outside playing with her friends, she was actually feeling hurt and angry.

Your mom — maybe without intending to — drove a wedge between the two of you, and your dad worsened matters by forming a separate little club with Joanne.

Parents shouldn't do this. Neither should have a favorite. I think someday that, if you and Joanne ever improve your relationship, you'll both realize that your parents erred and that your jealousy of each other comes from this sad kind of botched family relationship. Now that your parents are older, maybe you can both realize that there's more advantage to each of you being on each other's team than by hurting one another as your parents' special friends.

It took three years before these words, which had produced an emotional expression of relief, were actually translated into movement in these siblings' relationship. The effects of such groundbreaking discussions are rarely immediate and often require a fortuitous confluence of happenings in the family. For this case, realization of the idea that the sisters could be friends depended partly on the fact that both women discovered each was in therapy and that each had come to a similar understanding of the parents' problems.

CONCLUSION

Patients are often astounded when they realize that sibling rivalry does not merely come forth from an innate wellspring of blackhearted malice.

Transferring the emotional intensity from the sibling relationship to a broader context of parental failure may strike some readers as tough on parents. But it is my belief that the idealization of parents must be reduced if patients are asked to risk improving sibling relationships. Although the therapist cannot be sure of what "actually happened" years ago, the explanation one makes of childhood events often makes more sense to the patient than the simplistic and blameful sibling versions of one another's wrongdoing. The therapist simultaneously empathizes with the pain of each of the adult children and helps the patient to mourn for the lost opportunities and unhappy years. In the long run, the patient can come to view the parents and all family members as responsible for what happened, yet, at the same time, as victims of a system of relationships which made it difficult to give the advantage of a solid sibling bond.

Therapists of adult siblings can help them achieve greater freedom of choice with one another—to grow closer, to become less painfully enmeshed, or to actually break away. Validating their birthright to an unencumbered relationship sets the stage for healing and maturation, allowing brothers and sisters to be more genuine, forgiving, and perhaps affectionate.

REFERENCES

Bank, S. (1988). Parental Favoritism. In F. F. Schachter, *Siblings: Bridging the research-practice gap*. Haworth Press.

Bank, S., & Kahn, M. D. (1980-81). Freudian Siblings. *Psychoanalytic Review, 67* (Winter): 493-504.

Bank, S., & Kahn, M. D. (1982). *The sibling bond*. New York: Basic Books.

Cicirelli, V. (1977). Relationship of siblings to the elderly person's feelings and concerns. *Journal of Gerontology, 32*(3), 317-322.

Dunn, J. (1985). *Sisters and brothers*. Cambridge, MA: Harvard University Press.

Dunn, J., & Kendrick, C. (1982). *Siblings: Love, envy and understanding*. Cambridge: Harvard University Press.

Kahn, M. D. (1986). The sibling system: Bonds of intensity, loyalty, and endurance. In M. A. Karpel (Ed.), *Family resources* (pp. 235-258). New York: Guilford.

Kahn, M. D., & Bank, S. (1981). In pursuit of sisterhood: Adult siblings as a resource for combined individual and family therapy. *Family Process 20*(1), 85-95.

Masson, J. (1984). *The assault on the truth: Freud's suppression of the seduction theory*. New York: Farrar, Straus, and Giroux.

Miller, A. (1981). *Prisoners of childhood*. (Ruth Ward, Trans.). New York: Basic Books.

Miller, A. (1984). *Thou shalt not be aware*. Hildegarde & Hunter Hannum. (Trans.). New York: Farrar, Straus, Giroux.

Spence, 1982. *Narrative truth versus historical truth*. Rutgers, New Jersey.

17

Blueprints from the Past: A Character Work Perspective on Siblings and Personality Formation

Sandra Watanabe-Hammond

Traditionally, our therapeutic work attends to parents' impact on development and to the long-range effects of the family of origin. I find that siblings can also have a unique role in shaping the personality as well as the expectations for and patterns of intimacy. Indeed, it appears that siblings are often the first partners in life, the first "marriages" where primary intimacy can be learned. Parental marital relationships are imprinted, with the children learning by observing and often being drawn into the system. Siblings, however, live out the issues of intimacy in their own relationship. In this "sibship" they learn how to adapt around a peer on a daily basis.

Sibling couples participate in their own private world, bounded by an unmonitored, complex emotional life. Powerful sibships can be either nourishing or toxic; for some people they are both. Brothers and sisters develop patterns of love and hate, care and abuse, loyalty and betrayal. There are power struggles, sexual possibilities, interdependencies, role experiments, and divisions of emotional and instrumental labor. All of these will shape future adult functioning, perceptions, expectations, self-care, and self-worth. In other words, here is where many people directly learn some of the basics about who they are—or dare not to be—as individuals, partners, parents, and peers. What they may derive can be positive and easily incorporated into adulthood. However, it may also distort the fabric of their being, rendering them incapable of establishing a satisfactory adult life.

This has become apparent to me through Cast of Characters Work, a theoretical and clinical orientation I have developed over the past 15 years (Watanabe, 1984, 1985, 1986, 1987). Character Work conceives of the personality as a naturally organized group of distinguishable entities, or persona, which I call *characters*, who function together as a unique, highly complex, inner system. In a personality, all characters have importance, no matter how infrequently seen on the "outside" or how maladaptive they may appear to be, for each contributes to the whole person, to what it means and what it takes to be living that particular life. All have their own concerns and degrees of power in the system. Some function strictly internally and are experienced as a voice, a feeling, a fantasy life, a set of rules, etc. Others live at the interface with the world, dealing little with inner politics, while others may do border patrol duty or mediate transactions. Among them all, however, exists an intricate network of information, beliefs, actions, feelings, vulnerabilities, and protections. This rich systemic linkage among them makes possible a sustained relationship between the inner life of the characters and life in the moment, although the moments can be fraught with indecision, ambivalence, confusion and incongruity among the characters. Such conflict seems to happen most frequently when the whole person does not have access to or understanding of the differences among the characters and is therefore subject to the unresolved conflicting interests, feelings, and actions within the inner system. Such complexity does not spring to life all-of-a-piece, but evolves over time and is bounded by the experienced necessities of each character's formative relationships and situations. Indeed, it appears that in order to simply accommodate normal development, life's many traumas, and enculturation into family and society, a process of actual differentiation is necessary in the personality. Although people are generally not conscious of this differentiation within their own personality, the process of internally becoming discrete, viable characters begins at an early age and continues until there are, on average, five to ten characters. These characters have distinct functions, survival skills and mannerisms as well as particular ages, genders, attitudes and physical appearances. They even have names, such as old nicknames, family names, or names with meanings that are not immediately apparent. It may take time for all of these precise distinctions to come clear, but with attention to detail their lives and realities will become illuminated. In this sense, Cast of Characters Work is like viewing a drop of blood under a microscope, and can be as useful to psychotherapy as microbiology is to medicine. What can be seen with the "microscope" of Character Work are the characters' particular natures and specific survival functions, which have been derived from living through events unique to this individual's life. What can also be seen are the workings of the inner system, which draw the individual characters together into a unique human being. Characters in different people are recognizable to each other because of the common nature of the human experience. But no human being, with all characters accounted for, is truly like another, for no two people have the same system of characters and no individual has the same life as another.

In this matter Character Work is more in the tradition of existential philosophy and psychology than in the lineage of scientific psychology and medical psychiatry. However, many theories of personality, such as William James' pluralism, Freud's formulation of id, ego and superego, Jung's archetypes, Berne's transactional analysis, Assagioli's psychosynthesis, and the Watkins' ego-states, have attempted to delineate personality components. Despite this, there is little general acknowledgment these differences within a single person represent real, nonpathological differentiation and actual multiplicity. Indeed, many ancient philosophers showed more awareness of this phenomenon than most thinkers and clinicians during the past century.

Character Work has also been viewed as a developmental model, since most Characters evolve and emerge during the formative years. This is a period when sibships have their primary effect. Knowledge of those times, as recorded in the character system, serves as the blueprint which can be followed in therapy. Within the blueprints are the details of each character's governing beliefs and survival mastery. However, the blueprints are not the same as memories, for memories do not have regulatory functions. The relevant meanings, emotional codes, and information concerning survival seem to have been extracted during the original experience and installed within the operating system of the character network as a blueprint for living. What appears to be left in conscious memory is the story itself from a particular character's perspective, or bits and pieces of images, sounds, smells, tastes, textures, movements, or bodily sensations. All memories are important, though, because they can be used as route-markers and clues to the operating blueprints within the character system. Indeed, I have found little use for a typology of characters or a classification of character systems, for phenomenological self-descriptions lead to direct comprehension of reality and meaning rather than theoretical comprehension of a type of disorder.

For many people, the first recognizable sign of their characters is the great variation in emotion they experience, often around the same situation or relationship and often felt as conflict, ambivalence or indecision. Another initial sign is the experience of hearing inner voices busily coaching, distracting, commenting, criticizing, commanding, or even keeping the person up at night with heated arguments or critical reviews. Often such voices are ignored, feared, or deemed a nuisance, when in reality they are an indication of the life within this unique organization of characters called the self. However, since people operate at the interface with the outside world so efficiently, most are only vaguely aware of the processes and generally unaware of the realities of the characters and their intricate, precise network.

All of the characters live together as a functional unit, each being affected by the beliefs, feelings, and behaviors of the others. This marks a distinction between the typical personality and multiple personality disorder (MPD) (Kluft, 1983). Despite the same basic materials (a variety of characters who have evolved over time within an internal organization geared to survival), the MPD sufferers experience amnesia and dissociation as regulators of life, not the simultaneity and awareness of other people. This discontinuity protects the individual from full knowledge of the violent abuse most likely suffered as a child, but also leaves the MPD sufferer frighteningly devoid of time linearity and the continuity of life itself.

This differs substantially from the norm, where rarely does one character operate completely outside the awareness, assent, or cooperation of the others. This enables the person to adapt, to change in a changing world by having available the mastery of numerous characters to deal with the complexities of life. The placement of the characters within the system and their access to the outside are determined by the blueprints from the past. Various roles, situations and people bring out or stimulate different characters. Each character can make a person feel entirely different, perhaps confident or calm, perhaps angry or insecure. The characters can also be directly called upon to apply their survival skills to a situation at hand. At times characters themselves will jump to the forefront, or just as easily leave it, as they deem necessary. These switches are either disconcerting or relieving to other characters and just as often experienced as unsettling or comfortable to people on the outside. In these various fashions, each character contributes his or her own mastery to the overall adaptability and survival potential of the person.

Experiencing a balance between safety and risk is paramount to growth and continued mastery. If a situation is more risk-filled than that character is used to, or the perceived need for safety greater than before, then the old survival skills will not be able to restore the critical balance. It now only produces fear, pain, anxiety or frustration. The character's mastery, at this point, has come to its natural limit. Without this experimental edge, the character stops growing and becomes set in time, thereafter perceiving and acting from that age and emotional posture. If there is no other character available with a different approach to the same situation, then the whole system recalibrates for continued survival, allowing another character to take over or a new one to emerge out of interaction *with* a new situation itself. Because of this, each character embodies the perceptions and definitions of the situation being mastered as well as the particular survival skills developed in the situation. Eventually each character's being represents a particular cluster of history, memories, feelings, beliefs, intellect, meanings, attitudes, behaviors, bodily sensations, gestures, use of language, sense of humor, and ways of causing pleasure and pain, as well as the survival skills and mastery. Because of this, each new character or combination of characters has a different way of being in the very same situation, another viewpoint perhaps, or another approach which provides the needed balance between safety and risk.

When the characters are experienced collectively, the array of information produced simultaneously by their filters and the ensuing survival tactics determine the individual's complex functioning and consciousness at any given moment. There may be agreement among the characters as to the nature of the situation and how to be in it. This can lead to a flexible, adaptive presentation or a rigid, monochromatic approach to life. There can also be disagreement about whose assessment of the situation is correct and whose response will prevail, reflecting the significant differences among the characters' worldviews and methods of mastery. These differences between how situations and relationships are experienced and handled cause the familiar internal sensations of indecision, anxiety, self-doubt, conflict, ambivalence, immobility, or incongruence. Like a family, characters love and war with one another, learning to rely upon or distrust each other, protecting, undermining, ignoring, or obeying one another. Eventually, however, an intricately woven system of characters evolves, with substance, meaning, and depth emerging through the interplay of characters.

Because Character Work isolates and focuses on the individual threads in the tapestry of a personality, the power of intense sibling relationships can readily be seen. Frequently, there are specific characters who are wrapped up in this original sibship. Parents and others have had little or no influence on these characters. Hence, their histories and current functioning clearly reflect the shaping, issues, and survival strategies of the early relationships with a brother or sister. Both positive and negative experiences with a sibling can provide tensile strength and resilience for the whole person. Traits such as compassion, trust, playfulness, humor, self-liking, and the capacity to love can be found in the weave of a personality, even if there are characters who had few positive experiences in a difficult sibship.

A therapist working with the Cast of Characters, though, focuses on untying the knots and tangles from the negative experiences in certain characters lives, while making use of the specific strengths and traits of other characters to assist in these delicate procedures. By knowing the characters involved and the beliefs which govern the systemic mechanisms among them, it is possible to bring the original blueprints to light and see what is keeping a person stuck or a marriage from changing. This is particularly important when attending to sibling issues, for often these are the very issues obscured in family mythology or by the current locus of pain. Perhaps time itself has moved an individual far from a critical experience in survival and being, yet that event from the past still holds power over life today. Bringing into awareness the characters involved in the sibship and the blueprints drawn at that time provides the needed access to the actual living process where time is irrelevant and unspoken realities exist.

Many characters live embedded in the sibships from childhood,

with no distinction between *then* and *now*. In therapy, the kid characters in the sibship work on the sibling relationship as well as on their
own business. To feel safe enough to do their own work, they need a
trustworthy, age-appropriate link to the therapist. For some kids, this
means a caring, nourishing relationship with the therapist; for others
it means keeping the therapist at a safe distance and not having that
distance violated. The therapist's use of language must also be adjusted
when talking or playing with kid characters. Further, the therapist may
use her/his own characters in more direct and flexible ways than is usually the custom, including having his or her own kid characters upfront
during the work. Kids can often talk more easily to other kids, but are
inclined to seek safety, nourishment and approval from a grownup. This
is true in therapy with kid characters as well, so being prepared to do both
can enhance the therapist's connection to a child character.

Once connected, there is much that can be done in therapy sessions
with the kids to locate the blueprints drawn during the years within
the sibship. A sample of these therapeutic steps are: making the
details of their lives known and their realities comprehensible; detoxifying their fears with acceptance and safety; talking with them about
what is their "fault" or their sibling's "fault" versus what their parents
did not supply in the way of nurturing or boundary-setting; presenting a different sort of sibling model for them to experience through
your own kid or adolescent characters. In order to permit and accept
the necessary changes in the internal interactions and power structure, the kid character must be provided internal safety and acceptance *as a child*. Most likely this has been lacking in the inner system,
for we see many survivors of damaging sibships tyrannized by their
own terror and pain when such safety is not present. Ultimately, the
work with the therapist leads to unhooking from the original sibship
so that there is freedom to be in the world more comfortably. In the
process, the child character will often be transformed from a liability
to an asset, from an energy drain to an energy resource. However,
before such a good resolution among the characters can be achieved,
the sibling story must be told. The kids must return to the site of the
damage to do their transformational work before leaving it behind.

THE STORY OF MOLLY AND HER BROTHERS

As a child, Molly lived with two brothers, Will and Ricky, a very
proper mother, and a father whose work took him around the world

for long periods of time. All three children, by outside standards, had become successful adults, highly educated and productive. Molly appeared to be a competent woman who had recently divorced and continued to work with behavior-disordered children as a special education teacher. She also had custody of her son and together they lived in a house she was repairing herself. She entered therapy because of difficulties in a relationship with a man whom she loved.

What rapidly emerged in her work was a world of inner chaos and pain, masked by two characters. One had done an excellent job of guarding the border, keeping the inner and outer worlds separate. The other, *Berky Too*, had applied her relentless, 10-year-old energy to the "doings" of Molly's life, such as teaching, home repairs, artistic projects, parenting, and gardening. In fact, just about everything that had needed doing, *Berky Too** did. She had no awareness of limits and often exhausted or physically hurt Molly by doing too much too fast, as if she were in a competition that she *had* to win.

Inside, however, was a totally different world. Upon approaching the interior, we encountered intense emotional storms everywhere. It was hard to distinguish anyone or anything, at first, as rage and fear swirled around a core of homicidal fury, suicidal despair, impenetrable pain and intense sexual feelings. It took much of Molly's courage to look at the terror of her inner life and the world of her youth which had produced it. She had been profoundly harmed there, which had caused her characters to become so misshapen that the fabric of her life had thereafter been distorted. Her therapy took hard work, with each of her characters going through profound transformations. It also took a very long time—eight years—which is quite unusual. They were productive years, though, and necessary to do the "re-wiring," as Molly called it. A large amount of the initial work was spent quieting the storms inside of each character's world, trying to comprehend what had happened and what it had cost her to survive.

We found that a remarkable amount of the pain and inability to have anyone other than *Berky Too* in the outside world was derived from her relationships with her brothers. As is the case with many powerful sibling relationships, what mattered most to Molly's charac-

---

Berky Too is a character's name. All such names appear in this text in italic. These names were chosen by the characters themselves and usually have special significance to the characters. They also serve to distinguish one character from another, which is quite necessary once you have more than one character to address.

ters had taken place outside of parental and societal view and control. She remembered her father egging his children on with pride in their fierce fighting; she remembered her mother tying the lamps to the wall so they would not get broken in the brawls. Of her brothers, she had little but trace memories. These are the remains of an emotion, a mood, a rhythm, a sound or a smell; the remnants of events; the flashes of images too far away to grasp fully. Sometimes individual characters can fill in the details and content for themselves or for other characters, sometimes not. Hers could not, so the roots of her inner life, beyond the influence of her parents, remained a mystery for some time. However, as therapy progressed, she was able to generate images and pictures which, together with the trace memories, led the way back to her brothers and the blueprints which governed her life thereafter.

The most potent of these was a drawing of a girl-child curled up in fear at the base of a volcano. Three males in black-hooded robes were pouring molten lava onto her. We returned to this picture and its striking images time and again. It provided the major metaphor for Molly's belief that her brothers had somehow harmed her profoundly. For *Rose*, a five-year-old character who spent years working on the horribly tangled knots in her being, this was the key to her reality. It told her that to survive she had had to hide any sign of life. Because she existed at the very core of Molly's being, *Rose* affected Molly's life immensely. Daily she had been traumatized by *Berky Too's* interactions in the world, for experience told her that everything in the world was bound to feel like life with Will and Ricky. During therapy, she was able to recognize and accept her own governing belief that her brothers would always be able to intrude into her being and that anyone would, without warning, be cruel to her. This was the central information about *Rose* that had been entered into Molly's blueprints for life. Around these survival-governing beliefs had grown her reality. *Rose* had few detailed memories to back up her sense of this, but after a year of therapy she had begun to trust her own instincts about herself and her life.

Only after talking with Ricky about what she was doing in therapy did the facts behind the beliefs come to light. It turned out that he and Will had abused her with impunity. As a toddler learning to walk, she had regularly been tripped with sticks. She had been routinely attacked by Ricky after he had suffered an attack from Will.

Sometimes they had jumped her from behind, ambushing her. As a child of five or six (*Rose's* age), she had been lured to their treehouse, where they told her they were "going to fuck" her. These were the headlines to some of the stories Ricky recounted to Molly. How appalled, yet relieved, she was to hear all of this. What was real to her had also proved to be true.

The children's private life had been influenced by their relationships with their parents, but had been strictly bounded by their own unbridled emotional intensity, the boys' physical and sexual aggressiveness, and her child's desire to be included. The pain and fear which had been inherent in these situations for *Rose* had also served to catalyze *Berky Too* into a competitor determined to win by joining. By age ten she had become such a fierce fighter that her brothers backed off, left her alone. Unfortunately, she behaved the same way at school, for she knew no other way to be with playmates. Meanwhile, *Rose* remained immobilized in the war zone, unable to escape, for submission had already been entered into her blueprint for survival. Eventually, *Berky Too* had evolved into a hyperproductive fireball of energy, who often ran Molly emotionally and physically into the ground.

One of the other characters who evolved out of these years was *Tammy*, who could manage to make herself disappear, only to reappear in a homicidal or suicidal rage, triggered in a flash by reasons unknown to Molly until the blueprint code had been broken. For years she had been kept under wraps in favor of *Berky Too's* solution to survival with her brothers. It was only later in Molly's life that *Tammy* had mysteriously appeared. She could make Molly's blood run cold with fear about what she could do, and frightened other people as well. No one, on the inside or out, could make sense out of *Tammy* until the brother-code had been broken.

As we have noted, the connection with her brothers first appeared coded in the volcano drawing. Although it had been easy for her to see hooded males as the three males from her family of origin, this initially had little transformational impact. Information not connected to a particular character's being-world could not be experienced as useful, freeing knowledge. The meaning of these images and their specific coding in the blueprints had to come from her characters' comprehension of what had happened to make them who they were. Only after this had happened, and the characters had become willing to examine their old beliefs and survival tactics, did Molly find herself in a position to change her life.

As is generally true for characters, Molly's characters had devised solutions to their problems which in turn had become themselves problematic, adding another layer of complication to an already complicated, problematic life. By the time she entered therapy, the origins of these problematic solutions had been so deeply buried that no simple interventions could make a dent in the processes which governed her being. What did make a difference for Molly was going through the precision work with her characters, combined with the good fortune of having one of her brothers remember and willingly share what had happened. Many people never receive such a gift and have to proceed in therapy with only their own trace memories to guide them. This is not as bad as it seems, because it is not critical how accurate these memories are. It is what is *recorded* as the experience that determines the governing beliefs and enters the blueprint of the inner reality, which produces the survival and filtering mechanism still in use today.

In a session to which members of her family of origin had come from around the country, Ricky's stories were recounted. Her father refused to believe them, saying, "It must have been some neighborhood boys, not my sons!" He maintained his denial in the face of validation from his sons. By this point Molly's characters knew in their heart what had shaped their realities. Now those experiences could slowly be released as Molly's guiding templates to living. She was beginning to see that the world was not necessarily the same as her family, although she had no idea what rules other people used to govern their interactions. Slowly, she began to learn.

For example, *Rose* had always been upset at work despite other characters' competency and success. However, once Molly had her brothers' treatment in mind, *Rose's* "unreasonable" fear of her students made some sense. Day in and day out, *Rose* had spent 14 years with one aggressive, behavior-disordered "brother" after another. All of *Rose's* reactions to them had taken place on the inside, where her survival mechanisms were grounded in the mastery of chaos and abuse. Thus, while operating many times removed from current situations, *Rose* had experienced toxicity, felt pain, and lived in fear as if she were in direct contact with her brothers through this host of brother-surrogates. However, as she began to heal, *Rose* could consider the possibility that these children were not her out-of-control brothers; they were not to be feared just because they were in proximity to *Rose*.

Eventually Molly's other characters developed empathy for *Rose*, which led to some internal comfort and boundary-setting. This was a great relief to *Rose* and opened the way for her transformation into being just a kid. It took a while for the others' skills and her trust to build, but eventually they risked venturing into the world with her under their protection with trips to the park, a brief excursion to a store, being with sympathetic friends. Bringing the real outside world and the real inside world into congruence was difficult, but it finally happened. The students were no longer tripping the alarm and setting off *Rose's* old survival mechanisms derived from life with Will and Ricky.

This same transformation also occurred with Paul, Molly's son. Most of her characters were younger than Paul and had difficulty conceiving of themselves as "Mother," despite their primary parental responsibility for him. The characters who operated so effectively in the world had had little to do at home except work on their projects and keep Paul and Al, her former husband, from getting too close. Home had always been the haven for those of Molly's characters who rarely appeared in the outside world. There they could come out. However, this put them into interaction with Paul. One can imagine what it was like with *Rose* in constant pain and fear, leaving *Berky Too* to simultaneously care for and compete with Paul. To complicate things further, *Tammy* would spring out of oblivion in a tornado of rage when she experienced Paul as Ricky, for Paul resembled Ricky in looks, build and manner. The characters had, at different times, felt terrified, helpless, and furious with Ricky and could not help feel the same towards Paul, despite their love for him, because the blueprints from the past had been structuring the present. This problem had surfaced soon after Paul's birth, when *Berky Too* had felt it necessary to keep him in the basement when he cried so she would not be interrupted while writing her thesis. Throughout his childhood, Paul had been nurtured perfunctorily, with little physical contact and cuddling. As he grew older, Molly's characters occasionally inflicted their temper tantrums on him with much yelling and *Tammy* attacking him physically.

Only after arriving at a sense of their own histories and blueprints did Molly's characters realize how thoroughly they had misused Paul's young, male presence. It had been the recipient of misplaced revenge on Molly's brothers. Through Molly's consistent use of a Character Work journal, in which every character got to write for herself, they crystalized their fears and concerns about the damage this could have done to Paul's "little ones." They discovered, among other things, that often they had had to choose the lesser of two evils—to physically attack Paul with *Tammy's* murderous rage or to separate *Tammy* from Paul. They had chosen the separation as often as possible. Realizing the choices that Molly now had as a parent helped relieve their guilt as they came to grips with what needed remedying in Paul's life. In order to repair the damage done, they "reparented" their own son for about three years before he reached puberty.

We began this reparenting process with two joint sessions, held when Paul was about nine. He knew his Mom's characters and had found her more understandable because of it. So he chose to present his own three characters to her and to me: a three-year-old named *Jamie*, a nine-year-old named *Frank*, and a 15-year-old named *Jonathan*. They each spoke with Molly about what was bothering them. *Jamie* had always felt like a baby, not because he liked being one, but because he " . . . had never had enough." *Frank* had been a "regular kid . . ." but found it " . . . hard to spend time with other kids without smacking them." He knew no other way to interact when feeling disadvantaged, and had even smacked his mother on occasion. *Jonathan* had felt older because he had grown up fast with Molly as his mother, and had felt responsible for her fragile well-being. Mostly, this had meant keeping Paul's other two characters away from her as much as possible. This had served to protect them from her as much as it had protected her from them, although it had also isolated them. What it had not done was to free *Jonathan's* energy for himself. With this information, Molly and I planned the reparenting of Paul's characters. At times, it was difficult to get past her little ones' fears and furies, but with perseverance and enough coaching, Molly succeeded admirably. The bonus was that it furthered *Rose's, Berky Too's* and *Tammy's* release from the determining power of their past, as well as Paul from his.

CHARACTER WORK

Such ability to wrap up old business is usually dependent on the right character doing the necessary, precise work. To reach this place, numerous things must happen. Foremost is the therapist's willingness to meet the characters face to face and accept them on their own terms, without trying to correct or adjust them to approximate theory-derived specifications. Taking the character's reality seriously, as it is self-described, encourages accurate self-representation and the character's discovery of his or her own survival value.

In order to discover these realities, I conceive of myself as entering their inner system as a visitor. I have never been there before; they live there. Naturally they are the best guides to their own realities, and there is much to learn about who they are and what it means to be living as they do. I listen responsively to their stories of life in their family, their trials and tribulations, their successes and failures, their philosophies and prejudices. I ask questions and reflect back what they have said, often helping them discover the meaning and purpose of what they have revealed about themselves. I make comments designed to elucidate their experience as distinct from others.

People are generally relieved by what they discover once they become acquainted with their characters. Their findings bring clarity of meaning and purpose to previously confusing aspects of their lives. As characters become distinct from each other, they make themselves distinguishable to me as well. For instance their different voices, facial expressions, ways of moving, mannerisms, postures, energy levels, responses to issues, and senses of humor make them easily identifiable. Thus they begin to materialize in the world as they have lived for a lifetime on the inside. The illumination provided by the inside-out nature of Character Work reveals that characters who have survived damaging lives can still be full of strength, humor, playfulness, generosity, and compassion, as well as other traits. Everything (including non-admirable traits of a character) is to be valued and respected, for everything has contributed to the richness of the whole as well as the survival of the whole.

It seems that there are no superfluous characters in this living network of a person, no matter how self-destructive, hostile, manipulative, depressed, powerless, or irrelevant they appear to be. For better or worse they have developed into an interdependent living system with a set of beliefs which are the organizing principles around which life has been woven for strength and safety. These beliefs are recorded in the hidden blueprints as the guiding lessons of life. They are also integral to the filters which connect the intricate inner network with the outside world. These filters match an "event" in the present to the emotional blueprint from the character's past. This gives the present event recognizability and meaning, thereby cuing the mastery developed in the past. This circular process constantly affirms the necessity for each character's beliefs and behaviors, assuring an internal sense of continuity as the characters apply their own survival tactics to a world held constant by their own filters. The filters are often found layered and interconnected from one character to the next, arranging and rearranging the information for each character's use. There may be a few such constellations of filters, reflecting the interconnections of sets of characters who function together.

Learning about these interconnections and the value of each character takes a persistent phenomenology on the part of the individual as well as the therapist. But to accurately comprehend their particular lives, each person must retrieve the meanings and beliefs which have been stored in their blueprints. The clues are found in: the stories from the past; snapshots, drawings and movies; the body itself in the form of pains, ailments, energy patterns, rhythms, tensions and the quality of touch. In an effort to go where lives are retained, techniques such as storytelling, moviemaking, "mapmaking," kinetic group sculpture, art, dance, body-work, and music are integral to character work. For instance, it may take a variety of modes to gain awareness of and precisely locate the knots within their being/history, for such information may have been taken in through events, touches, sounds, etc. Within the safety of therapy, it is possible to follow the routes back to the origins of these blocked, knotted places, even back through previously closed or dimly lit passageways to those dark, moist recesses where the potent sibships are often kept intact.

Once the characters have become engaged in the process of rediscovering the sibling connection, the therapist can move with them through any of the following aspects of the work: unraveling the mysteries of the characters' origins as they learned to coexist with a sibling in the formative years; uncovering the specific damage done in the sibship; discovering how their shape and purpose evolved with the changes in their external lives; illuminating the workings of the inner system as it organized to accommodate the sibship; revealing the governing beliefs and survival strategies derived from life with a sib; seeing what was encoded in the filters and blueprints; comprehending how all of this shows up in their current lives.

The therapist must be willing to go where the character goes, despite how painful or scary it appears to be. By staying in contact with the characters and making it safe for the journey to continue, we place our trust in them. From the therapist's trust they are implicitly learning to trust themselves and each other as the best resources for and authorities about their lives.

Out of this will come clear images of the characters' collective lives. Generated by describing the details of purpose and being, these images can reveal the living process as clearly as a drawn map and are regularly transposed into actual maps, drawings, dances and group graphics. The latter are kinetic sculptures used to produce a "living" hologram of the complex inner system, with each character having a player to voice his or her own uniqueness within the system. All of the characters' concerns, fears and points of views can be seen simultaneously, which is an utterly unique and revealing experience. However, all of the graphic modes manifest the subjective experience of the characters for their own objective consideration, putting their life into a new perspective. Such systemic subjective-objectivity often leads to internal self-corrections which appear to be actual transformations of energy and inner connectedness among characters.

This is the level of change that people describe as living "right", or becoming "more like myselves."

In our next story we see some of this unfold in a different manner than it did in Molly's life. The power of this next sibship was so strong that the characters had been rendered virtually immobile and no mate could be successfully chosen by either brother or sister. The invisible marriage stayed intact for years into adulthood.

THE STORY OF MARK AND SARA

A young man in his thirties was unmarried and considered himself homosexual. He had not associated either of these states with his childhood relationship to his older sister, who now lived in another city. They had grown up on a farm, isolated from other children for many years. Their extremely close relationship had seemed very natural and pleasing to the family. It had been considered quite unremarkable, in fact. Only upon meeting one of Mark's characters, *Peter*, did it become clear that they had been sexual with one another for about six years of their childhood. This was shocking news to those characters in Mark who had the job of currently representing him in the world. They had been aware of a vague discomfort and guilt associated with Sara, their sister, but had never understood why. The memory had been obscured from clear view by the lives and activities of those characters who had come later.

Here is what they learned from *Peter*, age ten: "We played all of the time, even when we were doing our chores together. They [parents] left us alone a lot and we shared all of our secrets way into the night in our attic room where we slept. . . . We really had a good time together and did 'it' a lot whenever we could. It was great to be together 'cause it felt so good. . . . It wasn't so much fun, though, when she got grown up in her body. It got kind of yucky to me and scary too. I didn't like it then and besides, I'd rather bike a few miles to my new friend's house. He was more fun." *Peter's* story led to two other characters: *Becky* and *Micky*.

Becky was a 16-year-old female character who had been intensely identified with her sister. She explained: "We are like twins and would do anything for each other." Throughout the years *Becky* had remained connected and "true to my sister. It really upsets me when another woman is interested in Mark. I make it hard for them [women] to get close to him." Consequently *Becky* had become quite bitchy, "queenly," easily hurt, and often hysterical when criticized or threatened. She tended her vanities and fretted that other characters had to find her " . . . a beautiful young [male] lover before I'm no longer attractive." Yet, he had never seemed to be found. To comfort herself, *Becky* had often wished that her sister "could be here so we could talk like we used to. I know she could help. I miss her so much." At the core, she had been fearing the future, the passage of time. She had not wanted "to grow old alone without my sister and without ever having felt true love." She blamed *Peter* for having hurt their sister and for making it hard to "meet someone I could love, 'cause *Peter* doesn't care about love or me or Sara anymore."

Micky, a sad, lonely, vulnerable boy of five, was the next character to emerge. He, like *Becky*, spoke only in the present tense about his life and pain. "I know my sister Sara loves me and I love her lots but I can't be with her right now. They won't let me. They are very, very angry with me, I just know it. It's for something I did but I don't know what I did wrong. Maybe I'm just bad. But they shouldn't have made Sara go away 'cause of that. It was so mean to do that. I'm crying still about that and I can't help it, 'cause I've got no one now and I just know that I'm all Sara has and that she's lonely too. . . . I wish Sara would hold me now and read me stories, but they don't like me wanting that either. I want to die — and real soon, too, you'll see!" *Micky*'s despair and wish to be dead had to be taken seriously. His whole world had been with Sara; holding on to it and maintaining it had become his survival mechanism. From within his world view, *Micky* had not been able to understand what had happened in Mark's life. All he knew was: that he was being kept from Sara as punishment for being bad; that *Peter* and *Becky* squabbled a lot which frightened him; that other characters were mean to him; and that mostly he had no place where he was accepted and comfortable in Mark. All of this had kept him vulnerable and, as he said, "I don't even have any parents to turn to like other kids."

Micky had no memories of Mark's parents, only of Sara. *Peter* and *Becky*, though, had been aware of their parents' presence. In trying to socialize Mark, their parents usually had managed to increase the tangle among these characters. For example, they had chided him for not playing boys' games. *Becky* had felt exposed and vulnerable to the criticism. *Peter*, however, had felt wrongly accused and had pro-tested loudly to his parents that he had not been "playing with girls' stuff! I was just messing around." Then he would internally attack *Becky* for "being so stupid!" *He* had been playing with Sara; *Becky* had been playing like Sara. As time went on, such turmoil would catch *Micky*'s attention and he would think that they had been angry at him or that Sara had been disparaged by *Peter*. In either case he would cry in fear and despair, and then he *would* get yelled at. Eventually, *Micky*'s pain and fear would often set off *Becky*'s anxie-ties about dying before her time, and *Peter* would then attack her again for being so "disgusting." *Peter* had believed that if he did not keep them "in line," the whole world would know that he was a "damn fag," for that is what he felt like. Keeping up his guard had become a major survival job for him. So around and around they twisted, until they had become an incomprehensible, noisy, painful, fear-ridden knot inside of Mark. They had all wanted to be connect-ed on the outside but lived at such odds with one another that noth-ing safe and satisfying seemed possible to them collectively.

Peter had wanted to be friends with men, not sexual partners — sex was still "yuck" to him. *Becky*, although desperate for love, had been too self-absorbed and unwilling to be with another woman. *Micky* had remained thirsty for love, but wanted to die because he could no longer get love from Sara. He had decided to die rather than experience the pain of loss. The loss of Sara, no matter how necessary, had remained unimaginable because her inner presence had been so encompassing to their life and vital to the organization of their network. All of this had effectively rendered them unavailable for intimacy with anyone other than Sara.

None of this had ever been uncovered in years of traditional therapy, because no one had ever gotten past *Alfonse*, another character in the cast of nine. Experienced by the kids as mean, he turned out to be just an old curmudgeon, imprinted from a great-uncle bachelor-farmer. He had been eternally worried about the "kids" for they were his responsibility. It had been more than enough to let them move to the city and go to work; anything else was unthinkable and quite nervous-making for him. He envisioned himself eternally stationed behind the curtain at the window, frequently peeking out to see if they were safely home. Their riding a bus to and from work was about as much excitement and uncertainty as he could handle. One can imagine how he felt about therapy.

Change was just against *Alfonse's* principles; he had already let them change about as much as he could tolerate. Finally, though, he agreed to come to a session to warn me off. Facing away from me and addressing me as "Young Whippersnapper," he informed me of how disastrous it would be for them to have a social life, let alone a sexual one—especially with a man. "It would be the end of 'em! If I didn't keep a close watch on 'em no tellin' what they'd do. Probably go off in all directions and stay out all hours—11, maybe—and forget what's important. I don't let 'em bring nobody home—won't have it! I told 'em to stay with Sara on the farm after their Pa died, but they didn't listen. So now I have to look after 'em and I have enough to do without your 'help,' thank you!"

Needless to say, we had to deal immediately with this crusty old character's rejection of the process the others desired. They wished to be released from a painfully isolated life riddled with confusion, fear, hysteria, and self-destructiveness. It had kept Mark from being sexual or loving with anyone other than Sara. After a couple of meetings we came to terms. *Alfonse* agreed to monitor the process and let me know when he thought we were "going too far," which meant whenever he got anxious. *Alfonse* and I had many talks during the course of therapy, as one might expect. Because of this, the kids were granted the time to uncover their stories, to confront what the past had taught them about survival and acceptability, and to realize how inextricably bound to Sara they had remained.

Eventually they invited Sara to join their sessions, for she was right there in the inner "family" with them. During the joint meetings she learned how powerfully Mark was still joined to her. Sara, like Mark, had felt that their alliance had ended when they had physically parted, for at that time they both had keenly felt its passing. The idea of an unresolved "marriage" had caught her by surprise, but also seemed to address as many unaddressable issues in her own life as it had in Mark's. And so she began her own parallel work in therapy.

Sara soon made discoveries that brought precise comprehension to her situation. Of Sara's seven characters, four had been forged by the relationship with Mark. Their filters and governing beliefs had been calibrated and then "set" in the privacy of her life with him. Collectively these characters had produced her experience of being "in the world," her feelings of self-worth, and ultimately her capacity for self-care. Three of these four characters were still loyally attached to her brother and had been unable to sustain other connections. The fourth, a male named *Jason*, had struggled against the relationship in anger and frustration. He had felt used and betrayed by Mark, yet dependent upon him to keep their sexual secret.

The most poignant of the characters formed in the sibship was a young girl, *Jilly*, who yearned to be close to someone but feared it equally as much. Her experience of closeness had formed during sexual times with her brother and that is what she recapitulated in order to feel connected in her present life. But it never felt the same as with Mark. The strong, unspoken bonds she and Mark had had could not be manufactured with a stranger. These loving bonds had grown between Sara and Mark over the years, providing the necessary security for *Jilly* to feel intimate and safe with him. That intimacy and security did not magically reappear with others, as she hoped it would.

To make matters worse for *Jilly, Jason* constantly whispered to her that Mark had deserted her and that it was bound to happen again. And so she lived with constant ambivalence, wanting to be touched and loved, but fearing the consequences. Of course, *Jason*'s prediction always came true because *Jilly*'s own powerful governing beliefs dictated: that no one could love her as Mark had; that she was desertable; and that she had no power over what happened to her. This had always been enough to assure no experience would lead to a sustained relationship and that each experience would rub up against her open wounds from the loss of Mark. What might be felt as hurt by another was felt as harm to *Jilly*. And so she lived in fear of wanting desperately what was bound to damage her some more.

Like Mark, who had been waiting with increasing panic for " . . . my life to begin" . . . , Sara had felt that " . . . somehow my life has never been my own. I feel so damned will-less and I just hate that! Alcohol numbs me and sex makes me feel worse. . . . I used to think that sex and booze were my problems; now I think they must have been my solution. It never occurred to me that the real problem is that we [characters] just keep trying to live out our old patterns with Mark." With these new self-understandings, Sara returned to sessions with Mark in an effort to resolve their old marriage. They had been bound to each other and the bind was circular and complete. Without conscious awareness, they had shaped themselves to fit each other's love and limitations. These sibs had truly been alone in a private world with little to modulate it from the outside. They knew how to function intimately within that world, but nowhere else and with no one else. This had remained so, despite their years of separation. They now could see that letting go was imperative, for without it they would be unable to develop the mastery better suited to their adult lives.

For about three months in joint sessions they worked on debonding and releasing. From the historical blueprints which still governed their characters' systems and determined the maps of their intricately enmeshed lives, they knew where the knots and tangles were located. With these blueprints and maps as guides, they released each other, character by character, from the entwining past. There was pain and laughter and pain again, as they moved through their intense emotional and sexual bonds, unbraiding their lives as they went. As the threads were carefully rewoven into the present, the future became theirs without the plying of pain and fear, love and hate, which had bound them together. For the first time in many years the majority of their characters began to live in the world. By letting go of their past's governing hold, new beliefs and new mastery flowed from the energy released into Sara's and Mark's lives. Four years after therapy they were both continuing to blossom.

CONCLUSION

The characters described in our two stories, like so many others in entangled sibships, had mastery over *now* based on rendering *now* the same as *then*. They remained caught up in their own survival issues presented constantly by the old, faulty filters. This is not unique to these characters, but represents how people go round and round in their own knots of pain and fear as if living in a reconstruction of the original sibling system. Often a great deal of pain in the present is generated by recapitulation of pain in the past, all for the sake of maintaining known mastery and therefore survival.

In pointing out the flaws of this naturally elegant way of organizing a life around powerful formative experiences, such as a potent sibship, I am not implying that all sibships are toxic. However, if there is serious unfinished business in the dark recesses of their past, then the updated version will be at best uncomfortable or ritualized. Returning to that private world in which they had shaped each other's lives can release the adults from the old survival habits forged so long ago.

By description, character work can seem a tedious way to go about therapy. In reality, it is a fascinating enterprise which can yield results quickly or can be carried out over years, if necessary, and never be a futile exercise. In order to engage in this form of therapy, though, I have found that the patience of a master puzzle-worker, the curiosity of a child, the respectfulness of a curator, and the eye-for-detail of a detective are the most necessary and useful skills. The more willing the therapist is to work in this manner on the fluid edge of life, without having to know everything beforehand, without preconceived notions about what is being uncovered, the fuller each character materializes and the more quickly the blueprints will be revealed. It is a matter of making room for the details and surprises, with the therapist's knowledge held as an enriched background to be relied upon as needed.

If left to their own timing and style, most characters will pursue what is more important and relieving, becoming totally absorbed in unraveling, sorting, and reweaving the threads of their own lives as if the work were visible before them. All of the characters described in this chapter worked in such a manner, making their transformations possible.

378   *Siblings in Therapy*

REFERENCES

Kluft, R.P. (1983). Hypnotherapeutic crisis intervention in multiple personality. *American Journal of Clinical Hypnosis, 26*, 2, 73–83.
Watanabe, Sandra (1984). Cast of characters work: Exploring the naturally organized personality. Unpublished; presented at the First International Conference on Multiple Personality/Dissociative State, Sept.
Watanabe, Sandra (1985). Exploration systemique de l'organisation naturalle de la personalite: travail clinique sur la gamme des personnages (dramatis personae). *Systemes Humains*, 1, 4, automne.
Watanabe, Sandra (1986). Cast of character work: systemically exploring the naturally organized personality. *Contemporary Family Therapy, An International Journal*, 8, 1, spring.
Watanabe-Hammond, Sandra (1987). The many faces of paul and dora. *The Family Therapy Networker*, Jan.–Feb.

18

Siblings and the Family Business

Robert Carroll

As a family psychiatrist in full-time private practice, I have sometimes asked myself, "How do I make my work more meaningful, more profitable, and less draining?" I have been involved in many standard alternatives—university faculty appointments, independent research, supervision groups, etc. These certainly have provided a richness and variety of experience; however, none of them has given me the opportunity to get off my duff, out of my chair, and into the world of lights, sounds, and human activity (other than therapy) which seems so alluring to me.

It was in this context that family business consulting appeared to me as a viable alternative (or at least a counterpoint) to the full-time clinical practice of family psychiatry*. It was my hope that working with family businesses would be a way of getting out of my office and into the world.

MY FAMILY'S BUSINESS

When my maternal grandparents emigrated from Russia some 70 years ago, they established a small grocery store in Brooklyn, New York. As my mother and her three siblings grew up, they supplied both labor and motivation for keeping the business going. The four

*My thanks to Will McWhinney, Ph.D., who, as a consultant to organizations in general and family businesses in particular, went into a consulting partnership with me, taught me a new language, and served as a skillful guide. Throughout this chapter, the pronouns "we" and "us" refer to Dr. McWhinney and myself.

brothers and sisters worked in the store after school and in turn the business provided them with sustenance. It is part of my family's mythology that this grocery store fed my family through the Depression. It is also part of the mythology that my grandfather would extend credit to the neighborhood women to help them through difficult times; however, as my grandmother told it, Grandpa may have had other motives as well.

Family life and business life were intimately intertwined; indeed, they were inseparable. When I was seven, my parents and sister and I lived with my grandparents next to the grocery store. I remember cold winter afternoons in the back of the store, dissolving rock candy in warm, steaming milk as my grandfather waited patiently until it was "just right." I also remember stealing some change from the cash register. Even at the time, I knew stealing was wrong, but curiously I did not equate stealing from the cash register with stealing from my grandfather. When my mother found out, she said I had upset my grandfather, but she was the one who appeared upset. I learned that taking money had far greater implications between my grandfather and his daughter and between my mother and me than between him and me directly. My grandfather and I never discussed the event and stayed close until his death 20 years later. Money had always served as an important currency of relationship in my family.

As a child, I was aware of my family's business as crucial in the forging of our family relationships. My daily interactions, relationships with my mother, and sense of myself as part of and continuous with my family's history were all inextricably woven into the fabric of the family business context. Now, as an adult, I am undertaking the task of working with other systems like the one in which I was raised.

FAMILY BUSINESSES

Family businesses account for approximately 95% of all businesses in the United States. There are some 12 million family held companies in this country employing approximately half the private sector work force and accounting for half the gross national product. Family businesses can be very small "Ma and Pa" operations like my own family's business or very large. More than 150 of the Fortune 500 largest companies are family owned businesses — Hughes Aircraft

Company, Mars, Inc., and Hallmark Cards, Inc., to name a few (see
generally, Danco, 1982; Dyer, 1986; Rosenblatt et al., 1985; Stern,
1986).

Of late, a number of family business situations have been well
publicized (e.g., Prokesch, 1986). The following brief sketch of the
Sebastiani family business, as reported in the media (Leslie, 1986),
serves to introduce a number of the salient themes I will be discussing
in this chapter. Note particularly how the family business serves as
context for the negotiation of relational dynamics and how family
and business issues intimately intertwine. Please refer to the genogram in Figure 1.

The Sebastiani winery was founded in 1904 by Samuele Sebastiani
and under the direction of his son August became the 11th largest
U.S. wine producer. August, frequently in consultation with his wife
Sylvia, ran the winery as a low overhead operation producing cheap
jug wines. Sam, their eldest son, had always assumed he would eventually take over the business. He began working there in 1965, intending to move quickly into positions of greater responsibility;
however, he was frequently frustrated by his father's seeming unwillingness to acknowledge his input.

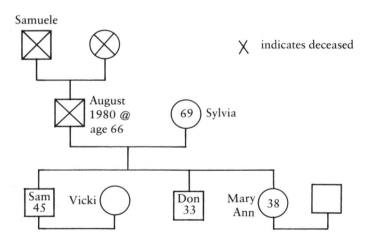

FIGURE 1
Genogram of Sebastiani Family as of 1986

In 1980, August died, leaving 94.6% of the business to Sylvia and management responsibility for the company to Sam. In what his mother later identified as a break with tradition, Sam aggressively set about to upgrade the winery's image, improve the marketing strategy, and produce a higher quality product. At the same time, he was increasingly sensitive to the needs of his employees and good community relations. By 1985, the winery had achieved critical acclaim, but was suffering losses. Nonetheless, it had apparently weathered the worst of a bad time in the industry generally and was in a position to begin to realize a profit in the higher quality market to which Sam had directed his efforts.

Meanwhile, however, family relations were deteriorating. Sam had removed his mother from her responsibility for food presentations and given the job to his wife, Vicki. He was in conflict with his younger brother, Don, who as a State Assemblyman drew unfavorable attention to the winery through questionable political judgments. Sam was also at odds with his sister, Mary Ann.

In a bid for greater control of the company, Sam sought backing from his mother; instead—apparently at Don's urging—she fired him and made Don chief executive officer of the company. He then placed a professional manager (a nonfamily member) in Sam's place as president. The future of the winery is now uncertain and some predict it will be sold.

Several themes are apparent in this brief sketch of the Sebastiani's family business.

1. Family issues and business issues were inextricably interwoven, such that it made no sense to talk about, for example, the firing of Sam, the company's president, without knowing that he was fired by his mother and replaced by his brother. Similarly, it would be incomplete to speak of August's relationship with his children without knowing that Sam had been groomed to succeed August in running the business. Another way to state this is that the family business was more than the family plus the business or a business enterprise undertaken by the family; it was, in itself, a system in which family and business were tightly intertwined.

2. The family business provided a context in which family members interacted in actual day-to-day relationships. These actu-

al relationships reflected such factors as: birth order, e.g., Sam was the oldest son; gender, e.g., Sylvia was replaced by another woman, Sam's wife Vicki; and position in the company, e.g., Sylvia owned 94.6% of the business.

3. The actual day-to-day business interactions drew powerful additional meaning from the existing familial relationships. For example, August's grooming of Sam to succeed him may have been experienced by Sam as affirmation by his father, by Don as a choice of his brother over him, or by Mary Ann as male favoritism. Similarly, Vicki's role as first lady to Sam may have felt to Sylvia like a betrayal by her oldest son, and Don and Mary Ann's usurpation of the company may have seemed to Sam to be a rivalrous overthrow of an older brother by his younger siblings.

4. The events of the final firing of Sam by his mother in collusion with her two younger children were themselves continuous with and evolved out of the shared history of these family members. This is the family legacy as it is passed on from generation to generation. It can be concretized in the form of property or manifested in the relational themes enacted between family members. Sam's break from the family tradition of producing inexpensive table wines and the replacement of his mother as the winery's matriarch may have been experienced by other family members as violations of this family's legacy.

5. Rather than finding a way to utilize the business as a resource for the ongoing and developing needs of this family and its members, they let it become a bone of contention. In the struggle to control the business, not only did the Sebastiani family jeopardize the business, but the family itself was also torn apart.

In the following pages I will focus on three components of relationship among family members—the *actual, transferential*, and *family legacy*—by substantiating and detailing their existence in sibling interaction. I will then discuss the value of the family business as a context for viewing family interaction in general and sibling relationships in particular. The family business as a resource in family development will then be addressed, the issue of sibling rivalry will be discussed, and finally, I will detail a strategy for clinical intervention in the family system.

SIBLINGS

When one considers the multiple structures and forms of expression of sibling relationships, it is apparent that there is "no standard, unitary sibling bond" (Bank and Kahn, 1982, p. 296). Rather sibling bonding represents a spectrum of diverse relationships, all of which have the potential for powerful meaning in the lives of the involved brothers and sisters. As such, the sibling bond is a bond of multipotentiality within which relational themes such as intimacy, dependency, rivalry, and fairness can all be enacted.

Sibling relationships are *committed* relationships. Commitment in this sense is not necessarily undertaken consciously or by choice, but by virtue of the fact of brotherhood and sisterhood and by the familial and socioculturally determined implications of that fact. To call someone your brother or your sister is meaningful, whether or not you intend it to be so. This commitment remains a potential resource for the family and its members throughout the life cycle. It is, in fact, more likely that on your deathbed you will be with your brother or sister rather than with your spouse (Kahn, 1983, 1986).

It is frequently stated that the sibling bond is a "horizontal" bond, that is, it is a bonding between members of the same generation and as such implies a peer-like relationship, as opposed to the "vertical" bond of intergenerational relationships. However, within the horizontal structure of these bonds there is much room for differentiated interaction.

There is an *actual* relationship between siblings. The actual relationship encompasses such factors as birth order, gender, and number of siblings. It also includes whether siblings live in the same home, share the same biological parents, or work as partners in the same business. The actual relationship is characterized by a certain commonsense, matter-of-fact quality which is, in the main, observable in day-to-day interactions. If an older sister nursed a younger brother through a childhood illness, or if one brother hires another's daughter to work in his company, these are also a part of the actual relationship. The actual relationship can be more or less affectionate, problematic, or meaningful.

Concurrent with their actual relationship, siblings can transfer onto one another unresolved issues with their parents, thus adding a *transferential* dimension to the sibling relationship. Transference is commonly defined as "the unconscious attribution to significant others, including the psychiatrist, of feelings and attitudes that were originally associated with important figures in the patient's early life" (Kaplan and Sadock, 1985, p. 485). In general, the transference relationship is considered to be a projection of a relationship with a parent onto a relationship with a therapist. In fact, as the above definition suggests, transference can reasonably be taken to be a projection of any significant relationship onto any other. There may be no better way for a person to resolve issues with parents of dependency, nurturance, intimacy, etc., than by transferring these issues and working them through in their relationship with a brother or sister.

At the same time, siblings can enact other aspects of the ongoing, historically rooted family drama. For example, mistrust between siblings in one generation is frequently replicated between siblings in subsequent generations. On the positive side, honesty in business can be a tradition in families over many generations. Siblings share a common intergenerational family history and become heirs to a shared *family legacy* (Boszormenyi-Nagy and Krasner, 1980; Boszormenyi-Nagy and Krasner, 1986; Boszormenyi-Nagy and Spark, 1984). In order to enact, propagate, and at times resolve ongoing themes in the family legacy, siblings will frequently undertake the exploration of these themes in shared interaction with one another.

To reiterate, sibling relationships and interactions contain *actual*, *transferential*, and *family legacy* dimensions. In fact, particular interactions may have aspects of all three dimensions, moreover, in my experience resolutions are more stable when they make sense in all three.

In the following example, two brothers' dissatisfaction with one another is multiply determined by issues which reverberate along each of the three dimensions of interaction. This family came to us for consultation because of the antagonistic relationship between the two brothers.

Example 1

In 1958, Max, age 60 at the time of our consultation, founded a law firm specializing in immigration and naturalization law. His older son, John, age 34, has worked with him for seven years, and his younger son, Jim, age 28, has been in the firm for two. Because of his tenure with the firm, John has access to new clients and the privilege of delegating cases to his younger brother, his junior partner. These are facts of the actual relationship between the brothers.

Jim is getting annoyed with John because of the "unfairness" in their relationship, while John does not "understand what Jim's problem is." Here is where the transferential aspect of the brothers' relationship to their father comes into play. Jim has always felt his father favored his older son, while John has identified with their father and tended to treat Jim as an unreasonable child.

Max himself is an immigrant, having come to this country with his parents when he was a child. The family legacy theme of helping those in need (particularly immigrant families) is part of the original reason that the two brothers went into law and now work with their father.

Jim's dissatisfaction is determined by the actual relationship of being a junior partner to his brother, the transferential issue of "whose side will Daddy take," and the family legacy belief that a man's value is determined by how well he serves the less advantaged. The simple solution to this dilemma was Jim's opening a branch of the family law firm in a nearby city. This put him in a better position to establish his path as an individual with the encouragement of both his father and his brother, while enabling him to continue the family legacy through the shared family law practice.

THE FAMILY BUSINESS CONTEXT

The family business is something family members do together. Because of the concreteness of the task of running a family's business, as well as the importance of its functions in providing for the ongoing and developing needs of the family and its members, the dynamic relational issues present in all families seem to stand in relief in the family business context. Because many family members are involved in the business as owners (whether or not they work in the business), managers, employees, consultants, etc., the family business is an arena in which actual relationships are negotiated. Because relational themes such as power, control, fairness, etc., are very much at the heart of running the business, as well as critical to healthy family development, the family business is rife with possibilities for transferential interaction. Finally, because most entrepreneurs want to see their creation kept alive in succeeding generations, there is a strong push to have their children join in and eventually take over the business. In this way, the business itself becomes a concrete manifestation of the family legacy around which other family legacy interactions naturally take shape.

However, the family business provides more than just a way to view family interaction; it also provides potential resources to serve the needs of the family. For instance, in a seminar held for families in business, we asked, "What are the functions of your family?" Typical responses included the raising of children to be adults, support of one another, holding and preserving certain principles, and serving the larger community. When we then asked participants, "What are the functions of your business?" they emphasized providing opportunity, making money, providing service or product, and employing people. When the functions of the business are juxtaposed with those of the family (see Table 1), a striking complementarity can be seen. The business can provide opportunity for the family members into and throughout adulthood; it can generate money to support the family; it can provide a service or product in accordance with the principles and values of the family's business practice; and it can employ people as a way of serving the larger community. In other words, if properly designed, the family business potentially provides resources to serve the ongoing and developing needs of the family.

It is important to emphasize that the ongoing and developing needs of a family and its members are exactly that: needs change as individuals develop and the family grows into new configurations, at the same time one must be aware that businesses also follow a sequence of developmental stages (Danco, 1982; Greiner, 1972).

An entrepreneurial couple with young children is at a different

Table 1

Business Functions	Family Functions
Provide opportunity	Raise adults
Make money	Support one another
Provide service or product	Hold and preserve principles
Employ people	Serve the larger community

family developmental stage than a couple in their sixties with mature children. Over the years a business might be designed to provide a steady family income and flexibility in childcare for young children, part-time work and skills development for adolescent children, capital to expand the company or fund independent business ventures for children in their twenties, or opportunity for children to assume ownership and control as issues of successorship and retirement come up for the original entrepreneurs.

Our consulting work with family businesses is based on matching the developmental needs of the family and its individual members with the business resources available given the developmental stage of the business. Even though we are primarily concerned with how the business can serve the family, we are aware that decisions based on good business practice must be observed. The role of planning coherently for the ongoing development of both the family and the business cannot be overemphasized.

It was curious to me that the juxtaposition of business and family functions in Table 1 yielded obvious complementarity that was not readily appreciated by the families before the exercise. In fact, the common wisdom is that family and business do not mix and should be kept as separate as possible. This attitude is reflected in advice by business consultants to keep family members out of business decisions, in the reluctance of therapists to openly discuss business issues (e.g., both the finances of the family and the business aspect of the therapy), and most importantly, in the apparent discontinuity between the functions of the business and the functions of the family as reported by the family members themselves.

Of course, the very strength of the family business enterprise rests on the commitment of family members to engage in the family business together. Consequently, the question is not how to separate business issues from family issues, but how to facilitate their harmonious interrelatedness. The complementarity of family and business functions is, as we have seen, inherent in the way family business members conceive of and identify the functions of their business and their family.

The resources of the family business become available when family business members realize:

1. The business can be planned and designed to serve the ongoing needs of the family and its individual members.

2. Family business members are engaged in the family business enterprise *together*.
3. Doing the family business together requires an attention to the ethic of *fairness* (Boszormenyi-Nagy and Krasner, 1980; Boszormenyi-Nagy and Krasner, 1986). In this context, the concept of fairness is contrasted with a notion of strict equality. As one mother put it, "I may love all my children equally, but I don't love them all the same."

These three issues frequently focus in the relationship between siblings. Sibling rivalry brings the issues of individual needs sharply into play, and the concepts of fairness and togetherness are critical to the resolution of rivalrous interaction.

SIBLING RIVALRY

When sibling relationships have been discussed at all in the psychotherapeutic literature, the emphasis has been on the rivalrous aspects of these relationships. (Bank and Kahn, 1982 have pointed out the reasons for this prevailing bias.) *Webster's* defines rivalry as "two or more striving for what only one can possess," e.g., a favored relationship with a parent or a particular role in the family business. Although there is certainly much sibling interaction that can be construed as rivalrous, much of what is called sibling rivalry might be better understood by analyzing the interplay among the actual, transferential, and family legacy components of sibling interaction. In the family business context sibling interaction might take the form of competition for a favored position; however, our analysis might reveal that the individual siblings are trying to satisfy quite different actual, transferential, and family legacy needs. Thus, they are not necessarily competing for "what only one can possess." Once individual goals are understood in terms of real needs and motivations, it may be that they are not mutually exclusive.

The family business context can provide resources which are both flexible and concrete enough to address different individual needs. In our first example two brothers were competing for a favored position in their relationship with their father and in their day-to-day business dealings with one another. The resources of the business were flexible enough to allow for a redefinition of the seemingly irresolvable rivalry by directly addressing the differing developmental needs of the brothers. In the next example, the two brothers were also engaged in "rivalrous" interaction; however, an analysis of the different components of interaction revealed a different dynamic and suggested a quite different solution.

Example 2

Two brothers, Dirk, 35, and Stephan, 32, worked together with their father in a metal works business. The business was founded by their paternal grandfather. Dirk and his father had never worked anywhere else, while Stephan was in the merchant marine and had worked on the docks until he joined the family business two years before I saw the family in consultation. Although Dirk and Stephan had been "best friends" growing up, Dirk was not eager to have Stephan in the business.

On a day-to-day basis, there was a division of responsibility, with Dirk in charge of the foundry and Stephan in charge of purchasing, shipping, and receiving. Dirk could not tolerate Stephan's interference in the running of the shop and almost got into a fistfight with his younger brother when Stephan fired one of the shop's workers, albeit for good cause. Their father managed the whole operation but was unable to intervene effectively in the struggle between his sons. The father's suggestions to further separate responsibility—to keep the boys apart—only made the brothers' interaction more antagonistic.

In the course of the consultation, it became apparent that for Dirk the business was more than day-to-day management, ownership of assets, or a way to make a living. It was a concrete manifestation of what he viewed as his legacy from his grandfather, an inventor who started the business as a means of producing the parts he needed for his inventions. Dirk recounted his childhood in the back room of the foundry in awe of his grandfather's creations, for which he had "won three patents!" Since the preservation of this legacy was an issue of self-identity for Dirk, no acceptable solution would be possible unless this dimension were adequately taken into account. Although for Stephan, too, the family business provided opportunity, his need for a secure job to support his wife and a new baby was quite different from Dirk's.

In the course of consultation, Dirk himself suggested that he take his grandfather's room for his own office, displaying the three patents as diplomas on a wall and saving a place for the first of his own. Dirk had been displacing his unresolved legacy issue into the actual relationship with his brother, resulting in what might have been mistaken for sibling rivalry. These brothers weren't "striving for what only one could possess." In fact, they were each striving for entirely different ends. Dirk was looking for a sense of self through identification with his grandfather's legacy. Stephan was attempting to establish himself in a secure position in the business so that he could provide for his family. The seemingly rivalrous nature of the relationship was an artifact of a legacy issue being displaced into the actual component of the brothers' interaction. With this legacy issue identified, and at least for now resolved, the brothers were able to negotiate their remaining differences.

Example 2 illustrates the potential power of the family legacy component in sibling interaction. The next example, of a family business involving two sisters, demonstrates ways in which transferential issues in a sibling relationship can become inextricably linked with an actual relationship of closeness and caring. Resolutions in such problematic relationships must come from an appreciation that transferential and family legacy components of interaction cannot always be separately identified and resolved; indeed, they may constitute a large portion of what has been meaningful between siblings over their lives. Intervention must be respectful of this reality.

Example 3

Two sisters, Sally and Lil, work together in a family business selling textile products. The older sister, Sally, both owns and runs the business, while the younger sister's talents in sales have made her indispensable to the company's financial growth. Lil owns no stock but draws a salary; in addition, she is "taken care of" by Sally through bonuses and other rewards. This relationship, originating in childhood, when their mother frequently delegated parenting functions to the older sister, has continued throughout adulthood. As Sally, age 70, nears retirement, Lil, age 60, is becoming uncertain about her own future and increasingly less content to simply rely on Sally's taking care of her. However, Lil is reluctant to confront her older sister for fear of jeopardizing their relationship. Sally, who has no children of her own, continues to assume a maternal attitude toward Lil, and neither sister wants the business issues to cause a rift in their family.

These sisters' powerful relationship of mutual caring and support included a significant transferential component. Lil had transferred her maternal relationship onto her older sister and Sally had transferred her own need to be "taken care of" onto her younger sister through projective identification. That is, the older sister was caring for *herself* by experiencing real need in her younger sister, projecting her own need onto it, and then "taking care of" this younger sister. The business became a vehicle for Sally's continuing to care for her younger sibling into adulthood and old age. It also served as an affirmation of Lil's "filial" loyalty and devotion to her older sibling.

But what of Lil's discontent? Doesn't this represent a need for individuation from the older sister? Most forms of psychotherapy are practiced with a bias towards the primacy of the individual. Individuation and differentiation from family are valued over the common family connectedness, intimate relatedness, and subordination of individual ego that doing things *together* may require (Carroll and Carroll, 1985; Schutz, 1951). In this case, the business relationship was a true expression of the sisters' caring for one another. It was something that they were doing together.

The consultants' suggestion that Lil be given some formal ownership of the business was met with resistance from both women. They were not resisting individuation, but instead enacting their own concept of family relatedness, i.e., family members trust and take care of one another. This concept of family relatedness was critical to each woman's individual sense of self.

There may be an error in assuming that there is something wrong with a relationship just because it has a strong transferential element. Lil's discontent was more properly viewed as concern about her own security when Sally retired rather than a belated assertion of a need for individuation. Lil had come to realize that she needed to have some definite sense of her financial future. Accordingly, Lil was urged to explain her needs to her older sister. The two women then worked together in negotiating a contract for the sale of the business in such a way that both would be suitably provided for. It will be interesting to see what legacy issues are being created for the younger sister's two daughters, now in their early thirties.

CLINICAL INTERVENTION — SUCCESSION AS A COMMON ISSUE IN FAMILY BUSINESS DEVELOPMENT

In most family business situations involving siblings, members of other generations are also on the scene. A typical — in many ways the most common — situation revolves around succession in the family business, i.e., to whom, how, and on what terms the business will be transferred to the next generation. In order to continue developing, a family business, like a family, must arrange for orderly transfer of control from one generation to the next. While a succession dispute may involve the siblings, the dynamics must be seen in the larger relational context of the intergenerational family system.

It has been our experience that certain common problems arise in the development of family business systems, such as the roles of female family members in the business, and how to deal with significant nonfamily members of the business as well as succession to the next generation. Given this commonality, a group experience provides a useful context for family business members to define relevant issues. The experiences of each family business can catalyze new solutions for the others. Additionally, families in business are not as a rule psychologically sophisticated, and so the sharing of experiences in the commonsense language of everyday life can add to the comfort level of what is typically an intense exploration of the participants' personal lives.

The overall construction of the course we offer at UCLA to families in business is based on the idea that there are three developmental lines to consider — the individual, the family and the business — and that impasses which occur in family businesses can be understood in terms of the interweaving of these three strands.

For example, the issue of succession in a family business has to do with entrepreneurs' willingness to see retirement (or redefinition of their involvement with the business) as a necessary next step in their personal lives, the lives of their families and as good business practice. If, however, there are no suitable family members to take the reins, or if there are several, a crisis may ensue. Since this impasse could have been predicted well in advance, planning makes sense. If, on the other hand, a crisis situation already exists, it can be useful to tease apart the personal, family, and business developmental issues so that they can be approached anew. In this process, the actual relationships among family business members are made explicit, transferential issues become apparent, and the family legacy can be tapped as a potential for understanding. We then encourage these families to utilize the business as a resource in their personal and family development and as a vehicle in their planning for the future.

Example 4

John, age 72, is the owner and chief executive officer (CEO) of a company with total sales of about $10 million per year. It employs about 25 people, including his son Warren, age 38, who is general manager, his daughter Meg, age 40, who is comptroller, his wife Anne, age 70, who works part-time in the office, and his grandchild who does part-time yardwork after school. The company was founded by John's father in 1922 and barely survived the Depression. Please refer to the family genogram in Figure 2.

Five years ago John had a heart attack. At the time he came to see us he was still concerned about his health, but he didn't seem to want to face the implications of his illness and age. Although he insisted that he wanted to retire and spend more time with his wife, something she has wanted since his illness, he had made few changes in his daily work habits.

Warren was divorced and without children. He was asked by his father to join the firm just after the heart attack, with the obvious implications that his father needed him and that he would soon take over running the company. Warren gave up a career as a teacher to prove himself in business and to help his father. His older sister, Meg, had worked for the firm as bookkeeper and then comptroller during the past 12 years. Like Warren, she was a part owner of the company. However, her primary business interest was to have a continued steady income and the long-term survival of the business as a place of opportunity for her two children (ages 7 and 13).

Anne had helped John develop the business; she had acted as the

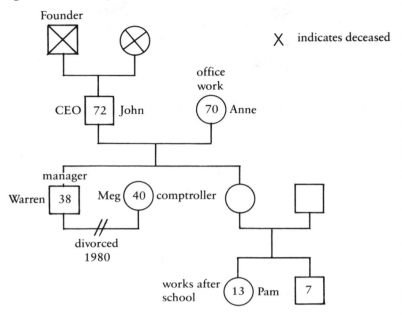

FIGURE 2
Example 4 Family Genogram

company bookkeeper until Meg took over 12 years ago. Anne's direct involvement had decreased in recent years. She felt trapped between her husband, who was holding tightly to the reins of the business, her son, who was chomping at the bit, and her daughter, who was concerned that the conflict between her father and her brother would jeopardize the security that the business provided. Although Meg had an ownership interest in the business, she did not want to run it on a day-to-day basis. She was eager for Warren to take over as CEO, but concerned that her needs might be overlooked in the pending transfer of control. As a consequence, Meg was frequently annoyed with both her father and her brother.

When this family began our course, it was Warren who identified the problem as being "My old man always wants his own way." John was aware of some friction between himself and Warren, but thought that was "just the way it is when you work with your son." There was some mutual irritation displayed between Warren and Meg, although they both seemed willing to hear one another's point of view. Anne seemed generally tense and uneasy.

The clinical intervention over the next weeks consisted of a series of exercises which the family members did both as course work and as homework. Each member constructed a timeline and used it as a way of talking about his/her own life story, what was important to him/her individually, and what his/her hopes were for the future. They then collectively constructed their family genogram, including extensive discussions of the emigration from Ireland by the grandparents, family stories and family values, and disappointments from the past and hopes for the future. Finally, a chart of the structure of the business was drawn, including all family members who had ever worked in the business, tales of founding the business, other family business ventures which had failed or succeeded, etc. All of these exercises were juxtaposed with didactic material about the stages of individual adult development, the family developmental life cycle, and the family business as an ongoing family resource. Exercises such as role plays, role reversals, etc., were also included where appropriate. Gradually, the following set of stories emerged.

John saw himself as a child of the Depression who had to scrape to survive in the business his father had started. His identity had become intimately fused with his role as owner and manager of the business. Although John very much wanted his children to take over the business, he was caught by not being able to let go.

Warren had come into the business four years earlier, after developing another career. He had always been adamant that he would not go into the business; however, when his father became ill he changed his mind. His decision was probably influenced both by his desire to help his father and by the opportunity to take things over quickly, perhaps more quickly than he was able.

Meg had never wanted to run the business because of her dual role as career woman and mother to her two children. Having seen how hard her father had to work, she chose to invest her time in the business as part owner and employee, but not attempt to take over for her father. Nonetheless, when her livelihood and the potential opportunity for her children was at stake, she knew she needed to become more involved.

Anne's stake was in facilitating her husband's retirement in such a way that he felt free to travel. She also wanted to assure a resolution to the situation that would satisfy both of her children. From the point of view of family development, it was about time for the older generation to move on and for the next generation to assert itself.

At one meeting we did a role play of this family in which John and Warren reversed roles. The next week John made a suggestion to his children. He was learning that he had personal and family developmental needs, but it was critical that his decisions make good business sense. John saw that he needed to redefine his priorities, but he would not give up control of the business until Warren had proved himself capable of running it. John told Warren of a project which he had always wanted the company to undertake, but had delayed for lack of time. It would both diversify their activity and expand their markets in ways that were consistent with the general trends in the industry.

During the year following the course, Warren took the idea and developed it with his own style and flair, showing particular skill in his marketing ability. Warren had adequately proved himself so that John could go into semi-retirement, and he and Anne went to Europe for the summer. Upon follow-up we learned that Warren had taken over the role of CEO. From Meg's point of view this was an adequate solution. It assured a continuity in family ownership of the company, a secure position for Meg, and potential opportunity for her children.

CONCLUSION

It has been about four years since I became interested in working with family businesses. The field itself is just beginning to organize, and the relative inputs from family therapy, organizational design, business management, law, accounting and others are still being negotiated. It is clear to me that the family systems perspective is a critical piece in understanding the relational dynamics so powerful in the family business enterprise.

In this chapter, I have focused on sibling interaction in the family business context to highlight the actual, transferential, and family legacy components of this interaction. I have suggested ways in which the family business might provide resources to resolve intersibling conflict by serving the developmental needs of the families in general and siblings in particular.

REFERENCES

Bank, S. P., & Kahn, M. D. (1982). *The sibling bond.* New York: Basic Books.

Boszormenyi-Nagy, I., & Krasner, B. (1980). Trust beyond therapy: A contextual approach. *The American Journal of Psychiatry 137*(7), 767–775.

Boszormenyi-Nagy, I., & Krasner, B. (1986). *Beyond give and take.* New York: Brunner/Mazel.

Boszormenyi-Nagy, I., & Spark, G. M. (1984). *Invisible loyalties.* New York: Brunner/Mazel.

Carroll, S. L., & Carroll, R. S. (1985 April). The functions of symbiosis. Paper presented at UCLA conference, "Self in Context," April 27.

Danco, L. A. (1982). *Beyond survival: A business owner's guide for success* (4th ed). Cleveland, OH: The Center for Family Business, University Press.

Dyer, W. G. (1986). *Cultural change in family firms.* San Francisco: Josey-Bass.

Greiner, L. E. (1972). Evolution and revolution as organizations grow. *Harvard Business Review,* July-August, 37–46.

Kahn, M. D. (1983). Sibling relationships in later life. *Medical Aspects of Human Sexuality 7*(12), 94–103.

Kahn, M. D. (1986). The sibling system: Bonds of intensity, loyalty, and endurance. In M. A. Karpel (Ed.). *Family resources: The hidden partner in family therapy.* New York: Guilford.

Kaplan, H. I., & Sadock, B. J. (1985). *Comprehensive textbook of psychiatry* (4th ed). Baltimore, MD: Williams & Wilkins.

Leslie, J. (1986, April). A wine family feud. *Los Angeles Times Magazine.*

Prokesch, S. (1986, June). The family business, new perspectives, new respect. *The New York Times.*

Rosenblatt, P. C., de Mik, L., Anderson, R. M., & Johnson, P. A. (1985). *The family in business.* San Francisco: Josey-Bass.

Schutz, A. (1951). Making music together: A study in social relationships. *Social Research 18*(1), 76–97.

Stern, M. H. (1986). *Inside the family held business: A practical guide for entrepreneurs and their advisors.* New York: Harcourt Brace Jovanovich.

19

Sibling Issues in Cotherapy and Coauthoring

William J. Doherty

Until recently, the insights of literary artists into the sibling relationship have surpassed those of behavioral scientists. A prominent theme in drama from Plautus' Latin plays to Shakespeare's *The Comedy of Errors* was the misidentification of twins who had been tragically separated in early childhood. Each carried the image of the other throughout life, feeling complete only when reunited in adulthood. For the dying poet Keats, his sister "walks about my imagination like a ghost." Here I will speak to the "ghosts" of sibling relationships that walk about us in close professional relationships, and to the continual reconnecting required to develop and maintain close relationships with both siblings and professional colleagues.

As seen elsewhere in this volume, sibling relationships, although never entirely ignored in contemporary psychology, have only in the 1980s received widespread and systematic study by researchers and therapists. Along with this growing appreciation of sibling dynamics in therapy has come the awareness that our own sibling bonds follow us into the therapy room and the conference room—and even look over our shoulder at the word processor. As I write these words, I picture my brother peering over my right shoulder, preparing a teasing remark about my needing all the help I can get.

This chapter discusses the connection between professional relationships and sibling relationships from two complementary perspectives: first, how relations with colleagues are similar to sibling relationships; and second, how issues in the therapist's own sibling experience may influence professional relationships, or what Bank and Kahn (1982) call "sibling transference." These issues are cast into a model for examining developmental issues in close professional relationships. Since there is little prior literature on these issues, this chapter is only an initial inquiry.

The conceptual framework for this exploration derives from recent literature on siblings (Bank and Kahn, 1982; Dunn and Kendrick, 1982; Schachter, 1985), and from the FIRO model of group development (Schutz, 1958). The core concepts to be used from the sibling literature are sibling identification and sibling deidentification.

As articulated by Bank and Kahn (1982), siblings tend to achieve one of three styles of identification with each other: *close identification*, which emphasizes similarity and denies differences; *partial identification*, which accepts both similarities and differences; and *distant identification*, which rigidly emphasizes differences between siblings. Schachter's work on sibling *deidentification*, on the other hand, emerged from hearing commonplace comments such as, "My sister is entirely different from me; she's like my father and I'm like my mother," and "My two children are as different as day and night; this one is like my side of the family, the other one is like my husband's folks" (1985, p. 415).

Sibling deidentification, then, refers to the tendency to define pairs of siblings (especially the first two siblings) as different, often opposite from one another. In several studies, Schacter has found a strong tendency for parents to assign very different global characteristics to their first and second children (Schacter, 1985; Schacter and Stone, 1985). Furthermore, she has observed that these characterizations are often linked to perceived qualities of one parent or the other or to one parent's family of origin or the other.

Not only are specific characteristics (e.g., quiet/talkative, sedentary/athletic) widely divergent for the first sibling pair, but there is evidence that parents contrast the global temperament—easy versus difficult—of their first pair of children in striking ways. Schachter and Stone (1985) found strong negative correlations between mothers' reports on the temperaments of their first two children, but little correlation between ratings of first and third child pairs or second and third child pairs. Finally, these studies suggest that more deidentification occurs for same-sex pairs than for opposite sex pairs, presumably because the family needs to more vigorously differentiate between same-sex children.

In *The Sibling Bond*, Bank and Kahn described a pattern similar to Schachter's sibling deidentification, namely, the process by which parents project positive and negative aspects of their own identities onto their children and onto the sibling relationship. Different siblings come to be "reservoirs" for different projections; thus, one child bears the "loving" side of the parents' personalities and the other bears the "hateful." As Bank and Kahn write, "For parents to cultivate a single characteristic in one child leaves the siblings with various other aspirations: some of these may be equally desirable (for example, lawyer), but others may be invidious (for example, family clown)" (1982, p. 57).

This sibling deidentification phenomenon has potentially important implications for family therapy (Schachter, 1985). The focus here, however, will be on ways in which this concept, along with sibling identification and the more familiar notion of sibling conflict, can help us understand the dynamics of certain professional relationships.

The Fundamental Interpersonal Relations Orientation (FIRO) Model was developed by Will Schutz (1958) in his studies of how small groups interact and develop over time. Schutz posits that when new groups are formed and expect to have a history together, they deal sequentially with issues of *inclusion* (membership, boundaries, roles), *control* (power, influence), and then *affection* (close interpersonal exchanges). Schutz recognizes that many issues are occurring simultaneously in groups, but believes that there are paramount themes at different stages of the group's development. According to the FIRO model, groups will deal adequately with control issues only after they have successfully handled inclusion issues, and will reach the point of affection or intimacy only when control struggles have subsided.

This model has been extended to family therapy by the coauthor team of Doherty and Colangelo, along with several of their colleagues (Doherty and Colangelo, 1984; Doherty, Colangelo, Green, and Hoffman, 1985; Doherty and Whitehead, 1986). The Family FIRO issues of inclusion, control, and intimacy will be used to organize the developmental issues in professional relationships of therapists. For the following discussion, *inclusion* is defined as interactions that relate to a professional pair's role patterns and to their individuality versus connectedness. *Control* interactions relate to conflict and negotiation in the relationship. *Intimacy* interactions relate to personally vulnerable and sharing exchanges between professional partners.

DEVELOPMENT OF PROFESSIONAL PAIRS

Our focus in this chapter is on dyadic relationships as opposed to group relationships, and on continuing partnerships rather than episodic collegial encounters or student-mentor relationships. The key factor is whether the individuals think of themselves and present themselves to the world as a pair, a team in which each person makes a contribution. If so, I propose that this professional relationship has, for good and ill, the flavor of a sibling bond, since it is at this dyadic level in sibling relationships that the most powerful identification and deidentification processes emerge.

Inclusion in Professional Relationships

Most therapists and scholars are trained to function autonomously, even though their training usually occurs in groups. Indeed, the hallmark of the well-trained therapist or scholar is thought to be the ability to confront the client or the word processor alone, without the immediate support of peers and mentors. Leaving training can be viewed as "leaving the nest" and "flying" on one's own as a professional. Newly launched birds try to fly far enough away from one another to prevent their wings from getting tangled.

Having accomplished this culturally-valued feat of functioning alone, the young therapist or scholar may have a still-precarious identity that can be threatened by forming a close partnership. (This might be a more stressful concern for men, who as a group appear more troubled by perceived threats to individual autonomy.) I have witnessed junior therapists in cotherapy who function so autonomously that one would scarcely imagine they are treating the same family. It is as if no pair bond has been formed, in the manner of two-year-olds in parallel play. Each therapist acts out his or her own training, leaving the family baffled.

Even some experienced therapists have great difficulty forming cotherapy partnerships with peers. Perhaps these therapists have never experienced satisfying mutuality with siblings. Bank and Kahn (1982) speculate that many middle-aged therapists, often firstborns in their own families, have convinced themselves that sibling relationships are not very important, in accord with their own lifelong difficulty in accepting the fact that they were "dispossessed" by siblings as the sole object of parental attention. In a similar vein, Heinz Kohut (1971) maintained that analysts who demand too vigorously that clients give up their symptoms tend to be oldest siblings who maintain an exaggerated sense of moral superiority over other sibling-like individuals.

Therapists with unresolved sibling issues may function well, however, with a student cotherapist, since they are more comfortable in parent-child type relationships. Their world view sees hierarchies and not partnerships, topdog/underdog and not dog/dog. This tendency to avoid a meaningful cotherapy bond between peers is likely to be most pronounced for same-sex partners who lack the culturally-defined complementarity of male-female dyads. However, even in opposite-sex cotherapy pairs, older brother/younger sister and younger brother/older sister issues are likely to emerge, with results that are difficult to manage unless the partners are willing to examine this dynamic in their relationship.

In relationships between academic colleagues, the parallel dynamic often occurs with authors who spend a productive writing career without ever coauthoring with a peer. Academic departments tend to be organized sociometrically in a vertical fashion, with each professor collaborating little with other professors and much with student advisees and research assistants. Coauthoring tends to follow working relationships: We coauthor with people with whom we discuss ideas and data. As in a family where parents are closer to the children than to each other, the faculty in many professional and academic programs relate to one another primarily through their students. The peer bond either does not take or does not hold.

In the contemporary family therapy world, senior therapists and faculty who have different therapy models seem to keep themselves steadfastedly unaware of their peers' ongoing ideas and work. They often do not look at each others' videotapes or read each other's writings. They don't inquire about workshops being given or accolades obtained. They don't refer to each others' work and often express unmixed disdain for colleagues who are regarded by the rest of the community or the profession as important contributors to the field. At the top levels of the family therapy field, the implicit message from the founding fathers and mothers is to disregard the work of their sibling founders.

So far I have emphasized the barriers to the formation of close, sibling-type partnerships. For professionals who do form ongoing bonds with peers in cotherapy or coauthoring, the sibling inclusion issues of identification and differentiation become important. Now that they are becoming a *we*, how will they define the two *I*'s and the common *we*. How complementary versus symmetrical will they become in their working styles? In Bank and Kahn's (1982) terms, will they develop close identification, partial identification, or distant identification? Each pair is confronted with tradeoffs between individual identity and team unity. The distant, rigidly differentiating or disowning identification is not likely to lead to an ongoing professional partnership, and indeed, may last only as long as required in a training context. This compares to some sibling bonds which are held together by parents' insistence, only to disintegrate on an interactional level (though not psychologically) after the parents give up or die.

Close identification that idealizes the professional relationship and denies differences may offer the therapist or scholar a sense of the perfect, conflict-free bond with a peer that had never existed with a sibling. This kind of identification may occur most frequently in unequal professional relationships in which the junior partner idealizes the senior partner, who in turn views the other as an admirable, younger clone. This is akin to the hero worship by the younger sibling of an approving older sibling (Bank and Kahn, 1982). Unfortunately, of course, the development of professional autonomy—not to mention genuinely new ideas—is stifled in this closely identified professional pair, if they maintain the rigidity of their relationship.

Partial identification offers a middle ground between the extremes of identity loss and identity cutoff. Bank and Kahn (1982) refer to this as the blending of perceived likeness and dislikeness in siblings, along with some degree of dependence. Dependence in some form is necessary for the pair bond to develop, while acknowledgment of differences is necessary for the partners to bring their individual perspectives to the relationship. Presumably, most professional partnerships fall into this broad category of partial identification. Dependence seems inevitably to involve a degree of complementarity: The partners are dancing together with steps that blend in a dialectic process. A critical issue concerns how rigidly and stereotypically they define their complementarity. Is one therapist defined as the more nurturing and the other the more confrontive? Among coauthors, is one the creative thinker and the other the plodding writer?

This is where Schachter's work on sibling deidentification seems most useful for considering professional pairs. An extension of her work would suggest that professional pairs might tend to emphasize their differences—their complementarity—in order to maintain individual identities and avoid competing with one another. They might then take small differences and make them larger ones for the sake of the relationship. For example, most good therapists can both nurture clients and challenge them. When two good therapists become cotherapists, they may covertly decide who is the more "natural" at each activity, and then use these "natural" differences to create complementary styles in cotherapy.

For example, two female therapists started a group for women clients. Although both therapists were capable of warm, empathic responses, and both were able to confront clients when appropriate, one of them tended to be more openly expressive of positive feelings than the other. Group members came to assign them roles of "warm Mom" and "cold Dad." When the therapists, who were very good friends, became aware that the group was assigning these stereotypes, they experimented with trying opposite behaviors: The warmer one became more confrontive and the sterner one more supportive. However, this switch did not work: The group perceived "Mom" as being temporarily cranky and "Dad" as being temporarily in a good mood. The therapists decided to accept the roles assigned to them by the group. Because they functioned separately in the rest of their professional roles, the therapists did not view the "deidentification" process in this group as stifling their development as therapists. But they were impressed with the power of the group projective process, which, by the way, tapped their own preferred ways of presenting themselves to the world.

When these defined differences take gender-stereotypic directions in male-female cotherapy teams, covert messages may be sent to cli-

ents about the abilities of men and women. In the marriage enrichment area, one famous cofacilitator couple begins their workshops by
telling the group that one of the pair is better at sensing the group's
feelings and the other is better at steering the content of the discussion (guess which is male and which female). This issue touches the
debate in family therapy field concerning sexual politics. Feminists
such as Virginia Goldner (1985) and Kerrie James and Deborah
McIntrye (1983) have called for an examination of the ways in which
family therapists perpetuate traditional sex roles by ignoring the social dimensions of family life and of therapy. The culturally-based
split between instrumental (masculine) and affective (feminine) tasks
can be reproduced in the therapy room by cotherapists who do not
question their need for sibling complementarity. An additional danger for the therapists is that they might internalize this complementarity, each concluding that he or she is "really" best at gender-stereo-
typed therapeutic interventions and "not so good" at others.

These identification issues occur not only in the subjective experience of the partners and in their interactions, but also in the view-
points of clients, readers, and professional colleagues. Thus, even
though the professional pair may feel themselves healthily interdependent, their "audience" sometimes projects different wishes in defining the pair's relationship. If the partners are not careful, they will
begin to live out the fantasies of their clients or colleagues.

A personal example: My frequent coauthor and sometime cotherapist Mac Baird and I were presenting a workshop together. The person
introducing us, who knew us mainly through our published collaborative writing, told the group that they were about to hear from Dr.
Doherty and Dr. Doherty. Mac and I (especially Mac) made a bit of a
fuss, as did the audience, and the introducer apologized. She proceeded to give my biographical data: "The first speaker will be Dr.
Doherty, who . . . . (accolade, accolade, etc.)." Then, to our dismay,
she said, "The second speaker will be Dr. Doherty, who . . . . " In a
classic Batesonian slip, she was telling the world how she defined our
relationship. Mac thanked her for the compliment but said, "I think I'll
stick with Baird." I commented, "It could have been worse: Dr. Baird
and Dr. Baird." I believe that we were able to respond with humor
because the slip did not touch a basic fear that we were undifferentiated, but rather came across as an indicator of the fusion others create
when two names are spoken so frequently in the same breath. Thus,

Rodgers gets credited with the lyrics and Hammerstein with the music.

Since I moved to a state where Mac Baird grew up and trained, I have had at least a dozen professional colleagues welcome me "back" to my home state, where I have never lived. When I comment that I never lived in Minnesota before, they look puzzled and say, "I guess it was just Mac who did." A final example of this Doherty and Baird fusion occurred at a conference on family systems medicine, the topic about which Mac and I have written. One of the conference participants wrote and delivered a humorous commentary on how many years it takes for a participant at this annual family systems medicine conference to get to the "inner circle." "In the first year," she said, "you don't know anyone but those you came with. In the second year, you begin to recognize some of the 'gurus,' and you think you know which one is Doherty and which one is Baird." Thirty minutes later, in an open forum discussion, I raised my hand to be acknowledged by the chair, whom I have known for five years. He looked at me and said, "Yes, Mac." Right then it stopped being funny, as evidenced by my resort to adolescent humor in response: "I'm Doherty; Baird is the ugly one." I have become impressed with the power of third parties to define professional partnerships, and I now better appreciate why many professionals prefer to publish alone or with junior colleagues.

As Bank and Kahn (1982) and Schachter (1985) point out, complementary identification and deidentification are neither good nor bad in themselves. It is a matter of the perceived content of differences and how inflexibly they are held. Schachter (1985) writes about the devil-versus-angel definition of sibling pairs. She found that deidentification between first child pairs occurs in most families, but that in families being treated in therapy the content of the defined differences ranged on a good-versus-bad continuum. The nonclinical families, on the other hand, tended to use less judgmental descriptors, e.g., quiet versus talkative, mechanical versus artistic, athletic versus musical.

For cotherapists and coauthors, then, the key seems to be whether each partner can be defined with positive, though sometimes complementary, characteristics, and whether each is locked inflexibly into this descriptor or is free to express a wide range of behaviors. Can the therapist who is "more structured" sometimes "go with the flow" without distressing the cotherapy partnership? Can the female cotherapist who is seen as "mother" also be "father," and can the male therapist be permitted to "mother"? Can the highly academic coauthor range into storytelling without threatening the more metaphorically-inclined partner? And can the latter present logical arguments without stepping on the tightly-wrapped toes of the partner?

I suggest that sibling identification and deidentification in one's family of origin play a role in how these issues are played out in professional relationships. To the extent that a therapist's sense of self is bound up with being different from a sibling, then that therapist may seek out cotherapists with complementary characteristics who will allow him or her to "shine" in the ways defined in the family of origin. Trouble may arise when the cotherapist begins to demonstrate symmetrical characteristics, as when the loosely structured cotherapist becomes more structuring, or the less academic partner begins to publish.

> For example, a male cotherapy team had implicitly embraced the complementary identification of one being more skilled at interviewing techniques while the other was better at "gut reactions" to the family. In particular, it was important to the more senior therapist that he be seen as more technically competent because of his longer years of training; however, he greatly valued his partner's ability to track underlying emotional processes in therapy. A threat to this complementarity occurred when the less technical partner received a consultation from an out-of-town expert who was skilled in a new technique called circular questioning. When the therapist used circular questioning in the next cotherapy session without warning the partner, the partner felt his identity threatened. He remained aloof from the circular questioning process during the session, a stance that was highly noticeable to the cotherapist and presumably to the family. Afterward, the partners discussed what had occurred and were able to begin redefining their roles to allow greater symmetry in their knowledge and skills.

These inclusion issues, in my view, are the fundamental building blocks of the cotherapy and coauthoring relationships. The partners confront similar inclusion issues to those they deal with in their own sibling experiences, namely, how much of self to surrender to the relationship, how much to hold onto, and how to define oneself in relation to the qualities of the partner. Healthy sibling and professional relationships involve a balance between autonomy and belonging, between complementary behaviors and symmetrical behaviors. A litmus test in both relationships may be whether the partners retain their ability to engage in behaviors that they deemphasize for the sake of complementarity in the relationship, or whether they curtail the flexibility of their professional skills—such as the coauthor who never learns to spell or the cotherapist who never learns to confront fathers—for the sake of complementarity in the professional relationship.

CONTROL IN PROFESSIONAL RELATIONSHIPS

An implication of the Family FIRO model is that control problems and power struggles in professional relationships often stem from unresolved inclusion issues. That is, the presence of difficulties in issues of identification, individuality versus connectedness, and role patterning are likely to spill over into overt or covert conflict over how much influence each partner will exert in the relationship.

Just as sibling conflict among children is most apt to occur for the benefit of their main audience—the parents—power struggles among professional partners frequently seem related to issues of prominence in the eyes of clients or a larger professional audience. Struggles over "air time" in cotherapy may be compared to siblings' efforts to dominate the family conversation. Struggles over primary authorship seem similar to siblings' efforts to gain the biggest possible slice of the prestige pie in the professional family. Of course, they can also be efforts to establish dominance over the professional partner. An additional important third party to professional conflict can be the supervisor or employer, who in an organizational "parental" role can generate conflict among professional siblings by playing favorites and selectively sharing secrets. I know one organization where peer relationships were torn beyond repair following a series of such triangulations by an administrator who actively undermined sibling-type relationships among the staff.

Just as Bank and Kahn (1982) describe healthy aspects of sibling conflict in families, control conflicts probably are part of many professional relationships in relatively innocuous, even helpful, ways. Well-functioning partners learn to act out their power struggles in a way similar to well-functioning siblings of the human or animal variety: poke and push and mock-bite, but don't be too serious, don't draw blood, and make sure each person "wins" some of the battles.

Sometimes, for example, with my coauthors I sense a norm that neither of us should win all the disagreements about wording and organization. If the "giving in" seems to be getting too one-sided, the "winner" looks for opportunities to "lose" some disagreements. Similarly, for cotherapists it may be important that each person both win and lose some strategy struggles — "win" being defined as convincing the partner to change and "lose" meaning giving in to the partner. Otherwise, a distorted complementary one-up/one-down pattern may be created in which the one-down partner uses indirect means of exercising control or gives up the relationship.

For some professional pairs, control issues cripple the partnership. Some researchers have never published their data because they cannot agree on primary authorship. I have seen clients bewildered by the ongoing power struggles of the cotherapists, sometimes rationalized as good for modeling constructive interpersonal conflict. Some married couples experience difficult power struggles in their professional partnership, particular if the perceived imbalance in professional expertise conflicts with a marital norm of equality. In a traditionally stereotyped example, the therapist wife will not play one-down to her more experienced therapist husband because to do so would feel like a surrender of a hard-won sense of equal power at home. I have watched videotapes of marital cotherapy teams where the therapists' power struggles were more apparent than the clients'.

When professional partners are experiencing difficult control issues, the most useful way to initiate change is to examine their lingering inclusion issues: How are they defining their roles? How much autonomy does each member need and feel? How complementary have they become, and is this interfering with their flexibility? How are the clients or the audience defining their relationship in such areas as prominence and influence? How are sibling issues from their families of origin being activated in the professional relationship? Exploration of these issues may provide the key to understanding how the partners got themselves into difficult control problems and lead to ideas for realigning their partnership in healthier ways.

INTIMACY IN PROFESSIONAL RELATIONSHIP

Affection or intimacy in the FIRO model refers to close interpersonal exchanges in which people reveal themselves as vulnerable, unique personalities. In the Family FIRO model, intimacy is possible for an ongoing relationship only when inclusion and control issues have been successfully handled. Many siblings never reach a high degree of intimacy, even though their bonds of caring and identification are strong, because they have not worked through personal and interpersonal issues, making it very difficult to sustain intimate dialogues. In order to become psychologically intimate, the siblings would have to be willing to examine together their jealousies, resentments, loves, hates, and desires to be similar to and different from each other.

Professional pairs, especially cotherapists, may have strong potential for the development of intimacy. To the extent that they are well-bonded as a team and can deal with control issues constructively, their work provides them with rich opportunities for the kind of risk-taking and self-disclosure that nurtures intimacy. They share affectively charged interactions with clients, and they support and challenge each other before and after sessions. When dealing with especially difficult clients, the cotherapists' own personal and interpersonal issues sometimes are evoked in powerful ways that invite intimate exchanges.

As Binns (1984) has pointed out in an article on "The Challenges of Cotherapy," the intensity of a male-female cotherapy relationship can lead to erotic attraction that can threaten other relationships of the partners. Just as siblings are expected to reserve their sexual interactions to peers outside the family, cotherapists presumably try to keep psychological intimacy from spilling over to physical intimacy. (The exception is cotherapy pairs who are already couples, in which case the cotherapists may have to keep their intimacy from spilling over into the therapy session and leaving the clients feeling excluded.) The intimacy of male-female cotherapy pairs in current professional culture, then, involves maintaining a boundary that protects other roles and relationships. The same would be true for gay and lesbian pairs. When siblings cross this boundary, it is incest. For cotherapy relationships, except in cases where the partners' definition of themselves as lovers is clear, sexual intimacy poses threats to their working relationship and to their outside relationships.

Even if the cotherapy relationship does not become sexually intimate, psychological intimacy can pose a threat to the primary relationships of the partners. Cotherapists have many of the goodies of intimacy — time together to talk about important matters, opportunity to share feelings and dreams—but few of the nitty-gritties that tend to dominate the lives of couples who live together—the bills, the housework, perhaps the children. To spouses hungering for some quality time with their therapist/mate, the intimacy of the male/female cotherapy pair can be quite threatening. Some spouses feel that their partner leaves the best part of self at the clinic—with the cotherapist. Working with this issue requires considerable commitment and finesse on everyone's part.

> An example is that of a male therapist whose non-therapist wife was home with two small children. He had a psychologically intimate relationship with a woman therapist with whom he often did cotherapy. He did all the personal "processing" of his emotional reactions to therapy with his cotherapist, and shared little of his work life with his wife. She began to be jealous of the woman therapist, who tried to include her when the three were together with questions such as, "Have you read anything interesting lately?" One time the wife replied angrily, "Only the back of the baby formula can!" as she ran crying out of the room. When the spouses finally talked openly about the problem, they concluded that the problem was not the closeness of the husband and his cotherapist but the lack of closeness that was developing between the married partners. They agreed that, among other things, the husband would share with his wife the emotional reactions he experienced in his work, rather than leaving the most interesting parts of himself at work.

It is because of the rich rewards and the genuine risks associated with intimate cotherapy relationships that many cotherapists experience grief and mourning at ending these relationships. Coauthoring relationships generally are much less intensely intimate, although those that develop over a career may become quite powerful in the inclusion domain and thus quite painful to lose. Similarly, when adult siblings experience psychological intimacy, they share a uniquely gratifying human relationship, the loss of which is intensely painful.

These last observations are intended to point out the inevitable costs of sibling-type professional relationships that achieve high levels of intimacy: Their formation always involves struggle over identity, their maintenance always involves persistence and conflict management, and their ending brings strong feelings of loss. Most of us, however, count ourselves lucky to have experienced such relationships in our careers.

CONCLUSION

Sibling bonds are our truly lifelong human connections. In them we forge our identity with peers and jointly experience the growth, maturation, and physical decline of the aging process. For many professionals, the intense partnerships of cotherapy and coauthoring replicate some of the powerful feelings and interactions of sibling relationships in childhood and adulthood. In this chapter I have called upon recent academic work in sibling relationships to suggest how a professional partnership can be profitably viewed as a sibling-type relationship. The clear implication is that our ongoing work on sibling relationships and professional relationships can work synergistically. Reconnecting with our own siblings can help us improve the quality of our professional relationships, and dealing with sibling transference issues in professional relationships can help us return with new perspective to our siblings. In my own case, it was a therapy experience with one of my siblings that opened my eyes to my lack of attention to peer issues in my professional relationships. It was as if I could go only so far with professional partnerships until I returned to older sibling issues that helped to form my identity and taught me to protect that identity by asserting my superiority.

To paraphrase Keats, our imaginations are peopled by the ghosts of all our brothers and sisters, the ones we are bound to in blood and family, and the ones we are bound to in the drama of therapy and the creation of the written word.

REFERENCES

Binns, M. (1984). The challenges of cotherapy. *British Journal of Guidance and Counselling, 12*, 154–165.

Bank, S. P., & Kahn, M. D. (1982). *The sibling bond*. New York: Basic Books.

Doherty, W. J., & Colangelo, N. (1984). The Family FIRO model: A modest proposal for organizing family treatment. *Journal of Marital and Family Therapy, 10*, 19–29.

Doherty, W. J., Colangelo, N., Green, A., & Hoffmann, G. S. (1985). Emphases of the major family therapy models: A Family FIRO analysis. *Journal of Marital and Family Therapy, 11*, 299–303.

Doherty, W. J., & Whitehead, D. (1986). The social dynamic of cigarette smoking: A family systems analysis. *Family Process, 25*, 453– 459.

Dunn, J., & Kendrick, C. (1982). *Siblings: Love, envy, and understanding*. Cambridge: Harvard University Press.

Goldner, V. (1985). Feminism and family therapy. *Family Process, 24*, 31–47.

James, K., & McIntrye, D. (1983). The reproduction of families: The social role of family therapy. *Journal of Marital and Family Therapy, 9*, 119–129.

Kohut, H. (1971). *The analysis of the self*. New York: International Universities Press.

Schachter, F. F. (1985). Sibling deidentification in the clinic: Devil vs. angel. *Family Process, 24*, 415–427.

Schachter, F. F., & Stone, R. K. (1985). Difficult sibling, easy sibling: Temperament and the within-family environment. *Child Development, 56*, 1335–1344.

Schutz, W. C. (1958). *FIRO: A three dimensional theory of interpersonal behavior*. New York: Holt, Rinehart, & Winston.

V

Facing the Problems of Aging

THE LATE YEARS

This last section includes chapters which examine siblings and old age from two perspectives — the children of the aged and the aged and their siblings. Sibling issues around aging are sorely overlooked, despite the fact that about half of the people over 65 years of age see at least one of their siblings every week. In fact, the ongoing rate of contact is incredibly high — 97% of elderly brothers and sisters value their connection sufficiently to keep it going by mail, phone, and personal contacts.

While settling scores with one's sibling(s) may be important in the middle years in order for each person to establish a satisfying identity, become successful, and have meaningful stable relationships, a different agenda emerges in the later years. The focus begins to switch from a preoccupation with correcting injustices from the past to find some solace and peace during the final years.

Old age not only provides the elderly with the opportunity to reconnect as the final links of their generation, but also provides brothers and sisters with a chance to rework old sibling issues in dealing with one or both of their aging parents. Crises in parents, psychological and physical, often bring their children face to face, forcing them to confront unresolved feelings towards each other, especially as they relate to parental favoritism. Given the lengthening of the life span, adult children today may face 20 — even 30 — years of caring for elderly parents, even well into their own retirement years. Such a long period of dependency strains the best of sibling relationships.

This later topic is sensitively dealt with by Tonti, who describes four evolving phases of change in the family with aged parents and the emergence of the primary caregiver from among the group of adult children. He then examines both supportive and conflictual relationships between the caregiver sibling and the siblings who are less involved in caring for the elderly parent.

Cicirelli gives a thorough summary of the literature on elderly siblings, looking at why and when the aged keep in contact with their siblings. He describes the characteristics of such relationships and how they may change over time. He offers suggestions for clinical practice, using the technique of reminiscence in dealing with the remnants of sibling rivalry. As Cicirelli shows, the life cycle, which often begins with two or more siblings being each other's closest companions, often ends in the same fashion.

20

Relationships Among Adult Siblings Who Care For Their Aged Parents

Mario Tonti

One mother can care for ten children, but ten children cannot care for one mother.

There is more than a little truth in this old saying. As more and more of our elderly population reach their seventies, eighties, and nineties, they turn to their families and to their children to assist them. This assistance can often begin as shopping or accompanying them to a medical appointment. As the elder's impairments increase it can extend to intensive care in the home of an adult child. Whatever the level of care the parents need, the children's ability to provide that care for their parents will depend, in large measure, on the quality of the siblings' relationship. By the same token, the realization of a parent's frailty and the need to provide care to that parent will have a significant impact on the relationships between siblings. As Bank and Kahn (1982, p. 16) have noted, "the sibling identity process is reactivated as elderly parents require extensive health care."

Awareness of a parent's frailty and need for care raises several key questions for the adult children. These questions speak to the issue of the children's commitment:

- Do the siblings feel a sense of obligation and/or commitment to care for their parents?
- Do they all feel this sense of commitment to the same degree?
- Who among the children feels a strong enough sense of com-

417

mitment/obligation to provide the kind of intense personal care that an elder may need?

- Has one sibling filled the caregiver role since childhood?
- How do the siblings take into account factors of birth and factors such as proximity to the elder and life situation in terms of available time and energy?
- What is expected of the siblings who are not the primary caregivers and how do they negotiate their roles with the caregivers?

In addressing these and other issues, I will first consider the phases families go through in recognizing and coping with a parent's frailty, highlighting the tasks and anxieties associated with the care of the elderly. Next, I will examine how the primary caregiver is chosen, the importance of this process to the parent, and its impact on the other siblings. Then some supportive and conflict-generating sibling responses to the familial challenge of caring for a frail elderly parent will be described, as well as patterns of control and conflict which hinder siblings' desire to care for their parents. Finally, I will discuss treatment techniques and clinical implications.

PHASES OF CHANGE IN THE AGED FAMILY

Most children are not prepared for their parents' becoming frail or disabled. Denial of the aging process is, on the whole, a positive adaptation allowing children to maintain relationships with parents unimpeded by fears of death or dependency. Nevertheless, awareness of normative aging phases facilitates planning and negotiations among siblings.

In our society improvements in health care have had an impact on the aging process. Gerontologists now discuss the elderly in two distinct groups: the young old, ages 65–75 years of age, and the old old, those over 75 years of age. The primary distinction between these two groups is their health (Shanas, 1985). The young old are seen as basically healthy and therefore quite self-sufficient, while the old old may experience a rapid decline in health. Often today's elderly lead active, healthy lives until a trauma causes them to decline dramatically in their health and functioning (Silverstone and Hyman, 1982, p. 61). The trauma can take many forms, for example, an acute illness, diagnosis of a serious illness, or loss of a significant person in their lives. Whatever the trauma, the impact on the children is powerful; it inevitably and inexorably changes the patterns of interaction between parents and children as well as among the children themselves. The result is awareness in the children of their parent's age and an increase in all family members of anxiety related to increased dependency and loss. All of the children will experience this increase in anxiety and will attempt, in their own style, to regain a sense of control over such feelings.

The following phases are not meant to represent all families and every situation; rather, they represent a set of norms for parents and children as they adjust to the changes brought about by advanced age.

First Phase

In most families, as aged parents require care, children will find themselves moving closer to one another and to their parents both physically and emotionally. In the first phase of this transition, the siblings may communicate more often and with more energy about their parent's situation. Initial plans may be discussed and a number of "what if" scenarios played out among the siblings. "What if Mom doesn't completely recover?" "Who will care for Dad now that Mom is gone?" "How are they ever going to stand being together now that Dad can't work anymore?"

Part of this initial dialogue will involve the children's own situations and capacities to handle stress and the realities of frailty. "I can't bear to see her like this; I keep remembering what she used to be like." Or, "This couldn't have come at a worse time—my husband is sick and my daughter is also having problems." In addition, old issues of rivalry and power between siblings may be reactivated. "Don't tell me what to do! She is my mother, too. Besides, who made you boss?" Or, "I know we will figure out how to deal with this crisis; we've dealt with others and we'll deal with this one." Whatever the specifics of their parent's illness or injury, the children must cope with the anxiety caused by the specter of their parent's increased dependency on them, on the one hand, and their desire, in most situations, to care for their parents, on the other.

In some families a pattern of distancing under stress may be seen. Siblings may speak to each other less often or try to hide their feelings of anger about the situation. This increased distance can be function-al in that it allows children to regain a sense of control over their feelings before they re-engage with their parents and siblings. Howev-er, if the distance increases or becomes rigidified, it can become problematic for all members of the family.

The Second Phase

In the second phase the needs of the parents increase, requiring physical intervention on the part of the children. During this phase life patterns of the children change. There is more physical contact with the parents, in order to monitor changes in their status or to do chores which they cannot manage. It is during this phase that the role of the primary caregiver begins to become evident in the family. Traditionally the primary caregiver has been one of the daughters living in close proximity to the ailing parent (Shanas, 1979). The role of the primary caregiver is to provide the support and services which the elders may need in order to maintain themselves in the communi-ty. In the second phase these services can include help with shopping, banking, housework, getting to appointments, and planning. Gener-ally, the parents remain in their own home and their adult children shuttle back and forth. While this is a stressful period for parents and children, the tasks remain fairly concrete and families can usually manage the tension caused by the changes in their routine.

The Third Phase

As the frailty of the elder increases or the trauma or loss becomes too difficult to manage, the family must recognize the necessity to reorganize itself in a more fundamental manner. This reorganization usually requires the elder's moving into the home of one child or, less frequently, vice versa. This move brings with it a new set of expecta-tions, stresses, and anxieties. The expectations originating from the family patterns are often generations in the making. These patterns create family rules concerning dependency and responsibility, rules which dictate the emotional cost of members moving too far away from the family or identify those who are to give or receive family support. These rules will be forged into the various family roles.

The stresses on the family during this phase are related to the increased intensity of the parent's needs for care. Tasks will include everything mentioned in phase two plus additional ones such as feeding, bathing, dressing, nursing, and being the prime source of activity and stimulation for the parent. The stress of this phase for adult children relates to several factors: the tasks themselves and multiple changes; grief associated with the loss of their independent parents; growing awareness of their frail parent's dependency; and the painful realization of the parent's mortality and the inevitability of death. All of these issues increase the tension in the family and, as we will discuss shortly, evoke powerful feelings and unusual behaviors among siblings.

The Final Phase

The final phase occurs when the needs of the elder become overwhelming or the capacity of the caregiver becomes stretched beyond limits. At this point the care of the elderly parent may be transferred to a nursing home or other care facility.

THE EMERGENCE OF THE PRIMARY CAREGIVER

The primary caregiver plays an essential role in the care of a frail parent. It is our belief that functional families create an environment which in turn produces a primary caregiver; the key struggles among siblings revolve around understanding and supporting the sister or sister-in-law who has taken on this role.*

The reader may ask, "Why a primary caregiver?" In order to understand the reason why, we must first consider the plight of the frail elder. As I have noted earlier, advanced age for most individuals is a time for accumulating losses—of loved ones and often of control over one's life. Most of us define our sense of self on the basis of what we can do and control as well as whom we love and who loves us. For frail elders the definition of self can no longer be based on accomplishments. As their circle of family, friends, and contacts shrinks, they must draw their emotional sustenance from fewer and fewer relationships. In addition, as the elder's losses increase, his or her need for care become more personal. In order to maintain a sense of

---

*We refer to the sister or sister-in-law since the vast majority of primary caregivers are daughters or daughters-in-law (Brody, 1981).

value and dignity, elders require an intimate relationship with one person who will provide both personal care and reassurance of individual worth. Often only a family member can provide this special kind of care.

How Does the Family Choose
A Primary Care Giver?

As we have already mentioned, the primary caregiver is almost always a daughter. Sons are rarely placed in the position of being the provider of hands-on care. Moreover, in families with several daughters, all other things being equal, the daughter who lives closest to the parent will take on the responsibility.

> Mrs. G. and her husband and new baby lived in a large, ramshackle house in a working-class neighborhood. Mrs. G. had recently invited her mother and father into her home to live. Mrs. G.'s mother had just had a leg amputated above the knee and her father was recovering from a heart attack. When we discussed the stress associated with caring for a newborn baby and two sick parents, Mrs. G. acknowledged the strain but said that she never hesitated in inviting her parents to come live with her.
> Mrs. G. is one of six children. When we asked why she was the one who felt this obligation, she said that she and her three sisters had all talked about where her Mom and Dad should live and each of the three sisters said that she would like the parents to come into her home. The deciding factor was that Mrs. G. lived much closer to the doctors and the hospital where her Mom and Dad received medical care. Since the visits were so frequent, it was decided by all the daughters that it would be best for the parents to live with Mrs. G., near their medical care.

While gender and proximity influence the choice of the caregiver, they are not the only factors. In many families the role of the caregiver child seems determined almost at birth.

> Mrs. D., the oldest of four siblings, was discussing her commitment to care for her disabled mother. "After Dad died, when Mom got sick, I knew I had to take over and care for her. It seems to me I have always been the one to pick up the pieces when things fell apart in our family. That's not to say that no one else cares about Mom. It's just that

everyone always knew that if Mom or anyone needed help I would be there."

The "born caregiver" often lives her life in tune with this role, even becoming a professional caregiver. In speaking to many groups of nurses and social workers, I have asked how many in the audience defined themselves as the caregivers in their families. An overwhelming majority of the women raised their hands.

There may be, of course, a relationship between the caregiver role and a daughter's proximity to her parents. People who define themselves in this role may feel an obligation to be close to parents who are aging so as to provide care and support. These women may be living away from their parents and decide that they must move closer in order to fulfill their role in the family.

> Mrs. J. and her husband had just accepted a transfer back to the area where she was raised. When asked what went into this decision, she stated that she and her husband had always wanted to return to their home town and now, with her parents growing older, the timing seemed right.

THE RELATIONSHIP BETWEEN CAREGIVERS AND THEIR SIBLINGS

A woman's ability to care for her parent is largely determined by the quality of support she receives from her siblings, spouse, and children, which in turn will be determined, in large measure, by the quality of the relationships within a family. As Cicirelli (1983) has suggested, "Helping behaviors flow out of the established attachment behaviors." Let us look at relationships which are supportive to the caregiving sister and those which are conflictual.

Supportive Relationships

Reciprocal Loyalty In their chapter, "Acts of Sacrifice: Loyalty and Caring," Bank and Kahn (1982, p. 114) describe relationships of reciprocal loyalty as ones in which "there is mutuality and a repayment of help and cooperation." In our experience with families fitting this description, the children, often sisters, view the task of support and caring for Mom and Dad not as the responsibility of one child but as a joint venture involving all the siblings. These children always speak glowingly of their relationships with their parents and with each other. While the parent may be physically present in one child's home, the care and tasks are divided as evenly as possible. Equally important is the fact that the emotional burden and concern for the parents are also shared. These situations are not very common; in fact, we have seen them only between sisters who feel close to their parents and to each other.

> Mrs. R. and her sisters decided that her home would be the most comfortable for her frail mother and father. She had a bedroom on the first floor which would allow her parents to move about with ease. Mrs. R.'s sisters all pitched in to support her in very active ways. They cooked and brought food for Mrs. R.'s whole family. They visited regularly and provided transportation for their parents to many medical appointments. Among these sisters there was a strong sense of reciprocal loyalty and it provided their mother and father with an exceptionally strong and loving support network.

Outside Siblings In Support of a Caregiver   More commonly, siblings are physically distant yet supportive to the caregiver. The distant position can be held by someone living a few blocks or many miles away. Great distances between parents and children is a reality in many American families. While studies estimate that in 1976, 75% of elders had at least one child living within one hour drive (Shanas, 1979), these same studies suggest that many children live well beyond the one-hour limit. These children often support their sister and parents through occasional visits, finances, and phone contact.

Distance, however, is not the only issue. Many siblings who live close by may sense the intensity of the relationship between their sister and parents and may choose to respond by adopting a secondary yet supportive role. It is important to note that there appears to be a gender difference in the impact of this "outside" position on sisters and brothers. Outside sisters appear to carry a stronger sense of guilt about their caregiving sister's sacrifices than outside brothers. This difference is understandable if one remembers that caregiving is, in our society, a woman's role. In supportive families a sister may feel she should be helping more even if she knows that she cannot. A brother may understand his sister's sacrifices, yet feel that he should assume the role of decision-maker or crisis-handler rather than primary caregiver.

Conflicted Relationships

In conflictual situations the roles discussed above may be the same, but problems of power and rivalry create very different situations.

Reawakened Sibling Rivalry The most frequent difficulty is the rivalry that occurs when one daughter takes over the care of a parent and is not supported by her siblings. Her brothers and sisters may not object to her assuming this responsibility but nevertheless engage in a struggle over how the care is provided. They may complain that their sister is not making the right decisions or is coveting the resources of their parents. Often underlying these issues is often a lifelong pattern of sibling rivalry that is reawakened by the crisis of aged care.

> Mrs. B. complained to the social worker that she was very concerned about how her mother, who was living with Mrs. B.'s sister after a stroke, was being treated. Mrs. B.'s sister refused to let Mrs. B. visit her mother, saying that every time Mrs. B. visited, the two sisters ended in a fight. These fights had to do with Mrs. B.'s desire to determine if her mother's complaints about poor food and little attention were valid. When she discussed these complaints with her sister, she would blow up and shout, "How dare you come here and criticize me! If you think you can do a better job you can take her home with you!" Mrs. B. explained that, although she would like to take her mother into her home, her husband refused to consider it. She went on to explain that she and her sister had always fought as children and had barely gotten along as adults. Now it felt like they were children again.

This example demonstrates the reawakening of sibling rivalry in the form of criticism between these sisters. Also evident is a parent who pits one child against the other. This, too, is probably an old pattern and one which now, at a time when the elder feels helpless and vulnerable, may give the mother a sense of control over the children.

Splitting of Responsibility and Authority The more common brother-sister conflict takes the form of splitting responsibility and authority in the care of a parent. In these situations the brother, often physically distant, tends to be given the authority in the parent's life, or in some cases the aged parent will imbued the son with an almost magical powers to "make things better." This instills a great sense of frustration in the daughter who provides the day-in and day-out care for her parent.

> Mrs. T. is sitting with her mother expressing her anger at her mother's lack of appreciation for all the hours she has spent caring for her. Mrs. T. explains that she is frustrated that her mother still insists on consulting her big, important son, who lives hundreds of miles away and to whom she speaks only once a week because he is so busy and so important. "It's as if he were a god. I can't take money out of the bank for her or make any decisions. She says, 'John will do it.' He can't do it. I'm here. I'm the one and yet all I hear is John, John, John." Mrs. T.'s mother sits angrily and says little as her daughter expresses her frustration.

In these situations the idealized son may be in agreement with mother as to his role in the family or he may want to change his position. In the former situation, if the alliance between the son and his mother does not allow the caregiving daughter any support, the tension between daughter and mother can become explosive. In the latter situation, if the son wants to shift power to his sister, the triangle can be broken by some direct communication between sister, brother, and mother.

FAMILIES WITHOUT CAREGIVERS

To this point we have described families which were sufficiently functional so as to provide one or more children who wished to care for their parents. There are, of course, situations in which a functional family cannot provide for its elders. The children's inability to provide intensive care for a parent may be a function of their own physical health problems, lack of space or other resources, or other difficulties. These families may turn to nursing homes or home care organizations to provide the resources they do not have. The inability to provide the hands on care to an elder does not disassociate the elder from the family or vice versa.

Differing from the above described families are those families with children who, because of a significant dysfunctional history or a trauma, cannot or will not organize themselves to care for their parents. A common pattern is that of the alcoholic family.

Mr. P., an active alcoholic since the age of 22, would often go on drinking binges and abandon his family for weeks at a time. He would then return home and resume his work and parental responsibilities. This life pattern was very painful for his children, since they grew up never knowing when to expect the next binge.

By age 62 Mr. P.'s body was suffering from the effects of years of abuse. In need of intensive home care, he turned to his daughter and two sons. Three of the children were in a longstanding alliance against their father. While they refused to take him into their homes, they did provide some care to him in his own apartment. When neighbors called in a protective service worker, the children resisted efforts to place their father in a nursing home because, as they stated quite openly, they did not feel he deserved more care than they were giving him.

These siblings' openness in admitting their desire to punish their father is extreme. Often the ambivalence or desire not to care for a parent takes more subtle forms.

Mrs. A. and her sister, Mrs. S., were struggling over who would care for their mother. Both made statements about their desire to care for her but were quick to add that their circumstances would not permit it. When pressed for family history, they described their relationship with their mother as abusive. She was an angry woman, especially when she drank. With the help of the social worker, both sisters were able to confront the fact that they felt few positive feelings for their mother and did not want to care for her. This disclosure was mutually supportive to the sisters, and strengthened their relationship enough so they could appropriately plan for their mother's care.

While alcoholism can impair an adult child's desire to care for a frail elder, it is not the only pattern which can hamper family functioning and sibling relationships. Another pattern which has the same effect is that of the overly controlling parent.

Mrs. R. and her three siblings were waiting downstairs for the social worker to visit their mother. When the social worker asked why they waited outside, Mrs. R. said that her mother never permitted more than one of her children at a time in her apartment. The visit had been arranged by the children because the landlord had called Mrs. R. and told her that her mother was too frail to live alone and needed their help. On the way up the stairs all of the siblings (who were in their forties and fifties) worried about how they would tell their mother and what they would do with her. By the time the social worker and siblings had reached their mother's door, all the children had made it clear that they could not possibly take their mother, as they were terrified of her. The social worker was greeted by a slight, frail-looking woman in her late seventies who immediately ordered her children to leave and demanded to know who the social worker was. With the social worker's intervention, the siblings were able to muster sufficient strength to confront their mother and deal with the question of her needing more care. When the mother saw that she could not use her divide and conquer tactics, she calmed down, and participated in the discussion.

This mother's longstanding pattern of control had caused her children a good deal of mental anguish. These siblings had never been able to gain enough support from each other to cope with their mother; only when there was a care crisis and professional intervention were they able to confront her.

INTERVENTIONS WITH THE CHILDREN OF FRAIL PARENTS

Counseling with siblings caring for their elderly parents is based on several key assumptions.

1. Many siblings seek professional intervention at this time because the family is in a crisis. The crisis may be establishing care for their parents or dealing with a situation that threatens the status quo of that care.
2. Conflicts between siblings often involve their parent. Whenever possible the treatment of choice should be family therapy or conjoint work with siblings.
3. The siblings, now adults, have a long history and find themselves confronting old patterns of sibling interaction. The therapist should not attempt to unravel years of conflict but instead focus on the tasks and challenges of elder care. Staying in the present, while keeping a sensitive eye on the past, will help siblings rise above the current struggle and develop new patterns of interaction.
4. The objective of work with siblings and their frail parents is to develop the best care system for all concerned. The desire and ability of siblings to provide direct care for their parents

must be determined. Then all concerned must participate in planning appropriately for the parent's needs.

Educational Interventions

Much of the anxiety siblings feel about their parent's situation stems from their lack of understanding of aging and its implications. Information about aging is required before families can plan appropriately for their parents or judge what they can or cannot commit to their parent's care. It is, therefore, essential for children to obtain information in the following areas:

1. Normal aging: What can parents and children expect to encounter as parents grow older? What are the implications of these developments?
2. Medical information: What medical problems are parents confronting? Does the medical care and advice the family is receiving seem authoritative? Does the family know the course of treatment and rehabilitation? Would more information or an additional perspective help?
3. Resource information: What is available in the family's community for support of an elder in terms of special housing, home health care, day care programs, community centers, etc.?

The above mentioned information alone will lower the anxiety of many families and free them to plan and provide appropriate care. However, when a parent suddenly requires assistance, even the most functional family will succumb to the stress of many unknown factors (see Silverstone and Hyman, 1982).

Mrs. J. and her three sisters were taking care of their 90-year-old parents, who still maintained an independent apartment. Although the sisters lived in different parts of the city, they were able to set up what they felt was a fair schedule of tasks and visitation. They had been living with this schedule for two years. Their parents had refused to leave their apartment and the sisters were committed to caring for them in their home as long as possible. The problem was that the schedule was taking its toll on the sisters and their families. Desperate at the thought that they might have to force their parents to move, they called a social service agency. During the meeting the parents and four children were informed of a home health care service which would relieve the sisters of a significant amount of work. The parents were pleased at the reduction of the burden on their children and the sisters were delighted that, for the time being at least, they could continue to support their parents according to their wishes.

Treating Siblings In Conflict Over the Care of an Elder

While education is a valuable intervention in all situations, some family relationships require additional strategies. In the previous discussion of siblings' conflictual responses to elder care, we noted two major types of sibling conflict: rivalry between siblings over their parent's care, and discord between siblings created by a parent's splitting of responsibility and authority. The distinction between these two types of conflicts is found in the site of control in the triangle created between the parent, the caregiver, and her sibling(s). In the former situation, in which there is excessive sibling rivalry, control is held by the sibling who uses the parent as a weapon in the battle with the other siblings. In the latter, the elder uses control to maintain or incite conflict between siblings.

What both of these situations have in common is the purpose for the power tactics. In both situations the family is confronting the experience of caregiving and the reality of dependence of the elder upon the children. The resulting dramatic changes in distance between family members will intensify the triangulation between siblings and parents. All families will, at this time in their development, experience a change in intensity of relationships; however, families which do not define being dependent on family members as acceptable will have greater difficulty. The therapist's task is to make the elder's dependence on the children acceptable, thereby reducing the need for intense triangulation.

There are several strategies for accomplishing this detriangulation. Here are just a couple:

(1) *Defining the parameters of care and commitment.* A good deal of the tension between siblings arises from the uncertainty regarding the extent of the commitment that is expected of them by their families. In many situations it is not possible to know exactly how much care a parent will need or for how long, but an informed therapist can

help children express their concerns about the open-endedness of their parent's needs and define some limits.

> Mrs. K., her sister, brother and their mother were meeting with a social worker in Mrs. K.'s home. Her mother had just moved in after falling and breaking her hip. Mrs. K. was expressing to her siblings her expectation that they would be there to assist their mother. She was angry at their lack of commitment and told them so. Mrs. K.'s mother repeated several times her dismay at being a source of conflict between her children. The social worker asked them what their fears were around moving into this situation. Mrs. K.'s sister said that she felt boxed in. She wanted to help but her husband and her family had to come first and that took a good deal of time. Mrs. K.'s brother said that he also was in a bind, what with work and his family responsibilities. Mrs. K. blew up and shouted "What about my family? I've got other responsibilities, but caring for Mom is my top priority!"
>
> The social worker interrupted the process and told the family that this type of tension was common in these situations. She stated that everyone in the family could not and need not make the same commitment. The worker then suggested that Mrs. K. state what kinds of assistance she needed. Mrs. K. talked about her schedule and the kind of care her mother needed, the social worker helped her brother and sister assign tasks and make commitments which felt manageable. Mrs. K.'s mother felt relieved that the conflict between her children was abating, and Mrs. K. stated that all she really wanted from her siblings was some support.

(2) *Improving communication.* Dysfunctional patterns of communication between siblings can aggravate an already difficult situation. We noted that conflict can be created by mixed messages between a caregiver and her siblings related to her ability and her authority to care for a parent. Sometimes it is sufficient for the therapist to contact the distant sibling and discuss the pressure the caregiver is under due to the elder's divide-and-conquer strategies. This contact is best done in a family session, but if the distance is too great a three- or four-way phone contact can be effective. However, in some families, where the alliance between the sibling and the parent against the caregiver is strong, clear statements may not be enough. The therapist may need to actively support the caregiver, to the point of considering alternative placements for the parent if the dysfunctional pattern does not subside.

Mrs. W. came into the office in tears. Her mother, who had been living in England, had come to live with her two years earlier. She was quite frail and had been on the verge of death several times. Mrs. W.'s tears came from her mother's incessant complaining about the care she was receiving and her mother's idealization of her son who still lived in England. Mrs. W. added that she and her brother had never gotten along and that his letters to his mother were filled with anger and accusations against Mrs. W. Several sessions were held with Mrs. W. and her mother. In addition, a letter was written to Mrs. W.'s brother stating the impact of the communication breakdown between his sister and him.

Despite these efforts, it soon became clear to the worker that the mother would never allow herself to appreciate the care she was receiving from her daughter. The worker finally raised the possibility of Mrs. W.'s mother returning home to England. When this option became a real possibility for the mother, it broke through the triangle, opening the lines of communication between Mrs. W., her brother and her mother. When faced with the prospect of caring for his mother, the brother stopped the accusations and began to offer some support to his sister. The mother reacted to the possibility of moving and to her son's loss of enthusiasm for caring for her by appreciating her daughter's efforts. Eventually, the mother did return to England, but not before the tension had eased considerably in the family.

Working With Siblings Who Will Not Care For Their Parents

In many of the cases seen in social agencies, siblings refuse to care for their parents. If these parents are frail and in need of intensive service, they have two options: home care, which is generally difficult to obtain in our country; and institutional placement. If siblings are clear about their refusal to provide intensive care for their parents, then the focus shifts to working with the parent to choose, if there is a choice, an available alternative. The elder may have to deal with the double stress of coping with both the change of living arrangement and the rejection by the children. More problematic yet are siblings who have ambivalent feelings toward their parents and who fight and accuse each other as a way to avoid acknowledging not wanting to care for their parent.

The social worker was conducting a meeting with the children of Mrs. B., aged 93. Mrs. B., suffering from Alzheimer's disease, had reached the point where she had little or no memory or awareness of where she was. The meeting began with her daughters' stating very clearly that their mother would not go into a nursing home. What followed was a series of testimonials to Mrs. B. from all of her children. This was followed by series of accusations, with each sibling explaining why caring for his/her mother was impossible and why the other sibling's reasons were all lies.

The worker interrupted and told the siblings they had probably waited too long to make a decision about how to care for their mother. She then spoke to the reality that providing care for their mother would be a very stressful task because of her end-stage Alzheimer's disease. The siblings felt some relief from the guilt they were heaping on one another and began to explore the options with the worker. During this discussion tempers occasionally flared, but the meeting ended with an agreement to have Mrs. B. live with her oldest daughter until a nursing home could be found.

While this crisis was easily resolved, there are situations in which siblings act out their feelings of anger and guilt towards their parents. These situations can perpetuate a pattern of conflict and pain and even lead to abuse and neglect of the parent.

CONCLUSION

The relationships between siblings are rarely tested as strongly as when children are asked to care for a frail parent. We have seen how this life stage can reawaken old conflictual patterns and raise new difficulties between sisters and brothers. But one should not lose sight of the fact that the majority of siblings do provide good care for their parents. In fact for most of these people, working with their siblings in support of their parents is a positive reaffirmation of their values as individuals and their strengths as a family.

REFERENCES

Bank, S. P., & Kahn, M. D. (1982). *The sibling bond*. New York: Basic Books.

Brody, E. (1981). Women in the middle and family help to older people. *Gerontologist, 21*, 471–480.

Cicirelli, V. (1983). Adult children's attachment and helping behavior to elderly parents: A path model. *Journal of Marriage and the Family, 11*, 815–825.

Shanas, E. (1979). Social myth as hypothesis. The case of family relations of old people. *Gerontologist, 19*, 3–9.

Shanas, E. (1985). Health, health resources and the utility of care. In R. H. Binstock and E. Shanas, *Handbook of aging and the social sciences* (696–726). New York: Van Nostrand Reinhold.

Silverstone, B., & Hyman, H. (1982). *You and your aging parents*. New York: Pantheon.

Tonti, M., & Silverstone, B. (1985). Services to families of the elderly. In A. Monk, *Handbook of gerentological services* (211–239). New York: Van Nostrand Reinhold.

21

Interpersonal Relationships Among Elderly Siblings

Victor G. Cicirelli

In most cases, relationships between siblings are not only maintained throughout life but assume considerable importance in old age (Allan, 1977; Cicirelli, 1980b, 1982; Ross and Milgram, 1982; Troll, 1971). Siblings provide psychological support for each other as well as more tangible helping and caregiving activities. Since sibling relationships contribute to an individual's adjustment earlier in life (Bank and Kahn, 1982a, 1982b), it seems logical to hypothesize that this would also be the case in old age.

Here we will consider interpersonal relationships among elderly siblings in the attempt to answer the question: Under what conditions is the sibling relationship of value in providing psychotherapy for older people? To gain a better understanding of the sibling relationship in later years, the following questions will also be considered: What do we know about sibling relationships among the elderly? How do sibling relationships change over time? How can theory be used to explain the sibling connections of the elderly? Finally, we will draw implications regarding the use of sibling relationships in clinical practice with the elderly. In particular, we will look at the strengths of the sibling relationship as a foundation for therapy and sibling readiness to help as an important resource for the clinician. Sibling reminiscence techniques will be described as a means of achieving therapeutic objectives.

UNDER WHAT CONDITIONS IS THE SIBLING RELATIONSHIP
OF VALUE IN PSYCHOTHERAPY WITH OLDER PEOPLE?

The increase in population of older people is now well-known (U. S. Bureau of the Census, 1983). Accompanying this rise in sheer numbers of older people in the nation has been an increasing concern for their well-being. However, while there has been a preoccupation with the physical problems of the elderly, relatively little attention has been focused on their mental health problems. The psychological stresses and strains of older people tend to be neglected. Depression as a result of illness or isolation is a major mental health problem of the elderly, for example. Some elderly people have longstanding psychiatric problems, while others have problems related to aging—adjusting to changed living conditions and family relationships.

There are no established methods for treating many of the psychological difficulties of old age, nor are there established guidelines to suggest when and how sibling relationships might be of value in therapy. Extensive and longitudinal research is needed. However, based on what is known about sibling relationships, we can identify possible problem areas where consideration of sibling relationships could be of value. The following discussion is merely a sample of such situations.

One such situation involves patients who have had longstanding family problems stemming from their families of origin. Conflicts and estrangements between siblings may persist from childhood years (Ross and Milgram, 1982) or be the result of certain critical incidents in the lives of siblings (Dunn, 1984). For example, one 79-year-old woman whom we interviewed had not spoken to her only brother since his refusal some 50 years earlier to assist her when her husband's sudden death left her virtually penniless with three young children.

Another source of conflict may involve long-term dependencies between siblings. Bank and Kahn (1982a, 1982b) note that sibling loyalties may at certain times become so intense as to be maladaptive and even disabling. Where there has been a sexual relationship between a sibling pair, whether abusive or by mutual consent, there are usually longstanding problems of dependency, guilt, fear, poor self concept, and anxiety (Bank and Kahn, 1982b; Finkelhor, 1980).

Still another situation comes about when early rivalries and aggressive actions between siblings are reactivated in old age (e.g., Berezin, 1977; Laverty, 1962) at times of crises or stress. A study by Gully, Dengerink, Pepping, and Bergstrom (1981) provides a basis for speculation in this regard, since early violent behavior involving siblings in the family was found to be predictive of later violent behavior toward others. Laverty (1962), in working with elderly people who displayed aggressive reactions toward family members or toward co-residents in institutions (ranging from excessive criticism and complaining to actual physical attacks), attributed such behaviors to unresolved sibling rivalry. Hostile impulses toward siblings or their counterparts become stereotyped and are manifested unconsciously under circumstances which threaten the gratification of the individual's needs.

When sibling relations are to be included in the treatment of the elderly client, does the literature suggest a particular therapeutic approach? Again, there are few clear guidelines. Approaches range from probing sibling relationships in the course of psychoanalysis (Rosner, 1985), through individual therapy (Bank and Kahn, 1982b; Kahn, 1983), to inclusion of siblings in family therapy (e.g., Kahn and Bank, 1981; Palazzoli, 1985) and family counseling (Herr and Weakland, 1979). The therapy can be done with all living siblings, with only a sibling dyad, or with a subgroup of siblings. With a close-knit family, it is more desirable to see the siblings together; otherwise seeing a subgroup or even a brother or sister in individual psychotherapy may be effective (Church, 1986; Kahn and Bank, 1981).

The use of reminiscence as an approach to therapy with older people has gained favor in recent years, beginning with Butler's (1963) work on the use of reminiscence in the "life review." Reminiscence in itself is simply thinking or talking about the past, or more specifically the act, process, or fact of recalling or remembering the past. While the life review incorporates reminiscence, it is a larger process in which past experiences are analyzed, evaluated, and reintegrated in relation to present events, values, and attitudes. Life review allows the individual prompted by the realization of impending biological decline and death to resolve old conflicts and come to grips with past mistakes through active personality reorganization. In this way he or she can achieve integrity in the latter portion of life (Butler, 1963; Molinari and Reichlin, 1985; Osgood, 1985).

Butler's thesis—that spontaneous reminiscence in the life review led to better adjustment (greater self-esteem, less depression, more positive view of others, and so on)—has been investigated in a variety of experimental and clinical studies. Reviews of such studies (e.g., Coleman, 1986; Molinari and Reichlin, 1985; Osgood, 1985) indicate that there is a great deal of evidence in support of the thesis. However, when the content of the reminiscence is highly negative or painful, so that the individual is unable to resolve or deal with past issues, the process can lead to a sense of despair. Also, when reminiscing in itself becomes obsessive in nature, as is often observed in institutional settings, it is an indicator of poor adjustment.

Coleman found that older people who reminisced and valued the activity maintained high morale, as did those who did not reminisce because they saw no point in it. On the other hand, those who reminisced but found the reminiscence disturbing and those who did not reminisce because they felt it would be depressing to think about the past tended to be maladjusted. The therapist can use guided reminiscence to gain an understanding of the older client's life history, to help the older person deal with painful memories or feelings of guilt about the past, to identify strengths that can be used in coping with the present, and to reach a more positive view of self.

Although older people reminisce a great deal about their childhood years, there is little in the literature dealing specifically with reminiscence of experiences with siblings. In a recent study (Gold, 1986), in which extensive open-ended interview techniques were used to investigate elderly people's sibling relationships over the life span, interviewees felt that the reminiscence process during the course of the interview was in itself quite valuable. It helped them to put their current relationships with siblings in a meaningful context, to understand present events, and to appreciate the significance of siblings in their lives. The relationships with siblings seemed to be particularly salient in the latter portion of life, with many of Gold's respondents expressing the view that they and their siblings were the last remaining members of their family and thus really appreciated each other. I have found similar themes expressed by elderly siblings (Cicirelli, 1985b), and have advocated the use of shared sibling reminiscence in the therapeutic situation as a means of resolving earlier conflicts while retaining a sense of security and rootedness in the original family setting (Cicirelli, 1985c).

Most siblings stand ready to help each other if needed (Troll,

1971) or at least profess such a willingness to help. The therapist can make use of this reservoir of good will to enlist siblings as allies in the treatment process. But to be skillful at doing so, one needs to understand the nature of the sibling relationship in old age.

HOW CAN THEORY EXPLAIN THE SIBLING RELATIONSHIPS OF THE ELDERLY?

Attachment theory (Ainsworth, 1972; Bowlby, 1979, 1980) contributes to our understanding of the sibling relationships in old age. Attachment refers to an emotional or affectional bond between two people; it essentially represents an internal state of being identified with, having love for, and having the desire to be with the other person. In infancy and early childhood, attachment is inferred from the child's behavior as it seeks to maintain proximity, contact, or communication with the parent. Somewhat later in time, a protective aspect of attachment develops, with the child taking measures to prevent the loss of the valued object. This protective behavior is distinct from attachment behavior and complementary to it, in that it is concerned with preserving or restoring the threatened existence of the attached figure rather than merely maintaining or restoring proximity. Examples of protective behavior are caring for the attached figure in time of illness, alerting the person to danger, and so on.

According to Bowlby, attachment does not end in childhood or early adolescence, but endures throughout life. Attachment behaviors are manifested in stage-appropriate ways through periodic communication, visiting, and responses to reunions, while protective behaviors are seen in helping and caregiving behaviors that attempt to maintain the survival of the attached figure and preserve the emotional bond.

Attachment is not restricted to the bond with the mother; multiple attachments to father, siblings, other family members, and friends can develop through such mechanisms as conditioning or self-promoted feedback (Hartup and Lempers, 1973; Troll and Smith, 1976). Thus, the bond between siblings can be regarded as arising from the attachment process. Some evidence exists for attachment to siblings in childhood (Dunn and Kendrick, 1982; Bank and Kahn, 1982b; Stewart, 1983), and the phenomenon has been extended logically to adulthood and old age. Troll and Smith (1976) devised a measure of attachment to study the dyadic bonds among family members and friends in adulthood. Attachment scores for university graduate students were higher for parents than for siblings, but were higher for siblings than for other kin. According to Troll and Smith, the attachment to siblings is a bond which can override separation and distance, even persisting after the death of the attached figure.

The media frequently report siblings who have gone to great lengths to reunite following an enforced or extended separation. Most maintain some level of contact, regardless of distance, through letters, telephone calls, and occasional visits. One 91-year-old man interviewed by this author corresponded weekly with a brother in Europe whom he had not seen since childhood. Bank and Kahn (1982b) provide numerous examples of strong sibling bonds throughout adulthood. My own unpublished data obtained from elderly subjects indicate that ties to deceased siblings remain as strong as those to siblings who are still living.

To explain the maintenance of the attachment bond over space and time, we can argue that the propensity for closeness and contact with the attached figure continues throughout life but is satisfied on a symbolic level (Cicirelli, 1983). Identification, the mechanism by which symbols are used to establish closeness and contact on a psychological level, is an essential ingredient of the affective bond. Through identification, the person can feel close to the attached figure by calling forth the symbolic representation of the person and experiencing a sense of closeness through the similarity of certain personality characteristics.

The individual can thus continue to feel a bond to the absent sibling by using the psychological representation. The symbolic contact can be supplemented from time to time with visits and other communications. Support for the role of symbolic processes in the development and maintenance of the attachment bond to siblings comes from a variety of sources (Bank and Kahn, 1982a, 1982b; Dunn, 1984; Ross and Milgram, 1982). Feelings of closeness to siblings are seen as originating in childhood, involving a symbolic representation of the child's place in the family; memories of early closeness and internalized shared values, goals, and interests have maintained the sense of continuity in spite of separation in adulthood.

The changing structure of the nuclear family is another factor contributing to the salience of the sibling relationship in later life.

The family system in adulthood and later life may be looked upon as composed of overlapping nuclear family systems, with the middle-aged adult taking the role of parent in the family of procreation which he or she heads and the role of child in the family of origin. Looking at the family in another way, the individual enters the family system as an infant. Both the system and the individual's roles within it change as the individual grows older. Beginning with the role of child in the family of origin, the individual "rises" in prestige and power within the system to assume the roles of spouse and then parent in the family of procreation, and finally the roles of grandparent and (possibly) great-grandparent. At the same time, certain roles are relinquished with time. When grandparents die, the role of grandchild is no longer available, and when elderly parents die, the role of adult child is given up.

The role of sibling, however, remains the same throughout the life of the sibling pair, once it has been defined in the family of origin. This continuity and constancy in a world of change appear to be satisfying to the siblings involved. However, there are changes in the family structure which affect the system of which the sibling dyad is a part. The family of origin gradually erodes over time as its members die and only fragments of the system remain, such as a sibling dyad. The parts continue to remain after the whole is gone, but the whole endures in the parts as memories and symbolic representations within the remaining individuals. Such a view helps to account for the value placed on sibling relationships by the elderly (Gold, 1986) and for the importance of reminiscence in their lives.

Some support for this view is found in an earlier study of topics of communication of elderly people with their brothers and sisters and their children (Cicirelli, 1985c). There was more discussion of old times with siblings than with adult children, indicating that siblings do play an important role in reminiscing. The fewer the remaining siblings in the family, the greater the extent of the reminiscing. As remaining members of their families of origin, siblings use reminiscences of old times together to evoke the warmth of early family life and to validate and clarify events and relationships that took place in earlier years. Such shared recollections (Rose and Milgram, 1982) appear to be a source of comfort and pride for the elderly, contributing to a sense that life had been lived in harmony with the family.

WHAT ARE THE CHARACTERISTICS OF SIBLING
RELATIONSHIPS IN OLD AGE?

Sibling relationships can be regarded as the total of the interactions (actions, verbal communication, and nonverbal communication) of two or more individuals who share common parents, as well as their knowledge, perceptions, attitudes, beliefs, and feelings regarding each other over the course of the relationship (Cicirelli, 1985b). In this view, sibling relationships consist of behavioral, cognitive, and affective components. Can it be said, then, that sibling relationships continue to exist in old age?

Previous research has provided ample evidence that the great majority of older people have one or more living siblings and that they are in frequent contact with at least one of these siblings (Allan, 1977; Cicirelli, 1980b, 1982; Leigh, 1982; Rosenberg and Anspach, 1973; Scott, 1983; Shanas, 1973). Approximately half of all people over age 65 see a sibling at least once a week. With the increasing longevity of the population, it seems likely that most older people will have living siblings until quite late in life. In very few cases do siblings lose touch with one another or suffer a complete break in the relationship; in fact, I found that only 3% of elderly people surveyed had lost touch with a sibling (Cicirelli, 1979).

Most older people profess feelings of closeness to their siblings. In a study of sibling relationships of elderly individuals over age 60 (Cicirelli, 1979), 53% reported feeling "extremely close" to the sibling with whom they had the most contact, while another 30% reported feeling "close." Only 6% did not feel close at all. Both men and women tended to name sisters and middle-born siblings as the ones to whom they felt closest. The affectional closeness of siblings has been supported by other studies as well (Allan, 1977; Cumming and Schneider, 1961; Ross and Milgram, 1982).

Closest feelings between siblings are found between siblings of working-class rather than middle-class families. It may be that economic hard times in working-class families contribute to stronger bonding among the children, as suggested by Bank and Kahn (1982b); different cultural expectations regarding family bonds at different socioeconomic status levels may also be a factor. Cultural expectations regarding sibling relationships apparently differ in certain ethnic groups; Johnson (1982) found stronger bonds between siblings in Italian-American than in non-Italian Protestant families. Siblings also reported considerable value consensus (Cicirelli, 1979; Ross and Milgram, 1982; Suggs and Kivett, 1983). In my study 68% of sibling pairs said they agreed about most things.

Ross and Milgram (1982) found that memories of earlier family events were a major factor in the maintenance of closeness among siblings, as well as visits, family rituals, and regular reunions. Get-togethers allowed siblings to reminisce about past experiences as well as to add further common experiences to their family history. Gold's (1986) interviewees reported some of the memories they shared with their siblings: things they used to do together, vacations, weddings, anniversaries, funny or crazy things they did as children, how they felt about each other in earlier years, their relationships with their parents, sad events, and negative feelings they had in the past.

The relationship between elderly siblings is generally a compatible one (Cicirelli, 1985b), with 88% of my sample reporting that they get along very well with their siblings, 74% reporting that they gain considerable or very great satisfaction from the sibling relationship, and 68% feeling able to discuss intimate topics with the sibling. However, only 30% talk over important decisions with a sibling. Thus, while most elderly siblings feel close and have a compatible relationship, a smaller proportion is able to share intimate details of their lives and disclose feelings and personal problems. If the relationship seems somewhat superficial for many siblings, it may be placed in perspective by considering Duck and Miell's findings (1986) that friendships are also conducted at the level of superficial chitchat and without "long, intense, private intimacies." Also, friendships between non-sibs are characterized by doubts and anxieties about the relationship's future, while siblings are freed from such doubts since their relationship is ascribed rather than voluntary.

Sibling rivalry is considered an important aspect of the sibling relationship during the childhood years by both psychotherapists and developmental psychologists. Some feelings of sibling rivalry persist into old age, although they may be expressed in more subtle forms, such as using the sibling as the standard of comparison for one's own activities and achievements (Troll, 1975). However, I (Cicirelli, 1985b) found a low level of rivalrous behavior among elderly siblings. Only 10% reported arguments, 6% reported bossing or attempts at domination by the sibling, 8% reported feelings of competi-

tion with the sibling (and that only rarely), and a few reported incidents of jealousy, hostility, snobbishness, and so on.

While the incidence of conflicts with siblings was low, about a
third of the siblings expected that sibling conflict would increase if
the siblings were to live together again. Other researchers (Berezin,
1977; Laverty, 1962) also found that sibling rivalry could be reactivated in certain situations later in life. Ross and Milgram (1980,
1982), using small group interviews in a clinical setting, found that
45% of people in adulthood and old age experienced feelings of
rivalry with their sibling.

Although the clinical interview appeared to stimulate more self-
disclosure than other types of interview methods, it may be that such
rivalrous feelings become overt in old age only in certain stressful
situations. For example, death of a spouse or other relative, questions
of inheritance, and other external events can provoke episodes of
rivalry. Other episodes may be internally exacerbated, as when an
older person's feelings of loneliness stir up long buried resentment of
a sibling's popularity. Another possibility to be considered is that
survey respondents tend to answer in ways deemed socially desirable,
which may mask actual rivalries. Bedford (1986), using an adaptation of the Thematic Apperception Test, found that older adults
revealed as many themes of sibling rivalry in their responses as did
younger adults, and that women expressed more conflict in the relationship with siblings than did men. She concluded that the projective
methodology was tapping feelings not typically reported. In general,
however, the evidence indicates that siblings value their relationship
highly in later years and seem to have developed ways of interaction
that avoid conflict and overt rivalry.

Another major aspect of the sibling relationship throughout life is
the help and support siblings provide for each other. In old age,
sibling help can include psychological support, on the one hand
(boosting morale, providing companionship, serving as confidants,
giving advice, aiding in decision-making, and so on), and instrumental help, on the other (homemaking, shopping, home repairs,
transportation, finances, care when sick, and so on). A few interview
studies have reported that siblings of the elderly are generally ready to
give aid in time of trouble, although their help may be called for only
on rare occasions (Allan, 1977; Cicirelli, 1979; Cumming and Schneider, 1961).

This general readiness to give help was illustrated in my study of the hospitalized elderly (Cicirelli, 1985a). About half of these elderly patients reported sibling visits, and a similar proportion reported telephone calls from siblings. Only 20% reported any kind of sibling help while in the hospital (e.g., taking care of mail, running errands, taking care of things at home, business arrangements, and so on), and only about 6% wanted or expected instrumental help from siblings once they returned home. In about half of the cases, they mentioned desiring psychological support from their siblings, such as visiting and companionship, love and caring, moral support, and prayers.

Townsend (1957) has provided detailed examples of situations where brothers and sisters provided a great deal of help (e.g., following the death of a spouse), appearing to substitute for a deceased or missing family member. Nevertheless, I (1979) found that most help in families was exchanged in a vertical, rather than collateral, direction, with children (after the spouse) viewed as the primary source of help in old age. One can view the family support network of the elderly as a substitution hierarchy, with the spouse first in line to give help, followed by adult children, then siblings, grandchildren, and other kin. When a primary helper in the hierarchy is unavailable or unable to carry the load alone, the next kin member in the hierarchy is preferred. If the need for help becomes too great for the spouse or children to handle, or the normal scheme of family obligations is disturbed for some reason (loss or absence of spouse or child), siblings undertake to fulfill that obligation. Indeed, some 60% of the elderly regarded their siblings as a source of support to be called upon in a crisis, although only 7% or fewer (depending on the type of help) regarded a sibling as a primary source of help.

In further statistical investigation of variables leading to sibling helping behavior in old age, feelings of sibling attachment (the affectional bond) and existing visiting patterns were found to be related to helping behavior, while feelings of obligation and perceived need for help were not. Scott (1983) also found that siblings gave relatively little assistance in old age compared to that given by children, although help was greater when a brother or sister fell ill, needed transportation, or needed to make an important decision. Further, the balance of help exchanged between siblings was approximately equal (in contrast to the imbalance in help given and received between generations). Three generalizations emerge from the research on sibling helping: Siblings appear to play a complementary role to spouse and adult children in giving help; they play a greater role in giving psychological support than in offering instrumental help; and help is greater in time of illness or other crisis situations.

Whether the sibling relationship leads to more positive adjustments and greater life satisfaction in old age is open to question, with both positive and negative evidence in the existing literature. Various researchers have pointed out the positive value of good sibling relationships for the older person. Cumming and Henry (1961) found that elderly with living siblings had higher morale than those who did not. Ross and Milgram (1982) concluded that the sibling relationship was of great value to the elderly, while I (1977, 1980a) found that those elderly with more frequent interaction with siblings maintained a greater sense of control in life. Men with sisters had a greater sense of emotional security in life, while women with sisters were stimulated and challenged in their social roles.

In contrast, a large-sample study (Lee and Ihinger-Tallman, 1980), controlling for a number of possible confounding variables, failed to find a significant relationship between frequency of interaction with siblings and morale of the elderly. A more recent study among rural elderly (McGhee, 1985) confirmed Lee and Ihinger-Tallman's findings regarding the lack of effect on life satisfaction of frequent sibling interactions, but found that the mere availability of a sister was a significant predictor of life satisfaction in women and approached statistical significance among men. Thus, it appears that any positive effects of a relationship with siblings on morale and adjustment derive from the simple existence of the relationship and not from the frequency with which the siblings interact. Relationships with sisters seem to be particularly important, whether it is a sister-sister or a sister-brother bond. One could attribute this to women's greater interest in family relationships; however, Gold (1986) found that brothers initiated sibling contact with sisters about as often as sisters contacted brothers. More likely, women's traditional roles as nurturers and their emotional expressiveness account for the importance of relationships with sisters.

HOW DOES THE SIBLING RELATIONSHIP
CHANGE OVER TIME?

Relationships between individuals are not static, but may be said to follow a developmental course or "career," with changes in the relationship accompanying major life events, environmental and social changes (Ginsburg, 1986). This is of particular interest in the case of the sibling relationship, since it probably is the longest lasting of all human relationships. One needs to pay special attention to what happens to relationships at particular transition points in life, such as marriage, retirement, and death of a parent. In later life, what happens during the declining years is of interest, including death of a sibling, death of a spouse, illness, and the waning of one's sense of power and importance.

The sibling relationship begins in early childhood as basic attachments develop (Bank and Kahn, 1982b). Then the relationship begins a long "maintenance" phase during which the intensity of the relationship fluctuates as one sibling or the other encounters various life events (school, puberty, leaving home, marriage). Once they leave their parents' home, siblings tend to interact with lesser intensity, and they may not meet or communicate directly for extended intervals in adult life. Yet the relationship goes on, with other family members providing the linkage. For example, the mother may tell the other children in a family about what is happening in the life of their out-of-town sibling and relay information about them in telephone calls to the child who is out of town. Although intentional dissolution of the sibling relationship is rare, the relationship may end abruptly with the death of a sibling or gradually dissolve as functions decline near the end of life.

As might be expected, the number of living siblings for an individual declines over the last decade of life, dropping from a mean of 2.9 siblings in the seventh decade of life to a mean of 1.1 in the ninth decade (Cicirelli, 1980b). Findings with regard to the amount of interaction with siblings in old age are inconsistent. Most previous studies, reviewed by Leigh (1982), reported a decline in sibling interaction in old age. More recent data presented by Leigh, however, indicated that sibling interactions declined from a peak in the adolescent years to a plateau in middle adulthood and then rose in later years. This pattern of declining relationships with kin during the childrearing years followed by a resurgence of kin involvement after the children have left home has been called the "hourglass effect" (Shanas, 1979). One explanation for the increase in later life is that declining parenting and career demands leave more time for interaction with siblings. One older woman and her sister, along with their husbands, found that they were able to take weekend trips together at least once a month after their children had all left home. A man and his brother started some home improvement projects together after they both retired. Others simply found more time to drop in and talk.

If we examine the feelings of closeness and affection rather than the frequency of interaction, sibling relationships appear to grow more satisfactory with age. I found (1982, 1985b) that the percentage of interviewees expressing closeness or extreme closeness to the sibling with whom they had the most contact rose from 68% in middle age to 83% in old age. Indeed, closeness ratings increased each decade from age 30 to age 90. Findings in regard to compatibility with the siblings and positive trait judgments are similar.

Recent work attempting to relate significant events over the adult life span to multidimensional measures of the sibling relationship (Mosatche, Brady, and Noberini, 1983; Noberini, Mosatche, and Brady, 1984), although flawed, is of interest because it suggests that various dimensions of the relationship change in different ways over the life span. For example, activity and admiration relative to the sibling were highest in young adulthood, while positive affect and emotional support were lower in middle age and preretirement than in childhood, with positive feelings resurfacing in later periods. The latter findings also provide some support for Leigh's (1982) U-shaped curve of sibling interactions over the life span.

Although sibling rivalry can persist until the end of life, existing evidence (Allan, 1977; Cicirelli, 1982, 1985c; Ross and Milgram, 1982) indicates a decline in rivalry over the decades of late adulthood and old age. Ross and Milgram detected a greater incidence of rivalry than other investigators but nevertheless found that rivalry had diminished during the adult years. By late adulthood and old age, the renewal and repair of sibling relationships appear to take on great importance, with reasons for rivalry being reevaluated from a more mature perspective. We can conclude that rivalry may be reactivated under appropriate circumstances, but the overall trend is for rivalry to decrease with age.

The findings with regard to sibling helping behavior over the life span present a somewhat puzzling picture. It has already been noted that siblings play a complementary role to adult children in later years, giving relatively more emotional support than instrumental help. Siblings are generally ready to give aid in time of trouble, although their help may be called for only on rare occasions. The small amount of data that the author has collected showing helping behavior for different age groups (Cicirelli, 1979) indicates that, as age increases from the seventh to the ninth decade, the amount of sibling help received in 16 categories of instrumental and emotional support rises. We talked to women who drove their sisters for shopping, meetings, or doctors' appointments and to women who cooked and cleaned for widowed brothers; we talked to men who did home maintenance jobs for their elderly sisters or who helped with tax and insurance forms; we even talked to one 78-year-old man who cared for a brother suffering from Alzheimer's disease.

The amount of help siblings desire from one another also increases as people get older. Hoyt and Babchuk (1983) found that the likelihood of a sibling's serving as a confidant increased after age 75, while I (1979) found that older people desired more help from siblings as age increased. These findings suggest that ties with remaining siblings become especially important in the last stage of life. The fact that elderly siblings appear to rally in support of one another in spite of their own advancing infirmities indicates the value which they place on the relationship. The norms of help flowing to and from adult children and of self-reliance and equity in sibling relationships appear to minimize sibling helping behavior throughout much of life. But in later life, when other supports (e.g., spouse, adult children) may no longer be present or cannot give sufficient help, sibling readiness to help finds expression. Kahn (1983) regarded the trust and interdependence between siblings in later years to be one of the most important of human relationships.

IMPLICATIONS FOR CLINICAL PRACTICE

Although the foregoing review of sibling relationships in old age has been brief and somewhat limited, there are a number of implications which can be drawn for the practitioner who deals with elderly people with mental health problems.

First of all, the persistence of the sibling relationship (even when there has been little contact) and its value for the individual should not be underestimated. When interviewing one man in late middle age who had experienced a conflict-filled relationship with his two brothers for many years, we were surprised at how much he appeared to value the relationship: "Sure, I hate my brothers . . . but after all, they're family!" It appears that many older people derive great comfort from simply knowing that a sibling is available. Others gain a deep appreciation of the value of a close relationship with a sibling in their declining years.

Still another area of sibling relationships which has not been studied thus far is the pioneering function of certain siblings in the family. The first brother or sister to experience a major life event (e.g., retirement, loss of a spouse, chronic illness) serves as a role model for the others, demonstrating ways of coping (or failing to cope) with the event.

The therapist needs to be aware that a sibling relationship characterized by conflict and rivalry or broken off due to a misunderstanding can be a source of great distress to the aging client. At a time when most elderly are finding comfort in a closer relationship with siblings, the realization that a resolution of the conflict with a sibling is unlikely or impossible can lead to depression or despair.

A relationship with a sister seems to be a special source of support and strength in old age. This is likely to be the manifestation of the woman's traditional role as a nurturer and emotionally expressive person. However, whether a good sibling relationship is with a sister or a brother, the therapist can build on this foundation, making use of the strengths of the relationship to achieve therapeutic goals. If the relationship has been a bad one, the therapist can seek to facilitate a better relationship as an intermediate step toward other objectives.

The clinician can make use of sibling readiness to help when such help might prove useful. Although siblings play a secondary role to the spouse and adult children in giving instrumental and emotional support, the increase in sibling help among the oldest groups of elderly indicates that, when another sibling's need is clear, help is forthcoming.

If a therapist wishes to consider the sibling relationship as part of a treatment program, he or she first needs to determine whether to work only with the client or to bring together a sibling group. Since it may be unwieldly to work with an entire sibship group, the therapist needs to identify an appropriate subgroup of siblings. (Of course, if only one or two living siblings remain, the choice may be by default.) The therapist may choose to bring in the sibling to whom the identified patient feels closest or the one with whom there has been a problem. Bank and Kahn (1982b) formulated guidelines for selecting a subgroup of siblings for therapy based on the quality of the relationship and the degree of identification; these hold for elderly patients as well. It should be remembered that sibling help does not derive from a sense of obligation but from the strength of the affectional bond between the pair.

There are several ways in which reminiscence about the sibling relationship might be used. The therapist might ask a woman to reminisce about the past sibling relationship in an individual session in order to help her recognize both strengths and problem areas. A second method is to explore reminiscences about siblings as part of group therapy sessions composed of unrelated elderly clients. Or the therapist can bring together a small subgroup of siblings for what we have termed "shared sibling reminiscing." In such groups the siblings share memories in order to obtain a better understanding and appreciation of earlier events in their relationship. It would also be possible to use such reminiscence as a device to work toward resolution of conflicts and problems rooted in the past.

Reminiscence has been used successfully in group situations to improve the morale of the elderly person by bringing out positive memories of shared experiences. In one day care center for the elderly we observed, a life review group was one of the activity options. Although many of the clients were somewhat withdrawn in other center activities, they were animated while reminiscing about good times and humorous or silly activities with brothers and sisters in childhood and adolescence. This improved affect appeared to transfer to other activities as well. It should be noted, however, that participation in this group was voluntary, and day care clients who were disinterested or who had unhappy memories of the past were not urged to attend. If negative memories (such as conflicts and misunderstandings, situations involving sibling abuse, and violations of trust in critical situations) are to be brought up, a therapist should be present and ready to help the client deal with feelings and reactions. While at times negative experiences and feelings about siblings may require an extended period of treatment, at other times simply bringing them up can serve to clear the air and "unfreeze frozen misunderstandings" (Bank and Kahn, 1982b; Kahn, 1983).

> Sometimes merely looking at past sibling relationships from a new perspective can accomplish a great deal. At one nursing home where I

function in an advisory role, the staff was experiencing numerous problems with a new patient. The patient was an 82-year-old widow, partially paralyzed, who refused to participate in any of the many optional social activities. At meals, which were served in a group dining room, she complained constantly about her tablemates and insisted on being returned to her room as quickly as possible. She was hypercritical and verbally abusive to the nursing aides, which was beginning to create problems. The social worker at the nursing home was enlisted to deal with this behavior.

The patient's three adult children visited frequently and, although concerned about their mother's complaints and state of mind, were unable to suggest any specific ideas to improve the situation. It turned out that she had a 90-year-old sister who was also a patient in another section of the nursing home, but that she had a long history of conflict with the sister. The sister suffered from multi-infarct dementia but had periods of lucidity. The children's attempts to bring the two sisters together for a visit had resulted in either seemingly trivial arguments or stony silence, so they had abandoned the effort.

The social worker, however, thought that this was an avenue worth exploring, and one afternoon brought the two sisters together. She asked them to recall any specially good memories about growing up together. After some initial grumbling, they talked about certain holiday occasions and visits with other relatives. Later, the social worker commented to the patient that she seemed to have had some enjoyable times with her sister in the past. The patient then launched into a long litany of complaints about the sister, whom she felt had always tried to "boss" and dominate her and to snoop into her affairs.

When she brought the two sisters together again, the social worker asked them to talk about memories of everyday events in childhood. The younger sister complained, "She always tried to tell me what to do," whereupon the older sister said that the mother had frequently placed her in charge of her younger sister during the busy years when they were growing up, giving her a long list of things that she was not to allow the younger child to do. The older sister said that she never really liked to be in charge and had always felt that they had trouble getting along because of it. The patient sat in silence after this and the visit ended. Later the patient said to the social worker that she had never thought about how the older sister felt about things.

The next visit between the two sisters went somewhat better, and the two women were able to share some memories and feelings about the early events in their lives. Gradually the patient's adjustment to the nursing home improved; she related better to the aides and to her tablemates in the dining room and began taking part in some of the activities offered at the nursing home. She now seemed to look forward to visits with her sister, and the two women finally seemed to be able to talk together without conflict. Unfortunately, the older sister's periods of lucidity were becoming few and far between, which was a source of sadness to the family. However, the patient appeared to derive comfort from the fact that they had finally been able to understand each other better after so many years.

Because there are few well-established methods for the use of siblings in therapy with the elderly, the clinician needs to adopt an experimental approach, making and testing hypotheses about what will work and what will not, and collecting systematic data about results to share with others in the field.

REFERENCES

Ainsworth, M. D. (1972). Attachment and dependency: A comparison. In J. L. Gewirtz (Ed.), *Attachment and dependency* (pp. 97–137). New York: John Wiley.

Allan, G. (1977). Sibling solidarity. *Journal of Marriage and the Family, 39,* 177–184.

Bank, S., & Kahn, M. D. (1982a). Intense sibling loyalties. In M. E. Lamb & B. Sutton-Smith (Eds.), *Sibling relationships: Their nature and significance across the life span* (pp. 251–266). Hillsdale, NJ: Lawrence Erlbaum.

Bank, S. P., & Kahn, M. D. (1982b). *The sibling bond.* New York: Basic Books.

Bedford, V. H. (1986). *A comparison of thematic apperceptions of sibling affiliation, conflict, and separation at two periods of adulthood.* Paper presented at the 39th Annual Scientific Meeting of the Gerontological Society, Chicago.

Berezin, M. A. (1977). Partial grief for the aged and their families. In E. Pattison (Ed.), *The experience of dying* (pp. 279–286). Englewood Cliffs, NJ: Prentice-Hall.

Bowlby, J. (1979). *The making and breaking of affectional bonds.* London: Tavistock.

Bowlby, J. (1980). *Attachment and loss, Vol. III. Loss, stress, and depression.* New York: Basic Books.

Butler, R. N. (1963). The life review: An interpretation of reminiscence in the aged. *Psychiatry, 26,* 65–76.

Church, M. (1986). Issues in psychological therapy with elderly people. In I. Hanley & M. Gilhooly (Eds.), *Psychological therapies for the elderly* (pp. 1–21). London: Croom Helm.

Cicirelli, V. G. (1977). Relationship of siblings to the elderly person's feelings and concerns. *Journal of Gerontology, 32,* 317–322.

Cicirelli, V. G. (1979, May). *Social services for elderly in relation to the kin network* (Report). Washington, D.C.: NRTA-AARP Andrus Foundation.

Cicirelli, V. G. (1980a). Relationship of family background variables to locus of control in the elderly. *Journal of Gerontology, 35,* 108–114.

Cicirelli, V. G. (1980b). Sibling influence in adulthood: A life span perspective. In L. W. Poon (Ed.), *Aging in the 1980s* I: *Psychological issues* (pp. 455–462). Washington, DC: American Psychological Association.

Cicirelli, V. G. (1982). Sibling influence throughout the lifespan. In M. E. Lamb & B. Sutton-Smith (Eds.), *Sibling relationships: Their nature and significance across the lifespan* (pp. 267–284). Hillsdale, NJ: Lawrence Erlbaum.

Cicirelli, V. G. (1983). Adult children's attachment and helping behavior to elderly parents: A path model. *Journal of Marriage and the Family, 45*, 815–825.

Cicirelli, V. G. (1985a, December). *Effects of personal characteristics and family support on stress, coping, and outcomes of hospitalized elderly* (Report). Park Ridge, IL: Retirement Research Foundation.

Cicirelli, V. G. (1985b). Sibling relationships throughout the life cycle. In L. L'Abate (Ed.), *The handbook of family psychology and therapy. Vol. I* (pp. 177–214). Homewood, IL: Dorsey Press.

Cicirelli, V. G. (1985c). The role of siblings as family caregivers. In W. J. Sauer & R. T. Coward (Eds.), *Social support networks and the care of the elderly: Theory, research, practice, and policy* (pp. 93–107). New York: Springer.

Coleman, P. (1986). Issues in the therapeutic use of reminiscence with elderly people. In I. Hanley & M. Gilhooly (Eds.), *Psychological therapies for the elderly* (pp. 41–64). London: Croom Helm.

Cumming, E., & Henry, W. (1961). *Growing old*. New York: Basic Books.

Cumming, E., & Schneider, D. (1961). Sibling solidarity: A property of American kinship. *American Anthropologist, 63*, 498–507.

Duck, S., & Miell, D. (1986). Charting the development of personal relationships. In R. Gilmour & S. Duck (Eds.), *The emerging field of personal relationships* (pp. 133–143). Hillsdale, NJ: Lawrence Erlbaum.

Dunn, J. (1984). Sibling studies and the developmental impact of critical incidents. In P. B. Baltes & O. G. Brim, Jr. (Eds.), *Life-span development and behavior*. Vol. 6 (pp. 335–353). Orlando, FL: Academic Press.

Dunn, J., & Kendrick, C. (1982). *Siblings: Love, envy, and understanding*. Cambridge, MA: Harvard University Press.

Finkelhor, D. (1980). Sex among siblings: A survey on prevalence, variety, and effects. *Archives of Sexual Behavior, 9*, 171–194.

Ginsburg, G. P. (1986). The structural analysis of primary relationships. In R. Gilmour & S. Duck (Eds.), *The emerging field of personal relationships* (pp. 41–62). Hillsdale, NJ: Lawrence Erlbaum.

Gold, D. T. (1986). *Sibling relationships in retrospect: A study of reminiscence in old age*. Unpublished doctoral dissertation, Northwestern University, Evanston, IL.

Gully, K. J., Dengerink, H. A., Pepping, M., & Bergstrom, D. (1981). Research Note: Sibling contribution to violent behavior. *Journal of Marriage and the Family, 43*, 333–337.

Hartup, W. W., & Lempers, J. (1973). A problem in life span development: The interactional analysis of family attachments. In P. B. Baltes & P. W. Schaie (Eds.), *Life-span developmental psychology: Personality and socialization* (pp. 235–252). New York: Academic Press.

Herr, J. J., & Weakland, J. H. (1979). *Counseling elders and their families: Practical techniques for applied gerontology*. New York: Springer.

Hoyt, D. R., & Babchuk, N. (1983). Adult kinship networks: The selective formation of intimate ties with kin. *Social Forces, 62*, 84–101.

Johnson, C. L. (1982). Sibling solidarity: Its origin and functioning in Italian-American families. *Journal of Marriage and the Family, 44,* 155–167.

Kahn, M. D. (1983, December). Sibling relationships in later life. *Medical Aspects of Human Sexuality, 17*(12), 94–103.

Kahn, M. D., & Bank, S. (1981). In pursuit of sisterhood. *Family Process, 20*(1), 85–95.

Laverty, R. (1962). Reactivation of sibling rivalry in older people. *Social Work, 1,* 23–30.

Lee, G. R., & Ihinger-Tallman, M. (1980). Sibling interactions and morale. *Research on Aging, 2,* 367–391.

Leigh, G. K. (1982). Kinship interaction over the family life span. *Journal of Marriage and the Family, 44,* 197–208.

McGhee, J. L. (1985). The effects of siblings on the life satisfaction of the rural elderly. *Journal of Marriage and the Family, 47,* 85–91.

Molinari, V., & Reichlin, R. E. (1985). Life review reminiscence in the elderly: A review of the literature. *International Journal of Aging and Human Development, 20*(2), 81–92.

Mosatche, H. S., Brady, E. M., & Noberini, M. R. (1983). A retrospective lifespan study of the closest sibling relationship. *Journal of Psychology, 113,* 237–243.

Noberini, M. R., Mosdache, H. R., & Brady, E. M. (1984). Qualitative alterations in adult sibling relationships. Paper presented at the 37th Annual Scientific Meetings of the Gerontological Society, San Antonio, TX.

Osgood, N. J. (1985). *Suicide in the elderly: A practitioner's guide to diagnosis and mental health intervention.* Rockville, MD: Aspen.

Palazzoli, M. Selvini (1985). The problem of the sibling as the referring person. *Journal of Marital and Family Therapy, 11,* 21–34.

Rosenberg, G. S., & Anspach, D. F. (1973). Sibling solidarity in the working class. *Journal of Marriage and the Family, 35,* 108–113.

Rosner, S. (1985). On the place of siblings in psychoanalysis. *Psychoanalytic Review, 72,* 457–477.

Ross, H. G., & Milgram, J. I. (1980, September). *Rivalry in adult sibling relationships: Its antecedants and dynamics.* Paper presented at the 88th Annual Meeting of the American Psychological Association, Montreal, Canada.

Ross, H. G., & Milgram, J. I. (1982). Important variables in adult sibling relationships: A qualitative study. In M. E. Lamb & B. Sutton-Smith (Eds.), *Sibling relationships: Their nature and significance across the lifespan* (pp. 225–249). Hillsdale, NJ: Lawrence Erlbaum.

Scott, J. P. (1983). Siblings and other kin. In T. H. Brubaker (Ed.), *Family relationships in later life* (pp. 47–62). Beverly Hills, CA: Sage.

Shanas, E. (1973). Family-kin networks and aging in cross-cultural perspective. *Journal of Marriage and the Family, 35,* 505–511.

Shanas, E. (1979). Social myth as hypothesis: The case of family relations of old people. *Gerontologist, 19*(1), 3–9.

Stewart, R. B. (1983). Sibling attachment relationships: Child-infant interaction in the strange situation. *Developmental Psychology, 19,* 192–199.

Suggs, P. K., & Kivett, V. R. (1983, November). *Rural/urban elderly and siblings: Their value consensus.* Paper presented at the 36th Annual Scientific Meeting of the Gerontological Society, San Francisco.

Townsend, P. (1957). *The family life of old people: An inquiry in East London.* Glencoe, IL: Free Press.

Troll, L. E. (1971). The family of later life: A decade review. *Journal of Marriage and the Family, 33*, 263–290.
Troll, L. E. (1975). *Early and middle adulthood*. Monterey, CA: Brooks/Cole.
Troll, L., & Smith, J. (1976). Attachment through the life span: Some questions about dyadic bonds among adults. *Human Development, 19*, 156–170.
United States Bureau of the Census (1983). America in transition: An aging society. *Current Population Reports*, Series P-23, No. 128. Washington, DC: United States Government Printing Office.

Index

Abelsohn, D., 194, 195n
Abend, S. M., 20
Absen, A., 13
abuse
    and bonding, 12–13
    sexual, 140–41, 142, 152
    unresolved aspects of sibling, 18–19
access
    high-access relationship and eating
        disorders, 300–302
    among siblings, 94
activities
    of normal tilted families, 277
adjustment
    to disabled siblings, 168
    to divorce, 190–92
    of sisters of the institutionalized, 173
Adler, A., 47, 48
adolescent children
    and remarriage, 221–25
adulthood
    for children of divorce, 205–7
    ethnic patterns of relationships, 78–79
affection
    in groups, FIRO model, 401
    phase, therapy for alcoholic families, 251
affective
    disorders in gender-tilted families, 284
    tasks, cultural assignment of, 406
aged parents
    caring for, 417–34
    families without caregivers, 426–28
    primary caregiver for, 421–23
    siblings who refuse care, 432–33
aging, 415–16
Ainsworth, M. D., 439
alcoholics
    and care for aged parents, 426–28
    children of, 228–52
Alcoholics Anonymous, 248
Allan, G., 435, 442, 444, 448

alliances
    sibling, in eating disordered families,
        310–11
ambivalence
    in twins or close-in-age siblings, 14–15
Amenson, C. S., 286
Andersen, T., 316
anger
    redirecting, 348–51
    in siblings of the disabled, 178–81
    in siblings of the mentally ill, 318
Angst, J., 26, 49
anxiety
    about care for a handicapped sibling,
        174
    of young children in therapy, 104–5
archetypes (Jung), 358
Arensberg, C., 71
Aries, P., 102
Asian ethnic patterns, 71, 75, 78–79
assessment
    of incest, 143–49
    of young children in brief therapy,
        99–100
attachment
    defined, 439
    issue for younger stepsiblings, 225–26
    and symbolic processes, 440
    theory, 439
Attneave, C., 75
Atwood, G. E., 11
authority
    and care giving to aged parents, 425–26
autogenous orientation
    and birth order, 30
autonomy
    ethnic patterns of, 74–76
    of siblings in large families, 119–20
    of sibling subsystems, 193
    in tilted families, 293
Avis, J. M., 42

Babchuk, N., 449
Bach Institute (Minneapolis), 27
Bach, Jerome M., 27–29, 31, 33
Bailey, D. B., 167, 184, 185
Baker, L., 297, 298
Baker, R. I., 117, 118
Baldwin, A. C., 55
Bank, Stephen P., 3, 4, 8n, 10, 11, 19, 20, 37, 41–42, 94, 97, 119–20, 121, 135, 137, 138, 141, 167, 172, 175, 176, 177, 180, 181, 182, 183, 192, 193, 211, 215, 250, 259, 263, 264, 288, 294, 299, 300, 302, 304, 305, 306, 309, 319, 324, 325, 331, 339, 341, 342, 344, 351, 384, 389, 400, 403, 404, 407, 409, 417, 423, 435, 436, 439, 442, 447, 450, 451
Barker, R. G., 120
Barrett, M. J., 299, 300
Basch, Michael, 5
Bateson, Gregory, 316, 325
Baxter, J., 54
Beavin, J., 325
Bedford, V. H., 444
behavior control
    in tilted families, 293–94
Belenky, M. F., 27, 42
Bellah, R. N., 27
Bem Sex Role Inventory (BSRI), 276
Bem, S. L., 276
Berezin, M. A., 437, 444
Bergstrom, D., 437
Bernal, G., 34
Berne, Eric, 358
biases, clinical, 42
Binger, C. M., 177
Binns, M., 411
bipolar patients
    and female-tilted families, 286
Birtchnell, J., 55, 56, 57
birth order, 2
    and characteristics of children, 28
    and deidentification, 400–401
    differences, recognition of, 32
    and ethnic patterns, 70–72
    and family systems, 26–29
    and functioning, alcoholic families, 237–38
    and myth for sibling groups, 31–34
    and psychopathology, 71
    and responsibility in large families, 127–32
    and role of daughter of an alcoholic, 238–39
    and role of son of an alcoholic, 240
    and social behavior, 49
    and structure in the alcoholic family, 245

and student-teacher interactions, 57–58
birthright
    the adult sibling in individual therapy, 341–55
    defined (Bank), 339
black ethnic patterns, 75, 80–81
Blick, L., 151
blueprints from the past, 358–78
Bohannan, P., 209
Boll, E. S., 116, 117, 118–19, 120, 121
bonds, sibling, 384
    in the alcoholic family, 234, 247
    constructive dialectic in, 345
    debonding, 376
    defined, 37–38
    and friendship, 43
    intense bonds, 4, 11–12
    Sibling Bond, The (Bank and Kahn), 85, 95, 324, 401
    and transgenerational complementary roles, 94
    and violence, 13
Boone, S. L., 118
Boscolo, L., 300, 303, 320
Boskind-Lodahl, M., 287
Boskind-White, M., 298
Bossard, J. H. S., 116, 117, 118–19, 120, 121
Boszormenyi-Nagy, I., 192, 272, 385, 389
boundaries
    and large family systems, 122, 124–26
    parent-child, 149–50
    in professional relationships, 411
    in remarried families, 213
Bowen, M., 272
Bowerman, C. E., 117, 274
Bowlby, J. H., 61, 218, 439
Boyd-Franklin, N., 81
Brady, E. M., 170, 448
Breslau, N., 184
Brice, J., 72
Brighton-Clegborn, J., 6
Briskin, Liz, 25n
British-American ethnic patterns, 76, 78, 82–83
Brody, E., 421n
Browne, A., 151
Brown, H., 211, 215
Bruch, H., 284, 286
business, family, *see* family business
Butler, R. N., 437–38

Cain complex, 303
Cantelon, L. J., 287
care giving
    to aged parents, 417–34

and attachment, 439
born caregivers, 422–23
families without caregivers, 426–28
caretaking
and abuse, 19
for handicapped siblings, 171–75
by sons in alcoholic families, 240
caring for the aged
final phase, 421
first phase transition, 419
second phase transition, 420
third phase transition, 420–21
Carlson, D., 118
Carlson, J., 116, 117
Carroll, Robert S., 340, 379, 392
Carroll, S. L., 392
Carter, E., 210, 215
Casper, R. C., 297–98
Cast of Characters Work, *see* Character
    Work perspective
Cecchin, G., 300, 303, 320
centrality
and ethnic patterns, 74–75
of the siblings in large families, 119
change
in the aged family, 418–21
in the sibling relationship over time,
    446–49
Character Work perspective, 356–78
Cherlin, A., 209
Chicago Sun Times, 8
Child Guidance Clinic (Philadelphia), 286
Children of Alcoholics (COA), 228
Children's PACT (Parents as Co-Therapists)
    Model, 249
chronic mental illness
case study, 327–36
defined, 315
siblings as allies in treatment, 314–37
Church, M., 437
Cicirelli, Victor G., 344, 416, 423, 435,
    438, 440, 441, 442, 443, 444, 445,
    447, 448, 449
circular questions
in the Milan approach, 322–24
Clinchy, B. M., 27, 42
clinical families
size of, 115–16, 118
tilted, 283–87
closeness
late adolescence and early adult years,
    253–54
cognitive, defined, 232
Colangelo, N., 401
Cole, E., 135, 137
Coleman, James, 8

Coleman, P., 438
Coleman, S. B., 232, 237, 241
Collins, L. E., 31, 33
Combrinck-Graham, Lee, 90, 95, 190
commitment
to elderly parents, 430–31
in sibling relationships, 384
communication
dysfunctional, and care for aged parents,
    431–32
metacommunication of worth, 73
and the presence of a disabled child, 181–82
compatibility-noncompatibility theorem, 57
complementarity, 2
attachment and protection, 439
between family and business functions,
    387–88
and family burdens, 192
in professional relationships, 404–5, 408
in roles of siblings and adult children,
    448–49
in RSA's, 30
sibling, and marriage configurations,
    52–53
transgenerational, and sibling bonds, 94
in twins, 14
utilizing siblings' in treatment, 324–26
conceptualizations
of children of alcoholics, 232–33
configurations
sibling, 47–58
sibling, in large families, 116
tilted, defined, 273–74
conflict
and care of aged parents, 425, 430–32
among elderly siblings, 444
between generations, 70
in loyalties, remarried families, 213
in male-tilted families, 282
parental, and sibling positions, 54
resolution in eating disordered families,
    298
and sex of siblings, 48
sibling role, and divorce, 53
between siblings, 96–97
example, 107–8
connection
in eating disordered families, 311
sibling, 370–71
sibling, and symptoms, 259–60, 265–66
constructive dialectic, 345
contextual circumstances of incest, 138
control
in groups, 401
phase of therapy for alcoholic families,
    250

control (*continued*)
    in professional pairs, defined, 402
    in professional relationships, 410
Cook, H., 287
Coppersmith, E., 329
Cork, Margaret, 229
cotherapy and coauthoring, 399–414
counseling, *see* therapy
Cowen, E. L., 118
Coyne, J. C., 274
Creelan, P., 49
Crimes of the Heart (Henley), 273
Crisp, A. H., 284
Critelli, J. W., 55
Croake, J. W., 49
Crohn, H., 211, 215
culture
    and acceptance of a disabled child, 183
    of the alcoholic family, 248
    defining incest within, 136
    and family system theories, 27
    incest in art and legend, 135
    movies about sibling relationships, 13
    and sibling relationships, 23, 442–43
    social and gender role changes in, 60n
Cumming, E., 442, 444, 446
Current Population Reports, 115
custody
    in separation and divorce, 195

Dahl, B. B., 115, 129
Dally, P., 284
Danco, L. A., 387
Davis, J. M., 297–98
Dearth, N., 318, 324, 326
Deaux, K., 287
debonding, 376
deidentification, 305, 400–401
    in eating disordered families, 300–303,
        311
    in professional pairs, 405
    sibling, 10
deinstitutionalization
    of the mentally ill, 314
Dell, Paul, 297n
Dengerink, H. A., 437
depression
    and parental emptiness, 349–50
DeShazer, S., 265
developmental issues
    arrests, 6
    due to divorce and remarriage, 210
    and pathology, 5
    in the remarried family, 210
differentiation
    from a handicapped sibling, 177

digital communication, 102
DINKS, 9
direct service in large families, 120–21
dirty fighting through symptoms, 261
disabled individuals
    defined, 169n
    effects on family, 184–87
    psychotherapy with siblings of, 167–89
disowned sibling relationship, 344
dissociation, 359
divorce, 190–208
    and sibling configuration, 52–54
Doherty, William J., 340, 399, 401
Duberman, L., 211
Duck, S., 443
Duffy, T., 170
Dunn, Judy, 263, 301, 302, 345, 400, 436,
        439, 440
duplication theorem, 50–51, 53, 54
dysfunctional behavior
    in children of divorce, 205–7
    in children of recovering alcoholics,
        233–34
    communication in caring for aged parents,
        431–32
    of large families, 124–37

Eagle, M. N., 5
eating disordered family, 297–313
    and tilting, 284
Eckert, E. D., 297–98
ecogenic functions
    in family systems, 26, 42
ecological system
    and family problems, 34
    family relationships as, 26–29
egalitarian relationships
    cultural emphasis on, 13
ego-states (Watkins), 358
Elder, G. H., 117, 274
elderly siblings, 435–56
emotional expressiveness
    ethnic patterns of, 76–77
emotional match
    between a child and caregiver, 9
empathy, 4, 5
    for siblings, 345
Engel, G. L., 8n
Engel, T., 211, 215
Eno, M., 96, 98, 194
entitlements
    assumed, and adjustment to divorce,
        191–92
environment
    for development and maturity, 7
    family, and incest, 137

and maturity of self, 6
epistemology
linear, 5
masculine, and birth order, 27
masculine, and therapists' views, 42
equalizing through symptoms, 260
Erikson, E. H., 287
Ernst, C., 26, 49
Espenshade, T. J., 118
estrangement
in children of alcoholics, 237
disowned sibling relationship, 344
ethnic patterns
and adaptation, 80
of autonomy and individuation, 74–76
and sibling relationships, 66–87
experience amnesia, 359
extended family, 79
external conditions
inhibitions and sexual abuse, 142
for sexual abuse, 140–41
Eysenck, H. J., 118

fairness
in the family business, 389
and responsibility for sick siblings, 325–26
Falconer, Clark W., 254, 273, 276
Falicov, C., 79
Families Helping Families (Dearth), 317
family
dynamics, and incest, 138
history, of stepsiblings, 212–13
legacy, 385
and sibling interactions, 390–97
patterns in alcoholism, case, 241–45
and personality self-report inventories, 279
reaction to incest, 143–44
sexuality within, and incest, 150
and sibling relationships, cyclical, 69–70
and sibling roles, 49–50
family business, 379–98
clinical intervention in, 393–97
family constellations, 58–63
Family Constellation (Toman), 49, 63
family crisis, 105–6
example, 108–9
and sibling therapy, 97–98
Family Environment Scale (FES), 276
Family Satisfaction Scale (FSS), 276
family size, *see* size of the family
family structure
basics of, 46–65
morphogenesis of, 27
reorganization, in sibling incest, 149–51
and sibling therapy, 98–99

Faber, A., 263
Farber, B., 173, 184
fear
in siblings of the mentally ill, 317
Featherstone, H., 172, 175, 179, 184, 187
Feely, M., 176, 184
Feigon, J., 176
Ferriera, A., 29
filters, in Character Work, 369–70
Finkelhor, David, 135, 138, 140, 142, 143, 151, 436
Fisch, R., 265
Fishbein, H. D., 286
Fishler, K., 184
Fishman, H. C., 95, 122, 149
Fitzgerald, Scott, 344
flagging function of symptoms, 262
Forgotten Children, The (Cork), 229
for sexual abuse victims and offenders
treatment goals, 152
Framingham Day Hospital, 315–16
Frances, A., 137
Frances, V., 137
Freud, S., 47, 245, 358
on incest, 137
Freyn, W., 57
friendship
and sibling bonds, 43
and sibling configurations, 57
Friesen, J. D., 149
frozen image, 264
of an intensely connected sibling, 10
and misunderstandings, 344
roles in eating disordered families, 303
Fundamental Interpersonal Relations
Orientation (FIRO) Model, 401
fusion, as a cause for concern, 97

Garcia-Preto, N., 72, 81
Gardner, R., 103
Garfinkel, P. E., 284, 298
Garner, D. M., 284, 298
Garrett, G., 116, 117
Gasch, U., 56
Gedo, John, 5
gender
and caregiving, 173, 421n, 422, 424
and closeness among aged siblings, 442
and conflict, 444
and deidentification, 400–401
and eating disorders, 285
issues in male-female cotherapy teams, 405–6
power and preference through, 72–74
and responsibility for the handicapped, 171

gender (*continued*)
    and siblings relationships in old age, 446
    tilted families, 273–96
gender tilting, 273–96
    attitudes about, in normal families, 280t
    findings and beliefs about, 287–88
genogram, 79–80, 147, 381, 394, 395
German ethnic patterns, 76–77
Gerson, R., 147
ghosts, of sibling relationships, 399
Gilligan, C., 27, 42
Ginsburg, G. P., 447
Glendinning, C., 185
goals
    for the eating disordered patient, 305–6
    of sessions with young children, 103
    treatment, for sexual abuse, 152
Gold, D. T., 438, 441, 443, 446
Goldberg, Arnold, 5
Goldberg, S. C., 297–98
Goldberger, N. R., 27, 42
Goldner, V., 406
Gorski, T., 249
Gowers, S., 284
Graham, P., 116
Grakliker, B. V., 184
Greek ethnic patterns, 71, 73–74, 75, 76
Green, A., 401
Greiner, L. E., 387
Griffith, J. D., 192, 195
Grossman, F. K., 172, 176, 183, 184, 186
Groth, N., 136, 154
group therapy
    peer groups for children of alcoholics,
        230–32
    sibling, 326–27
Guerney, B. G., 119, 121, 263
Guernez, B., 94
guilt
    in siblings of the disabled, 178–81
    in siblings of the mentally ill, 317
    survivor, 172
Gully, K. J., 437

Haley, J., 102, 122, 129, 314
Hall, A., 284
Halmi, K. A., 297–98
Hamlin, E. R., 309, 310
handicapped, defined, 169n
Handy, L. C., 54
Harper, D. W., 287
Harper, J. M., 28–29
Harris, Ethan G., 254, 314
Hartup, W. W., 439
Hatfield, E. H., 34
Hayden, V., 171, 179

healing, in incest therapy, 151–65
Heiman, Marsha L., 22, 135
Helsel, E., 186
Henley, Beth, 273
Henry, W., 446
heredity and mental illness, 177
Herr, J. J., 437
Herz, F., 76, 83
hierarchy
    natural sibling, 106–7
    substitution, in the family support
        network, 445
high-access relationship
    and eating disorders, 300–302
Hines, P., 81
Hobson, W., 154
Hocevar, D., 117, 118
Hoffman, L., 297
Hoffman, G. S., 401
Hollingshead, A. B., 276
Holmes, J., 302
Holt, K. S., 173
Hoopes, M. M., 28–29
Horn, R. L., 117
Horton, P. C., 17
Hörwick, E., 57
hourglass effect, 447–48
Houseman, S., 20
Howe, M. C., 115
Hoyt, D. R., 449
Hurley, J. R., 117
Hyman, H., 418, 429
hypnotic trance states, 25–26
    see also trance

id, ego and superego (Freud), 358
identification
    and the absent sibling, 440
    and differentiation, 120
    and professional relationships, 404–5
    sibling styles of, 400
Ihinger-Tallman, M., 446
Illes, J., 185
impulse control, 140
incest
    in the alcoholic family, 239, 246
    blueprints from the past, 371–76
    case example, 155–65
    cultural barriers to, 137
    demographic study of, 138
    emotional, 239
    nurturance-oriented, 11–12
    and parental neglect, 346–48
    preconditions for, 139–40
    and sibling love, 20–22
    therapy, and ethnic patterns, 83

treatment of, 135–66
types of, 138–39
inclusion
  in groups (FIRO model), 401
  issues in professional relationships, 409
  phase of therapy for alcoholic families,
    250
  in professional pairs, defined, 402
  in professional pairs, 402–9
incomplete institution
  the step family as, 209
indentification
  in siblings of the disabled, 175–78
individuation
  in eating disordered families, 299, 309–10
  ethnic patterns of, 74–76
  and family size, 117–18
information
  and care for aged parents, 429–30
  need for, by siblings of the disabled,
    168–71
instantaneous relationships
  of stepsiblings, 212
institutionalization
  and adjustment of well siblings, 173
  of disabled sibling, 173
instrumental tasks
  cultural assignment of, 406
intense bonding, 4, 11–12
  and violence, 13
intergenerational alcoholism, 241–42
internal inhibitions, 141
interpersonal functioning
  of children of alcoholics, 233
intersubjective matrix, 1
intimacy
  defined (FIRO model), 410
  in professional pairs, defined, 402
  in professional relationships, 410–13
  sibling, and family alcoholism, 91
introspection, defined, 6
Iranian ethnic patterns, 72–73
Irish ethnic patterns, 66–69, 71, 77, 79,
    81–82
Isaacs, M. B., 194, 195*n*
Israel, E., 138, 147, 150
Italian ethnic patterns, 66–69, 77.

Jackson, D. N., 276, 281, 325
Ja, D., 71
Jalali, B., 70, 73
James, B., 141
James, Kerrie, 406
James, William, 358
Jesse, Rosalie C., 91, 228, 230, 232, 233,
    235, 241, 249

Jewish ethnic patterns, 75–76, 83–85
Johnson, C. L., 442
Johnson, Samuel, 72
Jung, Carl Gustav, 358

Kadambari, S. R., 284
Kagel, G. H., 274
Kagen, D. M., 287
Kahn, Michael D., 3, 4, 6, 8*n*, 10, 11, 17,
    20, 37, 41–42, 94, 96, 97, 119–20,
    121, 135, 137, 138, 141, 167, 172,
    175, 176, 177, 180, 181, 182, 183,
    192, 193, 211, 215, 248, 250, 259,
    263, 264, 288, 294, 299, 300, 302,
    304, 305, 306, 309, 319, 324, 325,
    331, 342, 344, 345, 384, 389, 400,
    403, 404, 407, 409, 417, 423, 435,
    436, 439, 442, 447, 449, 450, 451
Kamenske, G., 118
Kantor, D., 318
Kaplan, H. I., 385
Kassel, H., 56
Keeney, B., 34
Keith, D., 95, 101, 304
Kelly, George A., 232, 235
Kemper, T. D., 54
Kendrick, Carol, 263, 345, 400, 439
Kibert, R., 184, 186
Kidwell, J. S., 118
Kimball, S., 71
Kirkman, M., 177
Kivett, V. R., 443
Kleinman, A., 71
Kleinman, J., 210
Klein, S. D., 179, 184, 186
Klerman, F. L., 286
Kluft, R. P., 359
Knoblaugh, T. M., 194
Koch, R., 184
Koestler, A., 122
Kohut, Heinz, 5, 11, 245, 403
Koo, H. P., 192, 195
Krasner, B., 385, 389

Labenski, B. J., 318, 324, 326
Langenmayr, A., 57
Lankton, C. H., 40
Lankton, S. R., 40
large family systems, 115–34
  sibling roles in, 118–22, 124–25
  see also size of the family
latency aged children, 232, 250
  and parental remarriage, 216–21
  sibling predicaments in, 236–40
Latin ethnic patterns, 72, 77, 78–79
Laverty, R., 437, 444

Lawrence, K., 176
Layton, M., 42
Lee, E., 78
Lee, G. R., 446
Lehr, W., 318
Leichner, P. P., 287
Leigh, G. K., 442, 447, 448
Lempers, J., 439
Lerner, S., 126
Leslie, J., 381
Levinger, G., 55
Lewinsohn, P. M., 286
Lewis, Karen Gail, 90, 93, 96, 98, 105, 106,
    110, 193, 252, 255, 259, 264
Liebman, R., 303
life cycle
    adolescent children and remarriage,
        221–25
    adulthood for children of divorce, 205–7
    aging, 415–16, 435–55
    and divorce and remarriage, 210–11
    latency, 216–21, 236–40
    the middle years, 339–40
    and relationships in the family, 79
    in the remarried family, 214–15
    and sibling issues, 263–65
    of sibling relationships, 446–49
Lindholm, B. W., 118
Lin, T. Y., 71
*Living With a Brother or Sister With Special
    Needs* (Meyer, Vadasy, and Fewell), 169
Lobato, D., 177, 182
Löhr, G., 49
Loredo, C., 135
loss
    of family members, 47, 61–62
    of original families in remarriage, 212–13
    sense of, in tilted families, 294
Lucey, K., 154
Luterman, D., 175

McAdoo, H., 75
McCubbin, H., 115, 129
McGhee, J. L., 446
McGill, D., 76, 78
McGoldrick, M., 66, 68, 76, 77, 79, 147,
    210, 215
McGuire, Dennis, 90, 115, 116, 117, 121,
    129
McIntrye, Deborah, 406
McWhinney, Will, 379n
Madanes, C., 272
Madgett, M. E., 115
Madsen, R., 27
maps
    of familial relationships, 233–34

family, 29
family, and birth order, 28–29, 33
    myths as, 25
Marion, R. L., 175
marriage, and sibling roles, 51–57
Masson, Jeffrey, 342
Mayhew, J., 55, 56, 57
Mazlish, E., 263
Mednick, B. R., 117, 118
Meiselman, K., 136
memories, arbitrary nature of, 7
Mendelsohn, M. B., 55
Messinger, K., 184
metacommunication of worth, 73
metaphors
    in eating-disordered families, 304
    for sibling strife, Biblical, 3–4
metarules
    family, and birth order, 28
    and maintenance of the family myth, 30
Mexican ethnic patterns, 76
Michaelis, C. T., 182
Michalik, M., 247
middle child, 245
Miell, D., 443
Milan approach
    to treatment of the chronic client, 319–26
Milgram, J. I., 435, 436, 440, 441, 442,
    443, 444, 446, 448
Miller, Alice, 342
Miller, M., 249
Miller, S., 186
Minns, Karen Marie Christa, 142
Minuchin, S., 71, 94, 95, 119, 121, 122,
    149, 263, 272, 286, 287, 297, 298
mirroring, 5
Möckel, K., 57
Moitoza, E., 79
Molinari, V., 437, 438
money
    as a currency of relationship, 380
Montalvo, B., 94, 119, 121, 194, 195n, 263
Montare, A., 118
Moos, B. S., 276
Moos, R. H., 276
Mosatche, H. S., 448
motivation, and sexual abuse, 141
Mott, H. E., 318, 324, 326
multiple personality disorder (MPD), 359
Murphy, A., 170
Murray, H. A., 276
Murrell, S. A., 118
mutual regulation in large families,
    121
Myers, R., 171
mythologizing, 43

about sexual roles, 35–39
  by sibling subunits, 32–34
  and the stepfamily, 210
  and trance, 40
myths, 1
  of benign sibling incest, 137
  effects of birth order and trance on, 25–44
  family, and sibling issues, 361–62
  sibling legends, 343–44

Nasjleti, M., 141
Native American ethnic patterns, 75
needs, of siblings of the mentally ill, 317–18
neutrality, Milan approach, 321–22
Newell, N., 229
Newman, M. B., 171, 184
Nichols, W., 96, 98
Noberini, M. R., 448
Noddings, N., 42
normal family
  defined, 345
  tilted, 275–83
norms for sexual behavior, 140
nursery school
  field experiment in, 50
Nye, F. I., 116, 117
Nystul, M. S., 274

object constancy
  the search for, 18–19
  and sibling images, 9–10
offender
  interviewing, in incest assessment, 147–49
Ogle, P. A., 177
older siblings
  overresponsible, 127–29
Olson, D. H., 276, 278
Olson, T. D., 49
ordinality, *see* birth order
organizational features
  of large families, 123–24
Ornstein, Anna, 5
Ornstein, Paul, 5
Osgood, N. J., 437, 438

Paeschel, S., 170
Paguio, L., 177, 185
Palazzoli, M. Selvini, 286, 287, 298, 300,
  303, 320, 437
Papajohn, J., 76
parental attitudes
  anxiety about therapy, 100–101
  and birth order, 26
  in families with a disabled child, 174,
    182–84
  favoritism, 351–54

scapegoating of mentally ill children, 319
parental problems
  and disturbed sibling relationships,
    344–45
  the parent/sib, 240–41
  separation, 190–208
  and stolen birthrights, 342–43
parentified roles, 97
  in the alcoholic family, 235–36, 238
  in large families, 116, 119
  of siblings of the disabled, 177
  of siblings of the handicapped, 171–75
parents
  care of, by children, 196–201
  as caretakers, 8–9
  in eating disordered families, 301–2
  interviewing, incest assessment, 146–47
peacemaking, through symptoms, 261
Pearce, J., 76, 78
peer
  groups for children of alcoholics, 230–32
  relationships and sibling roles, 51–57
Pellegrini, L. M., 318, 324, 326
Pepping, M., 437
Perlmutter, Morton S., 25, 29, 30, 31, 34,
  40, 42
persona, 357
  kid characters, 361–62
  survival tactics and, 360–61
  systemic linkage among, 357
personality formation, 356–78
Personality Research Form, 276
Pfouts, J., 97
Pinderhughes, E., 81
Pine, F., 4
Pinsky, H. J., 55
pioneering function, 450
pluralism (James), 358
Porter, F., 151
positive connotation
  Milan approach, 320–21
Powell, T. H., 177
Poznanski, E., 184
Prata, G., 300, 303, 320
Pratt, T. C., 308–9
precipitant
  immediate, of symptoms, 256–57
primary caregiver
  for aged parents, 421–23
process problems
  in eating disordered families, 298
professionals as siblings, 409
projective identification, 11*n*
Prokesch, S., 381
protecting, through symptoms, 260
pseudomutuality in remarriage, 211

psychopathology
  and birth order, 71
  and gender tilting, 287–88
  and tilted families, 283–87
psychosynthesis (Assagioli), 358
Puerto Rican ethnic patterns, 72

quasi-singletons, 61

Ranieri, R. F., 308–9
reality
  external, 7
  perceived, 23
  subjective, 7
  views of by siblings, 22
reciprocal obligation, 423–24
  ethnic patterns of, 75–76
recovery
  of children of alcoholics, 249–50
  problems in child of sober alcoholic,
    230–33
  and sibling messages, 258–59
Regan, R. A., 118
Reichlin, R. E., 437, 438
relationships
  actual, 384
  between caregivers and siblings, 423–26
  in Cast of Characters Work, 361
  components of family, 383–84
  family legacy, among siblings, 385
  professional, family models, 403–4
  third-party roles in defining, 406–7
  transferential, 384–85
relationship-seeking acts (RSA's), 30
reminiscence, 437–38, 451
repertory of characters, 360
responsibility
  and care for aged parents, 425–26
  by children for themselves, 203–5
  for disabled siblings, 171–75
  for parents in the sibling sub-system,
    196–201
  of siblings for one another, 201–3
Rhea complex, 13
Ritterman, M., 40
rituals
  of forgiveness, 342
  in the Milan approach, 322
Roberto, Laura Giat, 254, 297, 298, 299,
    302, 305, 308, 310
Rodstein, E., 211, 215
role confusion
  in tilted families, 292–93
roles
  of children in remarried families, 213–14
  family, of the mentally ill, 335–36

narrow, and large family problems,
    126–27
  of older siblings in large families, 124–25
  of siblings of the mentally ill, 318–19
Rosenberg, Elinor, 91, 96, 98, 209, 210,
    211
Rosenberg, E. B., 306
Rosenberg, E. G., 49
Rosenberg, G. S., 442
Rosenberg, M., 274
Rosen, E., 76, 83
Rosman, B. L., 119, 121, 263, 297, 298
Rosner, S., 437
Ross, Colin A., 254, 273, 276
Ross, H. G., 435, 436, 440, 441, 442, 443,
    444, 446, 448
Rotunno, M., 66, 77
Rutter, M., 116

Saba, G., 299, 300
Sachindran, C. M., 192, 195
Sadock, J. J., 385
safety of incest victims, 146
Sager, C., 211, 215
St. Pierre, J., 154
San Martino, M., 171, 184
Santiago, L., 135, 136, 137
Sargent, J., 303
Sarnoff, C., 232, 236
Sauer, J. S., 29, 31, 40
Schachter, F. F., 10, 263, 302, 303, 400,
    401, 405, 407
Scheidt, F. J., 55
Schmidt, R., 56
Schneider, D., 442, 444
Schreiber, M., 176, 184
Schubert, D. S. P., 116, 117, 118
Schubert, H. J. P., 116, 117, 118
Schuh, J. H., 55
Schumer, F., 94, 119, 121, 263
Schutz, A., 392
Schutz, W. C., 250, 400, 401
Schwartz, R. C., 126, 299, 300
Scott, J. P., 442, 445
Searcy-Miller, M. L., 118
selfobject, defined, 5
self psychology
  description of (Wolf), 6
  principles of, 5–6
  view of sibling relationships, 3–24
Seligman, Milton, 90, 167, 171, 174
separateness
  late adolescence and early adult years,
    253–54
  separating function of symptoms, 262
sex roles, *see* gender

sexuality
  intimacy in professional relationships,
    411–12
  myths about, 35–39
  in stepfamilies, 214
sexual play, defined, 136
Sgroi, S., 151
shame
  in siblings of the mentally ill, 318
Shanas, E., 418, 424, 442, 447
Shon, S., 71
sibling bonds, *see* bonds, sibling
Sibling Bond, The (Bank and Kahn), 85, 95,
    324, 401
sibling groups, 326–27
Sibling Information Network, 170, 170*n*
sibling rivalry, 354, 389–93
  and age, 448
  and care for aged parents, 425
  among children of alcoholics, 229
  among the elderly, 437
  in old age, 443–44
  overreaction to, 350–51
siblings with elderly parents
  counseling with, 428–33
sibling transference, 264, 400
Silver, M., 303
Silverstone, B., 418, 429
Simeonsson, R. J., 167, 184, 185
Simon, R., 42
size of the family
  change in, on remarriage, 214
  and clinical populations, 90, 115–16, 118
  and divorce, 195
  effects on psychosocial functioning,
    116–17
  of origin, and divorce, 53–54
Skeen, P., 177, 185
Sluzki, Carlos E., 7
Smith, H., 138, 147, 150
Smith, J., 439, 440
Smith, M. E., 55
Smith, Robert Marshall, 297*n*
social capital, defined, 8–9
social interactions
  and complementary sibling roles, 55,
    56–57
Solin, C., 143, 157
Solnit, A. J., 172
Sonnheim, M., 55
Spack, N. P., 298
Spark, G. M., 192, 272, 385
Spiegel, J., 69, 76
Squires, R. L., 287
Stark, M. H., 172
Steinman, S., 194

stepsiblings, 209–27
  relationships, 96, 211–15
Stern, D. N., 4
Stewart, R. B., 439
Stierlin, H., 297, 302
Stingle, S. F., 287
Stolorow, R. S., 4, 11, 20
Stone, R. K., 400–401, 407
Stress Situation Test, 235
Strodtbeck, F. L., 49
structure
  of large families, 123–24
  of latency, 232
    and children of alcoholics, 236–37, 250
  of sibling therapy, 104
substitution hierarchy
  in the family support network, 445
subsystems
  autonomous functions of, 193
  in large families, 117
  sibling, 119–20, 192
successful marriage
  and complementary sibling roles, 55–57
Suggs, P. K., 443
Sullivan, W. M., 27
supportive relationships
  and care for aged parents, 423–26
surrogate parents, *see* parentified roles
survival tactics and persona, 360–61
survivor guilt, 172
Sutton-Smith, B., 49
Swidlen, A., 27
symbolic-experiential family therapy
  and eating disordered families, 304
symbolic processes and attachment, 440
symmetry
  in professional relationships, 408
  utilizing siblings' in treatment, 324–26
symptoms
  connection through, 259–60, 265–66
  functions served by, 254, 259–62
  as messages, 255–72
    clinical examples, 266–72
  secondary benefits of, 257–58
  sibling connection to, 263
systemic linkage among persona, 357

Taggart, M., 42
Tarule, J. M., 27, 42
teacher-pupil relationships
  and sibling configurations, 57–58
Terrell, D. L., 118
Tew, B., 176
Thematic Apperception Test, 444
theorems
  compatibility-noncompatibility, 57

theorems (*continued*)
  duplication, 50–51, 53, 54
therapeutic context
  for eating disordered families, 306–8
  conversations with adult siblings, 346–54
therapeutic issues
  for sexual abuse victims and offenders,
    152
  for incest therapy, 144
therapist
  educative role of, 170–71
  reactions to young children, 101–3
  role in character work, 368–71
  role with young siblings, 105–7
  as selfobject, 5–6
  and sibling therapy, 41–42
therapy
  and family structure, 62–63
  for the large family, 122–24
  seeing siblings together, 96–99
  for remarried families, 215–16
  setting the stage for young children, 103–5
  and sibling groups, 34–42
  for siblings with elderly parents, 428–33
  value of, for aged siblings, 436–39
tilted family, 273–96
Timberlake, E. M., 309, 310
time-limited therapy, 110
  for mental illness, 316
Tipton, S. M., 27
Tolan, Patrick H., 90, 115, 116, 117, 121,
    129
Tolpin, Marion, 5
Tolpin, Paul, 5
Toman, Walter, 46, 47, 49, 50, 53, 54, 56,
    57, 60, 61, 192, 274, 293, 294
Tomm, K., 323
Tonti, Mario, 416, 417
Torrey, E. F., 314
Touliatos, J., 118
Townsend, P., 445
trace memories, 366
trance, 43
  and family myth, 31
  natural, 25–26
  in therapy, 26, 38, 40
transactional analysis (Berne), 358
transference
  defined, 385
  sibling, 264, 400
  in a sibling relationship, 391–93
transitional phenomena, 15–17
transitional sibling objects, 17
translating functions
  between siblings, 121–22
transmuting internalization, 15

trauma
  and functioning in the aged, 418–19
Travis, G., 173, 177
treatment goals, *see* goals
treatment phases
  healing, in incest, 151–55
  for incest therapy, 144
Trevino, F., 168, 171, 176, 182, 184
triangulation
  in therapy, 102
triple bind
  for siblings of the disabled, 179
Troll, L. E., 435, 438–39, 439, 440
Tuckman, J., 118
Turchi, B. A., 118
twinning, 1, 11
Twitchell, J., 138

Van den Berghe, P. L., 27
victim
  interviewing, incest assessment, 145–46
  resistance to therapy, and sexual abuse,
    142
  system stress, 81
violence, and intense bonding, 13
Visher, E., 211, 215
Visher, J., 211, 215
von Hintzenstern, G., 57
von Schlick, M., 53

Wagner, M. E., 116, 117, 118
Wald, E., 211, 215
Walker, L., 211, 215
Wallerstein, J. S., 194, 205, 210
Wallinga, C., 177, 185
Wasserman, R., 168, 176
Watanabe-Hammond, Sandra, 340, 356,
    357
Watkin, 358
Watzlawick, P., 265, 325
Weakland, J. H., 265, 437
Weissman, M. M., 286
Weitzman, M., 184
Welts, Eve Primpas Harriman, 66, 72, 76
West Indian ethnic patterns, 72
Wetzel, N., 76
Whitaker, C. A., 95, 304
White, M., 299
White, R. M., 274
Whiteside, M., 210
White, W., 298
Wikler, L. M., 29
Williams, O. J., 55
Wilson, M., 276, 278
Winawer-Steiner, H., 76
Winnicott, D. W., 10, 103

Wolf, Ernest S., 6, 9

youngest child
  in an alcoholic family, 246–47
  role in large families, 129–32
Ysern, E., 34

Zajonc, R., 117
Zemmelman, S. E., 194
Zilbach, J., 101
Zimmerman, N., 31, 33
Zuk, G. H., 121